The Jewish Values Finder

A Guide to Values in Jewish Children's Literature

Linda R. Silver

for the Association of Jewish Libraries

Neal-Schuman Publishers, Inc.

New York   London

Dedicated to Marcia W. Posner,
friend, mentor, and *mensch*.

Published by Neal-Schuman Publishers, Inc.
100 William St., Suite 2004
New York, NY 10038

Printed and bound in the United States of America.

The paper used in this publication meets the minimum requirements of American National Standard for Information Sciences—Permanence of Paper for Printed Library Materials, ANSI Z39.48-1992.

ISBN 978-1-55570-624-1

Contents

Foreword   v
Preface   vii
Acknowledgments   xi

  1   Jewish Children's Literature Comes of Age   1
  2   Awe and Reverence   11
  3   Contentment   25
  4   Decency and Ethical Conduct   31
  5   Honor and Respect   39
  6   Justice and Righteousness   47
  7   Learning and Wisdom   55
  8   Lovingkindness   63
  9   Observing and Beautifying Mitzvot   75
 10   Peace in the Home and in the World   111
 11   Peoplehood   121
 12   Perseverance   141
 13   Recognizing and Resisting Evil   153
 14   Remembrance   173
 15   Repairing the World   195
 16   Repentance and Forgiveness   203
 17   Saving Life   209
 18   Self-Worth   221
 19   Many Stories, Many Values   231

Appendix A: Glossary   241
Appendix B: Jewish Holy Days and Festivals   247
Appendix C: Sydney Taylor Book Awards   249
Appendix D: Jewish Publishers   255

Author Index   259
Title Index   273
Subject Index   289
About the Author   299

Foreword

As a researcher on children's services and former director of the Association for Library Service to Children, I sometimes receive requests from synagogues, parents, or educators in Jewish preschools or day schools looking for a comprehensive list of good children's books for a Jewish library collection. I've also received calls from individuals looking for good books with Jewish themes or events for a public school library or a community library in order to balance a collection and to raise awareness and sensitivity to Jewish-related themes and issues.

The Jewish Values Finder is the answer to these questions. Now there is a compilation of titles that can be selected to fill the expressed needs. Because of the variety of approaches to Jewish literature in *The Jewish Values Finder*, an individual can find just the right books for any collection. The arrangement is by values—a good choice because readers can search for books on a particular theme. The comparison among several books on a common theme (or among biographies) allows the selector to decide which of the books would fit into an existing collection or be the start of a new collection. Additionally, the title and author indexes give yet another approach to finding books.

The introduction defines, describes, and gives a history of how Jewish children's literature came of age. This valuable chapter can be used to enlighten library and education students and to edify other individuals interested in the history of children's literature. It may surprise some people to find that the history of Jewish children's literature follows much the same course as non-Jewish children's literature; for example, when the first realistic Jewish books for children began to be published in the 1960s, realism emerged in mainstream children's books as well. Scholars and others can explore these comparisons. The first chapter also includes an excellent list of selection criteria, which will help everyone choose the very best books for children.

This is one of those rare books that has multiple uses and offers a variety of ways to find information you need. It can be used equally well by professionals, parents, and grandparents. Enjoy!

Susan Roman
Dean and Professor
Dominican University
River Forest, IL
August 2007

Preface

Jewish teaching, law, tradition, and history embrace a remarkably constant set of beliefs and behaviors that can be considered Jewish values. These principles are not exclusive to Judaism—many religious and secular groups embrace concepts such as respect, justice, and self-worth. We all know that our worldviews can be influenced by the books we read, especially the stories we encounter as children. The titles in *The Jewish Values Finder* help teach and reinforce positive ideals through engaging and high-quality children's literature.

The number of Jewish children's books (defined as those that portray real or fictional Jewish characters interacting with discernible Jewish settings, experiences, practices, beliefs, or themes) published each year has more than doubled since 1990, to 160 in 2006. Despite this dramatic increase, few review sources cover these titles. Mainstream magazines review some books from large publishers, but their reviewers do not always recognize inaccuracies or inauthenticity. Publications from small Jewish presses and texts reflecting Orthodox views are rarely recognized in the general media.

If it is difficult to find information identifying high-quality Jewish books, it can be even more challenging to choose titles that support a particular Judaic concept. *The Jewish Values Finder* is the first wide-ranging guide to Jewish children's literature since Marcia Posner's last edition of *Juvenile Judaica* in 1995. It is based on the Jewish Valuesfinder Web site sponsored by the Association of Jewish Libraries (AJL). *The Jewish Values Finder* book includes additional titles and background information and uses value and age range as organizing principles to make it easy to find texts on a specific topic (such as a holiday or a specific Bible story) and to determine the titles that should be added to a particular collection. Browsing through any of the chapters will give readers an overview of the depth and breadth of the literature available, as well as help them select individual titles by grade range.

The Jewish Values Finder includes annotations on over 1,000 exemplary fiction, nonfiction, and picture books written for young people from preschool through high school age, arranged by grade level within the chapters. Each book meets the following selection criteria:

- **It meets recognized standards of literary and artistic quality within a range from acceptable to excellent.** The annotations point out weaknesses in literary or artistic quality when appropriate.

- **It has Jewish content exemplified by character, time, place, or theme, or it was originally written in Hebrew.** The Jewish content is presented accurately, authentically, and with sensitivity to Jewish concerns, without employing stereotypes or sentimentality. Where applicable, the books reflect a pluralistic view of Judaism, acknowledging racial and cultural differences, and avoid Christian conventions such as A.D. dates and Christian interpretations of the Bible. Some titles use Hebrew as well as English, but all can be read and understood by readers who do not know Hebrew.
- **To be fully appreciated by children, it merits introduction by a knowledgeable librarian, teacher, or parent.**
- **It has potential for use in the school curricula of Jewish and other schools in North America.**

The values, which were identified by drawing on numerous ancient and modern sources, are broadly conceptualized here. For example, the chapter on observing and beautifying *mitzvot* includes books on Jewish holidays, Sabbath observance and the dietary laws, prayer, and some Bible stories. The chapter on lovingkindness lists stories about kindness to animals as well as kindness toward one's fellow humans. In every case, the primary value exemplified in the text determines its placement within a given chapter. The majority of titles are in print. Out of print books are included when they are both especially valuable and readily available through secondhand or online sources. The Jewish Values Finder emphasizes up-to-the-minute recent works and older works that can be considered classics.

The Jewish Values Finder is written for adults who want to introduce a values-rich literature to children and teens in schools, libraries, churches, synagogues, and homes. Homeschoolers of every creed may also find *The Jewish Values Finder* useful. It may be used for book selection and collection development purposes, as a quick reference to identify a title embodying a specific concept, and as a source of ideas for curriculum enrichment, programs, and independent reading suggestions. Parents of any religion hoping to teach their children morals and ethics can use *The Jewish Values Finder* to identify books for family reading and for creating a home library.

ORGANIZATION

The first chapter, "Jewish Children's Literature Comes of Age," provides an introduction to the definition and history of Jewish children's literature in the United States. Chapters 2 through 18 each highlight a particular value. The last chapter lists short story collections, which by their nature illustrate multiple values.

Within the chapters, books are listed by grade level: preschool (ages 1–5), primary (ages 6–8), elementary (ages 9–11), middle school (ages 12–14), and high school (ages 15–18). Shaded boxes indicate essential titles recommended for first purchase. Every entry gives author, title, and publishing information. The annotations cover the general premise and plot, along with a critical evaluation of the book's limitations and strengths.

Because some of the annotations use Hebrew and Yiddish words, Appendix A, the glossary, allows readers to look up the meaning of unfamiliar words or terms. Since many Jewish children's books are about holidays, brief explanations of Jewish holidays are given in Appendix B. Additional appendixes list Jewish publishers and the winners of the Sydney Taylor Book Award, the most prestigious award for Jewish children's literature, given annually by the Association of Jewish Libraries. The body of *The Jewish Values Finder* includes annotations for many of these winners.

The great Spanish cellist, Pablo Casals, once said: "Each second we live is a new and unique moment of the universe, a moment that will never be again. And what do we teach our children? We teach them that two and two make four, and that Paris is the capital of France. When will we also teach them what they are?" Values-rich literature helps do just that—it awakens children's moral and ethical sensibilities, it teaches them to respect themselves, and, in the words of Micah 6:8, it teaches them "to do justly, to love mercy, and to walk humbly with God."

Acknowledgments

The author thanks her husband for relinquishing his time at the computer so that this book could be written and for his advice whenever it was requested. Thanks also to my colleagues at the Association of Jewish Libraries for their encouragement and support, and to my editor at Neal-Schuman, Elizabeth Lund.

CHAPTER 1

Jewish Children's Literature
Comes of Age

WHAT IS JEWISH CHILDREN'S LITERATURE?

Literature of Jewish content for children is characterized by its specifically Jewish dimensions, namely Jewish time, place, characters, and themes. Lois Lowry's *Number the Stars* is set during one of the most tragic times in Jewish history—the Holocaust. Aubrey Davis's *Bagels from Benny* takes place in a synagogue. Elijah the Prophet, usually in disguise, brings consolation and hope to the needy in countless Jewish tales. Isaac Bashevis Singer's *Why Noah Chose the Dove* shows how the dove exemplifies the Jewish virtues of modesty and peace.

Books of Jewish content are subject to the same standards of literary excellence as all other literature for children—a believable plot, well developed characters and setting, age appropriateness of content, a meaningful theme, creative artwork, and a style that piques readers' imaginations and intellects—but they also explore in varying degrees matters that are particularly meaningful to Jews. This may take the form of a retelling of a story from the Hebrew Scriptures (called by Christians the Old Testament), a folktale, fiction or non-fiction about the Jewish holidays, a biography of a famous Jew, or works, in different formats, that deal with Jewish beliefs, values, or experiences at some period, past or present, in the long spiritual and historical journey of the Jewish people. Books of Jewish content for children appear in all formats and are published by secular publishers as well as Jewish presses. Essentially, they are distinguished by a focus on issues that are central to the Jewish experience and by the authenticity and fullness with which they deal with these issues.

THE DEVELOPMENT OF JEWISH CHILDREN'S LITERATURE IN ENGLISH

As a part of children's literature written in English, Jewish children's books are a rather recent event, appearing first in the late nineteenth century in the form of textbooks and catechisms translated from Hebrew or other languages. As Jewish immigrants adapted to American life, particularly to the use of English as their first language,

1

the first Jewish publisher in America, the Jewish Publication Society, began seeking authors who could write in English about subjects that would appeal to children whose experience as American Jews was notably different from previous generations. The goal was didactic: To inculcate Jewish belief, knowledge, identity, and pride in young people as a way of ensuring that they would remain fully Jewish while becoming fully American. The books of Jewish content published before World War I were serious, inspirational, and stodgy, if not actually grim, in style and format.

Changes in American Jewish society in the years between the two world wars encouraged the development of a more modern form of literature for children. By 1920, the great wave of Eastern European immigration had slowed, and the American-born children of these immigrants were assuming their place in American society. Acculturation to American life had been a major challenge to immigrants and it still was to their children but in somewhat different forms. Concerns about material existence, such as earning a living, finding a decent place to live, and raising healthy children with enough food to eat, were replaced by what we would now call quality-of-life issues: The cultivation of a Jewish home and family life where Jewish traditions were transmitted from parents to children. As material needs were better met, the Jewish domestic ideology reflected an increased concern with family and the observance of home-based rituals (Joselit, 1994).

Women were at the center of this new domestic ideology. Magazines, books, child-rearing manuals, and advertisements proclaimed the housewife and mother to be the bearer of Jewish values and customs. Just as weddings, Bar Mitzvahs, and holiday table settings became more important, so did child rearing and children themselves. Jewish rituals that appealed to children, like the celebration of Hanukkah, became more emphasized and more elaborate. Jewish toys and games appeared and so did more children's books.

The first modern Jewish children's book was Sadie Rose Weilerstein's *The Adventures of K'tonton*, published by the Women's League of Conservative Judaism in 1935. Mrs. Weilerstein was the wife of a rabbi and she based much of her writing on the experiences of her own family. She had a natural gift for storytelling, imbuing her stories of Jewish holidays and Jewish customs with whimsy, fantasy, and a style whose rhythms followed the natural speech of children. K'tonton is the "Jewish Tom Thumb," a tiny boy born to a childless couple whose adventures always take place within a solidly Jewish milieu of family and community. There are several editions of the K'tonton stories, including a 50th anniversary volume, *The Best of K'tonton*, published by the Jewish Publication Society. In the introduction to this edition, Francine Klagsbrun writes about K'tonton's "special combination of mischief and morality, of Jewish observance and universal values"—an ideal to which American Jews have always aspired.

The Adventures of K'tonton ushered in a new era of literature that delivered its theme or message more subtly, with playful, child-centered attitudes, fanciful plots, exuberant characters, appealing formats, and a goal of engaging readers' emotions, intellects, sense of peoplehood, and spiritual imaginations. When color illustrations began to appear, books of Jewish content for children attained qualitative parity with their non-Jewish counterparts, although they remain, to this day, far fewer in number.

In the World War II era, books about prejudice and anti-Semitism began to appear. Some of the first, like John Tunis's *All American*, published by Harcourt in 1942, were not Jewish in content but they did explore the subject of religious and racial bigotry through characters who included Jews and African-Americans. These were virtually the first realistic and positively portrayed Jewish characters to enter secular children's literature. A milestone book in Jewish children's literature on the subject of anti-Semitism is Sulamith Ish-Kishor's *Boy of Old Prague*, an unforgettable exploration of Jew hatred with a Christian boy as the main character and narrator. Prejudice and anti-Semitism have remained prevalent themes in Jewish children's books, treated by such talented and well-known authors as Barbara Cohen, Robert Cormier, Kathryn Lasky, and Sonia Levitin and including such classic titles as Fran Arrick's *Chernowitz*, Cohen's *Molly's Pilgrim*, and Cormier's *Tunes for Bears to Dance To*.

The publication of Sydney Taylor's *All of a Kind Family* in 1951 marked an important milestone in Jewish children's literature because it—and the four sequels that followed it—were the first Jewish children's books to cross over into the mainstream. They are all about a family of Jewish immigrants—a mother, father, and five sisters—living in New York's Lower East Side on the eve of World War I. Together, the lively sisters share experiences, adventures, and celebrations like the birth of a brother and the marriage of two of their favorite (and non-Jewish) friends, an employee of Papa's named Charlie and the sisters' beloved public librarian. Throughout the stories, Jewish readers encounter characters and experiences with which they can identify, and non-Jewish children gain glimpses into Jewish holidays, lifecycle events, and the home life of a warm, loving family. Taylor based the stories on her own family and they spoke—and continue to speak—to all children in much the same way as Louisa May Alcott's *Little Women* or Laura Ingalls Wilder's books do. *All of a Kind Family* won the Isaac Siegel Memorial Award, the first children's book award to be given by the Jewish Book Council, and it also won the Charles W. Follett Award from its publisher. These awards helped establish the importance of Jewish children's books to both secular and Jewish publishers.

Books about the immigrant experience, often set in New York, have occupied a major place in Jewish children's literature since the publication of Sydney Taylor's books. Today, there is more attention being given to regional history as well. Esther Blanc's *Berchick*, involving a Jewish family homesteading in Wyoming, was one of the first, and there are now stories about Jewish immigrants and pioneers in South Dakota, Mississippi, Texas, Colorado, California, and other places far, far away from the Lower East Side.

The *All of a Kind Family* books continued a tradition started by Sadie Rose Weilerstein and others writers of her era, like Mamie Gamoran, in that they presented a portrait of the ideal Jewish family, adopting American ways and values while holding fast to Jewish tradition. In the 1960s, however, a new realism entered children's literature, both Jewish and secular, and children's books have not been the same since. In part, this new realism acknowledged that families were not all alike and were certainly not always ideal. A disturbing look at a Jewish family—and a much bleaker one than anything written previously—was taken by Sulamith Ish-Kishor in her novel, *Our Eddie* (Knopf, 1969). Its portrayal of an abusive Jewish father is searing and its ironic treatment of the disparity between his treatment of his family and the Jewish values he espouses is still unmatched. *Our Eddie* won the 1969 Sydney Taylor Book Award and it was followed, a few years later, by the publication of another shocking portrayal of an abusive Jewish father, Bette Green's *The Summer of My German Soldier*. Neither book has lost its power to shake readers over the years.

While *Our Eddie* and *The Summer of My German Soldier* mark the extreme of Jewish family dysfunction, many books explore conflicts in Jewish families over values and religious practice. *What Happened to Heather Hopkowitz?* by Charlotte Herman and *Confessions of a Closet Catholic* by Sarah Darer Littman are both stories with appealing adolescent heroines who search for a more authentic form of Judaism than the form practiced by their families. Sonia Levitin has explored the issue in two books for teens, *The Singing Mountain* and *Strange Relations*. Recently, there have been more books about intermarried families, single parent families, families in crisis, and families experiencing tensions between Jewish belief and assimilation.

In 1967, another milestone book, Isaac Bashevis Singer's *Zlateh the Goat and Other Stories*, was published. Although he had not yet been awarded the Nobel Prize for Literature, Singer was a renowned writer whose name drew wide attention to the collection of stories based on Eastern European Jewish folklore. Moreover, it was illustrated by the increasingly famous Maurice Sendak, who had won a Caledcott Award for his groundbreaking *Where the Wild Things Are* in 1964. After *Zlateh the Goat*, Singer wrote many more books for children inspired by Jewish lore, illustrated by notable artists like Leonard Everett Fisher, Anthony Frasconi, Nonny Hogrogian, and Margot Zemach. Following Singer's success, other authors and illustrators created such gems as Nina Jaffe's *The Uninvited Guest*, Eric A. Kimmel's *Hershel and the Hanukkah Goblins*, Howard Schwartz and Barbara Rush's *The Diamond Tree*, and Zemach's *It Could Always Be Worse*, to name just a few of the retellings of Jewish folklore that have delighted children of all backgrounds and ages.

Holiday books, following a trend set by Sadie Rose Weilerstein, still abound in Jewish children's literature. Stories and non-fiction are published by secular as well as Jewish houses. Eric Kimmel has written some of the best: *The Chanukah Guest* won the Sydney Taylor Book Award in 1990, *Gershon's Monster* won the same award in 2000, and *Wonders and Miracles: A Passover Companion* won a 2004 National Jewish Book Award. Author Sylvia Rouss and illustrator Katherine Janus

Kahn have created one of the most popular Jewish picture book characters, Sammy Spider, who explores the Jewish holidays with his loving mother and the human Shapiro family. One of the very few contemporary collections of poetry on Jewish themes for children is centered on Hanukkah: Karen Hesse's poignant story poems, *The Stone Lamp: Eight Stories of Hanukkah Through History*. Holiday settings are increasingly used to explore contemporary trends in American Jewish life, such as intermarriage, and to make multicultural statements. Eileen Cooper's *Sam I Am* is a well-written story about an adolescent boy with a Christian mother and a Jewish father, who searches for answers to questions such as "Who am I?" and "Where do I belong?" Patricia Polacco's and Michael Rosen's picture books show the sharing of holiday customs among Jews and their non-Jewish, racially diverse neighbors.

Fiction and non-fiction about Israel and Jewish-Arab relations have been an ongoing theme since the founding of the Jewish state in 1948. An early novel by Sally Watson, called *To Build a Land*, was followed by stories like *Samir and Yonatan* by Danielle Carmi, *The Secret Grove* by Barbara Cohen, *Snow In Jerusalem* by Deborah da Costa, and the 2004 Sydney Taylor Book Award winner, *Real Time* by Pnina Moed Kass, and by non-fiction like *Neve Shalom, Wahat al-Salaam: Oasis of Peace* by Laurie Dolphin and *When Will the Fighting Stop?* by Ann Morris. The tone of books about Israel over the years has changed from idealism and hope to anxiety and sadness, but recently, more upbeat and positive portrayals of life in modern Israel have begun to appear, such as Simone Elkeles's *How to Ruin a Summer Vacation* and Lisa Sandell's *The Weight of the Sky*. More picture books in Hebrew and English also are being published, and more secular picture books written in English are being translated into Hebrew. The explosion in the last few years of nonfiction series aimed at the school market has resulted in a plethora of inaccurate and biased books about Israel and the Middle East, making the selection of accurate and authoritative non-fiction difficult.

It has been said that Israel and the Holocaust are the two central issues in post-World War II Jewish consciousness. The publication of Anne Frank's *The Diary of a Young Girl* is undeniably a milestone in Jewish children's literature, and after it, several non-Jewish authors began to write about the Holocaust: It took almost 20 years from the end of World War II for Jews to write extensively about the Holocaust (Marcia Posner, *Jewish Book Annual*, 1992–1993) and many of the stories were based on personal experience, such as Esther Hautzig's *The Endless Steppe*, Sonia Levitin's trilogy consisting of *Journey to America*, *Silver Days*, and *Annie's Promise*, and Johanna Reiss's *The Upstairs Room*. From a hesitant beginning, the number of books for children and young people now being published about the Holocaust is huge. A recent trend is in illustrated books for older readers, including teens.

Today's world of Jewish children's literature includes specifically Jewish publishers and the publication of an increasingly larger number of children's books; Jewish book promotional events, such as Jewish Book Month; organizations that advocate for the advancement of Jewish books, such as the Jewish Book Council; a Jewish librarians professional association, the Association of Jewish Libraries (AJL); Jewish book review media; the development of specialists in Jewish children's literature; conferences devoted to it, in whole or in part; and Jewish children's book awards such as the Sydney Taylor Book Award given annually by the Association of Jewish Libraries. Lagging behind but now beginning to appear with greater frequency are authoritative bibliographies, studies, and electronic databases that focus on a particular aspect of Jewish children's books, such as folklore, Bible stories, or values. Both Jewish children's literature and the processes that legitimatize and support it have come of age.

SELECTING BOOKS OF JEWISH CONTENT FOR CHILDREN AND TEENS

Put simply and without mention of the criteria used to judge specific formats such as picture books, the general criteria for judging books of Jewish content for children and teens are listed below. For a fuller discussion of selection criteria, see *Excellence in Jewish Children's Literature: A Guide for Book Selectors, Reviewers, and Award Judges*, available on the Publications page of the Web site of the Association of Jewish Libraries (www.jewishlibraries.org) and reprinted in this guide with the permission of the Association of Jewish Libraries. The standard text, called *Children's Literature in the Elementary School, 7th ed.*, by Charlotte Huck, et al. (McGraw-Hill, 2001), is also an excellent resource and preferable to those often-tortured analyses written by academics.

- positive and/or authentic Jewish content
- compatibility of content with the principles of Orthodox, Conservative, Reform, or Reconstructionist Judaism
- compatibility of materials with institution's educational philosophy and curricular goals
- literary and artistic merit
- high degree of potential user appeal
- age-appropriateness
- accuracy, solid research, and reputable scholarship
- timeliness
- sensitivity to Jewish concerns
- inviting and "user-friendly" format
- favorable reviews

Some Jewish children's books, mostly those from secular publishers, are reviewed in magazines such as *Booklist* and *School Library Journal*. While these mainstream reviews are usually creditable, they evaluate books by general, not Jewish, criteria. The reviewers are not always knowledgeable enough to recognize inaccuracies or notice instances of inauthenticity—both of which are not uncommon. Reviews of books by Jewish publishers, especially small presses or those reflecting Orthodox

Judaism, appear infrequently in the mainstream media. It is not an overstatement to assert that the most comprehensive and reliable reviews of Jewish children's literature are found in two sources: the quarterly *Newsletter* of the Association of Jewish Libraries (AJL) and the quarterly *Jewish Book World*, published by the Jewish Book Council. Subscription information about both journals is available on their sponsoring organizations' Web sites: www.jewishlibraries.org and www.jewishbooks.org. *AJL Newsletter* reviews of books for children and teens are also found online in the Comprehensive Children's Literature Database (www.childrenslit.com) and, if recommended, are included in The Jewish Valuesfinder (www.ajljewishvalues.org).

An important aid in the selection of Jewish children's books is the Web site of the Association of Jewish Libraries (www.jewishlibraries.org). The Awards page includes extensive information about the annual Sydney Taylor medal winners, honor, and notable books, the Sydney Taylor Body-of-Work winners, and the Sydney Taylor Manuscript Awards. There is also a study guide to the *All-of-a-Kind Family* series by Sydney Taylor, a biography of Sydney Taylor, and specialized information for the media, publishers, librarians and educators, and booksellers. AJL produces its own publications, with some book selection and collection development guides among them. The most recent is a bibliography of classic Jewish books for children and teens; others include a downloadable brochure on judging excellence in Jewish children's literature, cited above. They can all be found—both those that are free and those that are sold—on the Publications page of the Web site. The Resources page includes a Bibliography Bank of annotated subject lists, suggested titles for reading clubs, and an FAQ (frequently asked questions) set that contains some information pertinent to book selection.

EXCELLENCE IN JEWISH CHILDREN'S LITERATURE: A GUIDE FOR BOOK SELECTORS, REVIEWERS, AND AWARD JUDGES

(Reprinted with permission of the Association of Jewish Libraries)

Introduction

When evaluating children's books of Jewish content, book selectors, reviewers, and book award judges always look for outstanding literary and artistic quality. Equally important is the merit of the book's Jewish content. Few books will meet all of the criteria for excellence identified in this guide, but the books of Jewish content that librarians select, reviewers praise, and judges award should approach the highest standards in both general literary criteria and those applied to Jewish children's literature.

Judging Jewish Content

Accuracy

Accuracy is essential in dates, spelling, identification of objects, and empirically verifiable facts. Interpretations are based on reputable scholarship. Conflicting points of view are balanced. The author's point of view, if partisan, is clearly stated.

The depiction of historical periods, event, or processes is not distorted or over-simplified. Careful research and editing are evident.

Age-appropriateness

A distinction must be made between "picture books," i.e., those aimed at younger readers, and "illustrated books," which are for older readers. Picture books are usually characterized by short sentences, playful language, and concepts complemented by clear, concrete illustrations. In illustrated books, the subject matter is more serious or abstract, the theme and language more sophisticated, and the illustrations may be somber or dark.

Authenticity

Jewish beliefs, characters, settings, and experiences should be portrayed without sentimentality, distortion, or stereotyping in words or illustrations. Authenticity is achieved when individuals are shown interacting with Jewish belief, tradition, history, and practice in a manner that is both truthful and respectful, although the perspective may be satirical or critical. Sometimes, there will be no explicit Jewish content, as in stories by the Hasidic masters that imply or assume a Jewish setting, characters, theme, or audience.

Depth of Jewish Content

Contemporary Judaism is pluralistic, and this is reflected in children's books. The content may range from fully observant to marginally Jewish. In the former, Torah values are central, and virtually all aspects of life are portrayed from a Jewish perspective. In more mainstream books, Jewish individuals are found in secular stories. Setting, theme, plot development, climax, and denouement do not depend on the character as a Jew but on a person who happens to be Jewish.

Positive Focus and Values

Jewish values are those that have a special emphasis in the Jewish tradition and are often tied to Jewish texts. However universal they may be, there is a particularly Jewish way of looking at them, and they are a vital, living force in Jews' lives. Whether serious or lighthearted, Jewish children's literature should have something Jewish to say to readers. While positive content is desirable, but not always possible, a positive Jewish focus will tell the reader "L'chaim, choose life."

Sensitivity

Literature of Jewish content should promote respect for and understanding of Judaism. The use of Christological terms like "A.D." and "Old Testament" should be avoided, along with Christian interpretations of the Bible and proselytizing. It should also be recognized that not all Jews are Caucasian or Ashkenazic in origin. Sensitivity to this issue includes an awareness of cultural and racial differences among Jews, as well as differing levels and forms of Jewish observance.

JUDGING LITERARY AND ARTISTIC EXCELLENCE

Fiction

- characterization
- point of view
- plot
- setting
- style
- theme

Non-Fiction

- accuracy and authenticity
- content and perspective
- illustrations and format
- organization
- point of view
- style

Picture Books

- age-appropriateness
- book design
- format
- harmony between words and pictures
- illustrations extend and enhance the story
- illustrations are technically accomplished
- illustrations are original, not trite or commercial

Illustrated Books

- accuracy and authenticity
- age-appropriateness (usually for older readers)
- format and design are appropriate to content
- illustrations are integral to plot, subject, or theme
- well-written and engrossing narrative

COLLECTION DEVELOPMENT GUIDELINES

Decisions about which books of Jewish content for children to select will depend, of course, on the library's mission and collection development policy. With some minor differences, the collection development policies of Jewish and non-Jewish libraries typically consist of the following elements:

Definition of Library Users: The library's collection development policy will identify the populations served by the library. If the library is part of a larger institution, such as a school or religious congregation, the policy will describe how the library supports the institution's mission, e.g., if the library will support the curriculum of the school, preschool, adult education classes, etc.

Guiding Philosophy: The philosophy of the institution of which the library is a part (e.g., Orthodox, Conservative, Reform, or Reconstructionist) is the basic guide to selecting materials.

Collection Formats: The collection development policy will describe the formats included in the collection, e.g., hardcover and paperback books, graphic novels, magazines, DVDs, online databases, etc.

Scope: The collection development policy will describe the scope of the collection with a focus on materials that reflect the movement with which the library is associated, its users' interests, and its space and budgetary limitations, e.g., non-scholarly works for children and adults, kosher cookbooks only, books published by Jewish publishers, popular magazines and newspapers, etc. Decisions regarding the inclusion of secular materials and of juvenile as well as adult materials are part of the scope of a library collection.

Weeding: The collection development policy will describe in general terms the criteria for weeding.

Gifts and Donations: The collection development policy will include a statement about gifts and donations.

Complaint Procedure: In a synagogue library, procedures to deal with complaints about materials almost always involve the rabbi. In a school, the education director and the rabbi are part of the process.

A library whose mission is to serve a community's entire Jewish population and whose collection consists mainly of books of Jewish content may select all or most of the titles in *The Jewish Values Finder: A Guide to Values in Jewish Children's Literature*. The library of an Orthodox Jewish day school may select mainly books written from an Orthodox point of view, just as libraries affiliated with the Conservative, Reform and Reconstructionist movements of American Judaism may select those titles that best reflect the tenets of their congregations. Libraries that serve either Jewish day schools or supplementary schools will choose books that support their schools' curricula and grade range.

Non-Jewish libraries' use of this guide will also be shaped by their missions and collection development policies. A public library serving a culturally diverse clientele will select titles—in greater or lesser amounts, depending on demographics and budget—as part of its multicultural collection. On the other hand, a public library serving a homogeneous population may select books of Jewish content as a way of increasing its users' understanding of religious and cultural diversity. School libraries with a values-oriented curriculum will choose books based on the values they impart. Home libraries oriented around values will be enhanced by the inclusion of titles listed in this guide. College and university libraries may decide to select all of the Sydney Taylor Book Award winners, honor books, and notable books as models of the best in American Jewish children's literature. It is the author's hope that there is something for everyone to use and enjoy!

REFERENCES

Joselit, Jenna. 1994. *The Wonders of America: Reinventing Jewish Culture.* New York: Hill and Wang.

CHAPTER **2**

Awe and Reverence

"Holy, holy, holy! The Lord of Hosts! His presence
fills all the earth!"

Tanakh

PRESCHOOL

Abraham, Michelle Shapiro. *Good Morning, Boker Tov.* Illus. by Selina Alko.
New York: UAHC Press. 2001.

A companion to *Good Night, Lilah Tov*, this is intended for parents to use with preschoolers. The story begins with a child waking up and saying *"Modeh Ani,"* which is printed in Hebrew, transliterated Hebrew, and English. Each subsequent page shows the child greeting the day and thanking God for all the good things in it. The pastel illustrations are rendered in simple lines and flat colors, with most of the focus on the child's happy, innocent face. An audio CD is available.

Abraham, Michelle Shapiro. *Shabbat Shalom!* Illus. by Ann Koffsky.
New York: UAHC Press. 2003.

This short book provides an introduction to the blessings and traditions of the Sabbath meal for families with young children. It begins with the Hebrew blessing recited before giving *tzedakah*, followed by a short verse. The blessings for candle lighting, children, wine or grape juice, bread, and for after the meal all follow the same pattern: Hebrew, transliterated Hebrew, and English. The blessings are rendered in gender-neutral language, and both mother and son are shown wearing *kippot*. An audio CD is available.

Adelman, Nechama Dina. *Bedtime.* Illus. by Fayge Devorah Blau.
New York: Hachai. 2003.

A sweet, childlike book that explores a little boy's emotions as he is put to bed. Dovid doesn't like to go to bed so he keeps finding reasons to call his mother into his room. After they've sung their favorite bedtime song, Mommy changes the words to acknowledge the presence of God in their lives, and Dovid is finally ready for sleep, knowing that God is near. The bedtime rituals of an observant family are blended smoothly into the story, and the illustrations are soft and comforting.

Adler, Tzivia. ***The Sefer Torah Parade.*** Illus. by Ito Esther Perez.
New York: Hachai. 2005.

A little girl describes the festive parade that carries a new *Torah* scroll to her synagogue. Set in an Orthodox neighborhood and attractively illustrated, this simple story focuses on concrete details and shows the importance of the Torah to Jews. It is especially appropriate to read to children around the holiday of Simhat Torah, or when they are learning about how a *Sefer Torah* is written.

Baer, Julie. ***Love Me Later.***
Peoria, IL: Bollix Books. 2005.

Through personal vignettes that reveal a young child's perceptions of his small world, family and nature are celebrated. The large, impressionistic illustrations and stream-of-consciousness narrative express Abe's sense of wonder as he observes butterflies, insects, flowers, trees, and comments on his place in his family. Abe's Jewish identity is discernible only by his observations about a *mezuzah* and Hebrew prayer.

Benenfeld, Rikki. ***I Go to the Doctor.***
New York: Hachai. 2004.

This simple story is meant to ease young children's anxieties about going to the doctor. A little boy with a sore throat describes his experiences in reassuring terms, and the clear, realistic illustrations do their part to calm fears. On the road to recovery, the little boy, as well as his doctor, both thank God.

Benenfeld, Rikki. ***Let's Go to Shul.***
New York: Hachai. 2002.

Concepts and vocabulary related to the Orthodox synagogue are introduced via two young children who attend and joyfully participate in the service. Within the text, the translated Hebrew is not defined, but its meaning is contextually clear. A glossary explains the Hebrew words used in the story.

Bogot, Howard I. ***Becky and Benny Thank God.*** Illus. by Norman Gorbaty.
New York: CCAR Press. 1996.

A board book that celebrates the wonder of nature and its creator. The text is written in verse, and the illustrations, with their touch, feel, and see inserts, employ vivid colors, tactile interest, and clearly recognizable objects. Among the books about God for very young children, this is one of the most accessible.

Brichto, Mira. ***The God Around Us: A Child's Garden of Prayer.*** Illus. by Selina Alko.
New York: UAHC Press. 1999.

Simple four-line rhymes celebrate the presence of God in a child's familiar world.

Each poem is matched with a prayer in English, Hebrew, and transliterated Hebrew and enhanced by glowing, multicultural illustrations. A glossary lists the traditional uses of the blessings included in the book.

Brichto, Mira. *The God Around Us, Vol. 2: The Valley of Blessings.*
Illus. by Selina Alko.
New York: UAHC Press. 2001.

Prayers and blessings for many of the events that occur in the lives of young children are presented in Hebrew, transliteration, and English, accompanied by lively multicultural illustrations.

Bruna, Dick. *Caleb's Ride on Noah's Ark.*
New York: Big Tent Entertainment. 2004.

Young children familiar with Dick Bruna's many popular books will recognize his signature artwork: Basic shapes, bright colors, and heavy black outlines. The story, told in simple words and sentences, concerns a caterpillar that is an eyewitness to Noah and his ark. Caleb's childlike sense of wonder, paired with the text and illustrations, brings the biblical tale within the understanding of preschoolers.

Carlstrom, Nancy White. *Glory.* Illus. by Debra Reid Jenkins.
Grand Rapids, MI: Eerdmans. 2001.

An extended rhyming narrative praises God for creation, with vivid and fancifully colored full-page illustrations of creatures with wings, gills and fins, spots, wild mammals, and domestic animals. The author's choice of words to begin each poem, "Glory be to God for..." is derivative of Gerard Manley Hopkins, but few young children will know this. They may be perplexed by the unusual use of color: Purple elephants, a green rhinoceros, etc. No Jewish content.

Cohen, Deborah Bodin. *The Seventh Day.* Illus. by Melanie Hall.
Minneapolis, MN: Kar-Ben/Lerner. 2005.

In an imaginative retelling of the biblical creation story, God is personified as a potter, a painter, and a musician. Two children—not identified as Adam and Eve—are part of God's creation, which ends with a joyful *Shabbat.* The lyrical style of the story is matched by textured and fanciful illustrations. Not for those who insist on textual exactness, but child-centered and very attractive.

Downey, Lynn. *This Is the Earth That God Made.*
Minneapolis, MN: Augsburg Fortress. 2000.

A cumulative rhymed narrative and full-page color illustrations combine to sing the praises of the natural world and its creator. As the details build, a family is shown enjoying the world and giving thanks for its wonders. The publisher is Christian, but this is ecumenical except that the family kneels to pray.

Greene, Rhonda Gowler. *The Beautiful World That God Made.*
  Illus. by Anne Wilson.
Grand Rapids, MI: Eerdmans. 2002.

Dazzling color illustrations, full of curves and movement, are the highlight of this retelling of the creation story. The text is patterned after "This Is the House That Jack Built," and the language is spare and simple. The inclusive intent of the book is clear: Adam and Eve are portrayed as being of two different races. Not directed to a specifically Jewish audience, this is ecumenical in approach.

Greene, Rhonda Gowler. *Sing Praise.* Illus. by Janet Broxon.
Minneapolis, MN: Augsburg Fortress. 2006.

Sing Praise is loosely based on Psalms 148 and 150. It is a paean to God's creation, written in verse. The text is short and joyful. Animals, insects, sea creatures, birds, nature, and humans take part in the celebration, portrayed with large, vivid illustrations that are filled with color, life, and movement. Like *The Beautiful World That God Made* by Greene, this is a nonsectarian and multicultural treatment of a biblical theme.

Groner, Judyth. *Thank You, God! A Child's Book of Prayers.* Illus. by Shelly O. Haas.
Rockville, MD: Kar-Ben Copies. 1993.

Illustrated in soft pastels, this is a collection of simple prayers and blessings intended to awaken young children to the connection between prayer and Jewish values, beliefs, and history. Each is written in English, Hebrew, and transliterated Hebrew.

Krohn, Genendel. *Who Is the Builder?* Illus. by Tirtsa Pelleg.
Nanuet, NY: Feldheim. 2002.

The *midrash* about Abraham's search for God is retold here with a new setting and in a different time period. The little boy who realizes that the world around him must be the work of a Builder is dressed in fairly modern-looking garb. Successive double spread color illustrations, large and expressive, show him in the dark, moonlit night and the bright light of the sun, in idyllic meadows, in domestic scenes, and at twilight. Concluding that neither the moon, the sun, nor the stars made the world, he continues on his search until a voice from above says to him, "I am the Builder... I am *Hashem*. This whole world is Mine..." to which Abraham replies, "You made the beautiful world, You are my Hashem." Little children may need some adult guidance to realize that the Abraham of this story is Abraham of the Bible.

Kushner, Lawrence, and Karen Kushner. *Because Nothing Looks Like God.*
  Illus. by Dawn Majewski.
Woodstock, VT: Jewish Lights. 2000.

Where is God? What does God look like? How does God make things happen? Simple, one-sentence answers are spread over several attractively illustrated pages in reply to these questions—the sort that young children ask. The illustrations depict families of different races in a variety of outdoor scenes. Three board books have been made from this book. Their titles are: *How Does God Make Things Happen?*, *What Does God Look Like?*, and *Where Is God?*

LeTord, Bijou. **Noah's Trees.**
New York: HarperCollins. 1999.

A quietly told, charmingly illustrated version of the Noah story, focusing entirely on his obedience to God. Noah loves the trees he plants, waters, prunes, and protects, planning to give them to his three sons to use for their own children. But when God orders him to cut down the trees to build an ark, he readily obeys, bringing into the ark "little green saplings from the trees he loved the most."

Lindbergh, Reese. **On Morning Wings.** Illus. by Holly Meade.
Cambridge, MA: Candlewick. 2002.

This adaptation of Psalm 139 is written in rhyming couplets that express a child's faith in the nearness of God. Charming and sincere, the poem is enhanced by watercolor and collage illustrations that show four small children throughout their day. Written as a prayer and with no overt Jewish content, this reflects an idealized and universalized vision of children's spirituality.

Nutkis, Phyllis. **When the World Was Quiet.** Illus. by Patti Argoff.
New York: Hachai. 2004.

Based on *midrash*, this very simple story for preschoolers portrays the silence in the world when God gave Israel the *Torah*. Large, bucolic illustrations are accompanied by just a few lines of text, describing the sounds that did *not* occur: The cows did not moo, the ducks did not quack, etc. Acceptable and useful as a story for the very young for the holiday of Shavuot, but artistically mediocre, especially in the depiction of humans.

Paley, Joan. **One More River: A Noah's Ark Counting Song.**
New York: Little Brown. 2002.

This retelling of the biblical story of Noah is based on the lyrics of a traditional song with the refrain, "One more river, and that's the river of Jordan, one more river, there's one more river to cross." The author-illustrator has adapted the song into a counting book. The counting begins after the ark has been built and the animals start to climb aboard, not in pairs but singly. The illustrations, made from cut paper shapes and painted with a textured effect, are all double-page spreads so the animals are easy to identify and count. Preschoolers can see each numeral, count the animals, name the bright colors, and join in on the refrain.

Rosenfeld, Dina. **A Little Boy Named Avram.** Illus. by Ilene Winn-Lederer.
New York: Hachai. 1989.

Surrounded by the idols in his father's shop, a little boy named Avram (the future

Abraham) searches for the one God. Adapted from *midrash* and appealing to children despite mediocre illustrations.

Sasso, Sandy Eisenberg. *For Heaven's Sake.* Illus. by Kathryn Kunz Finney.
Woodstock, VT: Jewish Lights. 1999.

After his grandfather dies, a young boy searches for the meaning and whereabouts of the "heaven" that he hears adults talking about. Various people in his life give him answers, and he finally learns from his grandmother that heaven is inside us.

Sasso, Sandy Eisenberg. *In God's Name.* Illus. by Phoebe Stone.
Woodstock, VT: Jewish Lights. 1994.

A beautifully illustrated picture book that uses metaphor to reveal some of God's attributes. It shows young children the many different ways that humans perceive the Almighty, often from a personal frame of reference. There also is a board book version, but this version is preferable because the large size is a better format for the stunning illustrations.

Schwartz, Howard. *Before You Were Born.* Illus. by Kristina Swarner.
Brookfield, CT: Roaring Brook Press. 2005

This beautifully written and illustrated little story is adapted from *Midrash Tanhuma*, telling of the angel who gives an unborn baby a soul, teaches it all of the world's wisdom—including the entire *Torah*—and then removes all that knowledge at birth by touching the baby above the lip, causing it to forget everything and leaving the indentation above the lip that all humans bear. Told with the intimacy and simplicity of a bedtime story and warmly illustrated, it is an outstanding addition to picture books for the youngest child.

Wilson, Anne. *Noah's Ark.*
San Francisco: Chronicle Books. 2002.

The illustrations create a fresh look for the Noah's Ark story, which is told without embellishment or fictional elements and in a spare style that respects both the biblical account and the attention span of preschoolers. The full-page illustrations have flat, bright colors and simple lines. Together, the text and illustrations celebrate obedience to God and the world's beauty.

Ziefert, Harriet. *First He Made the Sun.* Illus. by Todd McKie.
New York: G. P. Putnam's Sons. 2000.

Colorful, childlike illustrations grace this cheerful version of the creation story. Based on an African-American folk song, the story is written in rhyming quatrains, each one spread over two pages full of color and winsome-looking animals. While there is no overt Jewish or biblical content to the story, it is charming and simple enough to read to toddlers.

PRIMARY

Cohen, Barbara. *Yussel's Prayer.* Illus. by Michael Deraney.
New York: Lothrop, Lee and Shephard. 1981.

A classic story for the holiday of Yom Kippur, showing how the heartfelt prayers of an illiterate shepherd reach heaven while the prayers recited by rote by less humble people do not. Attractively illustrated and good for reading or telling aloud. Winner of a Sydney Taylor Book Award.

Eisler, Colin. *David's Songs: His Psalms and Their Story.* Illus. by Jerry Pinkney.
New York: Dial. 1992.

Few books on biblical themes for children surpass this one in beauty and taste. The psalms that Eisler has selected resonate with meaning and are enhanced by his comments and by Pinkney's superb illustrations. This classic biblical poetry is an important part of every Jewish child's literary heritage.

Evans, Clay Bonnyman. *The Winter Witch.* Illus. by Robert Bender.
New York: Holiday House. 2005.

Call it Hanukkah, call it Christmas, call it Yule—it's all one light, according to this handsomely illustrated picture book with an interfaith message. Holiday tensions in an intermarried family set the plot in motion, and the illustrations carry it along with panache. An old woman—a witch, perhaps—convinces the protagonist, a young boy, that "no matter what you call it... it's a time to comfort others and shed light on darkness, whether from lights on a tree, menorah candles, or a glowing Yule log." This is not the meaning of Hanukkah, but children from intermarried families may find that it strikes a chord.

French, Fiona. *Paradise.*
London: Frances Lincoln. 2004.

Intense colors and illustrations inspired by Tiffany glass design flow across the pages of this picture book that tells the story of creation and then continues with Adam and Eve in the Garden of Eden. Most of the illustrations are abstract, using line and color to suggest images. The Garden is populated with recognizable animals, however, and Adam and Eve are shown naked at first and then clothed and bereft as they are exiled from it. The brief text is from the King James Version of the Bible.

Gellman, Marc. *Does God Have a Big Toe? Stories about Stories in the Bible.*
  Illus. by Oscar de Mejo.
New York: HarperCollins, 1989.

Modern *midrash* at its most successful is written by Rabbi Marc Gellman in this book and its sequel, *God's Mailbox.* Gellman's interpretations of a selection of stories from the *Chumash* are both funny and reverent, written with a smattering of modern slang but always true to the meaning of the original. From Adam's naming of the animals to Enoch's discovery of the "announcing tool, " (a *shofar*, or ram's horn), there are stories here to enhance children's appreciation of the Bible.

Greengard, Alison. *In the Beginning: Bereishit.* Illus. by Carol Racklin-Siegel.
Oakland, CA: EKS. 2000.

A handsomely illustrated Bible story picture book in Hebrew with English explanation on the opposite page. The English text is faithful to the Hebrew version. A Hebrew-English glossary and an exact translation follow the stories. The Hebrew and English print is framed in vivid color, with illustrations that are abstract but understandable.

Greengard, Alison. *Lech Lecha: The Journey of Abraham and Sarah.*
  Illus. by Carol Racklin-Siegel.
Oakland, CA: EKS. 2004.

The story is written in Hebrew and English, half a page each, alongside very handsome full-page illustrations. The text is short, a few lines to a page. The Hebrew, on the top, is taken from the Bible, and the English, underneath the Hebrew, is a simple translation. At the end of the book, there is a literal translation in English and a glossary that lists alphabetically all of the Hebrew words used, with their English translation and transliteration. Like the other books in this series, it is an excellent choice for bilingual programs.

Greengard, Alison. *The Tower of Babel: Migdal Bavel.* Illus. by Carol Racklin-Siegel.
Oakland, CA: EKS.

A handsomely illustrated Bible story picture book in Hebrew with English explanation on the opposite page. The English text is faithful to the Hebrew version. A Hebrew-English glossary and an exact translation follow the stories. The Hebrew and English print is framed in vivid color. The illustrations are excellent, but the anachronistic portrayal of dress, language, and building styles—French language and Victorian gowns—may trouble some adults.

Hoffman, Mary. *The Animals of the Bible.* Illus. by Jackie Morris.
New York: Phyllis Fogelman. 2003.

These brief retellings of nine Bible stories about animals are stunningly illustrated. Besides some well-known stories like Noah's Ark, Jonah and the Whale, and the Ten

Plagues, there are some less familiar ones like Jacob's Sheep and Elijah's Ravens. Notes "About the Stories" cite biblical references. The term "Old Testament" is used, and none of the characters are identified as Jews.

Liddle, Elizabeth. *Pip and the Edge of Heaven.* Illus. by Lara Jones. Grand Rapids, MI: Eerdmans. 2003.

Pip is a child who asks questions about God. As he matures, so do both his questions and answers. Pip sounds like a real child, and his questions are sincere and thoughtful. Although not Jewish, per se, the book does a good job addressing universal questions that children ask about God, and is a useful springboard for discussion.

Portnoy, Mindy Avra. *Where Do People Go When They Die?* Illus. by Shelly O. Haas. Minneapolis, MN: Kar-Ben/Lerner. 2004.

In this thoughtfully written, attractively illustrated book for young children, children ask adults—grandparents, parents, and teachers, among others—about where people go when they die. Although different answers are given, they do not conflict with one another and offer meaningful, developmentally appropriate options to the reader. An Afterword gives samples of other questions children might ask, with sample answers, plus suggestions for parents about how to talk to children about death.

Rael, Elsa Okon. *When Zayde Danced On Eldridge Street.* Illus. by Marjorie Priceman. New York: Simon and Schuster. 1997.

Zeesie is a little afraid of her stern, religious grandfather Zayde, and she reluctantly attends *shul* with him on the holiday of Simhat Torah. But a wonderful change comes over Zayde as he reveals how much he loves both Zeesie and the *Torah*. Set in the neighborhood of New York City's historic Eldridge Street Synagogue in the 1930s, its text and illustrations combine to tell an appealing story. Zeesie first appeared in the author's *What Zeesie Saw On Delancey Street*. Winner of a Sydney Taylor Book Award.

Rossoff, Donald. *The Perfect Prayer.* Illus. by Tammy Keiser. New York: UAHC Press. 2003.

This modern *midrash* is based on an interpretation of the *Shema*, which breaks the prayer into its component sounds: Shhhh for listening, Mmmmm for thinking and Aahhhh for discovering. The storyline is strong, although the language is obscure at times and the illustrations are uneven in quality. Better for telling than reading aloud.

Seeger, Pete. *Turn, Turn, Turn.* Illus. by Wendy Anderson Halperin. New York: Simon and Schuster. 2003.

Folksinger Pete Seeger's famous song from Ecclesiastes, with lyrics that use the King James Version of the Bible, is illustrated beautifully with circular pictures, each with many frames containing vignettes inspired by the words. An audio CD comes with the book, which is best for individual use.

Sheri, Shira. *Jonathan and the Waves/Yonatan v'Hagalim.*
Denver, CO: Milk and Honey Press. 2006.

A little boy thinks about God as he tries to overcome his fear of the ocean. Written in English on the left-hand pages and in Hebrew on the right-hand pages, this is one of several bilingual books from Milk and Honey Press. The stylized illustrations are softly colored, there is ample space around the type, and the book is both readable and attractive.

Wildsmith, Brian. *Exodus.*
Grand Rapids, MI: Eerdmans. 1999.

Wildsmith presents Exodus as a series of operatic tableaux, with each double-page drama set on an enormous stage where tiny human actors play out the story against a vast backdrop of Egypt and the desert. The author-illustrator uses a motif to represent God, and the text follows the biblical account fairly closely.

ELEMENTARY

Burstein, Chaya. *The Kids' Cartoon Bible.*
Philadelphia: Jewish Publication Society. 2002.

The author of several "Kids' Catalogs" turns her artistic and storytelling talents to the Hebrew Scriptures, retelling many stories from the *Tanakh* and illustrating them with captivating cartoons. While the narratives faithfully follow the biblical accounts, the dialogue, rendered in cartoon bubbles, is contemporary and slangy. This lighthearted approach is an excellent way to introduce elementary grade children to the Bible.

Cassway, Esta. *The Five Books of Moses for Young People.*
Lanham, MD: Jason Aronson. 1992.

Stories that represent central parts of the history and beliefs of the Jewish people are selected and retold in a style that is faithful to the Bible yet accessible to children. Cassway tells them in prose and poetry, capturing each story's essential elements and adding embellishments that appeal to children's imaginations. The large format allows for an ample sprinkling of delicate black-and-white illustrations and an attractive book design.

Chaikin, Miriam. *Angel Secrets.* Illus. by Leonid Gore.
New York: Henry Holt. 2005.

Like the author's other two books about angels, this is a collection of modern *midrash*—tales inspired not only by the Bible, but also by works of Jewish scholarship and mysticism. Envisioning a heaven that vibrates with God's holy presence and resounds with love and song, Chaikin populates it with angels of every sort, whose purpose is to be active in the affairs of the world. Written with humor and fanciful imagery, each story is illustrated by an impressionistic painting. An author's note about the stories, an introductory story that sets the stage for the others, and an appended list of sources and references add context and credence to a lovely collection.

Chaikin, Miriam. *Angels Sweep the Desert Floor: Bible Legends about Moses in the Wilderness.* Illus. by Alexander Koshkin.
New York: Clarion. 2002.

These 18 inventive stories are set during the Israelites' sojourn in the wilderness. Moses, Aaron, and Miriam are the main human characters, but the focus is on the angels who ease the hardships of the desert and give Moses spiritual sustenance. The stories are based on biblical and *midrashic* sources and are imaginatively embellished by the author, who cites the sources she used.

Chaikin, Miriam. *Children's Bible Stories from Genesis to Daniel.* Illus. by Yvonne Gilbert.
New York: Dial. 1993.

Among the many Bible stories retold for children and assembled into collections, this is one of the most accessible to a wide age range. Its many strengths include a succinct style, abbreviated stories that remain faithful to the originals, a felicitous selection of stories, and an outstanding format. Gilbert's delicate colored pencil drawings depict the central scene of each story and decorate the book with page borders. The pastel colors and almost pictorial detail draw readers' attention to each story.

Chaikin, Miriam. *Clouds of Glory.* Illus. by David Frampton.
Boston: Houghton Mifflin. 1998.

The stories in this collection range from creation to the *Akeda* and are all drawn from *Genesis*. In addition to biblical heroes and heroines, the author portrays angels of many types: The Heavenly Choir, the *Shehina*, and Satan. The woodcut illustrations are striking, and sources for each story are cited.

Horwitz, Brad. *B'Chol L'Vavchah, With All Your Heart: A Weekly Prayer Book.*
Minneapolis, MN: Minneapolis Jewish Day School. 2004.

Minneapolis Jewish Day School students had collected and illustrated the prayers in this modern presentation of the Jewish daily prayer book, which was edited and translated by Rabbi Brad Horwitz. Meant to be used in a morning *minyan*, the prayers are given in a gender-neutral translation of the Hebrew in large and attractive print. For non-Orthodox collections and readers. A companion volume for the Sabbath and festivals by Rabbi Julie K. Gordon was published in 2006.

Kelly, Sheila M., and Shelley Rotner. *Many Ways: How Families Practice Their Beliefs and Religions.*
Minneapolis, MN: Millbrook/Lerner. 2006.

Clear color photographs deliver most of the message in a large, attractive book that celebrates religious diversity while pointing out similarities in belief. The focus is on American families who practice Buddhism, Christianity, Islam, Judaism, Hinduism, or Sikhism. The photographs show their places of worship, religious practices, sacred books, symbols, music, food, and life cycle events.

Lester, Julius. *When the Beginning Began.* Illus. by Emily Lisker.
San Diego: Harcourt/Silver Whistle. 1999.

In this *midrashic* interpretation of the first three chapters of *Genesis*, Lester combines Jewish and African-American storytelling traditions. Creation here is an ongoing act in which God takes many forms: Male, female, white, black, animal. The writing is lyrical and metaphoric, filled with movement and color that Lisker's wonderful illustrations reflect. In these profound and provocative tales, Lester writes about serious matters with a gentle, seductive humor.

Lottridge, Celia Barker. *Stories from Adam and Eve to Ezekiel.*
  Illus. by Gary Clements.
Toronto: Groundwood/Douglas and McIntyre. 2004.

This compilation contains 32 Bible stories, some of which are rarely found in children's books. It is an attractive book, with heavy, creamy paper, plenty of white space, and full-page color pictures every few pages. The telling is straightforward, with a formal, biblical tone of voice. The drawings provide emotional immediacy and have a cinematic quality, employing dramatic perspectives and unusual points of view. The perspective is not strictly Jewish, but the author uses the term "Hebrew Bible" rather than "Old Testament" and the neutral dating "BCE." A solid, if not particularly exciting, addition to the Bible story collection.

Podwal, Mark. *The Menorah Story.*
New York: HarperCollins/Greenwillow. 1998.

A clearly written account of the two *menorahs* of Jewish tradition: The seven-branched menorah formed by God and given to Moses and the eight-branched menorah, or *hanukkiyah*, symbolizing the miracle of the oil during the holiday that came to be known as Hanukkah. The illustrations are deeply colored and symbolic, most with a menorah motif embedded in its image.

Podwal, Mark. *Jerusalem Sky: Stars, Crosses, and Crescents.*
New York: Doubleday/Random House. 2005.

"With wonders and miracles, the sky over Jerusalem touches the world below." Drawing on strands of legend, Podwal celebrates the sky above the city and the places in Jerusalem that are sacred to Jews, Christians, and Moslems. Each page of short, poetic narrative is faced by an illustration that blends the realistic with the symbolic. Podwal's talent as a colorist is fully apparent in the illustrations, which end with rainbows in the sky.

Sobel, Ileene Smith. *Moses and the Angels.* Illus. by Mark Podwal.
New York: Delacorte. 1999.

Stories about Moses and the angels who protected him for all of his 120 years. Starting with his birth and ending when God took his soul with a kiss, these highly imaginative stories are lyrically written and well-illustrated with Podwal's impressionistic paintings. As embellishments to the biography of Moses found in the *Chumash*, they draw on *midrashic* elements and add a touch of holy fantasy to the biblical text.

MIDDLE SCHOOL

Feiler, Bruce. *Walking the Bible.* Illus. by Sasha Meret.
New York: HarperCollins. 2004.

Accompanied by an Israeli archaeologist Avner Goren, the author walked (and drove and flew) to various places where the Bible may have happened: To the possible site of the Garden of Eden, to Mt. Ararat, where Noah's Ark is said to have rested, to places where Abraham and his family lived, to the Egypt of Joseph and Moses, and to Mt. Sinai. His lively account is studded with anecdotes, adventure, and awe. Black-and-white maps, photographs, and quotes from the Bible provide context. Based on an adult book of the same title by the author.

Gaskins, Pearl. *I Believe In... Christian, Jewish, and Muslim Young People Speak about Their Faith.*
Peru, IL: Cricket. 2004.

Interviews with Jewish teens from Orthodox, Conservative, Reform, unaffiliated, and interfaith backgrounds are included. Footnotes are used to correct the teens' errors or misconceptions, but several errors remain. The 15-year-old son of a Reform rabbi gives a particularly strong and positive testimony about his Jewish faith.

CHAPTER 3

Contentment

"Who is rich? One who is satisfied and happy with whatever he has."

Talmud

PRESCHOOL

Fuchs, Menucha. *Gavriel and the Golden Garden.*
New York: Judaica Press. 2003.

To teach a little boy the satisfaction that comes from work, his mother tells him a story about a man who isn't content with his beautiful garden because it's so much work. Like King Midas, he wishes it would all turn to gold, but after it does, he realizes how a real garden, despite the effort it takes, is the source of true contentment.

Getzel. *The Stonecutter Who Wanted to Be Rich.*
New York: CIS. 1990.

Expressive illustrations and a concise text tell the story of a man who was never content, no matter how often his wishes to be something greater were granted. Progressing from a humble stonecutter to a rich man, the sun, a cloud, the wind, and a lofty mountain, he eventually realizes that being a stonecutter is who he truly wants to be. A familiar folklore theme is delivered with zest.

Hirsh, Marilyn. *Could Anything Be Worse?*
New York: Holiday House. 1974.

In one of the best-loved of the Jewish tales, a man with a very crowded house consults his rabbi for advice. Following the rabbi's strange advice, he learns that misfortune is relative and that being content with what one has is best. There are many versions of this story, not all with Jewish content.

Johnson, Evelyne. *The Cow in the Kitchen.* Illus. by Anthony Rao.
Honesdale, PA: Bell Books. 1983.

Full-page, folkloric illustrations showing an evermore crowded house face each page of text in this reprise of a well-known folktale. After complaining that his house is too crowded, a man is told to bring all of his animals inside. After he ejects them, he starts to appreciate the relative quiet.

McGovern, Ann. *Too Much Noise.* Illus. by Simms Taback.
Boston: Houghton Mifflin. 1967.

Rollicking illustrations grace this version of a Jewish tale about a man who thinks his home is too noisy. The absurd humor and cumulative action make it one of several versions that delight young children while teaching them an abject lesson about contentment.

Rosenfeld, Dina. *Why the Moon Only Glows.* Illus. by Yehudit Holtzman.
New York: Hachai. 1992.

Why does the sun shine so brightly while the moon can only glow? This is a *midrashic* expansion of the account in *Genesis* 1:16 of the sky's "two great lights," which were originally of the same size until the moon, because of its pride and boastfulness, was reduced in size and brightness. It is told in verse by a father to his children as a bedtime story and gently illustrated in pastels.

Souhami, Jessica. *The Little, Little House.*
London: Frances Lincoln. 2006.

This new, handsomely illustrated version of a classic Yiddish tale has no Jewish content, although the author-illustrator acknowledges its origin in a note. The flat, brightly colored illustrations have a minimum of detail but, spread across the pages, they convey the full meaning of the story about a man with a crowded house who learns what true happiness really is.

Van Kampen, Vlasta. *It Couldn't Be Worse!*
Toronto: Annick Press. 2003.

In a one-room house live a farmer, his wife, their six children, and the grandparents. It couldn't be worse, the wife exclaims to the fishmonger. Because he is such a wise man, the farmer and his wife take his peculiar advice, bringing into the house first a goat, then a sheep, then a pig, and all the rest of the animals. Their evermore crowded house and the growing chaos are perfectly expressed by large, slightly exaggerated illustrations that brim with noise and humor. A non-Jewish version of a beloved folktale.

Zemach, Kaethe. *Just Enough and Not Too Much.*
New York: Arthur A. Levine Books. 2003

When Simon the fiddler decides that he wants MORE!, he fills his house with more and more stuff in all colors, shapes, and patterns. Charming watercolor and gouache illustrations portray the increasingly crowded house and Simon's realization that a simple life with good friends is really just enough.

Zemach, Margot. *It Could Always Be Worse.*
New York: Farrar, Straus and Giroux. 1976.

A classic Yiddish story is retold and illustrated with distinction by Margot Zemach. As the tale of a man with a very crowded house unfolds, the pictures extend across the double-page spreads, growing more rollicking and more boisterous as the house itself becomes more crowded. When peace is finally restored, the house itself looks at rest. This is one of several versions of a tale about rabbinic wisdom and contentment.

PRIMARY

Bernstein, Robin. *Terrible, Terrible.* Illus. by Shauna Mooney Kawasaki.
Minneapolis, MN: Kar-Ben/Lerner. 1998.

This version of a classic Yiddish tale takes on contemporary American dress. The family is a blended one, the rabbi is female, and the main character is a girl. It falls a little flat, lacking in originality and the charm of the *shtetl* settings.

Brodman, Aliana. *Such a Noise!* Illus. by Hans Poppel
Brooklyn, NY: Kane-Miller. 1989.

Droll, dynamic illustrations are the high point of this story of a man with a crowded house who learns, after he takes the rabbi's advice, that it could always be worse. The writing style is rather wordy, detracting from this familiar tale's humor and vitality.

Chapman, Carol. *The Tale of Meshka the Kvetch.* Illus. by Arnold Lobel.
New York: Dutton. 1980.

Nothing pleases Meshka: Her house is too small, her daughter neglects her, her son is lazy. After endless complaining, her tongue gets a "weird, tingly kind of itch"—a *kvetch's* itch, the rabbi tells her—and all of her complaints begin to come true, leading her to realize that her life wasn't so bad after all. Told with kindly humor, this wise look at human nature has illustrations that show Meshka's plight perfectly.

Edwards, Michelle. *Chicken Man.*
New York: Lothrop, Lee and Shepard. 1991.

Of all his jobs on the Israeli *kibbutz*, Chicken Man loves working in the hen house the most. He makes it look so pleasant that others envy him, and so a job transfer takes place. In each job he is assigned, no matter how arduous, Chicken Man always makes the best of it. Eventually, when it is clear that no one knows chickens like he does, he is transferred back to the hen house, and contentment is restored.

Fagan, Cary. *The Market Wedding.* Illus. by Regolo Ricci.
Toronto: Tundra Books. 2000.

A joyous celebration of love and community, set in an immigrant neighborhood in
Toronto during the 1920s. The dynamic illustrations breathe with life. The story,
based on one written by Abraham Cahan in 1898, pokes fun at pretension while affirming the importance of friendship and contentment with one's lot in life.

Forest, Heather. *A Big, Quiet House.* Illus. by Susan Greenstein.
Little Rock, AK: August House. 1996.

A well-illustrated version of the familiar Yiddish tale about how "it could always be
worse." Told partly in rhyme, it departs from the usual telling to feature a wise old
woman instead of a rabbi. More authentic versions of the story exist.

Fowles, Shelley. *The Bachelor and the Bean.*
New York: Farrar, Straus and Giroux. 2003.

In this version of a Moroccan-Jewish folktale, a grumpy old bachelor, an irritable
imp, and a nasty-tempered thief are the focus of interest. It is written with sly humor
and an understated sense of the ridiculous, telling the story of a magic pot that is
given to the bachelor by the imp and then stolen, not once but several times. When
the bachelor recognizes in the thief a woman after his own heart, "they were married
under the chuppah." The full-page, deeply colored illustrations reflect the Moroccan
setting and the characters' personalities, adding fanciful details and Jewish motifs.

Ganz, Yaffa. *The Story of Mimmy and Simmy.* Illus. by Harvey Klineman.
Nanuet, NY: Feldheim. 1985.

Two little girls, one rich and one poor, envy one another. After they change places,
they find they are no happier than before. This is an appealing exploration of the
question asked in *Pirke Avot* 4:1: "Who is rich? One who is satisfied and happy with
whatever he has."

Krohn, Genendel. *I Wish I Were King.* Illus. by Tirtsa Pelleg.
Nanuet, NY: Feldheim. 2003.

Wanting to be the most powerful person in the world, a humble stonecutter is transformed into a rich man, a king, the sun, the wind, etc., and finally into a mountain, at
which point he realizes that as a stonecutter who chipped pieces from the mountain,
he had been exactly what he wanted to be. The theme of this brightly illustrated version of a familiar Jewish story comes from *Pirke Avot:* "Who is rich? One who appreciates what he has. . ."

Levin, C. and M. Mykoff. *The Fixer.* Illus. by Aharon Friedman.
Jerusalem: Breslov Research Institute. 1996.

A poor but resourceful man relies on God's goodness to foil the king's plans to destroy his contentment. This illustrated story is part of a series entitled *A Children's*

Treasury of Rebbe Nachman's Tales, based on the mystical storytelling of the *Hasidic* master, Rabbi Nachman of Bratslav. Another collection of Rabbi Nachman's stories is Neil Philip's *The Pirate Princess and Other Fairy Tales*. A version with a female protagonist is Nina Jaffe's "Rachel the Joyful" in *The Uninvited Guest and Other Jewish Holiday Tales*.

Melmed, Laura Kraus. **Moishe's Miracle.** Illus. by David Slonim.
New York: HarperCollins. 2000.

On the eve of Hanukkah, a kind, poor man receives a magic frying pan that produces endless latkes. Moishe wants to feed the whole village, but his wife Baila has other plans. When they backfire, showing the contrast between greed and contentment, Baila learns a lesson that neither she nor the readers will forget. The deep, dusky illustrations dance with demons and glow with magic.

Pertzig, F. **Messes of Dresses.** Illus. by Tova Leff.
New York: Hachai. 1995.

A catchy story in rhyme that leaves no one in doubt about its message: *"Aizehu ashir, hasameach b'chelko"* or "Who is rich? He who is satisfied with what he has." (*Pirke Avot* 4:1). A sub-theme is modesty, since the characters are girls and the plot involves an excess of attention to one's appearance.

Schwartz, Ellen. **Mr. Belinsky's Bagels.** Illus. by Stefan Czernecki.
Watertown, MA: Charlesbridge. 1998.

"I make bagels. Bagels are what I make." Carefully defined illustrations in muted colors are an integral part of this story about a bagel baker who decides, after experimenting with other goodies, that he should stick to the source of his own and his customers' contentment. A lesson in being true to oneself is told simply and directly.

Suhl, Yuri. **Simon Boom Gives a Wedding.** Illus. by Margot Zemach.
New York: Four Winds Press. 1972.

"Once there was a man named Simon Boom who liked to boast: 'I buy only the best.'" Simon's quest for the best goes to extremes when he serves only the "purest, coolest spring water there is" at his daughter's wedding. Zemach's pastel illustrations capture the humor and absurdity of an engaging tale that shows the opposite of contentment.

Uhlberg, Myron. **Lemuel, the Fool.** Illus. by Sonja Lamut.
Atlanta: Peachtree. 2001.

Unlike the others in his fishing village, silly Lemuel dreams not of a good catch but of finding an enchanted city. He sails off in search of the city of his dreams, returns home without realizing it, and is astonished that all the people and places look so familiar. This droll, gentle, and beautifully illustrated story is based on a *Chelm* tale.

Ungar, Richard. **Rachel's Gift.**
Toronto: Tundra Books. 2003.

Rachel's mother, Selma the Cook, has just inherited her aunt's secret recipe for matzah ball soup and she is certain that the luscious smell will bring Elijah to their house this Passover. Among the people who drop in is a disheveled man with holes in his shoes that Rachel fixes while he sleeps. As Selma impatiently awaits Elijah, her husband notices that the wine in Elijah's cup has diminished and he and Rachel realize who the disheveled guest must have been. Selma is disappointed because she expected a big reward instead of the rose the guest left but Rachel reminds her that "sometimes the right little something can make a world of difference."

Wasserman, Mira. **Too Much of a Good Thing.** Illus. by Christine Carolan.
Minneapolis, MN: Kar-Ben/Lerner. 2003.

Set in Roman times, this picture book retells a *midrash* about the Emperor Antoninus and Rabbi Judah the Prince. Its themes, developed with flair in both the narrative and illustrations, are about contentment and separating the sacred from the secular. *Shabbat* and *Havdalah* are the main foci of the story.

Ziefert, Harriet. **The Cow in the House.** Illus. by Emily Bolam.
New York: Viking. 1997.

An old house is noisy because the bed creaks, the chair squeaks, and the roof leaks. The man who lives in it can't stand the noise so he follows a wise man's advice to bring in some animals. When the hee-haws, baa-baas, woofs, meows, and moos become more than he can bear, he removes the animals and thereafter lives in contentment with the creaks, squeaks, and leaks. An easy-reading version of the Jewish folktale is rendered in a simple vocabulary, short sentences with rhyming words, and with visual clues in the illustrations. Level 1 in the Viking Easy-to-Read Series.

CHAPTER 4

Decency and Ethical Conduct

"What is hateful to yourself, do not do to your fellow
man. That is the whole Torah; the rest is commentary.
Go and study it."

Talmud

PRESCHOOL

Forest, Heather. **Feathers.** Illus. by Marcia Cutchin.
Little Rock, AK: August House. 2005.

The popular Jewish tale about gossip is given a simplified treatment in this picture book. There is very little Jewish content, and the illustrations, which are bright, large, and numerous, look more Russian than Jewish. Less developed and less engaging than *Yettele's Feathers* by Joan Rothenberg, this can be read to preschoolers because of its shorter length.

Jules, Jacqueline. **The Ziz and the Hanukkah Miracle.**
    Illus. by Katherine Janus Kahn.
Minneapolis, MN: Kar-Ben/Lerner. 2006.

The Ziz, a big bird with a little brain, is taught both sharing and cooperation in this third picture book of the series. Unwilling to share the light of the lamp that God has given him, he lurches to a spot near the Temple and so becomes the vehicle through which the oil to light the *hanukkiyah* lasted for eight nights. Clumsy and garishly drawn, the Ziz is hard to love, but lesson-loving adults forgive his faults because the stories about him deliver such unambiguous messages about good behavior.

Rouss, Sylvia. **No Rules for Michael.**
Minneapolis, MN: Kar-Ben/Lerner. 2004.

To teach the importance of rules, Rouss tells a story set in a preschool classroom. Michael protests against the classroom rules, so the teacher suspends them. Michael then discovers that class isn't much fun without the order that rules give it and asks to have them restored. The teacher compares classroom rules to the Ten Commandments, explaining that God gave them to humanity for the sake of harmony and order. While it gets the point across from a perspective that young children will understand, this is a lesson, not literature.

PRIMARY

Cohen, Barbara. *Molly's Pilgrim.* Illus. by Daniel Mark Duffy.
New York: Lothrop, Lee and Shephard. 1983.

An immigrant child gains acceptance in school with the help of a caring teacher. Her mother's creation of small dolls that resemble Russian-Jewish immigrants instead of Thanksgiving pilgrims helps Molly and her classmates make the connection between Thanksgiving and the holiday of Sukkot. Children are moved by this story of a Jewish child who is different from her peers but who acquires a sense of self-worth and pride in her heritage. The revised version was published by HarperTrophy in 1998.

Cohen, Miriam. *Mimmy and Sophie All Around the Town.*
Illus. by Thomas F. Yezerski.
New York: Farrar, Straus and Giroux. 2004.

A sequel to *Mimmie and Sophie*, this is a charming collection of short stories in chapter book form about two sisters growing up in Brooklyn in the 1930s. Children and childhood are at the center, with adults as peripheral figures. While the setting is specific, the theme is timeless. The Jewish identity of the two sisters and their parents is only implied, however, and young readers may not discern it.

Davis, Aubrey. *Bone Button Borscht.* Illus. by Dusan Petricic.
Toronto: Kids Can Press, 1995.

A hungry beggar teaches a town full of selfish people how to share by showing them the secret of making delicious borscht. This splendidly illustrated story is excellent for reading aloud. Many children will recognize that it is a version of the tale of "Stone Soup." Set in a *shtetl* and with most of the action taking place in a synagogue, it is a good example of how a tale can be Judaicized.

Estes, Eleanor. *The Hundred Dresses.* Illus. by Louis Slobodkin.
San Diego: Harcourt Brace. 2004.

Two of the great names in American children's literature collaborated on this powerful story about intolerance, one of the first on the subject to be written for American children. Originally published in 1944, this new edition has a foreword by Eleanor Estes's daughter, telling how it came to be written. There are no Jews in the story; a

Polish child who is scorned and bullied by her classmates represents all nationalities. Barbara Cohen's *Molly's Pilgrim* bears a resemblance to *The Hundred Dresses* and both are well worth reading and teaching.

Hodes, Lauren. ***Thirty-One Cakes: A Hashavas Aveidah Story.***
   Illus. by Harvey Klineman.
New York: Hachai. 2003.

When a little girl named Estie helps her mother bake 31 cakes for their *shul's tzedakah* bake sale, she loses her gold ring in one of them. Not a child to mope, Estie writes a letter which she encloses with each cake, urging whoever finds her ring to perform the *mitzvah* of *hashavas aveidah* and bring it back to her. In a few days, four people appear at her door with stories of *hashavas aveidah* of their own to tell. The story ends with Estie affirming the importance of the *mitzvah*. Pleasant and upbeat.

Kimmel, Eric A. ***A Horn for Louis.*** Illus. by James Bernardin.
New York: Random House. 2005.

A heartwarming story based on a possible fact about the youth of the great musician, Louis Armstrong. Set in New Orleans, it is about a Jewish family who helped seven-year-old Louis get his first real horn. Armstrong alluded to this family in an unpublished memoir, and Kimmel fleshes out the story with warmth. Characters are individualized, the plot is believable, and the setting is vividly realized.

McDonough, Yona A. ***Hammerin' Hank: The Life of Hank Greenberg.***
   Illus. by Malcah Zeldis.
New York: Walker. 2006.

Although there are other juvenile biographies of the baseball player Hank Greenberg, this is the first that is accessible to younger children. As in the other collaborations between this mother-and-daughter (author-illustrator) team, McDonough's writing is clear, concrete, and amplified by many quotes. Zeldis's folk art brings the characters and settings to life. Vivid colors and strong, composed pictures convey both action and the times in which Greenberg lived. Readers who love sports will appreciate the list of vital statistics that is appended, along with a chronology of Greenberg's life and a glossary of baseball and Jewish terms.

Olivas, Daniel A. ***Benjamin and the Word.***
Houston, TX: Arte Publico Press. 2005

A bilingual (English and Spanish) story that confronts the issue of name-calling and prejudice. In the heat of an argument, Benjamin's best friend hurls an ethnic slur at him. The exact words are not revealed, but Benjamin is hurt and seeks solace from his father, who helps him understand that his Jewish-Hispanic heritage is something to be proud of. The ending is pat, the illustrations are pedestrian, but the issue is not one that is dealt with often in children's books.

Rothenberg, Joan. *Yettele's Feathers.*
New York: Hyperion. 1995.

A classic picture book about *lashon hora*. Yettele loves to gossip, not realizing that her words hurt others. When the townspeople who have been stung by her words stop talking to her, Yettele seeks the rabbi's help. He tells her to cut open her largest pillow and bring it to him. A gust of wind blows the pillow from her arms, and feathers fly everywhere; Yettele tries to pick them all up and stuff them back into the pillow but to no avail. "And so it is with those stories of yours," says the Rabbi. "Once the words leave your lips, they are as impossible to put back as those feathers!" Having learned a lesson, Yettele changes her ways. Full-page illustrations in gouache reflect the action and portray *shtetl* life. Written and illustrated with a droll, winsome touch, this is a beloved story.

Waldman, Debby. *A Sack Full of Feathers.* Illus. by Cindy Revell.
Custer, WA: Orca. 2006.

A traditional Jewish tale about *lashon hora* is given a fresh, new treatment in this vibrant picture book. Graced with bright, dancing acrylic illustrations, it is about a little boy who overhears bits of stories in his father's store and then spreads them among his friends without regard for their truth or for the people in the *shtetl* whom they might hurt. Observing Yankel, the rabbi decides to teach him a lesson. He gives him a bag of feathers, instructs him to leave one in front of each house, and then to go back and pick them all up. This isn't possible, of course; the feathers have all blown away. While trying to fulfill his mission, Yankel becomes dirty, wet, bruised, and discouraged. "They're gone," he tells the rabbi. "I can't get them back." Over a bowl of hot soup and some tasty *rugelach*, the rabbi gently explains to Yankel how it is the same with the stories he spreads: "Once you tell a story, you cannot take it back... make sure the next story you tell is your own." On a par with Rothenberg's *Yettele's Feathers*, this is a welcome addition to Jewish folklore collections.

ELEMENTARY

Bloom, Tzivia. *The Dreams Come True Club.*
Nanuet, NY: Feldheim. 2005.

Five observant Israeli boys—models of behavior—form a club to help others make their dreams come true. Danny, the main character, is exemplary in his tact, maturity, and respect for adults. Many Hebrew terms are used, and there is no glossary. Through the boys' adventures, values of friendship, loving one's neighbor, and helping people in need are reflected. Written in a light, humorous style, this will mainly appeal to Orthodox boys.

Deedy, Carmen Agra. *The Yellow Star: The Legend of King Christian of Denmark.*
Illus. by Henri Sorenson.
Atlanta, GA: Peachtree. 2000.

A beautifully illustrated tribute to the tolerance of the Danish people and their king, Christian X, who took many risks on behalf of the Jewish population during the German occupation in World War II. Although the story of King Christian wearing a yellow star is historically untrue, it is used here as a metaphor, which is enhanced by Sorenson's superb oil paintings.

Ducharme, Dede Fox. *The Treasure in the Tiny Blue Tin.*
Fort Worth, TX: Texas Christian University Press. 1998.

A Jewish immigrant boy searching for his father is joined, by chance, by a prejudiced country boy in a dangerous journey through the flooded Texas wilderness. Needing one another to survive, they overcome their differences. Early twentieth-century Texas-Jewish history is woven into a wholesome and readable story of tolerance. The Texas locale shows that not all Jewish immigrants settle in New York.

Glasthal, Jacqueline B. *Liberty on 23rd Street.* Illus. by Alan Reingold.
New York: Silver Moon Press. 2006.

A short, abundantly illustrated immigration story about a Jewish girl named Emma and a black boy named Ambrose who help one another in difficult times and also help the publisher, Joseph Pulitzer, raise funds for a pedestal for the Statue of Liberty. Emma and Ambrose are plucky characters whose adventures convey a feeling for New York in 1885.

Kacer, Kathy. *Home Free, Margit: Book One.* Illus. by Janet Wilson.
Toronto: Penguin Canada. 2003.

Margit and her pregnant mother escape Nazi-occupied Europe and settle in Canada, where Margit struggles to make friends, be like other kids, and become a "Canadian girl." The story explores Canadian immigration policy toward Jewish refugees, anti-Semitism, and the effects of Nazism on European Jews. Historical events and explanations impose on the narrative at times, but readers who enjoyed *Molly's Pilgrim* will enjoy this book. The first book in the Our Canadian Girl Series.

Kacer, Kathy. *Open Your Doors: Margit, Book Three.*
Toronto: Penguin Canada. 2006.

Readers were first introduced to Margit, an 11-year-old Jewish girl who escaped the Holocaust and settled in Toronto, in *Home Free.* Her story was continued in *A Bit of Love and a Bit of Luck.* The third installment begins in 1946, as Margit learns of the thousands of Jewish children who have been orphaned by the Holocaust. She is determined to convince her parents to welcome one of these children into their home. The short chapters, concise writing, and black-and-white drawings will appeal to middle grade children looking for easy-to-read chapter books. Part of the publisher's Our Canadian Girl Series.

Karwoski, Gail Langer. *Quake! Disaster in San Francisco, 1906.*
   Illus. by Robert Papp.
Atlanta, GA: Peachtree. 2004.

A young Jewish boy is the main character in this readable historical novel set in San Francisco at the time of the 1906 earthquake. Separated from his father and little sister and not knowing if they survived the quake, Jacob searches through the wreckage and refugee camps for them. He is joined by a Chinese boy searching for his family and by a stray puppy, whom he names Quake. Vivid scenes of the disaster are juxtaposed with issues of prejudice and altruism. An epilogue gives readers some background and factual material, including photographs.

Kubert, Joe. *The Adventures of Yaakov and Isaac.*
Nanuet, NY: Mahrwood/Feldheim. 2004.

Joe Kubert is well known to readers of comic books. This collection of stories features two Orthodox boys who face many tough situations, such as encountering bullies who make fun of their *kippot* and rescuing a child trapped in a car. They also explore some famous moments in Jewish history, including the Warsaw Ghetto Uprising and the Six Day War. Following each story is a review of the *Torah* lessons the story taught, and a set of questions. The illustrations are similar to mainstream comics, with bold colors and large, action-filled panels. Ideal for elementary and middle school boys, especially those who are reluctant readers.

Matas, Carol. *Rosie in Los Angeles: Action!*
New York: Aladdin. 2004.

When Rosie's father moves his family from Chicago to Los Angeles, he decides to make movies starring Rosie. When she inadvertently causes an accident during the preparation for filming their first Western, injuring their best rider, Rosie sets off a chain of events from which only she could emerge with style and grace. She and the injured rider's son must learn to get along, not just to finish the film but also to foil a pair of horse thieves. Spunky Rosie's story is filled with humor and action but not much Jewish content. A sequel to two other books about Rosie and her family in New York and Chicago.

Nislick, June Leavitt. *Zayda Was a Cowboy.*
Philadelphia: Jewish Publication Society. 2005.

An engaging yarn about a young Jewish boy from Russia who walks and works his way across Europe to escape the Czar's army, takes a ship to Galveston, Texas, and becomes a real cowboy, with a ten-gallon hat, chaps, spurs, lariat, gun, and horse. The charm of the story is in listening to Zayda tell it. Seldom does a written narrative capture human speech so well and seldom does the narrative style establish a character as effectively as this does. Each chapter stresses a separate aspect of Zayda's life as a cowboy, and a strong sense of Jewish identity permeates the entire story. Winner of the Sydney Taylor Manuscript Award and not to be missed.

Shalant, Phyllis. *When Pirates Came to Brooklyn.*
New York: Dutton. 2002.

This imaginative and well-written novel is set in a diverse, working-class neighborhood in Brooklyn in the early 1960s. Its rich plot involves a madcap friendship between two girls, and its theme explores prejudice and difference. The well-developed characters grow and change within the story, which captures both the particulars of childhood and larger questions that confront children.

MIDDLE SCHOOL

Arrick, Fran. *Chernowitz.*
Scarsdale, NY: Bradbury Press. 1981.

A high school boy named Bobby is harassed at school by a bully for being Jewish. As the verbal abuse and threats increase, Bobby's so-called friends desert him and he is left alone to cope and, eventually, to plan revenge. When his scheme to frame his adversary for a theft he didn't commit is successful, Bobby suffers guilt for retaliating. Serious issues are probed with sensitivity in a thought-provoking book.

Auch, Mary Jane. *Ashes of Roses.*
New York: Henry Holt. 2002.

An immigration novel set in the early 1900s that reveals the working conditions that many young women had to endure, told through the experiences of an Irish immigrant named Rose Nolan. The story culminates with the Triangle Shirtwaist Factory fire that took many lives. Throughout the story, ethical issues are raised, making the book a good lead into a discussion of ethics.

Kanefield, Teri. *Rivka's Way.*
Chicago: Front Street/Cricket Books. 2001.

Set in eighteenth-century Prague, this book tells of teenage Rivka's longing to leave the safety of the Jewish Quarter and venture outside into the larger world that fascinates her. When she does, disguised as a boy, she becomes friends with a Christian boy who helps her and, in turn, needs her help. One of a number of historical novels with a feminist sensibility, it is resolved very traditionally, when Rivka agrees to marry the young man her parents have chosen for her.

Levine, Gail Carson. *Dave at Night.*
New York: HarperCollins. 1999.

An orphan boy is separated from his older brother and sent to the Hebrew Home for Boys. To escape from its harshness, Dave sneaks out at night and becomes immersed in the swinging, vibrant world of the Harlem Renaissance. There he meets real people like Langston Hughes and Countee Cullen, plus a young Black heiress and a crook with a heart of gold. The story is based on the experiences of the author's father, and it brings both the 1920s and an important episode in America's cultural history to life.

Pasachoff, Naomi. *Niels Bohr: Physicist and Humanitarian.*
Berkeley Heights, NJ: Enslow. 2003.

Readers are given a glimpse into the mind and heart of the great Danish theoretical physicist, learning about his scientific career and achievements, as well as about his steadfast efforts to help German Jewish intellectuals fleeing Germany and Danish Jews who, like the half-Jewish Bohr, were marked for arrest by the Nazis. His sojourn in the United States working on the Manhattan Project motivated Bohr to speak out against the military use of nuclear power and promote international cooperation.

Schachter, Esty. *Anya's Echoes.*
McKinleyville, CA: Fithian Press. 2004.

Lea learns about her great-aunt's experiences during the Holocaust when Anya comes for a long visit. As Lea's friendship with Anya grows, conflict among her school friends grows, too. One friend is ostracized by the 'alpha' girl in the group, and Lea goes along with this, despite her unhappiness over the situation. Anya helps her sort out her values and, ultimately, do the right thing. The Holocaust episodes are handled rather flatly, but the contemporary issues are well drawn and will be appealing to readers of Lea's age.

HIGH SCHOOL

McCaughrean, Geraldine. *Not the End of the World.*
New York: Harper/Collins. 2004.

A suspenseful novel about Noah and the flood, told by Timna, Noah's daughter. She is a fictional character, not mentioned in the Bible, and this is a modern interpretation of the biblical story. Along with Timna, her three brothers, their wives, Timna's mother, and even some of the suffering animals tell the tale from their various points of view, each in a distinctive voice. Noah does not speak, and he is portrayed as a religious fanatic who is not as blameless as he is in the Bible. Powerful language and imagery are used to tell the story, which is horrific and tragic, but also a little hopeful. In a time of well-publicized natural disasters such as tsunamis and hurricanes, it is a timely and engrossing story.

Schorr, Melissa. *Goy Crazy.*
New York: Hyperion. 2006

High school readers will enjoy this entertaining and ethical look at mixed dating. As Rachel's romance with a non-Jewish boy (the "goy" of the title) progresses, her developing sense of Jewish identity eventually convinces her that interfaith dating is not a good idea. Strong Jewish values and serious issues add heft to a readable story, although its use of the word "goy" may put off some adults.

CHAPTER 5

Honor and Respect

"Who is honored and respected? One who honors and respects others."

Talmud

PRESCHOOL

Eisenberg, Ann. *Bible Heroes I Can Be.* Illus. by Roz Schanzer.
Rockville, MD: Kar-Ben Copies. 1990.

Young children are encouraged to emulate the hospitality of Abraham, the kindness of Rebecca, and the exemplary traits of several other biblical figures who serve as role models. Each figure is introduced in just a few lines, with an illustration that extends the brief text. There is also a slightly abridged board book version.

Goldberg, Malky. *What Do I Say?* Illus. by Patti Argoff.
New York: Hachai. 2005.

From waking up until going to bed, there are events in the life of the Jewish child that require special words. Some are common to all English speaking children: "Thank you" and "Excuse me," for example. Others assume a deeper level of Jewish observance: "*Modeh Ani,*" "*Baruch Hashem,*" "*Refuah Shelaimah,*" and "*Shema Yisrael.*" Bright illustrations and short verses capture the situation in which each expression is appropriate, and by lifting flaps, readers can find the right words if they haven't guessed them already.

McDonough, Yona A. *Eve and Her Sisters.* Illus. by Malcah Zeldis.
New York: HarperCollins. 1994.

A biblical verse and a colorful full-page illustration accompany each of 14 very short biographical sketches of women in the Bible. Although the meaning of the stories and the grandeur of the original text are sacrificed to brevity, this is an acceptable and visually attractive introduction for young children.

Renberg, Dalia. *King Solomon and the Bee.* Illus. by Ruth Heller.
New York: HarperCollins. 1994.

A humble bee helps King Solomon solve riddles put to him by the Queen of Sheba. The slightly exaggerated illustrations are lush and extend the meaning of the story, which delights young children who enjoy the mighty king's recognition that the little bee is worthy of respect. One of a number of stories adapted from legends about King Solomon.

PRIMARY

Edwards, Michelle. *A Baker's Portrait.*
New York: Lothrop, Lee and Shepard. 1991.

As a wise and subtle story about behavior, this does what good literature always does: It shows but never tells readers its message. Michelin is a young artist who paints her subjects "warts and all." When she is asked to paint her fat and frumpy aunt and uncle, all she sees at first is how ugly they are. As she spends time with them, a different aspect of their characters emerges: Their kindness, their love for one another, their image of one another as beautiful. As the story progresses, wonderfully illustrated by Edwards in her inimitable style, children perceive that beauty is only skin deep and that character is more important than looks.

Greengard, Alison. *Rebecca.* Illus. by Carol Racklin-Siegel.
Oakland, CA: EKS. 2002.

The third in a series of Hebrew-English Bible stories, this story about Rebecca is excerpted from Chapter 24 of *Genesis.* It is told in easy Hebrew with vowel markings and also in English. The narrative is not a literal translation but there is one appended, along with a transliteration and a glossary. The illustrations are vibrant and attractive.

Hest, Amy. *The Go-Between.* Illus. by DyAnne Di Salvo-Ryan.
New York: Four Winds Press. 1992.

Lexi decides that her Gram and Mr. Singer, who sells newspapers across the street, should get together because they both love baseball. Acting as a go-between, she encourages them to become friends. To her surprise, romance blooms! A warm-hearted story that shows how responsibility can be guided by the heart as well as the head. Attractively illustrated.

Lieberman, Syd. *The Wise Shoemaker of Studena.* Illus. by Martin Lemelman.
Philadelphia: Jewish Publication Society. 1994.

Yossi the shoemaker is widely respected, so a rich man from Budapest invites him to his daughter's wedding. When Yossi appears in shabby clothes, his host thinks he is a beggar

(Cont'd.)

The Wise Shoemaker of Studena. (Continued)

and rudely turns him away. Deciding to teach the man a lesson, Yossi borrows some finery, returns to the wedding, and is welcomed now as the honored guest. When he pours wine into his pants, soup into his boots, and peas into his hat, the guests are appalled and finally his host demands an explanation. Yossi explains that he is feeding his clothes, because they are the reason he was invited, not for himself or his wisdom. Back home in Studena, Yossi tells his wife, "Fools see people's clothes; the wise see their souls." Bright, lively illustrations capture the absurdity of Yossi's actions.

Russo, Marisabina. *A Visit to Oma.*
New York: HarperCollins. 1991.

A beautifully illustrated, gently written story about a little girl and the special affinity she has for her very old great-grandmother. Although Oma speaks in a language that Celeste cannot understand, in their weekly visits Celeste imagines what it is that Oma is telling her about her life. Told subtly and illustrated in framed color pictures, generations are bridged as Celeste and Oma create their own form of loving communication. Although there is no explicit Jewish content, the story conveys to adults, if not to children, that the characters are Jewish.

Shollar, Leah. *The Key Under the Pillow.* Illus. by Harvey Klineman.
New York: Hachai. 2004.

Adapted from the *Talmud*, this is the story of Dama and his father, Nesina, who live in ancient Israel. The story involves Dama's refusal to disturb his father's sleep, although by doing so he foregoes a lucrative sale of gems. Later, he is rewarded when his cow gives birth to a red heifer, which is purchased for the same price he would have gotten for the gems. Dama's respect for his father is summed up in the words: "All my life I have been careful never to call my father by his name, never to sit in his place—and never to wake him from sleep." Modern children may honor their parents in other ways but this provides an objective lesson in the form of an engrossing and nicely illustrated story.

Stampler, Ann Redisch. *Shlemazel and the Remarkable Spoon of Pohost.*
Illus. by Jacqueline M. Cohen.
New York: Clarion. 2006.

An idler becomes a *mensch* in this delightful story by the author and illustrator of *Something for Nothing.* Shlemazel blames his idleness on bad luck: He's so unlucky that even if he tried to work, something terrible would happen. Moshe the tinker devises a scheme involving a spoon that he tells Shlemazel will help a man find all the treasure he will ever need. And so it does, because by the story's end, Shlemazel has earned himself a wife, respect, and a trade. Sparkling dialogue and folkloric illustrations convey the setting, characters, actions, and theme to perfection.

Wildsmith, Brian. *Joseph.*
Grand Rapids, MI: Eerdmans. 1997.

A retelling of the story of Joseph and his brothers who sold him into slavery in Egypt. The unexceptional writing, which follows the biblical text in showing Joseph's experiences as a slave and his rise to a position of great influence, is enhanced with intensely colored and richly detailed illustrations.

ELEMENTARY

Caseley, Judith. *Praying to A. L.*
New York: HarperCollins/Greenwillow. 2000.

Thirteen-year-old Sierra Goodman's father has died, and she looks to her hero, Abraham Lincoln, as a model for ways to cope. The author writes convincingly about being 13 and about Sierra's sorrow and anger at losing her father. Braiding American history together with Jewish and Cuban culture and family life, the story is absorbing. Although Sierra's family is only peripherally Jewish, there is a good feeling about her Jewish experiences with her father. Children of mixed marriages will find positive identification with Judaism and Jewish family values here.

Griffis, Molly Levite. *Simon Says.*
Austin, TX: Eakin. 2004.

This is the third in a series of books set during World War II. The series heroine, 11-year-old Rachel Dalton, is bright and curious about life. This story is about one of her best friends, Simon Green, whose secret is his own identity. He is Jewish and was sent from Europe to live with strangers in America. As he remembers his history, he discovers a link to his repressed emotions and to the people around him. When swastikas appear around town, Rachel and Simon work together to find the villain. Simon's dilemma is serious and engaging, and Rachel is intrepid and naive about the wider world. Together they make a worthy team.

Grossman, David. *Duel.*
New York: Bloomsbury. 2004.

A novel by the well-known Israeli writer, David Grossman, told in the first person by 12-year-old David. He has an elderly friend in a nursing home who is challenged to a pistol duel by another elderly man who accuses him of stealing a painting. To prevent either man from being harmed, David must think fast! He becomes a sleuth, unraveling the mystery of the men's past in Germany and their love for a beautiful woman. An interesting plot and setting, along with sound Jewish values. Translated from the Hebrew by Betsy Rosenberg.

Manushkin, Fran. *Daughters of Fire: Heroines of the Bible.* Illus. by Uri Shulevitz.
San Diego, CA: Harcourt/SilverWhistle. 2001.

Drawing on both the Bible and legend, the author portrays eleven heroines of passion and purpose, representing Jewish history from the period of the patriarchs to the Persian era. Richly colored illustrations capture the drama of each story.

Ross, Lillian Hammer. *Daughters of Eve: Strong Women of the Bible.*
   Illus. by Kyra Teis.
Cambridge, MA: Barefoot Books. 2000.

The women Ross writes about are Miriam, Zipporah, the daughters of Zelophehad, Ruth, Abigail, Huldah, Judith, and Esther. In these stories, women are given the names, voices, and ability to act that they do not necessarily have in the Bible. Each chapter begins with a page of historical background to provide some context. The attractive color illustrations show people of different races. As a contemporary "take" on the Bible, this is worthwhile.

Yolen, Jane. *The Prince of Egypt.* Illus. by Michael Koelsch and Larry Navarro.
New York: Penguin Putnam. 1998.

The animated movie of the same title is reinterpreted as an exciting story for children. Like the movie, it takes liberties with traditional, biblical accounts. The prose is fluent, passionate, and respectful. Color illustrations are based on scenes from the movie.

MIDDLE SCHOOL

Bell, William. *Zack.*
New York: Simon and Schuster. 1999.

In this riveting story, Zack, a mixed-race teenager, goes on a journey in search of his African-American roots. Comfortable with his Jewish identity and relatives, he has been mysteriously denied any knowledge of the other side of his family. The Jewish content of the story is slight, but the exploration of prejudice is powerful.

Dahlberg, Maurine F. *Play to the Angels.*
New York: Farrar, Straus and Giroux. 2000.

In Vienna in 1938, 12-year-old Greta studies music with her teacher, Herr Hummel, in preparation for an important recital. Herr Hummel is a mysterious but kindly figure, and he helps Greta develop self-confidence. When it turns out that he is fleeing the Nazis under an assumed name, Greta risks her life to save him. Jewish characters are not central to the story but it is interesting and suspenseful just the same.

Pinsker, Marlene. *In the Days of Sand and Stars.* Illus. by Francois Thisdale.
Toronto: Tundra Books. 2006.

A handsomely illustrated and well-designed collection of short stories about biblical women: Eve, Naamah, Sarah, Rebecca, Leah, Rachel, Dina, and Yocheved. Each story is meant to honor its subject for qualities that give her strength and grace. The writing is uneven, so some of the stories are unnecessarily cryptic.

Watts, Irene. *Finding Sophie.*
Toronto: Tundra Books. 2002.

For the first seven years of her life, Sophie Mandel has lived with her Christian mother and Jewish father in Germany. For the next seven and all through World War II, she is living in England with a foster parent she fondly calls Aunt Em. At age 14, Sophie feels thoroughly English but she knows that her future is uncertain once the war is over. At war's end, she learns that her mother has died and that her father is recuperating from imprisonment in Dachau. She is torn between her duty to him and her fervent desire to stay in England. A chance encounter with Marianne, an older girl she met on the *Kindertransport*, links this novel with the previous two in Watt's fine trilogy: *Good-Bye, Marianne* and *Remember Me*.

Whiting, Jim. *The Life and Times of Moses.*
Hockessin, DE: Mitchell Lane. 2005.

This slim, heavily illustrated account of Moses and his times combines the biblical record with modern scholarship. Chapters are arranged chronologically, from Moses' birth to death. The usual pattern in each chapter is to give the biblical or traditional account, followed by modern interpretations. Although differences between Jewish and Christian beliefs are noted, the terms "BC" and "Old Testament" are used and quotes from a Christian version of the Bible are used. An acceptable secular presentation.

HIGH SCHOOL

Bat-Ami, Miriam. *Two Suns In the Sky*.
Asheville, NC: Front Street/Cricket Books. 1999.

An intense and well-written historical novel set in Oswego, New York during World War II. The refugee camp at Fort Ontario was the only one established on American soil during the war. Told in alternating voices, the story of a romance between a Jewish refugee boy and an Irish-Catholic local girl is portrayed with sensitivity.

Sachs, Marilyn. *Lost in America.*
New Milford, CT: Roaring Brook Press. 2005.

A notable author returns to a character whose experiences in France during the Holocaust she portrayed in *A Pocket Full of Seeds*. Here, the orphaned teenager Nicole arrives in New York to begin a new life. It is a bittersweet one because, despite all of the amazing new things she discovers—like new friends, banana splits, and high heeled shoes—her family's tragic fate is never out of her mind and it hurts her to feel that Americans simply aren't interested. Written in a concise style, the novel shows Nicole's gradual adjustment to America and her growth as a young woman. Filled with humor, pathos, and the author's admiration for the woman on whom Nicole's character is based, it is a story that young teenage girls will take to their hearts.

Ward, Elaine. *Old Testament Women.*
New York: Enchanted Lion. 2004.

Part of the Art Revelations Series, this consists of art depicting women of the Hebrew Bible. Most of the painters are Old Masters, and a short biographical sketch of each painter represented by a major work is given.

CHAPTER 6

Justice and Righteousness

"Let justice well up as waters, and righteousness
as a mighty stream."

Tanakh

PRESCHOOL

Cousins, Lucy. ***Noah's Ark.***
Cambridge, MA: Candlewick. 1993.

The simplicity of the text and bright gouache artwork make this a captivating version of the Bible story for very young children. Bright colors and spare phrasing introduce the tale charmingly. There is also a board book version available.

Gerstein, Mordicai. ***Noah and the Great Flood.***
New York: Simon and Schuster. 1999.

Fanciful legendary elements embellish Gerstein's retelling of the Noah story. The oil-on-vellum illustrations are rich in detail and full of life; the narrative is lively and lyrical. There are several departures here from more traditional tellings: Noah is red-haired, elemental figure instead of an old man with a long, white beard; the wicked people are portrayed as ogres; and angels are prominent. Like Gerstein's other retellings of Bible stories, this uses strands of legend to enrich the narrative and provide a stage on which the illustrations have a major part.

Jules, Jacqueline. ***Noah and the Ziz.*** Illus. by Katherine Janus Kahn.
Minneapolis, MN: Kar-Ben/Lerner. 2005.

The Ziz, a giant bird from Jewish legend, was the main character in *The Hardest Word*, where he learned to say "I'm sorry" after making many messes. In this second story, the Ziz helps Noah build the ark but he is careless and too much in a hurry. Does he learn the error of his ways? Indeed he does, with a great deal of preaching.

Kuskin, Karla. *The Animals and the Ark.* Illus. by Michael Grejniec.
New York: Simon and Schuster/Atheneum. 2002.

Karla Kuskin wrote the poem that comprises the narrative of this delightful book in 1957. Now it has been illustrated with splashy, rollicking watercolors and packaged in a creatively designed format. With no explicit biblical content, it recapitulates the story of the Flood emphasizing the animals and the practical problems of so many crowded together in one small ark. Reading this aloud to a group will take some practice but it is well worth it.

Lenski, Lois. *Mr. and Mrs. Noah.*
New York: Random House. 2002.

Originally published by Crowell in 1948, this is typical of many of the books by the talented author-illustrator whose work helped establish modern children's literature. It is quite small—about the size of a board book—and tells the story in direct and economical style. The figures in the illustrations resemble dolls; each illustration depicts only the essential details, using black outlines, flat primary colors, and pale backgrounds. Artful in its simplicity, this follows the biblical narrative and is a charming introduction to the story for preschoolers.

Reinhart, Matthew. *The Ark.*
New York: Simon and Schuster/Little Simon. 2005.

The biblical story of Noah is told with a few *midrashic* embellishments, each passage dominated by stunning pop-up scenes. Because of the motion obtainable in pop-up art, Noah and his sons actually hammer, birds fly, lightning flashes, and tigers roar. Especially appropriate for displays or storytelling.

PRIMARY

Backman, Aidel. *The Money In the Honey.*
New York: Merkos. 2003.

An attractively illustrated story based on midrash about a rich woman who hides her money in a jar of honey. Her greedy neighbor steals the money and a young shepherd named David—the future King David—helps her get it back.

Brodman, Aliana. *The Gift.* Illus. by Anthony Carnabuci.
New York: Simon and Schuster. 1993.

A sweet, almost too good to be true, story about a child who foregoes many of the things she wants to buy with her Hanukkah *gelt* and gives it instead to a poor street musician. The large, luminous illustrations are very popular with little girls and they give the story a this-world quality that it is otherwise lacking.

Cohen, Barbara. *Even Higher.* Illus. by Anatoly Ivanov.
New York: Lothrop, Lee, and Shephard. 1987.

The retelling of an I. L. Peretz story about a man who is skeptical of the rabbi's reputed saintliness. When he follows the rabbi to see what he is up to, he discovers the true extent of his righteousness and becomes one of his most faithful followers. Set in a *shetl* just prior to the High Holidays, this demonstrates how *tzedakah* and *tikkun olam* are ways of reaching heaven.

Greengard, Alison. *Noah's Ark.* Illus. by Carol Racklin-Siegel.
Oakland, CA: EKS. 2004.

A handsomely illustrated book, written in Hebrew with an English translation on the opposite page. The English text is faithful to the Hebrew, which is somewhat abbreviated from the original story in *Genesis*. A Hebrew-English glossary and an exact translation follow the story.

Jaffe, Nina. *In the Month of Kislev.* Illus. by Louise August.
New York: Viking. 1992.

One of the best picture books for Hanukkah, this is the story of a rich but stingy man who wants to charge the children of a poor man for merely smelling his *latkes*. The judgement of the wise rabbi to whom he takes his case exposes the error of his ways and everyone in the town benefits. The strong woodcuts depict both the action and the emotions of the story.

Janisch, Heinz. *Noah's Ark.* Illus. by Lisbeth Zwerger.
New York: North-South Books. 1998.

A new perspective on the Bible story is given by slightly surreal illustrations that show sunken towns from an underwater perspective and mythical as well as human figures scurrying for higher ground. More than many versions of the tale for children, this one suggests the loss of human life that is implicit in the biblical account.

Kimmel, Eric A. *Zigazak! A Magical Hanukkah Night.* Illus. by Jon Goodell.
New York: Doubleday/Random House. 2001.

A pair of devils make mischief in the *shtetl* of Brisk until the rabbi puts an end to their escapades. This jolly story transmits the traditional message that sparks of holiness can be found in unlikely places. The rollicking illustrations recall Kimmel's *Hershel and the Hanukkah Goblins*.

Pinkney, Jerry. *Noah's Ark.*
New York: SeaStar/North-South Books. 2002.

The biblical flood story is told on an epic scale in this gorgeously illustrated version.

It follows the biblical account closely, showing Noah to be God-fearing and obedient. The dignified narrative places attention on the relationship that exists between nature, humans, and God. The dramatic illustrations set human endeavors in a sweeping natural setting. Pinkney is an African-American artist who has shown his artistry with Jewish themes before, as in Goldin's *Journeys with Elijah.*

Prose, Francine. *You Never Know: A Legend of the Lamed Vavniks.*
    Illus. by Mark Podwal.
New York: HarperCollins/Greenwillow. 1998.

With a light touch and glowing, impressionistic illustrations, the story is told of poor Shmuel, the shoemaker whose prayers save the town of Plotchnik from drought and flood. Inspired by legends of the 36 righteous people whose identity must be kept secret, this portrays abstract themes of goodness, justice, and humility with simplicity and great child-appeal.

Shollar, Lean. *Shadow Play: A True Story of Tefillah.* Illus. by Pesach Gerber.
New York: Hachai. 2006.

Retold from the *Talmud* and from commentaries of the *Baal Shem Tov*, this is a rather cryptic story of the effectiveness of prayer when it is uttered by righteous people. The illustrations capture the action and setting well, but the heavy use of Hebrew terminology and rather esoteric concepts limit the story's audience.

Singer, Isaac Bashevis. *Elijah the Slave.* Illus. by Anthony Frasconi.
New York: Farrar, Straus and Giroux. 1970.

Found in many versions, this retelling of an Elijah story is distinguished by the economy and dignity of its language and the impact of its color woodcuts. A poor and virtuous scribe is helped by Elijah, who commands the scribe to sell him as a slave. As a slave, Elijah builds a palace overnight and wins his freedom. The prophet here is a commanding figure, bringing solace to the righteous by working miracles.

Spier, Peter. *Noah's Ark.*
New York: Doubleday/Random House. 1977.

A wordless version of the Noah story, except for the words of the Dutch poem on which it is based printed at the very beginning. Spier's illustrations chronicle the entire saga, from the animals assembled and hoping to board, through the rain pouring down in amazingly evocative watery sheets, to the burdens of Noah and his family doing their daily tasks, to disembarkation and the planting of a new earth under the rainbow. The earthiness, humor, and minute detail of the pictures tell many stories. Winner of a Caldecott Medal.

ELEMENTARY

Altman, Linda Jacobs. *The Importance of Simon Wiesenthal.*
San Diego, CA: Lucent. 2000.

Part of a series of biographies of famous modern figures. Information is presented in a clear and concise manner through the use of sidebars, captioned black-and-white photographs, chapter notes, a bibliography, and an index. This biography brings to light the personal history of a Holocaust survivor, Simon Wiesenthal, and his passionate determination to hunt down Nazi fugitives for prosecution.

Beneduce, Ann Keay. *Moses: The Long Road to Freedom.* Illus. by Gennady Spirin.
New York: Orchard Books/Scholastic Press. 2004.

The story of the *Exodus* is retold in a narrative form that pales in comparison to the splendor of the accompanying illustrations. Large and lavishly spread throughout the book, they provide the drama that the text lacks. A central Passover theme—unleavened bread—is left out of the narrative.

Cassway, Esta. *The Prophets for Young People.*
Lanham, MD: Jason Aronson. 1995.

Stories from the section of the Hebrew Bible called *Nevi'im*, or Prophets, are retold for children in lyrical prose and poetry. The author's embellishments make the stories accessible by relating them to readers' experiences, and the black-and-white illustrations are engaging.

Hodges, Margaret. *Moses.* Illus. by Barry Moser.
San Diego: Harcourt Brace. 2006.

A spare and dignified retelling of the story of Moses' life from birth to death. The narrative closely follows the Bible, adding only enough fictional elements to provide background and transition. Moser's full-page framed illustrations match the text and depict some of its critical events, such as the beating of the Hebrew slave and the parting of the Red Sea.

Jaffe, Nina, and Steve Zeitlin. *The Cow of No Color.*
New York: St. Martin's Press. 1998.

The authors have compiled these stories with a common theme of justice from around the world. Pat conclusions are avoided; the reader is asked to reflect on the stories' moral implications. Only a few of the stories are of Jewish content, but the theme of justice is central to Judaism.

Matas, Carol. *Rosie in New York: Gotcha!*
New York: Aladdin, 2003.

The first in a trilogy, this is the story of 11-year-old Rosie who lives in a New York tenement in 1909. When her mother gets sick, Rosie must go to work in a factory.

There she becomes involved in union activity, including a strike. Treating themes of social justice and social responsibility, the story provides an interesting look into immigrant life on the Lower East Side.

Schwartz, Ellen. **Yossi's Goal.** Illus. by Silvana Bevilacqua.
Custer, WA: Orca, 2006.

Set in Montreal in 1891, this is the story of Yossi, an immigrant boy who works hard to earn money to buy hockey skates, so he can be just like the other boys. When the working conditions at the sweatshop where his father works produce dire consequences, Yossi gives up his savings to buy food for his family. He also becomes involved in the walkout from the factory that his sister and her fiancée organize to draw attention to the plight of workers. Black-and-white pencil sketches, a glossary, and an author's note enhance the historical content.

MIDDLE SCHOOL

Altman, Linda Jacobs. **Impact of The Holocaust.**
Berkeley Heights, NJ: Enslow. 2004.

A title in the Holocaust In History Series, this shows how the enormity of the Holocaust resulted in a new type of international law that holds aggressors accountable to an international court. It also discusses the founding of the United Nations, the struggle for a Jewish homeland, Germany's post-war de-Nazification program, the Eichmann trial, and the establishment of *Yom Hashoah* (Holocaust Remembrance Day) and many Holocaust memorials throughout the world.

Amler, Jane Frances. **Haym Solomon: Patriot Banker of the American Revolution.**
New York: Rosen. 2004.

This biography of the man who helped finance the American Revolution focuses almost entirely on his career in finance rather than on his personal life. The result is a dry account that is useful primarily for report writing.

Feder, Harriet. **Death on Sacred Ground.**
Minneapolis, MN: Lerner. 2001.

Vivi Hartman, a rabbi's daughter and teenage sleuth, uses Talmudic reasoning to solve a crime committed on the Seneca Reservation in New York State. Native Americans, Christian fundamentalists, and ultra-Orthodox Jews are all part of the plot. There are several other Vivi Hartman mysteries.

Mann, Kenny. **The Ancient Hebrews.**
Tarrytown, NY: Benchmark. 1999.

This short book is broad in scope, beginning with the ancient Hebrews and going on into

(Cont'd.)

> *The Ancient Hebrews. (Continued)*
>
> the Hellenistic period, the Diaspora, and modern times, including the State of Israel. The focus is on those characteristics of the Jewish faith and culture that enabled Jewish survival and gave a glorious legacy to the Western civilization. Copiously illustrated, with notes, sidebars, a chronology, and other aids to research.

Mayer, Marianna. *Remembering the Prophets of Sacred Scripture.*
New York: Phyllis Fogelman. 2003.

Who were the prophets? When and where did they live? What were their messages? This handsomely designed and illustrated book combines a succinct and graceful text with reproductions of artwork depicting the prophets. Virtually all of the art is of Christian origin, and there is a slight Christian slant to the vocabulary, such as the use of "Jesus Christ."

Morris, Neil. *The Life of Moses.*
New York: Enchanted Lion. 2003.

This oversize book, part of an art series, is a brief, pictorial account of Moses' life from birth to death, illustrated with paintings by the old masters. All of the art is captioned, and major works are numerically coded to identify their thematic and compositional features. The Christian origin of the art, as well as the text, gives the book a non-Jewish perspective, but the art inspired by Moses is well worth the attention.

Reeves, Mary Bell. *The Secret of the Mezuzah.*
Minneapolis, MN: Bethany House. 1999.

This engrossing mystery is set in Vienna and involves neo-Nazis. The main character, a teenage American boy, has a mother who works for the Nazi hunter, Simon Wiesenthal. The story is intended to reveal how submission to and cooperation with the Nazis allowed the Holocaust to happen. Bethany House is a Christian publisher.

MIDDLE SCHOOL

Rice, Jr., Earle. *Nazi War Criminals.*
Farmington Hills, MI: Lucent. 1998.

Accounts of six Nazi war criminals comprise this volume. An eclectic variety of sources are used, along with many primary and secondary source quotations, anecdotes and information in sidebar form, and numerous illustrations. A chronology, notes, bibliographies, a glossary, and an index are included. The point of view is that the Holocaust was a universal, not merely Jewish, human event.

Rogasky, Barbara. *Dybbuk: A Version.* Illus. by Leonard Everett Fisher.
New York: Holiday House. 2005.

A passionately written and dramatically illustrated version of the classic Jewish tale of broken vows and supernatural possession, based on S. Y. Ansky's famous play. Far more serious than the version of the story for younger children by Francine Prose and Mark Podwal, this conjures up elemental emotions in a mesmerizing blend of writing and art.

Welsh, T. K. *The Unresolved.*
New York: Dutton. 2006

The worst disaster in New York City's history before 9/11 was the fire aboard the *General Slocum* steamship in 1904, in which over 1,000 people died. The narrator of this lyrically written novel is one of the dead: The ghost of a teenage girl who lingers in the world until she can bring those responsible for the fire to justice and clear the boy she loves from charges that he had started it. The setting in what was then called Kleindeutschland, and later the Lower East Side, is richly populated with memorable characters, both good and bad. A sub-theme of anti-Semitism—the accused boy and his father are Jews—enriches an unusual story.

CHAPTER 7

Learning and Wisdom

"Happy is the one who finds wisdom...Its ways are
ways of pleasantness and all its paths are peace. It is
a tree of life to those who cling to it."

Tanakh

PRIMARY

Kimmel, Eric A. *Tuning Up: A Visit with Eric Kimmel.*
Katonah, NY: Richard C. Owen. 2005.

An array of photographs of Eric Kimmel, his friends, family, hobbies, and working environment provides an up-close-and-personal look at this well-known writer. His enthusiasm for writing is obvious and his narration does a good job of clarifying the writing process. There is no explicit Jewish content, although Kimmel mentions his grandmother, her *menorah*, and a family *dreidel*.

Lakin, Patricia. *Albert Einstein: Genius of the Twentieth Century.*
New York: Aladdin. 2005.

Einstein's "burning desire to know what was behind things" is the theme of this easy-to-read biography, which is part of the Stories of Famous Americans Series. The small format, large type, and ample white space make it comfortable for young children to read, and the writing and illustrations bring the subject to life. Of only partial use as an introductory reference book, with no table of contents or index.

Michelson, Richard. *Too Young For Yiddish.* Illus. by Neil Waldman.
Watertown, MA: Talewinds/Charlesbridge. 2002.

A story inspired by the work of Aaron Lansky, founder of the National Yiddish Book Center. It involves a young boy and his grandfather, from whom the boy learns to cherish Yiddish books. The sepia-tone illustrations are nostalgic, and the audience for the book—with a format that will attract younger children and a story more likely to have meaning to older ones—is hard to gauge.

Oppenheim, Shulamith Levy. *Rescuing Einstein's Compass.* Illus. by George Juhasz.
New York: Crocodile/Interlink. 2003.

An illustrated story about a little boy named Theo who meets Albert Einstein, "the most famous man in the world," takes him for a ride on his sailboat, and jumps into the lake to retrieve Einstein's treasured compass when it falls into the water. The story is based on several Einstein-related incidents in the life of the author and her husband. It is charmingly written and illustrated, although there is no Jewish content.

Schotter, Roni. *The Boy Who Loved Words.* Illus. by Giselle Potter.
New York: Schwartz and Wade/Random House. 2006.

An ebullient illustrated story that celebrates words. Selig is a boy who loves words, collects them, and cherishes them. He consults a Yiddishe genie who advises him to find a "poipose." That purpose is to spread words like a Johnny Appleseed of words and as he docs so, lovers adore one another, apologies restore friendships, teachers impart wisdom, and artists create masterpieces. Words appear everywhere in the story: Scattered through the illustrations, on the endpapers, in a glossary, and especially in the narrative. The Jewish content is not explicit, but Selig's family and certainly the Yiddishe genie imply it.

Silverman, Erica. *Raisel's Riddle.* Illus. by Susan Gaber.
New York: Farrar, Strauss and Giroux. 1999.

Large, handsome illustrations help tell this Jewish Cinderella story set in Poland during the holiday of Purim. The heroine is a learned girl who finds happiness and intellectual satisfaction with a rabbi's son because he appreciates her mind as much as her beauty. The climax depends on a riddle instead of a glass slipper.

Silverman, Erica. *Sholom's Treasure.* Illus. by Mordicai Gerstein.
New York: Farrar, Straus and Giroux. 2005.

Did Sholom Aleichem really have a mean stepmother? Did he compile a dictionary of her colorful Yiddish insults? Was he the boy making those grotesque faces behind the *melamed's* back in *cheder*? These are the kind of details, fascinating to children, that *Sholom's Treasure* deals with. Erica Silverman and Mordecai Gerstein have combined their gifts and knowledge of Sholom Aleichem to tell and show children some events—tragic and comic—from his early life. This charming story—part biography and part fiction—will introduce children to one of the great comic writers of our age and a prime chronicler of the Jewish people at the turn of the past century. Winner of a Sydney Taylor Book Award.

Ungar, Richard. 2004. *Rachel's Library.*
Toronto: Tundra Books.

Ungar's signature illustrations—intensely bright, filled with details, and suffused with a warm, humorous feeling—are the most successful element in this third

Rachel story. Set (nominally) in *Chelm*, it reveals no large truths about the human condition, as traditional Chelm tales do, but rather, provides a structure for Ungar to build a mildly pleasant story. Hoping to change their reputation as fools and show the world how wise they really are, a delegation of *Chelmniks* goes to Warsaw, where they expect to find a solution. Rachel goes along and identifies what they need: A library. So they go back to Chelm and build one, stocking it with books from their homes. Who can argue with the need for a library? Even so, the story is pallid.

ELEMENTARY

Allon, Hagit, and Lena Zehavi. *The Mystery of The Dead Sea Scrolls.*
   Illus. by Yossi Abulafia.
Philadelphia: Jewish Publication Society. 2004.

Cartoon-like illustrations and large color photographs of the Israel Museum's Shrine of the Book, plus an Israeli home, the Judean Desert, and artifacts associated with the Judean Desert sect face each page of text in this engaging book about the Dead Sea Scrolls, told as a mystery story. A fictional 11-year-old named Daniel is assigned to write a report about the Scrolls so he begins, wisely, at the Shrine of the Book. Daniel is helped by a guard, a librarian, and an archaeologist, as his quest takes him, with family, to Qumran, where the scrolls were found. For its glimpse of a present-day Israeli family, as well as for the abundance of information woven into the story, this is a welcome companion—for slightly younger children—to Ilene Cooper's *The Dead Sea Scrolls*.

Brown, Don. *Odd Boy Out: Young Albert Einstein.*
Boston: Houghton Mifflin. 2004.

An outstanding picture biography of Albert Einstein, revealing through a strong, well-focused text and charming illustrations the complex, brilliant scientist who emerged from an imperfect and lonely child. Considered weird by almost everyone, Einstein's Jewishness was only one of the reasons why he was at odds with family, teachers, and peers. Explanations of Einstein's intellectual development and discoveries are given in clear, yet poetic, language. The sepia-toned illustrations provide a feeling of European formality; the portrayal of loneliness followed by success and fame focus this memorable biography.

Chaikin, Miriam. *Alexandra's Scroll: The Story of the First Hanukkah.*
New York: Henry Holt. 2002.

Readers gain a palpable sense of what life in ancient Israel must have been like, especially the difficulties of living under the Greco-Syrian occupation, in this historical novel. The focus is on Alexandra's aspiration to become a scribe and on her personal experiences during the *Maccabean* revolt. The descriptions of the customs practiced by Alexandra's family are fascinating and convey a sense of spiritual connectedness.

Delano, Marfe Ferguson. *Genius: A Photobiography of Albert Einstein.*
Washington, DC: National Geographic. 2005.

Using a straightforward style and many attractive photos, along with easy-to-understand diagrams of difficult scientific concepts, *Genius* provides a fascinating, complete biography of Einstein from his birth to his death. The author does a fine job in explaining how his religion and ancestry helped shape Einstein's character. Rounded out by a chronology, a thorough resources list, and a detailed index. Highly recommended.

Gormley, Beatrice. *Adara.*
Grand Rapids, MI: Eerdmans. 2002.

Adara is an adolescent girl, neither Israelite nor Aramean, who is caught in the warfare between the two peoples during the reign of King Ahab and Queen Jezebel. She serves as an intermediary between the adversaries, bringing knowledge of the one God to the Aramean elite. The story is based on an incident from *Kings* II, Chap. 5, in which the prophet Elisha cures the Aramean general Naaman of leprosy. An interesting look at a period of religious syncretism and cultural transition.

MacLeod, Elizabeth. *Albert Einstein: A Life of Genius.*
Toronto: Kids Can Press. 2003.

This photo biography is light, lively, and very readable. The importance of Einstein's work is conveyed without complex explanations, and the many photographs are well reproduced. Einstein's Jewish identity is addressed, although this is not a major focus of the book. A timeline and index are included.

Mahr, Aryeh. *Shmuel Ha Nagid: A Tale of the Golden Age.*
    Illus. by Esteve Polls.
Nanuet, NY: Mahrwood/Feldheim. 2005.

A graphic novel that is the first in a planned series about the life of Rabbi Shmuel Ha Nagid, a prominent *Talmudic* scholar as well as philosopher, poet, statesman, and warrior. It begins with his flight from Cordoba, Spain, and continues with his rise to power in Granada as vizier to the king. It is recommended for readers who are conversant in Hebrew or who are familiar with terms commonly used in the study of *Torah* and *Talmud*. Volume 2 was published in 2006.

Pirotta, Saviour. *Albert Einstein.*
Austin, TX: Raintree/Steck Vaughn. 2002.

A balanced and accurate brief account of Einstein's life and achievements. After giving an overview of scientific advances in the nineteenth century, the author provides a chronological account of Einstein, including his childhood, family life, and experiences in school—all set against a European background in the period of two world wars. A more in-depth treatment of Einstein and, specifically, his Jewish identity and involvement in Zionist causes is found in *Albert Einstein: Visionary Scientist* by

John Severance. However, this is an acceptable introduction on a somewhat easier level. Part of the Scientists Who Made History Series.

Rossel, Seymour. **Sefer Ha-Aggadah: Volume Two.** Illus. by Judy Dick.
New York: UAHC Press. 1998.

Based on the classic collection of legends and stories of which Hayyim Nachman Bialik was the co-compiler, this features stories about Honi, Hillel and Shamai, Rachel, the wife of Hillel, and Beruria the scholar, as well as biblical figures. Stories exemplify concepts such as the importance of *Torah* study, observance of the Sabbath, and the importance of charity. The first volume was published by UAHC Press in 1996.

Singer, Isaac Bashevis. **Naftali the Storyteller and His Horse, Sus.**
   Illus. by Margot Zemach.
New York: Farrar, Straus and Giroux. 1976.

A collection of eight stories, including several set in *Chelm* and several based on events from Singer's childhood. Naftali, the title character, is very much like Singer himself: A storyteller who keeps the past alive. His story is a celebration of books, learning, and imagination—one that every storyteller should know. In the other tales, imps and fools appear along with Singer's family, his experiences at *cheder*, and the inquiring mind of a child who became a great writer. Margot Zemach's scratchy black-and-white illustrations capture the essence of each story.

Stone, Tanya Lee. **Ilan Ramon, Israel's First Astronaut.**
Brookfield, CT: Millbrook Press. 2003.

The circumstances of Ilan Ramon's death add poignancy to this brief biography. Combined with an account of Ramon's life, career, and dedication to the space program is information about the space shuttle, space experiments, and the jobs that astronauts do on it. Many photographs add to the appeal.

Weil, Sylvie. **My Guardian Angel.**
New York: Scholastic. 2004.

An outstanding historical novel set in eleventh-century Troyes, France, in the household of Rabbi Solomon ben Isaac, the great Jewish sage, Rashi. Historic, religious, and everyday domestic events are portrayed through the experiences and thoughts of 12-year-old Elvina, Rashi's granddaughter, whose love of learning sets her somewhat apart from most of her contemporaries. Elvina is a charming, spirited, and believable heroine whose acute perceptions bring the time in which she lived to life. The crisp narrative style weaves setting, plot, character, and theme into an appealing whole, with Jewish values giving the story ballast. Rashi's teachings are incorporated into the story, showing how they gave strength and affirmation to a small, vulnerable Diaspora community of 1,000 years ago. Translated from French by Gillian Rosner.

Weissenberg, Fran. *The Streets Are Paved With Gold.*
New York: Authors Guild. 2002.

This novel won a Sydney Taylor Manuscript Award when it was first published in 1990. It has now been reissued as an Authors Guild Backinprint.com Edition. Debbie Gold, the narrator, is 14, the only girl in a family of Jewish immigrants living in Brooklyn in 1922. The plot blends incidents that show the experiences of immigrants struggling in a new land with action involving Debbie's friends at school, her goals and aspirations, and her role in a hardworking Jewish family. Readers of today will recognize themselves in Debbie while appreciating the differences between then and now. Among the many values inherent in the Gold family and the story is a recognition that education is worth sacrifice.

Wells, Rosemary. *Streets of Gold.* Illus. by Dan Andreasen.
New York: Dial. 1999.

These vignettes, based on Mary Antin's *The Promised Land* and beautifully illustrated by Dan Andreasen, tell in Mary's words of the hardships faced by Russian Jews, the journey to the United States, and of the joys of American life. Mary's joy in being able to go to school is very appealing and may surprise modern children who take it for granted.

MIDDLE SCHOOL

Abrams, Judith Z. *The Secret World of Kabbalah.*
Minneapolis, MN: Kar-Ben/Lerner. 2006.

A clearly written introduction for young people to Jewish mystical tradition of *Kabbalah*, explaining how it is much more than wearing a red string around your wrist. The author, a rabbi, discusses basic Kabbalistic concepts, several different approaches to its study, and gives advice on how to find a good Kabbalah teacher. She shows readers how Kabbalah is something that is "hiding in plain sight" and gives examples of how it can be found in the *Torah*, in *gematria*, and in synagogue services.

Bankston, John. *Albert Einstein and the Theory of Relativity.*
Hockessin, DE: Mitchell Lane. 2003.

Part of a series called Unlocking the Secrets of Science, this book presents scientific and biographical information in a colloquial style. Although the facts are accurate, the absence of documentation and scientific drawings is a detriment. After a chapter giving historical background on physics, short chapters describe Einstein's work. Of slight Jewish content, this includes a chronology, a glossary, a list of books and Web sites, and an index.

Bankston, John. *Edward Teller and the Development of the Hydrogen Bomb.*
Hockessin, DE: Mitchell Lane. 2003.

Part of the Unlocking the Secrets of Science Series, this presents scientific and biographical information in the same, somewhat chatty, style as the other titles in the series. Documentation is lacking but the facts are accurate. After a chapter giving historical background on nuclear science, short chapters describe Teller's work. Of slight Jewish content, this includes a chronology, a glossary, a list of books and Web sites, and an index.

Bankston, John. *Lise Meitner and the Atomic Age.*
Hockessin, DE: Mitchell Lane. 2004.

Like other books in the Unlocking the Secrets of Science Series, this gives an overview of Meitner's work in nuclear physics and sets it in a historical context. It is simplified but accurate and portrays Meitner as both a human being and a scientist. Useful for reports.

Barron, Rachel Stiffler. *Lise Meitner, Discoverer of Nuclear Fission.*
Greensboro, NC: Morgan Reynolds. 2000.

A biography of the distinguished nuclear physicist who converted to Christianity as a young woman. It includes material on women's attempts to enter the scientific professions and on scientists who attempted to carry on their work under the Third Reich.

Feinstein, Edward. *Tough Questions Jews Ask: A Young Adult's Guide to Building a Jewish Life.*
Woodstock, VT: Jewish Lights. 2003.

Rabbi Feinstein addresses questions such as: "Why should people believe in God?" and "Is any of that stuff in the Bible true?" He does a creditable job of finding reasonable explanations and for putting the questions into perspective. Useful for kids preparing for their Bar or Bat Mitzvah, their rabbis, and parents. Also useful as an introduction to Jewish thought for a non-Jewish audience. The term "young adult" is somewhat misleading; the audience is actually adolescents.

Hamilton, Janet. *Lise Meitner: Pioneer of Nuclear Fission.*
Hockessin, DE: Mitchell Lane. 2003.

A well-organized and documented biography of the scientist who discovered nuclear fission. Meitner was an Austrian Jew who converted to Christianity. She had to flee Nazi Germany and spent years in Denmark. In this book, she is a remote and diffident figure whose devotion to science was total, despite being rejected for a Nobel Prize.

Napoli, Donna Jo. *Daughter of Venice.*
New York: Random House. 2002.

Set in Venice in 1592 and informed by a feminist sensibility, this is an engrossing and historically accurate novel about a girl from a noble family who wants to be a scholar. Her love for a young Jewish man is an important but not central part of the plot. A vivid picture of Venetian society is drawn, and Donata is based on Elena Piscopia, a Venetian woman who earned a doctoral degree from University of Padua in 1678.

Reef, Catherine. *Sigmund Freud: Pioneer of the Mind.*
New York: Clarion. 2001.

The life and work of one of the modern world's most important thinkers are illuminated in this carefully researched, superbly crafted biography. Freud was controversial during his lifetime and remains so: The author discusses his theories, points out their weaknesses and enduring strengths, and fairly represents the views of both his supporters and critics. This is done within the context of his family life and his position as a Viennese Jew, placing Freud's personal and professional life within a social history. Enhanced by excellent notes, an amazingly clear glossary, and black-and-white photographs. Winner of a Sydney Taylor Book Award.

Severance, John B. *Albert Einstein: Visionary Scientist.*
New York: Clarion. 1999.

An engrossing biography that covers Einstein's entire life—from birth in Ulm, Germany, in 1879 to his death in Princeton, New Jersey, in 1955—as well as his many contributions to physics. Einstein's Jewishness is integrated into the account of his life. The writing is lucid, making complex scientific concepts understandable, and there are many photographs and aids to use, such as a chronology, notes, and an index.

HIGH SCHOOL

Potok, Chaim. *The Chosen.*
New York: Ballantine Books. 1967; 1982.

A classic novel about friendship and the relationship between fathers and sons. After Reuven, a Modern Orthodox boy, and Danny, the scion of a *Hasidic* dynasty, become friends, their lives and the lives of their fathers become entwined in a way that gives each boy the courage to follow his own course in life. The tone is very serious, and much of the story charts the difference between the two modes of belief, but through the characters, a believable tale emerges.

Redsand, Anna. *Viktor Frankl: A Life Worth Living.*
New York: Clarion. 2006.

The life of one of the great psychotherapists of the 20th century is presented in this meticulously researched biography of Viktor Frankl. While studying neurology in Vienna, Frankl began to develop a new type of treatment that he called logotherapy. He tested his theories under the worst of conditions while imprisoned by the Nazis in a concentration camp. Surviving the Holocaust, Frankl wrote a book about logotherapy called *Man's Search for Meaning*, one of the most widely read and highly regarded psychology works of modern times. He lived and died as a believing Jew.

CHAPTER 8

Lovingkindness

"The world depends on three things: the study
of Torah, the worship of God, and acts of
lovingkindness."

Talmud

PRESCHOOL

Brett, Jan. ***On Noah's Ark.***
New York: G. P. Putnam's Sons. 2003.

A secular version of the biblical tale, narrated by Noah's granddaughter. Her description of the animals on the ark is enhanced by superb realistic illustrations by the author-illustrator of *The Mitten*, well known for her paintings of animals.

Gadot, A. S. ***The First Gift.*** Illus. by Marie LaFrance.
Minneapolis, MN: Kar-Ben/Lerner. 2006.

The first gift we are given is our name. In this story about names, a boy recalls his namesake and talks about names in general, including the different names by which a single person may be known. Full-page color illustrations use simple shapes and soft colors to support the text.

Koralek, Jenny. ***The Moses Basket.*** Illus. by Pauline Baynes.
Grand Rapids, MI: Eerdmans. 2003.

The role of Miriam, Moses's sister, is emphasized in this fresh approach to the biblical story. Her future as a prophet is foreshadowed by her prediction that Pharoah's daughter will take care of the baby Moses, and when this comes true, Miriam dances and sings in a manner reminiscent of her song of jubilation after the crossing of the Red Sea. The illustrations are in muted browns, blues, and greens and their formal style suggests Egyptian temple decoration. A good choice for reading aloud.

Reid, Barbara. *Two By Two.*
New York: Scholastic. 1996.

Among the many versions of the Noah's Ark story, this stands out for its rollicking verse and delightful clay-modeled illustrations. Excellent for reading aloud to a group of children who can participate by identifying the many different animals that crowd the ark.

Rosenbaum, Andrea Warmflash. *A Grandpa Like Yours; A Grandma Like Yours.*
    Illus. by Barb Bjornson.
Minneapolis, MN: Kar-Ben/Lerner. 2006.

A beautifully illustrated book for preschoolers on the joys of grandparents. Whether you call them zaydes, sabas, grandpas, pops, bubbes, savtas, or grandmas, their love of their grandchildren is shown in many ways. A menagerie of happy animals—elephant grandmas, a kangaroo savta, porcupine papas, snail sabas—cavort across the pages, portraying many of the wonderful Jewish things that grandparents do with and for their grandchildren. Told very simply in bouncy rhyme, the book reverses from the story about grandmas to the story about grandpas, all depicted in charming animal form.

Rosenfeld, Dina. *Dovid the Little Shepherd.* Illus. by Ilene Winn-Lederer.
New York: Hachai. 1996.

Taking care of sheep, tending to their needs, and looking after their welfare imbues Dovid with the skills of leadership and compassion that he will need as *Dovid HaMelech*. This is an appealing biographical sketch for the youngest children.

Rosenfeld, Dina. *Kind Little Rivka.* Illus. by Ilene Winn-Lederer.
New York: Hachai. 1993.

Based on biblical and *midrashic* accounts of why Rebecca was chosen to be Isaac's wife, this book shows her generosity and kindness. The bright, somewhat super-realistic illustrations help tell the story.

Schweiger-D'mil, Itzhak. *Hannah's Sabbath Dress.* Illus. by Ora Eitan.
New York: Simon and Schuster. 1996.

This flawless picture book based on a traditional story extolls the joys of the Sabbath while teaching the *mitzvah* of kindness toward others. The illustrations almost dance off the page. Translated from Hebrew.

Waldman, Neil. *The Two Brothers: A Legend of Jerusalem.*
New York: Simon and Schuster/Atheneum. 1985.

This version of a well-known legend shows how King Solomon came to build the Temple on the very spot where the two brothers discover that each has been looking after the needs of the other. The illustrations resemble ancient, sun-drenched frescoes.

PRIMARY

Aroner, Miriam. *The Kingdom of The Singing Birds.* Illus. by Shelly O. Haas. Rockville, MD: Kar-Ben. 1993.

"Long ago, in a little village in a faraway land, a gentle rabbi named Zusya wondered about the world he lived in... The more Zusya asked, the more he learned. Thus he grew wise in the ways of nature." Strikingly suggestive illustrations grace this story with a theme of kindness to animals.

Blanc, Esther Silverstein. *Berchick.* Illus. by Tennessee Dixon. Volcano, CA: Volcano Press. 1989.

Homesteading in Wyoming in the early years of the twentieth century, a Jewish mother saves the life of an orphaned colt whom she names Berchick. An unusually close relationship develops between the two, and after being the family pet, Berchick grows up to run wild and free. Winner of a Sydney Taylor Book Award.

Blanc, Esther Silverstein, and Godeane Eagle. *Long Johns for a Small Chicken.* Volcano, CA: Volcano Press. 2003.

This delightful story by the author of *Berchik* is set on a Nebraska homestead in the early 1900s. Mama saves a chick who is caught outside in a hail storm by making him a pair of long johns to cover his featherless body and nursing him back to health. Strong values are imbued in a humorous and appealing story.

Blitz, Shmuel. *The Artscroll Children's Book of Ruth.* Illus. by Tova Katz. New York: Mesorah. 2005.

A large-format, well-illustrated version of the Book of Ruth for children. It opens as a Hebrew book, left to right, with the biblical text on the right side of each page and the English on the left. Commentary according to the Orthodox Jewish thought is found throughout. A reverent, child-friendly, and useful version of the *Megillah* of Ruth.

Brandeis, Batsheva. *Faiga Finds a Way.* Illus. by Alexandra Levitas. New York: Hachai. 2006

Times are hard in Czarist Russia, but the spirit of lovingkindness that animates this short novel imbues it with hope. Part of Hachai's series for beginning readers, it has been preceded by *The Great Potato Plan*, *More Precious than Gold*, and *The Secret Tunnel*, all with historical setting and brave, religiously observant children as protagonists.

Burstein, Chaya. *Hanukkah Cat, Revised Edition.* Illus. by Judy Hanks-Henn. Rockville, MD: Kar-Ben Copies. 2001.

Amusing new illustrations add sparkle to this appealing story of a little boy who finds a kitten at the start of Hanukkah. The story of the *Maccabees* and Lenny's adventures with the mischievous kitten are deftly interwoven.

Fagan, Cary. *Ten Old Men and a Mouse.* Illus. by Gary Clement.
Plattsburg, NY: Tundra Books of Northern New York. 2007.

Ten old men gather each day in an old synagogue to pray. When they discover a mouse living among the holy books, they realize, after a half-hearted attempt to trap it, that they've found a new friend. After she presents them with a littler of mice, they release the mouse family into the woods and then pine for their friend. But as winter sets in, they hear a scraaatch... Delightful illustrations match the story.

Freedman, Florence. *Brothers: A Hebrew Legend.* Illus. by Robert Andrew Parker.
New York: HarperCollins. 1985.

The retelling of a legend about two brothers whose love for one another and acts of selflessness cause first confusion and then heavenly rewards. This version is a classic, told and illustrated with simplicity and beauty. Other retellings are *The Two Brothers: A Legend of Jerusalem* by Neal Waldman and *The Brothers' Promise* by Frances Harber.

Fridman, Sashi. *The Last Pair of Shoes.* Illus. by Seva.
New York: Merkos. 2005.

A well-illustrated, well-paced story on the theme of generosity. It is set in the past, during a time of war. Shalva, the narrator, recounts a story from his boyhood, when he was responsible for earning a living for his family while his father was at war. He learns his father's craft of shoemaking and helps not only himself but a stranger with that "last pair of shoes." Told without preaching, it is recommended for its strong Jewish values.

Gellman, Ellie. *Jeremy's Dreidel.* Illus. by Judith Friedman.
Rockville, MD: Kar-Ben Copies. 1992.

Set during Hanukkah, this appealing story celebrates the creativity of children and sensitively explores a parent's blindness. As a group of children make off-beat *dreidels*, Jeremy puts Braille letters on his. His classmates learn that Jeremy's father is blind and how his family deals with this disability.

Gerstein, Mordicai. *The Shadow of a Flying Bird.*
New York: Hyperion. 1994.

A legend of the Jews of Kurdistan, this is a poetic and touching evocation of the death of Moses. In telling of Moses's refusal to die, it also reflects the Jewish concept of struggling with God. Handsomely illustrated, it is appropriate for a wide age range.

Harber, Frances. *The Brothers' Promise.* Illus. by Thor Wickstrom.
Morton Grove, IL: Albert Whitman. 1998.

Originally set in or near Jerusalem during biblical times, this version of a traditional story about brotherly love is set in Eastern Europe. The writing is as spiced with Yiddish phrases as the pictures are seasoned with the flavor of *shtetl* life. As each brother strives to secretly help the other, the confusion is blamed on *dybbuks*, ghosts, and imps—those staples of Eastern European Jewish folklore.

Hershenhorn, Esther. *Chicken Soup by Heart*. Illus. by Rosanne Litzinger. New York: Simon and Schuster. 2002.

When Rudi's sitter, Mrs. Dinkins, gets a cold, he makes her the cure she makes for him. Seasoning the chicken soup with stories as he and his mama stir, Rudi remembers all of the good times he and Mrs. Dinkins have had together, despite the difference in their ages. The Yiddish-flavored style of the writing sounds as though Mrs. Gittel herself were telling it, while the illustrations reflect the story's warmth and humor. Winner of a Sydney Taylor Book Award.

Kosofsky, Chaim. *Much, Much Better*. Illus. by Jessica Schiffman. New York: Hachai. 2006.

Adapted from a traditional Elijah tale, this gentle story is about a mysterious traveler who rewards a childless couple's kindness by predicting a surprising future for them, one with a "sticky stained tablecloth" and "crumbs scattered on the floor." Attractively illustrated, it takes place within the Jewish community that once existed in Baghdad.

Levinson, Robin K. *Miriam's Journey: Discovering a New World*. Illus. by Drusilla Kehl. Teaneck, NJ: Gali Girls. 2006.

This easy chapter book is the first in a series called Gali Girls, which is meant to be the Jewish counterpart to the American girl series, with a doll representing each main character. Kindness, respect, charity, and honesty will be the themes of the stories showing Jewish girls in historical settings. In this book, Miriam and her family journey to America only to discover that they will not be admitted into the country because their father—the breadwinner—has died. Their struggle to gain entrance is at the heart of the story.

Marzollo, Jean. *Ruth and Naomi*. New York: Little Brown. 2005.

In her series of Bible stories, Jean Marzollo condenses details while preserving the story's spirit and meaning. The biblical account of Ruth and Naomi exemplifies *chesed*, and this is the predominant theme of the story, shown by Ruth and Naomi's caring for one another and by the kindness shown to them by Boaz. The lilting illustrations extend the story by showing several generations of redheads, starting with Ruth and culminating with the birth of David, future King of Israel. A chorus of rabbits comments on the story, adding a childlike point of view.

Polacco, Patricia. *Mrs. Katz and Tush.*
New York: Bantam. 1992.

A sentimental but sweet story about a friendship between an elderly Jewish widow and a little African-American boy. Larnel visits Mrs. Katz, looks after her, and gives her a little tailless cat whom she names Tush. As their lives entwine, Mrs. Katz and Larnel share food and holidays and a knowledge that their people's pasts both involved slavery and discrimination. After Larnel has grown up, he, his wife, and their children visit and put a little stone upon Mrs. Katz's grave. The bold, expressive illustrations capture characters' expressions and many other cogent details of the story.

Polacco, Patricia. *The Trees of the Dancing Goats.*
New York: Simon and Schuster. 1996.

When a scarlet fever epidemic threatens to ruin their Christian neighbors' Christmas, a Jewish farming family decorates little trees for them, using the carved animals that were meant to be Hanukkah presents. A warm story with expressive illustrations, this stresses interfaith harmony. As in so many of Polacco's books, the Jewish family appears more Russian than Jewish in dress, looks, and language.

Sandman, Rochel. *Perfect Porridge.* Illus. by Chana Zakashanskyi-Sverev.
New York: Hachai. 2000.

In a time of war, *Zayde* Mendel and *Bubbe* Hinda set out to help the hungry people around them. While Bubbe goes to collect bread, Zayde starts a big pot of porridge, despite the fact that he has never cooked. After several near-disasters, the porridge is delicious! A gentle story of piety, *Torah* study, and lovingkindness is told in this humorous and easy-to-read book.

Schram, Peninnah. *The Chanukah Blessing.* Illus. by Jeffrey Allon.
New York: UAHC Press. 2000.

The gifted storyteller, Peninnah Schram has drawn on Jewish oral tradition plus her own memories and experiences to create an original story for Hanukkah featuring Elijah. The plot follows a familiar pattern: Elijah in the guise of an old man is invited to share a poor family's meagre meal and, in return for their kindness, he leaves them with spiritual and material riches. The narrative is a bit choppy; this is a story better told than read. The illustrations are commonplace.

Schur, Maxine Rose. *The Story of Ruth.* Illus. by Gwen Connelly.
Minneapolis, MN: Kar-Ben/Lerner. 2005.

This pallid retelling of the story of Ruth and Naomi begins with the journey of Elimelech and his family to Moab to escape famine and continues through the biblical account to Ruth's marriage to Boaz. Departing from the biblical theme of *chesed*, it emphasizes the strength of the two women.

Shollar, Leah. ***Thread of Kindness: A Tzedaka Story.***
   Illus. by Shoshana Mekibel.
New York: Hachai. 2000.

Goodness rewarded is the theme of this traditional story about a poor family who use the six years of plenty given to them by Elijah to help others. The "thread of kindness" that the family sows throughout the community lasts "to this very day." Dreamy watercolors portray the *shtetl* setting and the story's meaning.

Silverman, Erica. ***Gittel's Hands.*** Illus. by Deborah Noure Lattimore.
Mahwah, NJ: Bridgewater. 1996.

Rumpelstiltskin meets Elijah in this mildly feminist recasting of familiar folklore motifs. Gittel is a kind, obedient daughter whose domestic talents are exaggerated by her boastful father and exploited by a greedy merchant. Challenged to fulfill some impossible tasks that her father bragged she could do, Gittel helps a dove, a cat, and a beggar (Elijah, of course) who, in turn, help her. Fanciful illustrations add to the story.

Stillerman, Marci. ***Nine Spoons: A Chanukah Story.*** Illus. by Pesach Gerber.
New York: Hachai. 1998.

This story of *mesirat nefesh* is told by a *zoftig* grandmother to her flock of round-faced, rosy-cheeked grandchildren. She recalls the grim circumstances under which her odd little Hanukkah menorah was made by women in a concentration camp barracks so that the children among them could observe the holiday. The illustrations of the prisoners, while somber, are softened to render the reality they represent less harsh to young readers. The contrast shown between past and present is very moving. Winner of a Sydney Taylor Book Award.

Sugarman, Brynn Olenberg. ***Rebecca's Journey Home.***
   Illus. by Michelle Shapiro.
Minneapolis, MN: Kar-Ben/Lerner. 2006.

An appealing combination of text and full-color illustrations tells the story of the Steins, who adopt a baby girl from Vietnam. Exploring the feelings of all the family members, the story also gently portrays how the new baby, Rebecca Rose in English, Rivka in Hebrew and Le Tai Hong in Vietnamese, will enjoy a triple heritage.

Swartz, Nancy Sohn. ***In Our Image: God's First Creatures.***
   Illus. by Melanie Hall.
Woodstock, VT: Jewish Lights. 1998.

All of God's creation gather to witness the creation of man and woman, and each gives the new humans a gift based on its own nature: Laziness from the lizard, curiosity from the chimpanzee, warmth from the sun, etc. God adds to these gifts goodness, love, and kindness so that humanity will live in harmony with nature. Deeply colored illustrations have fluid, sweeping lines.

Tal, Eve. *The New Boy/Yeled Hadash.* Illus. by Ora Schwartz.
Denver, CO: Milk and Honey Press. 2006

An attractive bilingual English/Hebrew picture book about the appearance of a new immigrant child in a kindergarten and how the teacher helps the other children accept him and make him feel at home. The story is set in Israel, and the new boy is Russian, but the child's behavior and the lessons taught could occur everywhere where children encounter someone different in school.

ELEMENTARY

Adler, David. *A Hero and the Holocaust: The Story of Janusz Korczak
   and His Children.* Illus. by Bill Farnsworth.
New York: Holiday House. 2002.

This short, dramatically illustrated biography of Janusz Korczak, the Polish physician, author, and humanitarian, is a good example of what is meant by the term "illustrated book." It is not a picture book, as that term is meant to describe a book for young children. The content of an "illustrated book" is on a higher level: Here, readers encounter the sad and heroic story of how Korczak cared for Polish-Jewish orphans and eventually accompanied them to the gas chambers. The narrative uses quotes from Korczak's diary and captures the grimness of wartime Warsaw. The illustrations are deeply colored and suitably somber.

Cohen, Barbara. *The Carp in the Bathtub.* Illus. by Joan Halpern.
Rockville, MD: Kar-Ben Copies. 1987.

Consider this a classic for Jewish children. It is timeless in its appeal and still popular with both children and adults. The plot, the writing style, and the evocation of an earlier time when gefilte fish was made and not bought are all heartwarming. So, too, are the illustrations which capture not just the two children's well-meant attempts to keep a carp that they name Joe, after a deceased neighbor, from the cooking pot but also the characters' love and respect for one another. Set shortly before Passover during the Depression, this highlights one food custom but does not explain the holiday.

Glaser, Linda. *Bridge to America.*
Boston: Houghton Mifflin. 2005.

After suffering deprivation and danger from Cossacks in their Polish *shtetl*, Fivel and his family finally get money from Pa to join him in America. With enough food to eat and warm clothing, Fivel—now called Phil—eagerly adapts to American life, despite times of feeling strange and foreign at school. Written with conviction, the story has a well-developed plot, believable setting, and strong characters, as well as a firm grounding in Jewish values.

Hest, Amy. *Love You, Soldier.* Illus. by Sonja Samut.
Cambridge, MA: Candlewick. 2000.

Katie is seven when her father leaves to fight in World War II, nine when she and her mother get the devastating news of his death, and ten when the war ends. Katie's story is told with artful simplicity and resonates with emotion. There are two other Katie Roberts books.

Kaplan, Kathy Walden. *Dog of Knots.*
Grand Rapids, MI: Eerdmans. 2004.

A beautifully written first novel about a girl named Mayim who lives in Israel at the time of the Yom Kippur War in 1973. She has had to leave her best friend and her beloved grandfather in Jerusalem when her mother gets a job in Haifa. In Haifa, Mayim makes many friends around the neighborhood, Jewish and Arab alike. She also develops a bond with a mysterious stray dog who lives in a *wadi*. The old dog is known to everyone in the neighborhood by a different name and they all help care for him. Mayim's affection for the dog helps her recover memories of her dead father—killed in an earlier war—which she feared she would never retrieve, and to gain courage. An unusual exploration of a child's feelings and a vivid rendering of a fraught time in Israeli history.

Provost, Gary, and Gail Provost Stockwell. *David and Max.*
Philadelphia: Jewish Publication Society. 2006.

Originally written in 1988, this classic story of friendship between a grandfather (Max) and his grandson (David) explores their relationship as it is tested by the appearance of a man whom Max swears he knew before the Holocaust. The revised version, besides having some updated vocabulary, assumes readers are more familiar with the Holocaust than they were when the book was originally published. It approaches the subject with greater emotion than in the original while still retaining all of the vitality of the original.

Ruby, Lois. *The Moxie Kid.*
Austin, TX: Eakin. 2003.

There's a Texas twang to the dialogue of a readable story that will attract a wide audience of readers, especially boys. It entails a mystery, but the main focus is on a friendship between a pre-adolescent boy named Jonathan and an old man who may or may not be named Mr. Canto Cantiberti. The child and teenage characters are especially convincing. Jonathan realizes soon after meeting Mr. Cantiberti that he stretches the truth, but late in the story he comes to understand that lies—or imaginative fabrications—are sometimes the "life-affirming errors" that make existence tolerable.

Taylor, Sydney. *All-of-a-Kind Family.* Illus. by Helen John.
New York: Follett. 1951.

Available in several versions, this is the first in a series of five classic Jewish children's books. The family is introduced, their relationships with one another and with other important people in their lives like the library lady and Papa's friend, Charlie, are portrayed, their life on the Lower East Side is explored, and their values are established. Taking place about 100 years ago, it suggests fundamental Jewish American themes to young readers through the timeless prism of a loving family and lively, believable children. The other books in the series are: *More All-of-a-Kind Family, All-of-a-Kind Family Uptown, All-of-a-Kind Family Downtown,* and *Ella of All-of-a-Kind Family.*

Weber, Ilse. *Mendel Rosenbusch: Tales for Jewish Children.*
New York: Herodias. 2001.

Mendel is a good and wise man with the power to become invisible and a special love of children. He uses his gift to help the poor and to right wrongs. These tales, by a Czech writer who was murdered at Auschwitz, paint a knowing portrait of small-town life and culture in pre-Holocaust central Europe.

MIDDLE SCHOOL

Avrech, Robert J. *The Hebrew Kid and The Apache Maiden.*
Los Angeles: Seraphic Press. 2004.

A coming-of-age story that follows a Jewish immigrant family across the untamed Southwest in the early years of the twentieth century. Ariel, who is *Bar Mitzvah* age, is the Hebrew Kid, and the Apache maiden is Lozen, the sister of the Apache warrior, Victorio, and a real person. Their relationship forms the central plot strand, but many other characters and adventures appear as well. Ariel's family lives according to Jewish teaching and applies it to the situations they encounter. Strong Jewish values animate this engaging historical novel.

Carmi, Danielle. *Samir and Yonatan.*
New York: Arthur A. Levine/Scholastic. 2000.

Frightened to be the only Arab child in the children's ward of an Israeli hospital, Samir withdraws into himself. Gradually Yonatan, the boy in the next bed, draws him into another world where the two boys can overcome sickness, fear, and conflict. An extraordinary exploration of the redemptive power of children's imaginations. Translated from Hebrew.

Kimmel, Eric A. *Be Not Far from Me: The Oldest Love Story: Legends from the Bible.* Illus. by David Diaz.
New York: Simon and Schuster. 1998

These robustly written stories, each centered on a biblical person, are based on

Tanakh and *Midrash* and encompass the five books of Moses, the Prophets, and the story of Daniel from the *Writings*. In creating these vivid portraits of heroes and heroines, Kimmel emphasizes God's love for Israel, which endures despite human frailty. The boldly colored, stylized illustrations suggest the drama inherent in these retellings of human encounters with God.

Kurtz, Jane. **The Storyteller's Beads.**
San Diego: Harcourt Brace. 1998.

A blind Jewish girl named Rahel and a Christian girl named Sahay, both Ethiopian, overcome mutual prejudice and suspicion as they help one another make the dangerous exodus out of war-torn Ethiopia into a refugee camp in the Sudan. Throughout the ordeal, Rahel comforts herself and Sahay with her grandmother's stories from the Bible and Ethiopian tradition, stories that give them both hope. An engaging story about friendship and cross-cultural relations.

Mack, Tracy. *Birdland.*
New York: Scholastic. 2003.

As the title suggests, jazz is a force in this moving novel that contrasts the sadness of a life within a grieving family with the vitality and sensation of life outside, in New York City. Stricken and overwhelmed by the death of their oldest son, 13-year-old Jed's family is eventually drawn out of their personal sorrow by connecting with the people and places of their neighborhood. Besides jazz, poetry and film-making are part of the story that, despite its subject, manages to be life-affirming and even humorous. Although the family is Jewish and Jewish values inform the plot, there is little that is overtly Jewish about the story.

Napoli, Donna Jo. **The King of Mulberry Street.**
New York: Random House. 2005.

Another superb novel by Donna Napoli, this one is set in New York's Five Points in the early twentieth century. An Italian Jewish child named Dom is the central character, and through the spirited story of his survival on his own, the experiences of many Italian immigrants to the U.S. are captured. As in Napoli's other books with Jewish themes, strong character and a good heart prevail.

Napoli, Donna Jo. *Stones in Water.*
New York: Dutton. 1997.

A survival story and a powerful indictment of war, this book is propelled by a plot unusual in World War II fiction: The kidnapping of Italian boys by their country's German allies for forced labor. Roberto and his Jewish friend, Samuele, must live by their wits to evade Nazi cruelty. The stoicism with which Samuele confronts his fate is matched by the courage of both boys as they perform small, furtive acts of kindness to alleviate the misery of Jewish prisoners whose treatment by brutal guards is even worse than their own. Winner of a Sydney Taylor Book Award.

Schwabach, Karen. *A Pickpocket's Tale.*
New York: Random House. 2006.

Ransomed from the depths of London's Old Bailey prison, an orphaned Jewish pickpocket named Molly is transported to the colonies to be the indentured servant of a kindly Jewish family in New York. Historical details, including frequent use of "Flash," a dialect spoken by thieves, are skillfully combined into a fascinating historical novel.

CHAPTER 9

Observing and Beautifying Mitzvot

"The commandment is a lamp, and the teaching is a light."

Tanakh

PRESCHOOL

Adelson, Leone. ***The Mystery Bear: A Purim Story.*** Illus. by Naomi Howland.
New York: Clarion. 2004.

A charming picture book about a hungry bear cub who is drawn by the smell of food from his cave into the midst of a Purim celebration. Howland's illustrations, like those of her book, *Matzah Man*, are filled with humorous action and story-enhancing details. A note about the holiday of Purim is appended. Two other funny picture books about bears who wander into Jewish holidays are *Once Upon a Shabbos* by Jacqueline Jules and *The Chanukah Guest* by Eric A. Kimmel.

Araten, Harry. ***Two by Two.***
Rockville, MD: Kar-Ben Copies. 1991.

A collection of short Bible stories for preschoolers, illustrated with simple shapes and primary colors. Because each story is only a page long and the writing rather dry in style, this is strictly for introductory purposes.

Baum, Maxie. ***I Have a Little Dreidel.*** Illus. by Julie Paschkis.
New York: Scholastic/Cartwheel. 2006.

A large, bold design enhances the text of this picture book, which consists of the words to a familiar Hanukkah song. Following the illustrated song are a recipe for potato *latkes*, directions for playing *dreidel*, and a musical score.

Benenfeld, Rikki. ***Let's Go Shopping.***
New York: Hachai. 2005.

Reflecting the everyday experiences of young children, this is part of the Toddler Experience Series, which also includes *I Go to School, Let's Go to Shul, I Go to the*

Doctor, and *I Go Visiting*. The point of view is Orthodox, so on their shopping trip with Mommy, the two children make sure they do *mitzvot* like holding the door open for a woman pushing a stroller and checking for the *kosher* labels on the food they buy. Their excursion takes them to the kosher butcher shop, the grocery store, the fish market, the produce market, the bakery, the Judaica gift shop, and the ice cream parlor. Hebrew words like *bris* and *brocha* that are used in the story are defined in the glossary. Cheerful illustrations match the cheerful text.

Capucilli, Alyssa Satin. **Biscuit's Hanukkah.** Illus. by Pat Schories.
New York: HarperFestival. 2005.

This Hanukkah board book is a welcome addition to the popular series about a puppy named Biscuit. It is a different story than *Happy Hanukkah, Biscuit*, where the puppy gets into all sorts of mischief celebrating Hanukkah at a friend's house while the adult dog, Sam, watches calmly. The message here is that on Hanukkah, we share stories, songs, delicious food, games and time with our friends. Although the story is slight, an appealing cover, sturdy board pages and good-size pictures in bright primary colors will engage preschoolers.

Capucilli, Alyssa Satin. **Happy Hanukkah, Biscuit!** Illus. by Pat Schories.
New York: HarperFestival. 2002.

A popular character in an easy-to-read series, Biscuit celebrates Hanukkah with some friends. Clear, insipid illustrations tell the story, augmented by one or two lines of text describing each scene and a flap to lift to discover Biscuit's latest mischief. No information is given about Hanukkah's history or meaning.

Carter, David. **Chanukah Bugs: A Pop-Up Celebration.**
New York: Little Simon. 2002.

An amazingly clever pop-up book that features a *shamash* bug, a storyteller bug, the dizzy *dreidel* bug, golden *gelt* bugs, sizzling *latke* bugs, dancing bugs, and *Bubbe* Bug with a holiday feast. For the eighth night, a *hanukkiyah* lit by bugs pops up from the centerfold.

Chwast, Seymour. **The Miracle of Hanukkah.**
Maplewood, NJ: Blue Apple/Chronicle. 2006.

Teachers of young children often look for Hanukkah picture books that tell the story unembellished with fictional details. Here is a straight account of the holiday in a clever, step-page format, with stylized pastel illustrations that follow the text in showing what the Jewish tradition says about Hanukkah.

Cisner, Naftali. **Count with Mendel.**
New York: Judaica Press. 2003.

A board book that uses Jewish holidays and symbols to introduce the numerals one through ten. The text is in rhyme, and the illustrations are cheerful. Mendel is an Orthodox Jewish boy with *side locks* and a *caftan*. A similar book by the same author is entitled *Get Ready for Shabbos with Mendel.*

Cohen, Santiago. *It's Hanukkah!*
Maplewood, NJ: Blue Apple/Chronicle. 2003.

Eye-catching illustrations are the most important feature of this slight story about Hanukkah. Bright colors contrast with black backgrounds, and candle flames are rendered in foil, intensifying in color as the number of candles in the menorah increases. Very little information about Hanukkah is given.

Cooper, Alexandra. *Spin the Dreidel.* Illus. by Claudine Gevry.
New York: Little Simon. 2004.

A novelty board book, with softly colored illustrations showing a family surrounded by symbols of Hanukkah: A *hanukkiyah, latkes,* and *dreidels.* How to play the dreidel game is simply explained, and through the spine of the book an actual plastic dreidel is inserted, not for playing but at least for twirling.

Dion, L. N. *The Opposites of My Jewish Year.* Illus. by Julie Olson.
Minneapolis, MN: Kar-Ben/Lerner. 2005.

The concept of opposites is very effectively presented through the basic symbols and texts of Jewish holidays. Part of a series of board books for the youngest Jewish child. Other titles are *The Colors of My Jewish Year*, *The Shapes of My Jewish Year*, and *The Sounds of My Jewish Year.*

Emerman, Ellen. *Is It Shabbos Yet?* Illus. by Tova Leff.
New York: Hachai. 2001.

Originally published in 1990 with illustrations by Toby Vegh, this new edition retains the same text and pagination as the original. Malkie is a little girl who wakes up on Friday eagerly waiting for *Shabbos* to begin. Throughout the day, as she helps her mother clean, shop, cook, bake *challah*, set the table, give *tzedakah*, light the candles, and say the blessing, Malkie keeps asking, "Is it Shabbos yet?" At last the long awaited time arrives and the story ends with a "Good Shabbos" from Malkie. A version of this story in Yiddish was published in 2006.

Emerman, Ellen. *Just Right: The Story of a Jewish Home.*
    Illus. by Sarah Krantz.
New York: Hachai. 1999.

When an Orthodox family moves into their new home, the youngest child feels that something is missing. As they discover what it is, the objects that make a Jewish home are identified. A similar picture book for the same age group is *The Place That I Love* by R. G. Cohen, published by Hachai in 2006.

Finkelstein, Ruth. *Big Like Me! A New Baby Story.* Illus. by Esther Touson.
New York: Hachai. 2001.

This sweet story is about a little boy named Benny who tries to teach his newborn baby sister all of the things that his big brother has taught him. When he succeeds in putting her to sleep while softly singing the *Shema*, he feels the pride of being a big brother himself. A perfect story for preschoolers with younger or older siblings or a baby on the way.

Fridman, Sashi. *When I Fell into My Kiddush Cup.* Illus. by Sarah Krantz.
New York: Merkos. 1999.

As an observant family gathers to celebrate *Shabbat*, a little boy falls into his *kiddush* cup, embarking on a fantasy adventure that reveals how kiddush is made at weddings, during Passover and Purim, at a *bris*, and for *Havdalah*. Told in rhyming verse with simple pictures.

Fuchs, Menucha. *Four Good Friends and a Boat.* Illus. by Estie Hass.
New York: Judaica Press. 2005.

Part of the Menucha V'Simchah Series adapted by Shoshana Lepon, this has spill-proof laminated pages, a short, simple story, and abundant illustrations. Each story is on a theme of friends helping friends, friends giving to friends, friends being kind to friends, and dealing with childhood fears. The characters are modestly dressed, each with a head covering. Aimed at an Orthodox audience but useful in other early childhood settings. The second title in the series is called *Guests Deserve the Best.*

Gellman, Ellie. *Tamar's Sukkah.* Illus. by Shauna Mooney Kawasaki.
Rockville, MD: Kar-Ben Copies. 1999.

In board book form, this shows a little girl decorating her *sukkah* with help from friends. On each double-spread page "something seems to be missing" until Tamar realizes that "a sukkah full of friends is exactly what a sukkah should be." A pleasant introduction.

Glazer, Devorah. *A Touch of the High Holidays: A Touch and Feel Book.*
    Illus. by Seva.
New York: Merkos. 2002.

A board book for preschoolers that lets them touch holiday objects such as "sweet, sticky honey" and "the smooth book cover." Curiously, *Sukkot* and *Simchat Torah* are included as High Holidays. The text is very short and rather cryptic so explanations from adults will be needed.

Goldin, Barbara Diamond. *Night Lights: A Sukkot Story.* Illus. by Laura Sucher.
New York: UAHC Press. 2002.

This year, Daniel and his older sister get to sleep overnight in the *sukkah* alone! Daniel is scared and ashamed of being scared. When his sister helps him think of the stars in the sky as nightlights, he is able to overcome his fear. This was originally published in 1995, with imaginative and fanciful illustrations by Louise August. The illustrations in this new edition are softer, less scary perhaps, but also less evocative.

Gold-Vukson, Marji. *The Numbers of My Jewish Year.* Illus. by Joni Oeltjenbruns. Minneapolis, MN: Kar-Ben/Lerner. 2006.

One *shofar*, two apples, three *Torah scrolls*, four *dreidels*, five trees, six *hamantaschen*, seven people at a *Seder*, eight Israeli flags, nine kids playing a Lag Ba'Omer game, and ten commandments symbolize a selection of Jewish holidays and deliver the concept of counting. Part of a the publisher's Very First Board Book Series, this has clear, colorful illustrations and a few lines of explanatory text to help preschoolers count their way through the Jewish year.

Greenberg, Kay. *Josh and Alisha Celebrate Chanukah.* Illus. by Cory Correll. Rockville, MD: Stop and Smell the Roses. 2000.

Through scented stickers included in the back of this book, children are encouraged to use their sense of smell to enhance the simple story of a family's Hanukkah celebration. The text is short and unembellished, the illustrations are realistic, and the book is spiral bound. Suitable for the visually impaired.

Groner, Judyth, and Madeline Wikler. *My Very Own Haggadah.*
    Illus. by Sally Springer.
Minneapolis, MN: Kar-Ben/Lerner. 1999.

Originally written in 1974, this popular *Haggadah* is written with the interests, learning capacity, and attention span of young children in mind. The *Seder* service, including songs, lasts about one hour. There are activities to engage children in the observance of Passover prior to the Seder and after it. Illustrated in black and white, it can also be used as a coloring book.

Grossblatt, Ruby M. *Who's That Sleeping on My Sofabed?* Illus. by Sarah Krantz. New York: Hachai. 1999.

The *mitzvah* of *hachnosat orchim* is imparted through this appealing story for preschoolers. Yoni is looking forward to sleeping in a bigger bed but his parents' guests keep getting his sofabed. When grandma comes and Yoni offers the sofabed to her, his parents realize he is ready for a bigger bed of his very own.

Hildebrandt, Ziporah. *This Is Our Seder.* Illus. by Robin Roraback. New York: Holiday House. 1999.

This introduction to the Seder was written for preschoolers and includes most of the important symbols: *Elijah's Cup, matzah, maror,* and *afikomen*. The illustrations showing a somewhat disheveled family celebrating Passover at a table that accumulates more and more dishes add humor.

Holland, Cheri. *Maccabee Jamboree: A Hanukkah Countdown.*
  Illus. by Roz Schanzer.
Rockville, MD: Kar-Ben Copies. 1998.

Modern-day, multicultural children dressed as *Maccabees* have fun on each of the eight nights of Hanukkah, making cards, exchanging gifts, singing songs, etc. The counting is done in descending order, from eight to one. On the brightly illustrated pages, each numeral is depicted, and preschoolers can see and count the objects represented by each number.

Holub, Joan. *Apples and Honey: A Rosh Hashanah Lift-the-Flap Book.*
  Illus. by Cary Pillo.
New York: Puffin. 2003.

Cheerful, full-page pictures in pastel tones show a family preparing for and observing *Rosh Hashanah.* The text is mostly in rhyme and there are several flaps to lift on every page. A short glossary is appended along with directions for making an apples-and-honey dish.

Holub, Joan. *Company's Coming: A Passover Lift-the-Flap Book.*
  Illus. by Renee Andriani.
New York: Puffin. 2002.

The emphasis in this lift-the-flap book is on food and fun. On each double-spread page, there is a four-line verse surrounded by an illustration showing a cheerful, celebrating family consisting of grandparents, parents, kids, and a cat. Sturdy flaps open to show more aspects of the *Seder*, including the foods on the *Seder* plate and the hunt for the *afikomen*. The pace is fast, the tone is light, and the content slight. Preschoolers will enjoy it.

Jules, Jacqueline. *Clap and Count: Action Rhymes for the Jewish Year.*
  Illus. by Sally Springer.
Minneapolis, MN: Kar-Ben/Lerner. 2001.

A charming and useful collection of action rhymes, finger plays, tickling jingles, and other activities for knee and foot, hand and fingers, clapping, and counting. They are all holiday-related and arranged as such. Some are original, some traditional, and some are adapted from other sources. The illustrations are bright and clear, depicting the use of fingers, feet, and bodies and enhancing the theme by decorating each rhyme with holiday motifs. This is a must for preschools.

Kimmelman, Leslie. *Dance, Sing, Remember.* Illus. by Ora Eitan.
New York: HarperCollins. 2000.

Outstanding illustrations decorate this introductory holiday collection. For each holiday, a page or two of basic information and a few activities are given.

Kimmelman, Leslie. *Hooray! It's Passover!* Illus. by John Himmelman.
New York: HarperCollins. 2000.

A board book for preschoolers, this includes many of the elements of the *Seder*, including the foods and the story of the Exodus, ending with the search for the *afikoman*. It is an abridgement of a 1996 book of the same title.

Kimmelman, Leslie. *The Runaway Latkes.* Illus. by Paul Yalowitz.
Morton Grove, IL: Albert Whitman. 2000.

In a delightful take-off on "The Gingerbread Boy," three crisp, brown latkes roll out of Rebecca Bloom's frying pan. Off they go, through the town, causing everyone to join in the chase, including the rabbi, the cantor, and the mayor. There is no serious message here, just a joyful celebration of *Hanukkah* for young children to applaud. This is a good example of how a story can be "Judaicized," that is, adapted to Jewish time, place, people, and meaning. Other Jewish versions of the same nursery tale are *Matzah Man* by Naomi Howland and *Runaway Dreidel* by Leslea Newman.

Klein-Higger, Joni. *Ten Tzedaka Pennies.* Illus. by Tova Leff.
New York: Hachai. 2005.

By counting backwards from ten to one, this simple story shows a little boy's pennies being used for *tzedakah*. Short verses tell the story, and bright, realistic pictures add details. Paired with *The Very Best Place for a Penny* by Dina Rosenfeld, this conveys the *mitzvah* of tzedakah to young children in an engaging manner. The characters are Orthodox Jews, as in all of Hachai's books, but the story's appeal is nonsectarian.

Kropf, Latifa Berry. *Happy Birthday, World: A Rosh Hashana Celebration.*
Illus. by Lisa Carlson.
Minneapolis, MN: Kar-Ben/Lerner, 2005.

In an attractively illustrated and appealing board book for very young children, the basic observances of Rosh Hashanah are compared with something that most young children will have experienced and enjoyed—a birthday party. Important holiday symbols and customs are imparted very effectively.

Kropf, Latifa Berry. *It's Challah Time!* Photographs by Tod Cohen.
Minneapolis, MN: Kar-Ben/Lerner, 2002.

Color photographs of real children in a real Jewish preschool capture the fun of preparing for *Shabbat* and the atmosphere of a rich learning environment. The *Shabbat* blessings and a recipe for *challah* are included. This is a first of a series of delightful holiday books by Kropf and Cohen; the others are *It's Hanukkah Time!*, *It's Seder Time!*, *It's Sukkah Time!*, *It's Purim Time!*, *It's Shofar Time!*, and *Happy Birthday World!*

Levine, Abby. *This Is the Dreidel.* Illus. by Paige Billin-Frye.
Morton Grove, IL: Albert Whitman. 2003.

This simple Hanukkah story loosely follows the cumulative rhyme scheme of "The House That Jack Built," progressing through all eight days of the holiday with the activities of a little boy named Max and his family. The identification of the letters on the *dreidel*, the inclusion of *tzedakah* as a holiday custom, and the lack of emphasis on gift giving are nice touches.

Levine, Abby. *This Is the Matzah.* Illus. by Paige Billin-Frye.
Morton Grove, IL: Albert Whitman. 2005.

A Passover picture book with text that loosely follows the cumulative rhyme structure of "The House That Jack Built." It shows a little boy and his family as they prepare for Passover, celebrate the *Seder*, and anticipate all the *matzah* treats they will eat throughout the holiday. A strength of the book and of the cheerful illustrations is that they link the Exodus to modern Jews, emphasizing that "we" and not "they" went out from Egypt. Similar to *This is the Dreidel* by the same author and illustrator, this is good for reading aloud to children who already know something about Passover.

Levy, Sarah G. *Mother Goose Rhymes for Jewish Children.*
    Illus. by Jessie B. Robinson.
New York: Bloch. 1945.

A collection of jingles about the Jewish holidays, Israel, and everyday life. Hebrew words appear in many of them, and there is an extensive glossary that defines each word and gives its pronunciation. The two color illustrations are sprightly and, like the jingles, sweet and somewhat quaint. Published before the State of Israel was established and one of the first modern Jewish picture books, the jingles in this classic deserve to be introduced, selectively, to today's young children.

Lieberman, Channah. *Happy Birthday to Me!* Illus. by Patti Argoff.
New York: Hachai. 2006.

There are two versions of this book: One with a pink cover for girls and the other with a blue cover for boys. Lively, attention-absorbing illustrations and a colorful format are the highlights of the story, told in rhyme. When a child thinks that her (his) family has forgotten her birthday, she decides to make a party for herself. Just as she realizes that she forgot to invite any guests, the door bursts open and family and friends flock in. The birthday celebrations are in the Orthodox mode, so the child's preparations involve *Torah* stories, Jewish songs, *brochot*, and a *tzedakah* box.

Lissy, Jessica. *A Blue's Clues Holiday.* Illus. by Dan Kanemoto and Jennifer Oxley.
New York: Simon Spotlight/Nick Jr. 2003.

Characters from the popular Blue's Clues television show celebrate Hanukkah by making and lighting *menorahs*, learning a little bit about the holiday, frying a batch of *latkes*, playing *dreidel*, and singing a couple of songs. All are portrayed in cartoon style except for the teenage boy who is Blue's friend.

Lister, Claire. *My First Jewish Holidays Library.*
New York: DK. 2003.

This is a boxed set of three board books, two of which were previously published: *My First Passover My First Hanukkah* plus *My First Shabbat*. Photographs of holiday symbols and children dressed in ancient garb illustrate the text. The format is rather busy and a bit longer than most board books, but the clear illustrations are useful for explaining the holidays to younger children.

Livney, Varda. *What I Like about Passover.*
New York: Simon and Schuster/Little Simon. 2002.

This cheerful board book expresses a young child's liking for each item on the *Seder* table and for being with friends and family. It doesn't even hint at the Passover story, however. Introductory.

Manushkin, Fran. *Hooray for Hanukkah!* Illus. by Carolyn Croll.
New York: Random House. 2001.

An old-fashioned family's Hanukkah celebration is described, night by night, by the *hanukkiyah*. This is a novel twist, but unfortunately the narrative is not as effective as the large, warm illustrations. The pedestrian storyline makes this a second choice for holiday reading.

Medoff, Francine. *The Mouse in the Matzah Factory.* Revised Edition.
    Illus. by Nicole in den Bosch.
Minneapolis, MN: Kar-Ben/Lerner. 2003.

What is *shmura matzah* and how is it made? A short explanation is followed by a story that gives a mouse's view of each step in the process, from wheat field to oven. This revised edition of a book first published in 1983 retains the charm of the story but replaces the rough but vigorous two-tone illustrations with disappointingly bland ones. The addition of color is welcome but the look is commercial and lacking in any Jewish tam. Keep the original of this country mouse/city mouse Passover story.

Nerlove, Miriam. *Shabbat.*
Morton Grove, IL: Albert Whitman. 1998.

Told in rhyme by a little girl whose family is shown celebrating the Sabbath at home and at synagogue services, the story begins with the meaning of *Shabbat* as the day when God rested and ends with *Havdalah*. Blessings are included, as well as an appended summary about *Shabbat*.

Nerlove, Miriam. *The Ten Commandments for Jewish Children.*
Morton Grove, IL: Albert Whitman. 1999.

Nerlove retells the story of Moses receiving the Ten Commandments and then lists each one with a brief explanation, ending with the comment that these commandments are as important today as they were long ago. Full-page pictures—all in color—are clear, realistic, and in a pastel palette.

Newman, Leslea. **The Eight Nights of Chanukah.** Illus. by Elivia Savadier. New York: Harry Abrams. 2005.

A joyously illustrated, lighthearted romp through the eight days of Hanukkah, featuring a multicultural cast of characters. As the text progresses so does the action in the pictures, extending across each double-page spread, showing people of different ages and races celebrating. No messages or lessons—just holiday fun conveyed through what appears to be effortless artistry.

Newman, Leslea. **Matzo Ball Moon.** Illus. by Elaine Greenstein. Boston: Houghton Mifflin. 1998.

Bubbe arrives to make her special chicken soup and *matzah* balls for the family *Seder*. Her granddaughter Eleanor is her assistant and trainee. This appealing Passover story embodies the loving bond between generations and the continuity of Jewish traditions. Soft illustrations maintain the tone of the text.

Paluch, Beily. **Braid the Challah.** Illus. by Patti Argoff. New York: Hachai. 2004.

The text of this board book—just a few words to a page—rhymes, and the clear, cheerful illustrations show children acting out the words with body language that real children can easily imitate. A simple but effective introduction to some of the joys of the Sabbath.

Paluch, Beily. **I Am a Torah.** Illus. by Patti Argoff. New York: Hachai. 2004.

The text of this board book—just a few words to a page—rhymes, and the clear, cheerful illustrations show children acting out the words with body language that real children can imitate. Considering the shortage of stories for the holiday of *Simhat Torah*, this will be welcomed by preschool teachers.

Pearlman, Bobby. **Passover Is Here!** Illus. by Christel Desmoinaux. New York: Simon and Schuster/Little Simon. 2005.

A lift-the-flap book that tells of a little boy's preparations for Passover. There is a flap on almost every page, revealing more information and details about the holiday. More text than is usual in this type of book and harder vocabulary may confuse some younger readers. God is never mentioned. An additional purchase.

Randall, Ronne. **The Hanukkah Mice.** Illus. by Maggie Kneen. San Francisco: Chronicle. 2002.

A rhyming picture book that follows the quest of a mouse family for the "wondrous Hanukkah lights." Each night, they find a different source of light: A candlestick, shiny chocolate *gelt*, etc., until on the eighth night, they find all of the candles in the *hanukkiyah* burning brightly. On the left side of every cardboard page is a folded-over flap with a small cutout that reveals Hanukkah symbols made of shiny paper foil.

Rauchwerger, Diane. ***Dinosaur on Hanukkah.*** Illus. by Jason Wolff. Minneapolis, MN: Kar-Ben/Lerner. 2005.

"There's a dino knocking on my door, it's Hanukkah, you see. He's come to decorate our house and celebrate with me." So begins this cheerful picture book that is written in short, rhyming passages and illustrated with cartoon-like humor. Through the antics of the dinosaur and his young host, some familiar Hanukkah customs are depicted, and an atmosphere of playfulness prevails. The series also includes *Dinosaur on Passover* and *Dinosaur on Shabbat*.

Rosenfeld, Dina. ***Five Alive! My Yom Tov Five Senses.*** Illus. by Tova Leff. New York: Hachai. 2003.

Toddlers and preschoolers are shown how they can see, hear, smell, taste and touch the holidays of Rosh Hashanah, Yom Kippur, Sukkot, Simhat Torah, Hanukkah, Purim, and Shavuot. The simple story is told in rhyme that succeeds in highlighting a central aspect of each holiday. The illustrations are bright and cheerful.

Rosenfeld, Dina. ***Get Well Soon.*** Illus. by Rina Lyampe. New York: Hachai. 2001.

A little boy wants to perform the *mitzvah* of *bikur holim* but he's too little to visit the hospital, and his parents don't want him to catch germs. Sending a card or making a phone call doesn't satisfy him, so when his big sister gets a headache, he visits her in her bedroom and finally feels proud that he could do the *mitzvah* after all. Bright, cheerful illustrations of an observant family accompany a simple, pleasant story.

Roth, Susan. ***Hanukkah, Oh Hanukkah.*** New York: Dial. 2004.

The words of the familiar Hanukkah songs are spread, a phrase at a time, across the pages of this winsomely illustrated picture book. As children sing the song, they can observe a family of mice celebrating Hanukkah. The mice are the focal point of very creative collages made with cloth, paper, different textures, and pretty colors. The full song with music completes this charming book for young children.

Rouss, Sylvia. ***The Littlest Pair.*** Illus. by Holly Hannon. New York: Pitspopany. 2002.

Written in rhyme, this book is about a little girl who watches her mother and older sisters light Sabbath candles and wishes she had her own pair of candlesticks. To her delight, in school the next day the teacher gives the class candlesticks to decorate. Abby combines themes from the candlesticks lit by her mother and sisters and brings home a pair that "lit up that *Shabbat* night." The illustrations are vivid and full-page.

Rouss, Sylvia. *Sammy Spider's First Passover.* Illus. by Katherine Janus Kahn. Rockville, MD: Kar-Ben Copies. 1995.

Sammy Spider is more interested in watching the Shapiro family prepare for Passover than he is in learning from his mother how to spin a new web. After he helps Josh find the *afikomen*, Sammy realizes that he has spun a beautiful new web using all the shapes his mother taught him. The enjoyment of reading about "silly little Sammy," seeing a family prepare for Passover, learning about triangles, circles, and squares, and appreciating the bright color collages that depict the story are all part of the fun for a preschool audience. This is but one of a series of holiday stories about Sammy Spider, each embodying a simple concept. The others are: *Sammy Spider's First Purim, Sammy Spider's First Rosh Hashanah, Sammy Spider's First Shabbat, Sammy Spider's First Sukkot,* and *Sammy Spider's First Haggadah.*

Sanders, Nancy I. *Passover.*
New York: Children's Press. 2003.

This *matzah*-size book is filled with easy-to-understand yet accurate information about Passover for reading aloud to preschoolers and for independent reading by primary grade children. The format is inviting, with clear type, plenty of white space, color illustrations, and color accented captions. Two of the illustrations show families of non-European origin at their *Seders*. Part of the True Book Series, it has a glossary and an index.

Schon, Ruchy. *Who Am I?* Photographs by Ruchela Roth.
Nanuet, NY: Feldheim. 2006.

Winsome photographs of toddlers posed and dressed in costumes representing occupations are the focal point of this slightly oversized board book, which ascribes a *mitzvah* to each occupation. The bright, inviting format and simple rhyming text make this a good choice for reading to very young children.

Schotter, Roni. *Hanukkah!* Illus. by Marilyn Hafner.
New York: Little Brown. 2003.

The original and slightly longer version of this board book was published in 1993. The illustrations, with an old-fashioned look, are its most appealing feature. They show a family celebrating Hanukkah in a house filled with love.

Schotter, Roni. *Passover!* Illus. by Erin Eitter Kono.
New York: Little Brown. 2006.

Five-year-old Moe feels the excitement of Passover as he participates with his family in the preparations, including setting a place at the *Seder* table for Izzy, Moe's dog. The family who appeared in *Hanukkah!* now celebrates Passover, their story told in verse and illustrated with loose, pastel pictures. A slight book for young children that assumes some prior knowledge about the holiday.

Schuh, Mari C. *Passover.*
Mankato, MN: Pebble Books/Capstone. 2003.

A small book, illustrated with full-page color photographs and part of the Holidays and Celebrations Series. Children with no knowledge of the holiday will get an acceptable introduction to Passover and how it is celebrated in North America. Each page of large-type text is faced by an illustration. Factual and user-friendly.

Schwartz, Betty. *Where's My Dreidel?* Illus. by Varda Livney.
New York: Simon and Schuster/Little Simon. 1999.

To help Max find his *dreidel*, readers can lift the flap on each page of this very simple story. In doing so, they find various symbols of Hanukkah: The silver *menorah*, *latkes*, *gelt*, and a present from Grandma—a *dreidel*.

Smith, Dian. *Hanukkah Lights.* Illus. by JoAnn Kitchel.
San Francisco: Chronicle Books. 2001.

This little story shows a family lighting one Hanukkah candle per night, telling about it in a rhymed refrain and simple, explanatory sentences. Its most eye-catching feature is the gold metallic paper that forms the candle flames, but the winsome, boldly outlined illustrations are also appealing. The sturdy cardboard pages are easy for small hands to turn.

Sollish, Ari. *A Touch of Passover.* Illus. by Boruch Becker.
New York: Merkos. 2004.

A touch-and-feel book that invites preschoolers to touch the leather *Haggadah*, feel the bumpy *matzoh*, rub the leafy green *maror*, and stroke the silken *afikomen* bag. A very simple text links the symbols to the *Passover Seder*. There is also a version in Spanish, entitled *Un Toque De Pasaj.*

Stone, Tanya Lee. *D Is for Dreidel.* Illus. by Dawn Apperley.
New York: Price Stern Sloan. 2002.

Each letter of the alphabet is tied into a Hanukkah-related concept. Although plotless, this alphabet book gives a well-rounded picture of the Hanukkah holiday. It includes a dollop of tradition, food, history, spiritual meaning, and values. An acceptable introduction to Hanukkah.

Stone, Tanya Lee. *P Is for Passover: A Holiday Alphabet Book.*
    Illus. by Margeaux Lucas.
New York: Price, Stern Sloan. 2003.

The letters of the alphabet are used to describe 26 characteristics of Passover, from *afikomen* to zzzzz (the sleepy sound at the end of the *Seder*). Religious, historic, and humorous aspects of the holiday are shown, all with a light touch and colorful illustrations.

Tanner, Suzy-Jane. *The Great Hanukkah Party.*
New York: Harper Festival. 1998.

A slight, lift-the-flap book for preschoolers that introduces Hanukkah through the story of a family of bears that finds common holiday objects and symbols throughout their house. The bright, cozy illustrations are appealing.

Topek, Susan Remick. *Shabbat Shalom.* Illus. by Shelly Schonebaum Ephraim.
Rockville, MD: Kar-Ben Copies. 1998.

A board book that introduces young children to *Havdalah*, the ceremony that ends the Jewish Sabbath and welcomes in a new week. The childlike illustrations show a family preparing for and observing *Havdalah* as three stars shine in the sky.

Topek, Susan Remick. *Ten Good Rules.*
Rockville, MD: Kar-Ben Copies. 1992.

A very simple and attractively illustrated version of the Ten Commandments with the negative ones reworded into positive statements. Little children can count on their fingers, following the pictures, as the book is read to them. A revised version, with color photographs of real children by Tod Cohen, was published in 2007.

Vorst, Rochel Groner. *The Sukkah That I Built.* Illus. by Elizabeth Victor-Elsby.
New York: Hachai. 2002.

A clever adaptation for the holiday of *Sukkot* of "The House That Jack Built." Several elements are blended into the story: Highlighted vocabulary, the process of building a *sukkah*, and realistic family dynamics. The tale and the *sukkah* grow together, as does the humorous tension between the narrator's description of all the work he is supposedly doing and the depiction—in the illustrations—of all the work his family is really doing. The illustrations are naive but colorful and charming. Includes a short glossary and history of the holiday.

Zolkower, Edie Stoltz. *It's Tu B'Shevat.* Illus. by Richard Johnson.
Minneapolis, MN: Kar-Ben/Lerner. 2005.

This simple board book follows a little boy as he grabs a shovel, digs a hole, and plants a tree on *Tu B'Shevat*. As we watch, the boy and the tree grow older; he and his family picnic under its shade and enjoy the fruit it bears. Illustrated in lush pastels and written in verse, the narrative flows easily.

Zolkower, Edie Stoltz. *Too Many Cooks: A Passover Parable.*
Illus. by Shauna Mooney Kawasaki.
Rockville, MD: Kar-Ben Copies. 2000.

A karate-chopping, thoroughly modern *Bubbe* is preparing her *charoseth* for the Passover *Seder*. Each time Bubbie leaves the kitchen, a well-meaning relative tastes the *charoseth*, decides it is too bland, and adds a "secret ingredient" to pep it up.

Oddball ingredients are found as they rummage through the refrigerator. A humorous addition to Passover stories for young children.

Zucker, Jonny. *Apples and Honey: A Rosh Hashanah Story.*
　　Illus. by Jan Barger Cohen.
Hauppage, NY: Barron's. 2002.

Double-page spread illustrations of a family observing Rosh Hashanah will engage the attention of preschoolers. Each action is described by a few simple sentences. The ritual of *tashlikh* is explained as saying goodbye to the "sad things of last year by throwing crumbs into the river." A pleasant introduction, part of the Festival Time Series, which also includes: *Eight Candles to Light: A Chanukah Story, Four Special Questions: A Passover Story*, and *It's Party Time! A Purim Story*.

PRIMARY

Adelman, Penina V. *The Bible from Alef to Tav.* Illus. by Michael Jacobs.
Los Angeles: Torah Aura. 1998.

Each of the 21 Bible stories in this collection is associated with one of the letters of the Hebrew alphabet. Several Hebrew words are embedded within each story. With an appealing format and a few discussion questions at the end of each section, it is for individual or classroom use.

Bastrya, Judy, and Catherine Ward. *Hanukkah Fun: Great Things to Make and Do.*
Boston: Kingfisher. 2003.

Clear directions and color illustrations are the hallmarks of this Hanukkah activity book. Directions for making *hanukkiyot* candles, *dreidels*, a helmet and shield, plus a few recipes are included. Originally published in 1996.

Bredeson, Carmen. *Purim.*
New York: Children's Press. 2003.

Like other titles in the Rookie Read-About Holidays Series, this is a simple introduction to the holiday of Purim, illustrated with color photographs and told in short sentences, a few to a page. The pronunciation of some of the more unfamiliar words is given parenthetically in the sentence where they are used. The content briefly explains the history and meaning of the holiday and how it is observed, all enhanced by realistic photos.

Cleary, Brian P. *Eight Wild Nights: A Family Hanukkah.* Illus. by David Udovic.
Minneapolis, MN: Kar-Ben/Lerner. 2006.

Genuinely clever rhymes, several cuts above the jingles used in so many picture books, tell the story of an extended family's raucous eight nights of Hanukkah. It's an exaggerated version of many family celebrations, and the realistic illustrations, colored in a pastel palette with strong facial features on all of the characters, complement the plot and the style.

Cohen, Barbara. *Make a Wish, Molly.* Illus. by Jan N. Jones.
New York: Bantam Doubleday Dell. 1995.

A sequel to *Molly's Pilgrim*, this book shows Molly learning to reconcile Jewish and American traditions when a classmate's birthday party occurs during Passover. Once again, Molly's resourceful mother comes to the rescue. As in the earlier book, this is a sensitive portrayal of children's relationships with classmates.

Cone, Molly. *The Story of Shabbat.* Illus. by Emily Lisker.
New York: HarperCollins. 2000.

First published by Crowell in 1966 under the title *The Jewish Sabbath*, this new edition has eye-catching illustrations by Emily Lisker. The text traces the significance of the Sabbath throughout Jewish history, treating the subject with precision, historical accuracy, and reverence. An excellent introduction.

Cone, Molly. *Who Knows Ten? Children's Tales of the Ten Commandments.*
Revised Edition. Illus. by Robin Brickman.
New York: UAHC Press. 1998.

Originally published in 1965, this collection of stories about the Ten Commandments is well illustrated and attractively designed. Each of the commandments is stated and then followed by a short story that exemplifies its meaning. Some of the stories are based on traditional tales.

Dollinger, Renate. *The Rabbi Who Flew.*
Van Nuys, CA: Booksmythe. 2001.

Colorful gouache paintings in the author-illustrator's primitive style decorate this story about a saintly rabbi with holes in his shoes. The plot expresses the *mitzvah* of Jew helping Jew within an idealized *shtetl* setting.

Epstein, Sylvia. *How the Rosh Hashanah Challah Became Round.*
Illus. by Hagit Migron.
Jerusalem: Gefen. 1993.

When Yossi drops all the *challahs* that his father has carefully braided for Rosh Hashanah, he is mortified. The bakery customers scoff at the odd, roundly shaped loaves of bread until the rabbi's wife points out that there is a similarity between the new, round challahs and the endless happiness that we wish for one another at the New Year.

Erlbach, Arlene. *Hanukkah: Celebrating the Holiday of Lights.*
Berkeley Heights, NJ: Enslow. 2002.

A good introduction to the holiday for preschool through grade 3. The text discusses the history of the Jewish people and describes Judaism before giving a straightforward account of the origins of Hanukkah and the customs associated with it. Be aware that the menorah pictured is the one engraved on the Arch of Titus—a symbol of Jewish defeat and not related to the time of the *Maccabees.*

Fishman, Cathy Goldman. *Hanukkah.* Illus. by Mary O. Young.
Minneapolis, MN: Carolrhoda/Lerner. 2004.

Designed and written as an easy reader, this gives the history of Hanukkah and describes its modern day celebration. The sentences are occasionally choppy, but in general, the book is readable, with soft colored illustrations that reflect the text and help beginning readers understand it.

Fishman, Cathy Goldman. *On Shabbat.* Illus. by Melanie Hall.
New York: Simon and Schuster/Atheneum. 2001.

A holiday book, part of a series, that is both stylish and steeped in Jewish knowledge. The dreamy illustrations capture the spirit of the Sabbath. Other holiday books by the author and illustrator are: *On Purim, On Passover, On Rosh Hashanah and Yom Kippur,* and *On Sukkot and Simhat Torah.*

Flanagan, Alice. *Passover.*
Mankato, MN: Compass Point Books. 2004.

An acceptable introduction to Passover, with bright, attractive illustrations. Information about the origin, history, rituals, food, symbols, and meaning of Passover are given. Along with a table of contents and a short index, there is a glossary; words defined in it are printed in bold the first time they appear in the text. The book's strongest feature is its brief discussion of Passover's theme of freedom and some suggested activities to reflect that theme.

Ganeri, Anita. *Jewish Festivals Throughout the Year.*
North Mankata, MN: Smart Apple Media. 2004.

This is part of the Festivals Throughout the Year Series, which includes books on Buddhist, Hindu, Muslim, Christian, and Sikh festivals, as well as this one. The series originated in the United Kingdom. After short introductions to Judaism and Jewish history, it describes ten Jewish festivals, beginning with *Shabbat* and *Rosh Hashanah.* A few holiday-related activities are included. The photographs show observant Jews from a variety of backgrounds. The intended audience is not Jewish children: Jews are referred to in the third person as "they." However, the book makes a useful introduction to the Jewish religion in non-Jewish settings.

Ganeri, Anita. *The Passover Story.* Illus. by Rachael Phillis.
Mankato, MN: Smart Apple Media. 2004.

Large type and full-color illustrations are used to tell the story of Passover from the birth of Moses to the Exodus from Egypt to the Promised Land. A brief description of the holiday of Passover and the *Seder* meal follows, along with a recipe for *charoset* and the lyrics to the traditional Passover song, "Dayenu." The book is part of the Festival Series that also includes a book about Hanukkah. Similar in scope and content to *Festival of Freedom* by Maida Silverman, the presumed audience is public schools and libraries.

Geras, Adele. ***Rebecca's Passover.*** Illus. by Sheila Moxley.
London: Frances Lincoln. 2004.

As a grandmother and her grandchildren chat while preparing for Passover, information about the holiday and the *Seders* is imparted. This makes for a rather static narrative, although it is accurate and relatively thorough. Pastel illustrations support the text and provide it with visual reinforcement.

Glaser, Linda. ***Mrs. Greenberg's Messy Hanukkah.*** Illus. by Nancy Cote.
Morton Grove, IL: Albert Whitman. 2004

Irrepressible Rachel, who involved her lonely neighbor, Mrs. Greenberg, in celebrating Hanukkah in *The Borrowed Hanukkah Latkes*, does it again. This time she doesn't borrow ingredients but goes straight to the source—Mrs. Greenberg's immaculately neat kitchen—and turns it upside down as she and Mrs. Greenberg fry up a big batch of *latkes*. When Rachel's parents come to pick her up, they are horrified at how the house looks. Rachel herself is mortified. But Mrs. Greenberg doesn't mind it a bit—she enjoys the company! A very upbeat and cheerful picture book.

Goldin, Barbara Diamond. ***The Magician's Visit.*** Illus. by Robert Andrew Parker.
New York: Puffin. 1993.

Barbara Diamond Goldin retells an I. L. Peretz story set during Passover. The magician who visits a poor couple on the first night of the holiday is mysterious, and they don't know whether they should trust him or be frightened of him. The rabbi they consult tells them that if the magician's tricks result not in mere illusion but in real transformations, then he has powers for the good. Their *Seder* is the real thing, thanks to the magician—who may be Elijah—so they are able to celebrate a joyous Passover. This is excellent for reading aloud, because children enjoy the shivery sense of mystery that both the story and the illustrations convey.

Had Gadya: A Passover Song. Illus. by Seymour Chwast.
New Milford, CT: Roaring Brook Press. 2005.

Seymour Chwast's superb illustrations of the traditional Passover Seder song tell several stories at once. First is the one told by the cumulative chain folksong itself, with the characters accumulating across the top of the pages. Second is a story of preparations for the *Seder*. And third is a visual portrayal of life in a *shtetl*, capturing its looks and life in a way similar to what Phoebe Gilman did in *Something from Nothing*. An afterword by Rabbi Michael Strassfeld comments on the dual nature of the song: Its lighthearted qualities and its more serious implications, both religious and historical.

Heiligman, Deborah. *Celebrate Hanukkah with Light, Latkes, and Dreidels.* Washington, DC: National Geographic. 2006.

Uganda, Kenya, Poland, Peru, Israel, Italy, the United States, and Canada are some of the places where Hanukkah celebrations are pictured. Written with accuracy, simplicity, and clarity, the text describes the two miracles of the holiday: That of the *Maccabees'* victory over the powerful Greco-Syrian army, and the other of the oil that burned for eight days after the Temple was rededicated. There are color photographs on every page, celebrating both the holiday and Jewish diversity. The appended material is also informative.

Heiligman, Deborah. *Celebrate Passover with Matzah, Maror, and Memories.* Washington, DC: National Geographic. 2007.

The format and focus of the second book about a Jewish holiday in the Holidays Around the World Series is similar to the author's *Celebrate Hanukkah with Lights, Latkes, and Dreidels.* Engaging color photographs and a succinct text show Jews from different parts of the world preparing for and observing Passover. Some additional facts about the holiday are given in an appendix along with a recipe, an explanation of the foods on the *Seder* plate, a list of books and Web sites, and a map showing where the photos were taken.

Herman, Charlotte. *How Yussel Caught the Gefilte Fish.* Illlus. By Katya Krenina. New York: Dutton. 1999.

A rosy glow suffuses both the pictures and the story of this father-son tale. When his father takes him fishing for the first time, Yussel catches a pike, a carp, and a trout— but no gefilte fish. Taking the fish home, Yussel watches Mama work her culinary magic, seasoning the fish with the special spice of *Shabbat.*

Herman, Debbie. *Eight Lights for Eight Nights.* Illus. by Anne D. Koffsky. Hauppauge, NY: Barron's. 2003.

The story of Hanukkah is told in the first part of this activity book, and interesting facts about the holiday are provided by text boxes. The crafts that comprise the second part of the book are creative and easily made from common household items. Well illustrated and especially useful to teachers.

Herman, Debbie, and Anne D. Koffsky. *More than Matzah: A Passover Feast of Fun, Food, Facts, and Activities.* Illus. by Nancy Lane. Hauppauge, NY: Barron's. 2006.

This holiday activity book begins with the story of Passover, the text decorated with large realistic pictures and studded with boxed facts. An activity section comes next, consisting of nine or ten crafts, a few songs, and a description of the *Seder* plate foods. They are all illustrated attractively, and the craft directions are clear.

Hessel, Joui, and Steve Zorn. *The Hanukkah Family Treasury.* Illus. by Sarah Gibb. Brookfield, CT: Running Press. 2004.

An oversize and profusely illustrated collection of Hanukkah history, lore, legends, blessings, poems, and activities. Includes excerpts of text from the *Books of the Maccabees* and a rousing poem by Emma Lazarus.

Hest, Amy. *The Friday Nights of Nana.* Illus. by Claire Nivola. Cambridge, MA: Candlewick. 2001.

In this serene picture book, a little girl helps her grandmother prepare for *Shabbat*. The celebration of tradition provides an atmosphere of closeness and warmth, a contrast to the wintry world outside.

Hirsh, Marilyn. *Joseph Who Loved the Sabbath.* Illus. by Devis Grebu. New York: Viking. 1986.

One of many outstanding books of Jewish content by an author-illustrator whose untimely death robbed Jewish children's literature of a stellar talent. In this story, retold but not illustrated by Hirsh, Joseph works hard all week for a greedy taskmaster so that he can savor his one day of Sabbath rest. When Sorab, his employer, dreams that Joseph will inherit all of his wealth, he spends it all on one splendid ruby and then sails away with the ruby to keep it from Joseph. In true folklore fashion, the boat he is on sinks, the ruby is swallowed by a fish, and Joseph buys the fish, with ruby, to cook for a Sabbath meal. When he discovers the ruby and his newfound wealth, Joseph invites everyone to celebrate *Shabbat* with him.

Howland, Naomi. *Latkes, Latkes, Good to Eat.* Boston: Houghton Mifflin. 1999.

An Eastern European village is the setting of this Hanukkah tale of a poor girl who is rewarded for her generosity by receiving the gift of a magic frying pan. The illustrations are striking, and the story is reminiscent of "The Sorcerer's Apprentice."

Hoyt-Goldsmith, Diane. *Celebrating Hanukkah.* Photographs by Lawrence Migdale. New York: Holiday House. 1996.

A family associated with San Francisco's Temple Emanu El is the photographic subject of a book that is not only about Hanukkah but also about many of the symbols and practices associated with the holiday. Most of the narrative is written in the first person, told by 11-year-old Leora Wolf-Prusan, the family's oldest child. Although the text is clearly written and well organized with a glossary and index included, the color photographs are the book's highlight.

Hoyt-Goldsmith, Diane. *Celebrating Passover.* Photographs by Lawrence Migdale. New York: Holiday House. 2000.

The author and photographer have written a number of books like this one on various holidays, including Chinese New Year, the Day of the Dead, and Hanukkah. It features a real-life family and focuses on one of the children as a way of achieving a child-centered point of view. The color photographs are many and attractive, and the information is accessible through an index and glossary. This is an additional purchase for Jewish libraries and is best suited for children who know nothing about Passover.

Jules, Jacqueline. *Once Upon a Shabbos.* Illus. by Katherine Janus Kahn. Rockville, MD: Kar-Ben Copies. 1998.

Whether or not children are familiar with a variant of this story from the American South called "Sody Sallyratus," they will be captivated by this Yiddish-flavored version, set in New York, about a lost bear and a resourceful *bubbe*.

Kimmel, Eric A. *The Chanukah Guest.* Illus. by Giora Carmi. New York: Holiday House. 1990.

Old *Bubba* Brayna doesn't see or hear very well anymore. She has invited the rabbi to her home in the forest for *latkes* but welcomes, instead, a hungry bear who has been drawn by the delicious smell. Children find this story laugh-aloud funny, and Carmi's illustrations do much to extend the humor.

Kimmel, Eric A. *When Mindy Stole Hanukkah.* Illus. by Barbara McClintock. New York: Scholastic. 1998.

New York City's historic Eldridge Street *shul* is the setting for this story about a family of little people, akin to Mary Norton's *The Borrowers*, who live within its walls. When the synagogue's ferocious cat, Antiochus, threatens to ruin the family's Hanukkah, Mindy and Grandpa relive the story of the *Maccabees* to save the holiday. Humorous characters and an appealing story are illustrated with Victorian charm.

Kimmelman, Leslie. *Sound the Shofar.* Illus. by John Himmelman. New York: HarperCollins. 1998.

This informative and easygoing story, which follows a family's observance of the Days of Awe, is set in a Jewish community served by a modest synagogue with mixed seating and a female cantor. Nice touches are the pre-Yom Kippur food drive for the needy, discussion of fasting by children and family pets, and explanation of the attitude of reflection at a level that primary age children can understand.

Kline, Suzy. *Horrible Harry and the Holidaze.* Illus. by Frank Remkiewicz. New York: Viking. 2004.

Harry is a third grader who likes teasing his classmates and playing with slime. When his great-grandfather enters a nursing home, Harry and his friends share their holidays with the elderly people in the home. Harry's class celebrates five holidays: Hanukkah, Christmas, Kwanzaa, Three Kings' Day and Korean New Year. Each is explained briefly, and artifacts associated with them are shown. Written in short chapters with a simple vocabulary, this can be read independently by third graders, who will enjoy seeing reflections of themselves and kids they know in the story.

Koons, Jon. *A Confused Hanukkah.* Illus. by S. D. Schindler.
New York: Dutton. 2004.

An original *Chelm* story that cleverly uses elements of the traditional tales to satirize Jews who imitate Gentiles. This may be over the heads of younger children, but the story itself and wonderful illustrations will have great appeal. A funny, clever, and offbeat addition to Hanukkah picture books.

Krensky, Stephen. *Hanukkah at Valley Forge.* Illus. by Greg Harlin.
New York: Dutton. 2006.

During the grim winter at Valley Forge, a Polish-born Jewish soldier tells General Washington about Hanukkah, who draws parallels between the *Maccabees'* war against their foes with the American war against the British oppressors. Handsomely illustrated and designed, the book draws on some known historical references to evoke a compelling picture of Washington and of American courage. The text is dignified and the illustrations are outstanding. Winner of a Sydney Taylor Book Award.

Kripke, Dorothy K. *Let's Talk About the Sabbath.* Illus. by Joy Nelkin Weider.
Los Angeles: Alef Design. 1999.

New illustrations update an older book that explains the concept and observance of the Jewish Sabbath in informative and reverent fashion. The Sabbath is presented as a day for relaxation, reflection, study, and family togetherness—not a day of prohibition.

Krulik, Nancy. *No Matzah for Me!*
New York: Grosset and Dunlap. 2003.

The story of the Exodus is framed by the story of a modern day Hebrew school's Passover play. The plot involves a boy who is assigned to play the *matzah* when he really wants to be a superhero. How he combines the two makes for a child-appealing conclusion. The illustrations—and indeed, the entire format—are of the mass-market variety.

Lamstein, Sarah Marwil. *Annie's Shabbat.* Illus. by Cecily Lang.
Morton Grove, IL: Albert Whitman. 1997.

In six short, attractively illustrated chapters that begin with preparations for *Shabbat* and end with *Havdalah*, Annie and her family celebrate *Shabbat* at home, at synagogue, and with some stories from our past.

Lanton, Sandy. *Lots of Latkes.* Illus. by Vickie Jo Redenbaugh.
Minneapolis, MN: Kar-Ben/Lerner. 2003.

Lightweight but sweet, this story about Hanukkah puts the emphasis on fellowship, sharing, story telling, celebrating, and eating. The plot involves a group of older, single people who are invited to a Hanukkah party and cannot bring the food they were asked to bring. Their creative substitutes make the party. Warmly illustrated and set in the long ago.

Lewis, Patrick. *The Boat of Many Rooms.* Illus. by Reg Cartwright.
New York: Simon and Schuster/Atheneum. 1997.

Each stylized, large-eyed figure, whether human or animal, is sharply defined and distinctively composed upon the pages of this unusual version of the Noah's Ark story, written in several styles of verse.

Manushkin, Fran. *The Matzah That Papa Brought Home.* Illus. by Ned Bittinger.
New York: Scholastic. 1995.

Beautifully colored full-page illustrations and a cumulative rhyming story draw the attention of young children to the history and traditions of the Passover *Seder*. The large, realistic illustrations show a family from a bygone era and the repetition invites listeners' participation.

Manushkin, Fran. *Miriam's Cup.* Illus. by Bob Dacey.
New York: Scholastic. 1998.

Based on *midrash*, this story of Miriam's life and deeds is told against the background of a contemporary family's Passover celebration. Lavishly colored illustrations frame the tale, which elucidates the recent, feminist-inspired practice of placing a cup of water on the *Seder* table in Miriam's honor.

Manushkin, Fran. *Starlight and Candles.* Illus. by Jacqueline Chwast.
New York: Simon and Schuster. 1995.

The story of a family's preparations for the Sabbath and observance of it is a story of everyday events being made special by the holiness of the day. The meaning of *Shabbat* is woven into the story along with synagogue services and blessings. Strong, heavy-lined illustrations add interesting visual details.

Nason, Ruth. *The Jewish Faith.*
North Mankato, MN: Cherry Tree Books. 2005

Children who know nothing about Judaism will gain some rudimentary information from this attractive book, as they are taken on a visit with a Reform family to learn about some of the holidays and customs they observe. Sharp color photographs, a colorful book design, large type, and a list of vocabulary words along the bottom of each page create a useful and inviting introductory work. A two-page section for parents and teachers gives background information and suggests some activities and resources. Part of a series called Start-Up Religion, it is suitable for children with no Jewish knowledge or experience.

Nason, Ruth. *Visiting a Synagogue.*
North Mankato, MN: Cherry Tree Books. 2005.

Part of the Start-Up Religion series, this is an appealing, largely pictorial book for both Jewish and non-Jewish libraries. The text is sensitive to differences within Judaism, although the synagogue featured is Reform. Each double-page spread deals with a different aspect of the synagogue. The font is large and easy to read, and vocabulary words are highlighted. A section for teachers and parents gives additional information about Judaism. Activities in listening, reading, writing, and art are included. The companion volume is Nason's *The Jewish Faith.*

Polacco, Patricia. *Tikva Means Hope.*
New York: Doubleday/Random House. 1994.

It's Sukkot, and the Roths have invited two neighborhood kids, Duane and Justine, to sleep overnight in their *sukkah*. The fun of celebrating the holiday is short-lived, however, because the setting is Oakland and the crisis of the story is the devastating fire that burned over a thousand houses in the Oakland hills. Intertwining themes of community and kindness to animals, this features the author/illustrator's usual cast of multiethnic characters in a large, illustrated format. The story is compelling but it can also be frightening and is probably best read to children by parents or a sensitive adult who is prepared to offer genuine and convincing reassurances.

Rael, Elsa Okon. *What Zeesie Saw on Delancey Street.*
   Illus. by Marjorie Priceman.
New York: Aladdin. 1996.

Attending her first *landsleit* society party on New York's Lower East Side, Zeesie makes an impulsive decision and then regrets the harm it may cause. By discovering accidentally the importance of privacy and personal dignity, she also witnesses acts of true *tzedakah*. Set in the 1930s, this is an outstanding story, filled with strong values, believable characters, an engaging plot, and excellent illustrations.

Rosen, Michael. *Chanukah Lights Everywhere.* Illus. by Melissa Iwai.
San Diego: Harcourt/Gulliver. 2001.

A little boy guides readers through the nights of Hanukkah, describing his family's way of celebrating and beginning with the day before and going on to the days after. The narrator counts the lights shining all around the neighborhood. The text is gentle, inclusive, and cheerful, but the illustrations are the highlight, portraying an urban neighborhood with strong colors, defined shapes, and bold color. Like other books by Michael Rosen, this takes a multicultural approach.

Rosen, Michael. *Our Eight Nights of Hanukkah.*
　　Illus. by DyAnne Di Salvo-Ryan.
New York: Holiday House. 2000.

Softly colored illustrations of gentle-faced people of different races placed in a glowing winter holiday ambience set the tone for this feel-good story. In it, a young boy describes the way his family celebrates Hanukkah night by night. Lights, *latkes*, and *dreidel* spinning are part of the celebration but so are collecting gifts to give to the needy and sharing interfaith customs with Christian friends. The theme is one that runs through many of the author's books: It is about people of different religions respecting one another and living together in harmony.

Rosenthal, Betsy R. *It's Not Worth Making a Tzimmes Over!*
　　Illus. by Ruth Rivers.
Morton Grove, IL: Albert Whitman. 2006

"It's not worth making a *tzimmes* over," is Sara's Grandma's response to most problems. When Sara pours a little too much yeast into the *challah* dough and her attention is diverted while she and Grandma sit down to watch "The Blob," the dough overflows and threatens to engulf the entire neighborhood. After calls to the police and a quick trip on Grandma's motor scooter, Sara and Grandma find a way to control the dough and share delicious, fresh-baked challah with everyone. Droll illustrations lend quite a bit of humor to this warm and lighthearted story that is flavored with an ample sprinkling of Yiddish.

Rosinsky, Natalie M. *Hanukkah.*
Minneapolis, MN: Compass Point Books. 2003.

Introductory information about Hanukkah is conveyed through a simple text and clear, attractive photographs, one facing each page of text. Topics are stated in the form of questions: What is Hanukkah? How did it begin?, etc. There is a glossary, index, and list of resources. Acceptable when basic and simply presented information about Hanukkah is needed.

Schulman, Goldie. *Way Too Much Challah Dough.* Illus. by Vitaly Romanenko.
New York: Hachai. 2006

After a little girl adds too much yeast to the *challah* dough she is making, she takes a nap and dreams that it oozes all over the house and then out the door. The arrival of her *bubbe*, carrying two fresh loaves of challah, wakes her up and sets the stage for a joyous celebration of *Shabbat*.

Shulman, Lisa. *The Matzah Ball Boy.* Illus. by Rosanne Litzinger.
New York: Dutton. 2005.

In another take-off on the *Gingerbread Boy*, the *matzah* ball boy careens through the village, evading the *bubbe* who made him, the *yenta*, the rabbi, and a sly fox with a "voice as smooth as *schmaltz*," but not a poor man and his wife who invite him to their *Seder*, where he winds up in the soup! The illustrations by Rosanne Litzinger, who also illustrated the Sydney Taylor Award winning picture book, *Chicken Soup by Heart*, are rich and delicious.

Sievert, Terri. ***Hanukkah: Jewish Festival of Lights.***
Mankato, MN: Capstone. 2006.

Clearly written and well organized, this easy-to-read book gives all of the basic facts about Hanukkah and provides a few enrichment activities in the form of a *dreidel* craft and the address of the First Facts Web site. It is attractively illustrated with full-page color photographs and provides an overview of the holiday, its historical background, and aspects of its celebration. Part of the First Facts Series.

Sper, Emily. ***Hanukkah: A Counting Book in English, Hebrew, and Yiddish.***
New York: Scholastic/Cartwheel. 2001.

The format of this original Hanukkah book is important: Intensely bright colors upon black backgrounds, die cuts in the shape of candles, Hanukkah symbols that correspond in number to the number of candles on each page, color coding to indicate the gender of the Hebrew words, the guttural sound, the stressed syllables, and the language of the word. The spellings of numbers one to eight plus phrases that indicate the Hanukkah symbol, such as "three elephants," are given in English, Hebrew with transliteration, and Yiddish with transliteration. Following the counting pages is a brief account of Hanukkah, emphasizing the symbols that have been used throughout the book.

Sper, Emily. ***The Passover Seder.***
New York: Scholastic/Cartwheel. 2003.

The author of *Hanukkah: A Counting Book in English, Hebrew and Yiddish* has created something special for Passover. It will keep the reader busy, with flaps to lift, textures to rub, wheels to turn, and tabs to pull in addition to brief explanations of all the parts of the *Seder*, plus *Seder* vocabulary words expressed in Hebrew characters and English transliteration. The sturdy, colorful pages are made of cardboard with bright colors and easily identified objects.

Swartz, Daniel J. ***Bim and Bom.*** Illus. by Shelly Schonebaum Ephraim.
Rockville, MD: Kar-Ben Copies. 1996.

A rather sanctimonious picture book about two siblings' love for one another, their community, and the Sabbath. Based on a popular children's Sabbath song, the story reverses customary gender roles and portrays Bim and Bom as children who live alone and have jobs; Bim is a carpenter and Bom is a baker. Nicely illustrated but not a first choice.

Weilerstein, Sadie Rose. *The Adventures of K'tonton.*
New York: National Women's League of the United Synagogue. 1935.

The first modern Jewish children's book, *The Adventures of K'tonton* is also a true classic. It has delighted several generations with its tales of the mischievous, thumb-sized little boy named K'tonton, whose adventures introduce young children to Jewish customs, holidays, and values. Different versions of the K'tonton stories exist, some collected in a volume of favorites and a few others published as separate stories. No Jewish child should grow up without having met K'tonton.

Wilkowski, Susan. *Baby's Bris.* Illus. by Judith Friedman.
Rockville, MD: Kar-Ben Copies. 1999.

During the first eight days of her new brother's life, a little girl learns to be a big sister. The meaning of the *brit milah* is developed as the eight days of the story unfold, emphasizing peoplehood and continuity over the surgical aspects of the ceremony. The soft illustrations are outstanding, particularly in their expressive portrayal of characters' faces.

Zalben, Jane Breskin. *Beni's First Wedding.*
New York: Henry Holt. 1998.

Beni is one of the author/illustrator's bear characters and here he is asked to be the page boy in his Uncle Izzy's wedding. The story and illustrations show many Jewish wedding customs, from the *aufruf*, to the *ketubah* signing, to the breaking of the glass.

Zalben, Jane Breskin. *Pearl's Eight Days of Chanukah.*
New York: Simon and Schuster. 1998.

Arts and crafts take center stage in this story about a family of sheep. For each night, there is a story plus an assortment of recipes, songs, games, crafts, or other play activities. The illustrations are delicate and detailed. The crafts and cooking projects require adult assistance.

Zalben, Jane Breskin. *Pearl's Passover.*
New York: Simon and Schuster. 2002.

Subtitled "A Family Celebration through Stories, Recipes, Crafts, and Songs," this features a sheep family preparing for Passover by cleaning, greeting guests, reading the *Haggadah*, etc. The illustrations are charming and the activities are enjoyable.

Zalben, Jane Breskin. *Pearl Plants a Tree.*
New York: Simon and Schuster. 1995.

Inspired by Grandpa, Pearl plants an apple seed in a pot, waters it, and watches it grow. In the spring, Pearl and Grandpa plant the sapling and have a picnic. The characters are animals, and the illustrations are delicate. Not a first choice for reading aloud to a group because of its small size but fine for individual use.

Zelcer, Draizy. *Once About a Time.* Illus. by Vitaly Romanenko.
New York: Hachai. 2001.

A charming rhymed story that teaches about time by showing analog clock faces at different times of the day and by telling a story of a religiously observant town where every moment of the day is used to perform *mitzvot*. Oversized, bright illustrations complement the story and the concept.

ELEMENTARY

Adler, David A. *The Kids' Catalog of Hanukkah.*
Philadelphia: Jewish Publication Society. 2004.

An addition to the publisher's popular Kids' Catalog Series, this is filled with facts, stories, songs, games, jokes, recipes, crafts, and more. Despite their rather drab formats, all of the Kids' Catalog books are basic to their subjects, whether they are Bible, Israel, or Jewish holidays.

Agranoff, Tracey. *Kids Love Jewish Holiday Crafts.*
New York: Pitspopany. 2000.

An attractive book with craft ideas for the Jewish holidays. Some of the crafts are expensive and difficult. Each is accompanied by a photograph showing what the finished product will look like. Spiral-bound to stay flat.

Allen, Richard. *Parashah Plays.*
Denver: ARE. 2000.

This collection of 54 short plays represents the weekly *Torah* readings, reflecting their message and tone. They rely heavily on the biblical text itself and can be performed in classrooms, on stages, or at camps.

Ben-Zvi, Rebecca Tova. *Four Sides, Eight Nights: A New Spin on Hanukkah.*
    Illus. by Susannah Natti.
Brookfield, CT: Roaring Brook Press. 2005.

A perky collection of *dreidel* history, customs, and lore that is a little different from other books about Hanukkah because of all the offbeat information it includes. What, for example does the science of probability have to do with dreidels? Or Sir Isaac Newton? What are the origins of the dreidel and how do you play it? Written and illustrated with verve.

Berger, Gilda. *Celebrate! Stories of the Jewish Holidays.* Illus. by Peter Catalanotto.
New York: Scholastic. 1998.

For each of eight holidays, the author has written a story followed by short sections on the meaning of the holiday and how it is observed, plus some crafts and recipes. The format is large, readable, and attractive.

Blumberg, Marjie. *Avram's Gift.* Illus. by Laurie McGaw.
Rockville, MD: MB Publishing. 2003.

A well-illustrated short chapter book about an eight-year-old boy whose love of Judaism and his family motivate him to learn to blow the *shofar*. The story interweaves the Rosh Hashanah observance of a modern Jewish family with *shtetl* ancestors, immigration, and High Holiday rituals in a Rockville, Maryland, synagogue. McGaw's illustrations are photographically realistic and provide details that will enable middle grade readers to identify with the story.

Cato, Vivian. *The Torah and Judaism.*
North Mankato, MN: Smart Apple Media. 2004.

The origin, structure, content, teachings, use, and study of the *Torah* are explained in clear and absorbing prose. The emphasis is on Jewish religious concepts and practices, noting when practices differ. The physical *Torah* as well as the conceptual is discussed, including the work of a *sofer* and the way to treat the *Torah*. Sections on daily life and worship present Judaism as a living, vibrant religion relevant to contemporary life. A very useful introduction.

Cooper, Ilene. *Jewish Holidays All Year Round: A Family Treasury.*
   Illus. by Elivia Savadier.
New York: Harry Abrams. 2002.

The goal of this appealing book is to help families create holiday rituals that make their home celebrations special by choosing from the rituals, crafts, activities, and recipes included. Many of the illustrations are from the collection of New York's Jewish Museum.

Curtis, Sandra. *Gabriel's Ark.* Illus. by Spark.
Los Angeles: Alef Design. 1999.

This story of a mentally disabled child's *Bar Mitzvah* is told with tact and sensitivity. Supported by a loving family and tutored by an understanding rabbi, Gabriel overcomes his fear of anything new and becomes a *Bar Mitzvah* in a manner unique to his capabilities. The black-and-white, comic book-style illustrations are a detriment.

Fisher, Adam. *God's Garden: Children's Stories Grown from the Bible.*
Springfield, NJ: Behrman House. 1999.

A useful collection of original stories based on the weekly *Torah* portions. Each story includes a short summary of the *parashah*, a line or two of biblical text with citation, a statement about the values in the story, some discussion questions, and storytelling props. At the end of the book there is a glossary and an index to all of the values found in the stories.

Frankle, Pessie, and Yocheved Leah Perkal. ***Mrs. Honig's Cakes.*** Illus. by Tova Katz. Tampa, FL: Hamodia. 2004.

A collection of short anecdotes that illustrate moral lessons. The story is held together by a frame in which three young Orthodox Jewish girls visit their neighbor, Mrs. Honig, to share her baking and her stories. At the beginning of each chapter, the girls relate a problem they have encountered, and Mrs. Honig tells them a story that offers a solution, plus gives them each a piece of cake. The problems presented seem more relative to a sheltered community of 50 years ago than the present, and the style also is dated. Set in a girls' school, this will appeal primarily to Orthodox girls.

Ganz, Yaffa. ***The Adventures of Jeremy and Heddy Levi.*** Illus. by Avi Katz. New York: Pitspopany. 2003.

Originally published as two separate books, this revised and updated version tells humorous stories about a brother and sister whose good intentions and great ideas often go awry. Jeremy and Heddy cheerfully use Judaism to provide structure for their daily activities, as well as for their spiritual and emotional lives. An affirmative book for Orthodox readers and accessible to others.

Herman, Charlotte. ***What Happened to Heather Hopkowitz?***
Philadelphia: Jewish Publication Society. 1981.

One of the best novels ever written about a young Jewish teen in search of religious identity. Heather is introduced to traditional Judaism almost accidentally, when she stays with an Orthodox friend and her family while her parents are on vacation. Her attempt to live as an observant Jew—keeping *Shabbat* and *kashrut*, for example—is done in secret from her assimilated family until she finally realizes that she has to tell them the truth. Their reaction is not positive but, like all of the plot and all of the characters, it is genuine and believable.

Koss, Amy. ***How I Saved Hanukkah.*** Illus. by Diane de Groat. New York: Dial. 1998.

Fourth-grader Marla, the only Jew in her California school classroom, decides that she must learn more about Hanukkah. Delving into its history, meaning, and tradition, she infects her family with her zeal and the holiday spirit. Told in a breezy style, this affirms a rather secularized form of Jewish identity.

Lehman-Wilzig, Tami. ***Passover around the World.*** Illus. by Elizabeth Wolf Minneapolis, MN: Kar-Ben/Lerner. 2007

Passover customs of various countries are explored through stories, fact boxes, and recipes, with a map provided to show each location. Colorful illustrations and a lively text make this an interesting book for browsing and pleasure reading.

Milgram, Goldie. *Make Your Own Bar/Bat Mitzvah: A Personal Approach to Creating a Meaningful Rite of Passage.*
Hoboken, NJ: Jossey Bass. 2004.

Written for children preparing for their *Bar* or *Bat Mitzvahs*, this is a creative and well-organized guide that explains the event's rationale and meaning and encourages children to personalize it through writing their life story, honoring Jewish texts and traditions, finding community *tzedakah* projects to do, and more.

Moscowitz, Moshe. *Miracle Lights: The Chanukah Story!*
Chicago: Shazak Productions. 2004.

This cartoon-style graphic novel gives a thorough history of Hanukkah while managing to be light and humorous. The story of the *Maccabees* is told in contemporary language, including references to action figures and electrical appliances. The cartoons are done in vibrant colors. Following the story there are games, activities, a funny quiz, and brief examinations of Hanukkah traditions. A video is also available.

Musleah, Rahel. *Apples and Pomegranates: A Family Seder for Rosh Hashanah.*
Illus. by Judy Jarrett.
Minneapolis, MN: Kar-Ben/Lerner. 2004.

The Rosh Hashanah *Seder* originates with a *Talmudic* recommendation to eat pumpkins, fenugreek, leeks, beets, and dates on New Year. Basing this guide on *Sephardic* customs and those of her family's community in India, the author has created a spiritual celebration that children and adults can enjoy. Recipes, songs, and intriguing questions are included; attractive watercolor illustrations enhance the text.

Musleah, Rahel. *Why on This Night? A Passover Haggadah for Family Celebration.*
Illus. by Louise August.
New York: Simon and Schuster. 2000.
Intended to give children a central part in planning and participating in the Passover *Seder*, this includes every major part of the *Haggadah* in Hebrew, English, and transliteration. There are also superb illustrations, songs, games, crafts, recipes, and other ideas for making the *Seder* family-centered.

Podwal, Mark. *A Sweet New Year: A Taste of the Jewish Holidays.*
New York: Doubleday/Random House. 2003.

A small, beautifully illustrated book that relates food to 10 holidays. Podwal's art connects the sacred with the sumptuous, and the brief text facing each picture page gives just a few observations about the holiday. The color and design are a feast for the eye, and Jewish tradition is always in the foreground. Ideal for enriching factual material about the holidays and excellent as a gift.

Pushker, Gloria Teles. *Toby Belfer Never Had a Christmas Tree.*
   Illus. by Judith Hierstein.
Gretna, LA: Pelican. 1991.

In one of several picture stories based on the author's life, Toby Belfer never had a Christmas tree because she is Jewish. In the small southern town where the Belfer family lives, they are the only Jews and they proudly share their Hanukkah customs with their Christian neighbors, having a party, telling the story of Hanukkah, eating *latkes*, and playing *dreidel*. Toby and all the Belfers are appealing characters because they are so proudly and affirmatively Jewish without being self-conscious about it. The large illustrations of strong-featured, attractive people are an important part of the Toby Belfer books, and one cannot imagine the stories without them.

Rauchwerger, Lisa. *Chocolate Chip Challah.*
New York: UAHC Press. 1999.

This well-organized holiday cookbook provides safety tips, an illustrated index of cooking utensils, and a list of terms. Arrangement begins with the Sabbath, proceeds through the year, and closes with *Rosh Chodesh*. Each festival includes a religious and historical introduction. Blessings are grouped in the back of the book. The recipes are kosher.

Rush, Barbara, and Cherie Karo Schwartz. *The Kids' Catalog of Passover:*
   A Worldwide Celebration of Stories, Songs, Customs, Crafts, Food,
   and Fun.
Philadelphia: Jewish Publication Society. 2000.

Organized in relation to the *Seder*, this book is filled with information, stories, crafts, games, recipes, and songs. A drab, black-and-white format is offset by lively, informal writing, photographs of Jewish children, and a welcoming point of view.

Salkin, Jeffrey. *For Kids—Putting God on Your Guest List.*
Woodstock, VT: Jewish Lights. 1998.

This companion to the author's adult work on the same subject traces the origins of *Bar* and *Bat Mitzvah* in Jewish history, law, and custom. Writing in an easy, friendly style, the author—a rabbi—describes this rite as denoting the assumption of responsibility for performing the *mitzvot* that connect individuals to the community and to God.

Schecter, Ellen. *The Family Haggadah.* Illus. by Neil Waldman.
New York: Viking. 1999.

From pre-*Seder* preparations through the ceremonial conclusion, this offers practical suggestions and an outline for maximizing participation of adults and children. It is non-sexist, non-patriarchal, and non-nationalistic. Although pared down, the text retains most of the traditional highlights. Mainly in English.

Schur, Maxine Rose. *Day of Delight: A Jewish Sabbath in Ethiopia.*
   Illus. by Brian Pinkney.
New York: Dial. 1994.

Menelik, the son of an Ethiopian blacksmith, celebrates the Sabbath with his family in their village sometime before their exodus to Israel. The scratchboard illustrations add beauty to a gentle story. *When I Left My Village*, a Sydney Taylor Award winner, continues the family's chronicle as they escape and are airlifted out of Ethiopia to Israel.

Segal, Eliezer Lorne. *Uncle Eli's Special-for-Kids, Most Fun Ever, Under-the-Table Passover Haggadah.* Illus. by Bonnie Gordon-Lucas.
San Francisco: No Starch Press. 1999.

If Dr. Suess had written a Passover *Haggadah*, this is what it might have been like. Written to entertain children who might be bored with a long, traditional *Seder*, this *Haggadah* retains the structure of the *Seder*, using wacky rhymes and even wackier illustrations.

Steinberg, Judy, and Barbara Tabs. *Matzah Meals: A Passover Cookbook for Kids,* Revised Edition. Illus. by Bill Hauser.
Minneapolis, MN: Kar-Ben/Lerner. 2004.

Good advice for young cooks, plus suggestions and crafts for the *Seder*, are the prelude to this collection of recipes that range from the no-cooking variety for young children to more complicated ones for teens. Arranged by food category, with clear directions for each recipe, this revised version contains about 12 new recipes.

Stern, Joel. *Jewish Holiday Origami.*
Mineola, NY: Dover. 2006.

Twenty-four origami models based on Jewish holidays are diagrammed and photographed in this welcome addition to the Jewish origami books written previously by Florence Temko. They are arranged by order of difficulty and cross-indexed by holiday. The directions are clear, and the finished products are evocative of the holidays they exemplify.

Zalben, Jane Breskin. *The Magic Menorah: A Modern Chanukah Tale.*
   Illus. by Donna Diamond.
New York: Simon and Schuster. 2001.

An encounter with a Yiddish-spouting genie named Fishel changes a boy's mind about Hanukkah and family traditions. This humorous story provides an appealing picture of a contemporary Jewish-American boy and his family.

MIDDLE SCHOOL

Kimmel, Eric A. *Wonders and Miracles: A Passover Companion.*
New York: Scholastic. 2004.

The traditional order of the *Seder* is the organizing principle of this superbly written and illustrated anthology. The lucid narrative blends history, tradition, modern practices, and Passover's timeless meaning. It is extended by a fascinating selection of poetry, stories, and song lyrics, including a *K'tonton* tale and another about a protest rally on behalf of the Soviet Jewry. The illustrations and book design are outstanding and draw from centuries of *Haggadot*, manuscripts, ritual objects, sculpture, and paintings. A distinguished book for a wide range of interests and ages.

Rush, Barbara. *The Jewish Year: Celebrating the Holidays.*
New York: Stewart, Tabori, and Chang. 2001.

The laws, customs, practices, and folk traditions pertaining to the Jewish holidays, new as well as established, are accompanied by folk tales and attractive artwork. Rush's grasp of the subject is masterful; little children will enjoy having the stories told and read to them, and older folks will appreciate the holidays more for Rush's exploration of their meaning. Format and book design are also outstanding.

Rush, Barbara. *Passover Splendor: Cherished Objects for the Seder Table.*
New York: Stewart, Tabori, and Chang. 2004.

Haggadot, Seder plates, cups, and textiles are the cherished objects discussed and showcased in this handsome book. The accessible text gives the origin and history of Passover and the order of the *Seder* before proceeding, chapter by chapter, to lucid discussions of the historical and ritual significance of the objects themselves. Each illustration is clearly captioned, with its source given. It concludes with *Seder* blessings and songs.

HIGH SCHOOL

Levitin, Sonia. *Strange Relations.*
New York: Random House. 2007.

A teenage girl spends the summer in Hawaii with her religiously observant aunt and the aunt's large family. Not since *The Singing Mountain* has Levitin explored the varieties of Jewish practice in such depth. An absorbing story of good people striving for religious authenticity and learning to understand one another.

Roth, Matthue. *Never Mind the Goldbergs.*
New York: Scholastic/Push. 2005.

A coming-of-age story about an Orthodox Jewish girl who is chosen for a role in a new television series. Leaving her home and family for California, where the sitcom is being filmed, Hava tries to remain observant while testing the limits of observant life. The punk tone, with lots of swearing, will put off some readers—especially adults—but teens may find the rather improbable story offbeat and engrossing.

CHAPTER 10

Peace in the Home and in the World

"Seek peace and pursue it."

Tanakh

PRESCHOOL

Bogot, Howard. **Shalom, Salaam, Peace.** Illus. by Norman Gorbaty.
New York: CCAR Press. 2000.

A universalistic vision of peace, embracing Judaism, Islam, and Christianity, is conveyed through a brief, evocative narrative, repetitions of the English text in Hebrew and Arabic, multicultural illustrations with a Middle Eastern flavor, and an excellent design by Norman Gorbaty, the illustrator. The design is the highlight because it unifies the other elements and dramatizes the theme. Bogot's narrative portrait of a world at peace is sincere, concrete, and child-centered.

Coplestone, Lis, and Jim Coplestone. **Noah's Bed.**
London: Frances Lincoln. 2004.

A sweet picture book, charmingly illustrated, about Noah's grandson, Eber, who creeps into his grandparents' bed when a storm frightens him. Noah and his wife Nora keep telling Eber to stop tickling them, stop scratching them, stop snoring, stop pulling off the quilt. When Noah is ready to send Eber back to his own bed, they discover that lizards, birds, and lions—also afraid of the storm—have joined Eber under the covers. A young child's fear of storms and love of snuggling with adults for comfort is blended with the familiar Noah's Ark story in an entirely new way.

Ludwig, Warren. **Old Noah's Elephants.**
New York: G. P. Putnam's Sons. 1991.

A delightful version of an Israeli folktale, set on Noah's Ark in a time of crisis: The elephants are eating up all of the food and getting so fat that the ark is sinking. Poor Noah

(Cont'd.)

Old Noah's Elephants (Continued)

appeals to God, who tells him, "Tickle the hyena." It's one of those cryptic heavenly orders that works out in its own way, as animal after animal is affected by it. Warren Ludwig's illustrations delight children because of their humor, good nature, and expressiveness—each animal is distinctive and all of the figures invite closer looks; the two elephants' large, wise eyes are especially compelling. A classic folktale that is ideal for reading to young children.

Singer, Isaac Bashevis. *Why Noah Chose the Dove.* Illus. by Eric Carle.
New York: Farrar, Straus and Giroux. 1973.

As the animals vie to be taken with Noah on the ark, each one brags about its strength, its size, its cleverness, and so on. Only the dove does not compete, telling Noah that it doesn't think it is any wiser or better than any of the others. For its modesty, Noah chooses the dove to fly from the Ark and bring back news of the world. Singer ends the story with the words: "The dove lives happily without fighting. It is a bird of peace." Carle's illustrations present an array of animals with splashes of color, sometimes spreading across two pages.

PRIMARY

Da Costa, Deborah. *Snow in Jerusalem.*
   Illus. by Cornelius Van Wright and Ying-Hwa Hu.
Morton Grove, IL: Albert Whitman. 2001.

During a rare day of snow in Jerusalem, a Jewish boy and an Arab boy who live in the Old City experience a rare moment of friendship when they put aside their differences to help a stray cat. Ethereal watercolor and pencil drawings portray the earthly and the heavenly Jerusalem.

Goldin, Barbara Diamond. *A Mountain of Blintzes.* Illus. by Anik McGrory.
San Diego: Harcourt/Gulliver Books. 2001.

The holiday of Shavuot is coming, and a poor family of Jewish farmers in the Catskills prepare for it by saving their money so they will be able to make "a mountain of blintzes." While neither adult in the family manages to save a penny, each assuming that the other is doing it, the children leave nothing to chance and work secretly to earn enough to make the holiday joyful. Bouncy watercolors help capture the mood of the story, based on a tale from *Chelm*.

Jacobs, Laurie. *A Box of Candles.* Illus. by Shelly Schonebaum Ephraim.
Honesdale, PA: Boyds Mills Press. 2005.

The Jewish year forms the framework of a story about a little girl who gradually learns to accept her grandmother's budding romance with a neighbor and to become friends with him herself. Ruthie's emotions are portrayed genuinely, with feeling, and the resolution is believable. The Jewish flavor of the book is strong, with holiday observances integrated into the plot.

Jungman, Ann. *The Most Magnificent Mosque.* Illus. by Shelley Fowles.
London: Frances Lincoln. 2004.
An idealized story of interfaith friendship in medieval Cordoba, Spain. A Jewish boy, a Moslem boy, and a Christian boy are friends, making mischief around the Great Mosque until they are caught and punished. As men, they renew their friendship to collaborate on persuading the Catholic king to save the mosque instead of tearing it down. The illustrations are lovely, almost too lovely to convey the monumental stone grandeur of La Mezquita, the Great Mosque, which still stands, a Roman Catholic cathedral placed within its vast interior. Although it is historically dubious, the story is told and illustrated with verve and goodwill.

Older, Elfin. *My Two Grams.* Illus. by Nancy Hayashi.
San Diego: Harcourt Brace. 2000.
A cheerful story that portrays the narrator's two grandmothers, one Jewish and one Christian. Their lives are contrasted, as well as the customs and holidays they observe. The unifying event is the "First Traditional Grandmothers' Party" that the little girl gives, asking both *Bubbe* Silver and Grandma Lane to attend, bringing food that represents each one's religious tradition. The final picture of Grandma Lane eating *Bubbe* Silver's gefilte fish and horseradish is worth the rest of the book, which is upbeat but rather stereotyped.

Prose, Francine. *Dybbuk.* Illus. by Mark Podwal.
New York: Greenwillow. 1996.
A charming romantic comedy loosely based on the legend of the *Dybbuk* and S. Y. Ansky's play. Underlying Prose's version is the legend of the angels who, 40 days before the birth of babies, predestine their marriage partners. Podwal's illustrations, laden with Jewish objects, enhance the mystical tone.

Rouss, Sylvia. *Aaron's Bar Mitzvah: Growing Up Jewish with Sarah Leah Jacobs.*
Illus. by Liz Goulet Dubois.
Middle Village, NY: Jonathan David. 2003.
Sarah Leah Jacobs was introduced to readers in *My Baby Brother, What a Miracle.* In this story, the attention is on her older brother, Aaron, who just doesn't have time for Sarah as he studies for his *Bar Mitzvah.* Her feelings of rejection and jealousy over all the attention he is getting are recorded in cartoon bubbles that reveal her not-very-nice but completely believable thoughts. A humorous and perceptive look at sibling relationships.

Rouss, Sylvia. *My Baby Brother, What a Miracle!* Illus. by Liz Goulet Dubois.
Middle Village, NY: Jonathan David. 2002.

The arrival of a new brother puzzles Sara Leah Jacobs. She can't figure out why all her relatives make such a fuss over him. To her, he is less than special! Her thoughts are recorded in bubbles and are humorously juxtaposed with the adoring remarks made by others. Solid Jewish content runs through the narrative. The illustrations are pallid and fail to capture the humor of the story.

Sasso, Sandy Eisenberg. *Cain and Abel: Finding the Fruits of Peace.*
    Illus. by Joani Keller Rothenberg.
Woodstock, VT: Jewish Lights. 2001.

Bold splashes of color illustrate this interpretation of a Bible story that emphasizes the destructive power of anger. Running through the narrative is the *midrashic* tradition of nature's mourning for Abel.

Stampler, Ann Redisch. *Something for Nothing.* Illus. by Jacqueline M. Cohen.
New York: Clarion. 2003

In this ebullient trickster tale, a clever and peace-loving dog foils three rowdy cats who terrorize the neighborhood by playing upon their greed. All of the characters are animals, but the story is steeped in Eastern European Jewish tradition—reflecting, as the author notes in the Afterword, the triumph of the underdog over powerful uncertainties. The stunning illustrations complement and enhance the story. Excellent for reading aloud.

ELEMENTARY

Cooper, Ilene. *Sam I Am.*
New York: Scholastic, 2004.

Twelve-year-old Sam has a Christian mother and an agnostic Jewish father. When tensions emerge in his family at Hanukkah/Christmastime, Sam begins to wonder why people of different religions always fight. His own Jewish identity, not particularly strong, is given a jolt when his class begins to study the Holocaust. Interwoven with a school story is an authentic exploration of Sam's questions, the answers he gets, and the answers that he doesn't get. The conclusion offers no definitive choices but a satisfying sense that asking questions is as important as getting answers. The portrait of an intermarried family is drawn with honesty and open-mindedness.

Fagan, Cary. *Daughter of the Great Zandini.* Illus. by Cybele Young.
Toronto: Tundra. 2001.

This charming little story is set in Paris in the late 1800s. It features a feisty heroine named Fanny whom modern girls will admire. The plot involves Fanny's magician father, a journalist who claims he's washed up, and Fanny's lovesick brother, who would rather do anything than follow in his father's footsteps. The Jewish content is slight, but the plot, characterization, and style are sprightly.

Houghton, Sarah. *Elie Wiesel: A Holocaust Survivor Cries Out for Peace.*
Bloomington, MN: Red Brick Learning. 2004.

A high interest–low vocabulary biography in the High Five Reading Series, this book combines a bit of information about Elie Wiesel with color and black-and-white photographs in an attractive and inviting format. Serving both as an introduction to the Holocaust and to Wiesel's life and work as they were shaped by his experiences, this slight book is readable and attractive.

Hurwitz, Johanna. *Dear Emma.* Illus. by Barbara Garrison.
New York: HarperCollins. 2002.

Readers who met Dossi Rabinowitz in *Faraway Summer* and those meeting her for the first time in this sequel will enjoy her letters to her friend Emma Meade in Vermont. In them, Dossi confides in Emma about her life on the Lower East Side, her relationship with her new brother-in-law, and her aspirations. She also draws a vivid picture of life in New York City in the early twentieth century, including an account of the Triangle Shirtwaist Factory disaster.

Levitin, Sonia. *Annie's Promise.*
New York: Atheneum. 1993.

The three Platt sisters have adjusted well to America, but their parents retain their old-world ways. Annie, the youngest sister and narrator of this third book in the trilogy, experiences a turbulent thirteenth year as she struggles for independence. A summer at camp is a wonderful experience for a girl who loves nature and animals, but even there she encounters prejudice against Jews and also against her best camping friend, a black girl. All of the Platt family members are beautifully developed characters and, as the war ends, their emotions and reactions are sympathetically delineated. An outstanding conclusion to an outstanding series that includes *Journey to America* and *Silver Days*.

Penn, Malka. *The Hanukkah Ghosts.*
New York: Holiday House. 1995.

A manor house on the English moors is filled with ghosts and secrets. As she becomes involved with these ghosts, Susan forgets how unhappy she is to have been left with a great-aunt while her father is on a business trip. Hanukkah figures into the plot very marginally, as though it were a hook to hang a title on. Nevertheless, the story is engrossing, and girls who like fantasy will enjoy it.

Propp, Vera. *When the Soldiers Were Gone.*
New York: G. P. Putnam's Sons. 1999.

This is a poignant story about a hidden child and his gradual reintegration into his Dutch Jewish birth family after Holland is liberated from German occupation. The characters are decent and good-hearted and the plot is a quiet, reflective one. It would be a good followup to Oppenheim's *The Lily Cupboard*, which is also about a hidden Dutch child, set during rather than after the Holocaust.

Rinn, Miriam. *The Saturday Secret.* Illus. by Spark.
Los Angeles: Torah Aura. 1999.

A preteen boy plays baseball clandestinely on the Sabbath, in defiance of his religiously observant stepfather. His guilt feelings, plus evidence that his stepfather is really an okay sort of guy, eventually change his mind. The sports plot will appeal to boys, but the writing, illustrations, and format are pedestrian.

Rosen, Michael. *The Blessing of the Animals.*
New York: Farrar, Straus and Giroux. 2000.

Twelve-year-old Jared wants to take his dog to the blessing of the animals that the nearby Catholic church holds once a year. His mother is opposed—they are Jewish—so Jared and Mom agree to each get four other opinions to help Jared make the final decision. In this way, plot and character are developed, family and community relationships are revealed, and Jewish belief and identity are explored. A bit slow-paced, the story nevertheless is a believable portrait of the kinds of dilemmas that contemporary Jewish American kids encounter in a pluralistic society.

Yorinks, Arthur. *The Flying Latke.* Illus. by William Steig.
New York: Simon and Schuster. 1999.

Farcical in the broadest sense and marked by the offbeat comedy that is a Yorinks specialty, this book pokes fun at a bickering family's Hanukkah party. The narrative—mostly dialogue—parodies the idiocy of family arguments, which lead to the accidental launching of a *latke* into orbit. The characters are photographs of real people. Like all farces, this will appeal to some readers and leave others cold.

Zalben, Jane Breskin. *Paths to Peace: People Who Changed the World.*
New York: Dutton. 2006.

A collective biography that contains 16 one-page biographical sketches of people who tried to make the world a better place. Each sketch gives basic facts about the person's life and highlights the actions that characterize each person as a peacemaker. The symbolic illustrations are excellent. Of the 16 biographies, only Albert Einstein, Anne Frank, and Elie Wiesel are Jewish.

MIDDLE SCHOOL

Koss, Amy. 2001. *Stolen Words.*
Middleton, WI: Pleasant/American Girl.

Everything is going wrong on Robyn's vacation with her family in Austria. As recorded in her diary, Robyn's comments and observations are filled with both biting teenage wit and deep concern about her mother, who cannot get over the death of her sister. This is an engaging portrayal of a contemporary Jewish-American family.

Levitin, Sonia. *The Singing Mountain.*
New York: Simon and Schuster. 1998.

Contemporary Jewish identity and the search for religious authenticity are the intertwined themes of this engrossing novel set in California and Israel and portrayed through the lives of two teenagers and their family. To the consternation of his assimilated parents, Mitch becomes a *baal teshuvah* and decides to stay in Israel. Differences in Jewish belief are explored with the tact understanding that are typical of this author's explorations of pluralistic Judaism.

Lowenstein, Sallie. *Waiting for Eugene.*
Kensington, MD: Lion Stone Books. 2005.

This offbeat and ambitious story shows the effects of mental illness on a family and on individual creativity. It is set sometime after the Holocaust, and the protagonist's father is a survivor who is haunted by his memories. Few stories for children deal with the relationship between art and experience, much less mental illness, and this does it well. However, the author's universalistic approach to the Holocaust obscures both the family's Jewish identity and the Holocaust as a specific historical experience.

Metzger, Lois. *Missing Girls.*
New York: Viking. 1999.

The heavy toll exacted by lack of communication is the theme of this serious novel set in 1967. Two alienated girls become friends; Carrie's grandmother is a Holocaust survivor; Mona and her mother do not get along. The character development is strong, but Judaism is not central to the plot or theme.

Naylor, Phyllis. *Walker's Crossing.*
New York: Simon and Schuster/Atheneum. 1999.

Thirteen-year-old Ryan lives with his family on a ranch in Wyoming. His admired older brother joins a white supremacist group, and Ryan is forced to examine his own feelings about loyalty and honesty. Although there are very few Jewish characters, the subject of racism is explored with conviction, and Ryan is an appealing character.

Newbery, Linda. *Sisterland.*
New York: David Fickling/Random House. 2004.

Family secrets are revealed in this ambitious novel for teenagers. The most complex and closely guarded is the Jewish identity of an elderly woman suffering from Alzheimer's. Set in a small English city during World War II and in the present, the story also involves homosexuality, racism, interracial dating, and the Israeli-Palestinian conflict. Plot, setting, and characterization are skillfully blended to create a thought-provoking exploration of family and social issues. Some sex scenes and anti-Zionism will put off some readers.

Ostow, Micol. *Emily Goldberg Learns to Salsa.*
New York: Razorbill. 2006.

Emily Goldberg first meets her Puerto Rican mother's family at the funeral of her grandmother. Her mother and her family have been estranged since she married Emily's Jewish father. Emily stays on with her mother after the funeral and gets to know her relatives and the culture of middle-class Puerto Ricans, which is rather different from her own. The writing style is colloquial, filled with teenage jargon and references to teen lifestyle. Lacking in any depth of characterization, this may appeal to girls who like chick lit. It is remarkably similar in theme and narrative style to *How to Ruin a Summer Vacation*, but the Jewish elements are much less important and the point of view is more personal.

Rahlens, Holly-Jane. *Prince William, Maximilian Minsky, and Me.*
Cambridge, MA: Candlewick. 2005.

The "me" of the title is Nelly Sue Edelmeister, who lives with her Jewish mother and Gentile father in present-day Berlin. Beset by anxieties concerning her pending *Bat Mitzvah* and her parents' marital problems, Nelly falls in love with a picture of Prince William and decides to train for her school's soccer team so she can go to England and meet him. To help her overcome her lack of athletic ability, she gains the help of Maximilian Minsky, the Goth-garbed son of her father's mistress. Helping her sort out the issues of Jewish identity is her elderly friend, Risa, who dies during the course of the story. With a mature subtext about marital conflict and infidelity, this isn't for everyone, but it's likely that girls will enjoy reading it.

Rifai, Amal, Odelia Ausbinder, and Sylke Tempel. *We Just Want to Live Here: A Palestinian Teenager, an Israeli Teenager—an Unlikely Friendship.*
New York: St. Martin's Press. 2003.

Tempel, a German journalist, facilitated this exchange of letters between two teenagers living in Jerusalem. The Palestinian girl is constrained, the Israeli voluble and critical of Israeli society and the Sharon government. Between them, they present a reasonable sample of opposing views. Excellent for discussion of issues involved in the Israeli-Palestinian conflict, for a demonstration of free versus unfree speech (the Palestinian girl's family would not allow their real name to be used for fear of reprisals), and for what it suggests about the choices and life options open to young Israeli and Palestinian women.

Schwartz, Ellen. *Stealing Home.*
Plattsburgh, NY: Tundra. 2006.

Set in Brooklyn in 1947, there are two main characters in this appealing story. Joey is a nine-year-old, racially mixed orphan who is accepted neither by his African-American peers nor by some of the people in the Jewish community where he goes to live. He has learned to be tough, to look after himself, and to expect nothing from others, including the stern, disapproving grandfather whose home he shares. Jackie Robinson is the baseball hero whom Joey comes to love, even though he plays for the Brooklyn Dodgers instead of for Joey's favorite team, the New York Yankees. Through many scenes of baseball games, Robinson's stoic struggle against racism is portrayed, mirroring in some ways Joey's own.

CHAPTER 11

Peoplehood

"All Jews are responsible for one another."

Talmud

PRESCHOOL

Abraham, Michelle Shapiro. *My Cousin Tamar Lives in Israel.*
   Illus. by Ann D. Koffsky.
New York: URJ Press. 2007

After showing a boy's home in the United States and his cousin Tamar's home in Jerusalem, the simple story moves quickly through a few of the Jewish holidays in Israel, showing how Tamar observes them. As an affirmative introduction for preschoolers, emphasizing the normalcy of Israeli life, this focus on the holidays could be used in tandem with Groner's *Let's Visit Israel*, which takes children on a short tour of places in Israel.

Carmi, Giora. *And Shira Imagined.*
Philadelphia: Jewish Publication Society. 1988.

Wildly fanciful color illustrations, representing a child's imagination, alternate with realistic black-and-white sketches of places in Israel. They tell the story, along with a brief text, of an American family's visit to Israel. With each sight they see—Tel Aviv, Caesarea, a *kibbutz*, King David's Tower in Jerusalem, to name a few—Shira imagines that the stuffed toys from her bedroom back home are there, too. Young children delight in this classic picture book, which introduces them to Israel while appealing to their imaginations through familiar objects like toys.

Groner, Judyth. *Let's Visit Israel.* Illus. by Cheryl Nathan.
Minneapolis, MN: Kar-Ben/Lerner. 2004.

In what is now the simplest book about Israel in print, a little boy is the guide, taking readers from the Ben Gurion Airport to Jerusalem and the Old City, to a *kibbutz*, and then for a camel ride in Beersheva, a jeep ride through the dessert, to Eilat and a glass-bottomed boat, up the side of the mountain in a cable car to Masada, to the Dead Sea for a float, and then back to Jerusalem to the *Kotel*. Each site occupies a page with just one line of text and a bright, cheerful picture that shows young children what Israel looks like. Although very cursory, it is the right length and format for preschoolers.

Portnoy, Mindy Avra. *Mommy Never Went to Hebrew School.*
   Illus. by Shelly O. Haas.
Rockville, MD: Kar-Ben Copies. 1989.

Gently illustrated in black and white, this is one of the first books to deal with conversion to Judaism. It is for primary-grade children, told by a little boy whose mother is a convert. He explains why and how she did it and what it has meant to her. The issue of Christian grandparents is handled in a respectful way. An excellent introductory story.

Rosenfeld, Dina. *A Little Girl Named Miriam.* Illus. by Ilene Winn-Lederer.
New York: Hachai. 2001.

Part of the publisher's "Little Greats" series, this story of Moses' sister, Miriam, portrays her as endowed with the gift of prophecy from childhood. Wise and brave beyond her years, she stands up to Pharaoh, reads the riot act to her father and the other Jewish men who are planning to separate from their wives, and returns her baby brother, Moses, to be cared for by his own mother after Pharaoh's daughter has found him. Combining biblical accounts with *Talmud* and *Midrash*, the story is illustrated with flat, bright colors and exaggerated lines.

Rouss, Sylvia. *Sammy Spider's First Trip to Israel.* Illus. by Katherine Janus Kahn.
Minneapolis, MN: Kar-Ben/Lerner. 2002.

The ever-curious Sammy stows away on the Shapiros' trip to Israel. There, he uses his five senses to experience the country. With Sammy, children tour Israel: the Ben Gurion airport, Tel Aviv, a *kibbutz*, the Western Wall and Jerusalem, the Negev, Eilat, the Dead Sea, and the Galilee. As seen through Sammy's big, round spider's eyes, Israel is a diverse, colorful, and meaningful place for Jews. Kahn's collage and torn-paper illustrations are colorful and have just the right amount of detail for preschoolers.

Rouss, Sylvia. *Sammy Spider's Israel Fun Book.* Illus. by Katherine Janus Kahn.
Minneapolis, MN: Kar-Ben/Lerner. 2004.

Familiar to teachers and others who read the Sammy Spider books to children, this fun book reinforces the concepts introduced in *Sammy Spider's First Trip to Israel* through puzzles, games, mazes, crafts, and other easy activities.

Seidman, Lauren. *What Makes Me a Jew?*
Woodstock, VT: Jewish Lights. 2007

Is it the way that I look? Do Jews come from only one place on earth? Are Jewish people Jewish from the time of their birth? Are there ways to be Jewish with my family? These are some of the questions asked and answered in this colorful book. Young children will enjoy looking at the bright photographs of people who represent Jews of different races and ages behaving Jewishly. Inclusive in its outlook and age-appropriate in the Jewish behaviors that it portrays, the format is inviting, with large type printed in different colors and an all-around cheerful look.

PRIMARY

Alexander, Sue. *Behold the Trees.* Illus. by Leonid Gore.
New York: Arthur A. Levine/Scholastic. 2001.

Recalling the history of the land of Israel from Canaanite times to the founding of the modern state, this engagingly written and beautifully designed book has splendid illustrations that extend the text in chronicling the rise, trials, and achievements of the Jewish people as reflected by Israel's trees. A tribute to the Jewish National Fund is included. Excellent for reading during the holiday of *Tu Bi'Shevat* and when studying Israel.

Blumenthal, Scott. *The Great Israel Scavenger Hunt.*
Springfield, NJ: Behrman House. 2003.

An interactive, nicely illustrated trip through modern Israel, covering major cities and places. It is presented in the form of a scavenger hunt and includes pages on which children are to draw, write, and apply stickers. This will limit its use in libraries but not in schools or homes. A teaching guide is also available.

Fontes, Ron, and Justine Fontes. *Israel.*
New York: Children's Press. 2004.

This attractive introduction to Israel for primary-grade children gives about 10 sentences of information for each of 26 topics, from animals to *zayteem*. The Web sites listed at the back of the book are especially interesting: One spotlights Israel's lesser-known tourist attractions, and another gives a picture tour of Jerusalem, including the Chagall windows. The site about Jerusalem history is also good, although for children older than those for whom this book is intended. Part of the publisher's A–Z Series.

Gresko, Marcia S. *A Ticket to Israel.*
Minneapolis, MN: Carolrhoda/Lerner. 2000.

Simply-presented information about Israel is packaged attractively in this book for grades 1–3. The type is large, sentences are short, the coverage includes people, geography, religion, language, customs, and social life of both Jewish and Arab Israelis. The format includes photographs, some boxed information, and pictures showing the flag, Hebrew letters, a *shofar*, etc. Balanced in its brief mention of the Palestinian conflict, this is acceptable as an introductory work. Part of the "A Ticket to..." Series.

Grossman, Laurie. *Children of Israel.*
Minneapolis, MN: Kar-Ben/Lerner. 2000.

The author is a photographer who lives in Israel. These credentials contribute to a better-than-average book about Israel's children. Several pages, liberally sprinkled with excellent color photographs, are devoted to each child, his/her family, and lifestyle. Besides information about *Ashkenazic* and *Sephardic* Jews, secular Israelis, a modern Orthodox family, a *haredi* family, Ethiopians, Bedouins, and Muslims, glimpses are given of life in big cities, small towns, *kibbutzim*, caravans, and suburbs. Suitable as an introduction to Israel and good for browsing. An index and pronunciation guide are included.

Grossman, Laurie. *The Colors of Israel.* Illus. by Helen Byers
Minneapolis, MN: Lerner. 2001.

The author introduces this book by emphasizing the spiritual significance of Israel to Christians, Moslems, and Jews. Employing a theme of colors, she provides basic information about Israel's history, geography, climate, natural environment, agriculture, cities, *kibbutzim*, religions, and culture. The charming illustrations feature children of many backgrounds.

Hoffman, Lawrence A., and Ron Wolfson. *What You Will See Inside a Synagogue.*
    Photographs by Bill Aron.
Woodstock, VT: Jewish Lights. 2004.

Excellent color photographs accompany a lucid introduction to Reform, Conservative, and Reconstructionist synagogues. Jewish ritual objects, prayer, synagogue services, holidays, and lifecycle events are explored, along with the synagogue library. Scenes inside the synagogue show men and women praying together, with the women wearing *talliot* and *kipot*. The point of view is affirmative, inclusive, and positive. There is no glossary or index, but the pronunciation of Hebrew and Yiddish words is given, and the book is short and well-captioned enough to make locating information easy. The final two pages show six architecturally different American synagogues. This is part of a series that includes books on a mosque, a Catholic church, and a Hindu temple.

Kendall, Jonathan P. *My Name Is Rachamim.* Illus. by Alemu Eshetie.
New York: UAHC Press. 1987.

A Jewish Ethiopian boy named Rachamim tells the story of the life of the *Beta Israel* in Gondar, Ethiopia, of their hazardous journey to the Sudan to escape famine, and of "Operation Moses," the secret transport and resettling of the *Beta Israel* in Israel. His narrative, told simply and with conviction, describes the history and customs of Ethiopian Jews, their way of life, and their amazement at discovering that there were white Jews in a fabled land awaiting them. The black-and-white illustrations capture the flavor of the narrative and many of its essential details. This appealing introduction to the *Beta Israel* was one of the first written for children.

Manushkin, Fran. *Come, Let Us Be Joyful: The Story of Hava Nagila.*
    Illus. by Rosalind Charney Kaye.
New York: UAHC Press. 2000.

Children who have sung and danced to the song "Hava Nagila" will learn how it may have come to be transformed from a sad Yiddish melody to the musical embodiment of pioneering Zionism. An ebulliently written and illustrated story set in Israel before statehood. The authorship of the song is disputed; this is one version.

Mitten, Christopher, and Priya Seshan. *Israel.*
Austin, TX: Raintree/Steck-Vaughn. 2002.

This small book gives a bit of information about Israel's history, geography, government, cultures, and tourist sites. It is part of the Steadwell Books World Tour Series and it is the kind of book children might want to consult for taking a trip—real or imagined—to Israel. The color photographs are made to look as if they were photos in a scrapbook, with "taped on" captions. The emphasis is not on in-depth information but on a tourist-eye view of Israel.

Schuman, Burt. *Chanukah on the Prairie.* Illus. by Rosalind Charney Kaye.
New York: UAHC Press. 2002.

The story of an immigrant family who leaves Galicia in Poland and settles in Grand Forks, North Dakota, where a thriving Jewish community welcomes them. Based on real history, this is a delightful story about a little-known part of American-Jewish history. The title is a misnomer because only the concluding episode is set during Hanukkah.

Schur, Maxine Rose. *When I Left My Village.* Illus. by Brian Pinkney.
New York: Dial. 1996.

Language rich in metaphor describes an Ethiopian Jewish family's hardships and daring escape to Israel across harsh terrain and hostile borders. The main character is a 12-year-old boy, and the story brings dramatic recent history to life. Pinkney's strong illustrations add to the drama. A sequel to *Day of Delight: A Jewish Sabbath in Ethiopia* and winner of a Sydney Taylor Book Award.

Steiner, Connie Colker. *On Eagles' Wings and Other Things.*
Philadelphia: Jewish Publication Society. 1987.

After the founding of Israel in 1948, Jews from all over the world flocked there. In many cases, they were refugees from war and anti-Semitism; in others, they were ardent Zionists. In this moving story, Jewish children from Yemen, Tunisia, the United States, and Poland represent Jewish immigrants and refugees from all over the world who settle in Israel in fulfillment of the Zionist dream. Nicely illustrated, this is an age-appropriate introduction to Zionism.

Waldman, Neil. *The Never-Ending Greenness.*
New York: Morrow. 1997.

Illustrations in pointillist style are one of the striking features of this story about replanting the barren land of Israel. The narrator begins as a boy and ends as an old man, telling the story of coming to Palestine with his parents as refugees from the Holocaust, his hopes of filling the land with trees, and the eventual fruition of the Zionist dream of making the dry places bloom. The illustrations showing the Nazis are done in black and white, while the rest are in pastels that suggest hope and growth.

ELEMENTARY

Aretha, David. *Israel in the News: Past, Present, and Future.*
Berkeley Heights, NJ: MyReportLinks.com/Enslow. 2006.

Designed to help students write reports, this book is part of the Middle East Nations in the News Series. It has information on the geography, religion, culture, history, and economy of Israel, as well as on the Arab-Israeli conflict. As with many nonfiction series, there are editorial lapses, such as a photo caption identifying the animal that an Arab girl is riding on as a jackal instead of a donkey. Using a password that the book provides, readers are directed to the Myreportlinks.com Web page, with many links to government and mainstream journalism sources about Israel and the Middle East.

Benderly, Beryl Lieff. *Jason's Miracle.*
Morton Grove, IL: Albert Whitman. 2000.

Jason is one of those kids who wishes he could have a Christmas tree instead of Hanukkah. One night, a mysterious visitor appears who takes Jason back with him into the time of the *Maccabees*, where they join the battle for religious freedom and see the miracle of the burning oil. Boys who don't like to read fiction may enjoy the adventure.

Boraas, Tracey. *Israel.*
Mankato, MN: Bridgestone/Capstone. 2003.

Factual and objective, this short book for report writers in grades 3–6 covers Israel's geography, climate, wildlife, history, government, peoples, and daily life in a well-organized and accessible manner. Clearly drawn maps and text boxes, plus photographs and other illustrations, add visual interest and additional information. Appended material includes pictures of the Israeli flag and coat of arms, a timeline, glossary, brief bibliography, addresses and Web sites, and an index. Part of the Countries and Cultures Series.

Broida, Marian. *The Ancient Israelites and Their Neighbors: An Activity Guide.*
Chicago: Chicago Review Press. 2003.

An informative and interesting guide to the cultures of the ancient Israelites, Phoenicians, and Philistines. The time period covered is the Iron Age, from about 1200

BCE to 538 BCE. Presented in an informal, child-friendly style with two-color illustrations and maps, the text draws on historical, biblical, and archaeological sources to sketch the origins, religions, and daily lives of the three peoples. Each of the sections has chapters on history, architecture, clothing, language and writing, work, food, and religion—all amply illustrated with photographs of artifacts from each culture. Each section also has craft activities and recipes.

Burstein, Chaya. *The Kids' Catalog of Bible Treasures.*
Philadelphia: Jewish Publication Society. 1999.

A wealth of activities and information all relate the biblical world to the interests of modern-day children and provide multiple entry points into the fascinating and complex subject of the Bible. There are archaeological digs, Bible crafts, recipes, and projects, jokes, riddles—all designed to show children how the Bible influences our lives today. Illustrated with maps, drawings, and photographs.

Burstein, Chaya. *A Kid's Catalog of Israel, Revised Edition.*
Philadelphia: Jewish Publication Society. 1998.

Originally published in 1988, this is the most comprehensive, most ebullient introduction to Israel for children that exists. Illustrated with the author's pencil drawings, it combines history, geography, lore, crafts, songs, recipes, dances, stories, information, and more in a style that stresses Israel's multicultural nature. Children with no knowledge of Israel can read it with enthusiasm, browsing here and there as strikes their fancy, while children informed about Israel will find both confirmation of their knowledge and new insights.

Burstein, Chaya. *Our Land of Israel.*
New York: UAHC Press. 1995.

Although the CIP data calls this a textbook, it is also suitable for independent reading because it is written in Burstein's typically lively style, and because it gives an excellent overview of Israel, with each chapter able to be read independently of the others. Each chapter's subject is introduced by an Israeli who gives a brief, first-person account about something personal that relates to the chapter topic. Throughout the book, there are maps, charts, photographs, activities, Hebrew vocabulary, timelines, and other useful aids to understanding.

Finkelstein, Norman H. *Ariel Sharon.*
Minneapolis, MN: Lerner. 2005.

A brief and objective account of the life of Ariel Sharon, stressing his military accomplishments, his political career, and the controversies that have surrounded him. It is organized chronologically, written in a clear, direct, and unbiased manner, illustrated with black-and-white photographs, and appended with an index, a timeline, and a list of further readings and Web sites that include two very poor books about Israel.

Goldstein, Margaret J. *Israel in Pictures, Revised and Expanded.*
Minneapolis, MN: Lerner. 2004.

This substantially revised overview of Israel is part of the Visual Geography Series. It covers the land, history and government, people, cultural life, and economy of the country. Informational sidebars, color photographs, and maps augment the text. A timeline, list of fast facts, a page on the Israeli flag and national anthem, short biographical sketches of some famous Israelis, a list of Web sites and books, a glossary, and an index will delight elementary and middle school report writers. So will the fact that the book is keyed to Lerner's Visual Geography Series Web site, which expands the print information.

Gormley, Beatrice. *Miriam.*
Grand Rapids, MI: Eerdmans. 1999.

This elaboration of the biblical story of Moses' birth and adoption by an Egyptian princess is told from the perspective of his older sister. The author paints a fascinating picture of ancient Egypt and the temptations of assimilation that Jews have encountered in every era, fleshing out characters known from the Bible and exploring their feelings and motivations. Another less traditional, more provocative fictional treatment of Moses and his family, written for slightly older children, is Julius Lester's *Pharaoh's Daughter*.

Greene, Jacqueline Dembar. *Out of Many Waters.*
New York: Walker. 1989.

Escaping the friars who kidnapped and enslaved them, two Portuguese Jewish sisters struggle to get to Amsterdam to find their parents. In the course of this exciting story, they are separated, and Isobel becomes part of the small group of refugees who were the first Jews to settle in North America. *One Foot Ashore* continues the sisters' story, as Maria stows away to Amsterdam and becomes part of Rembrandt's household.

Gresko, Marcia. *Israel.*
Minneapolis, MN: Carolrhoda/Lerner. 2000.

The same chapter headings, illustrations, and number of pages as the author's Ticket to Israel book are found in this book for children in grades 3–5. Much of the text is also the same but it is expanded to include more information. The treatment is balanced, the format is attractive and there are a few reference aids: A pronunciation guide, a short bibliography, a metric conversion chart, and an index. This useful introductory work for the elementary grades is part of the Globe Trotters Club Series.

Heller, David. *We Gave the World Moses and Bagels: Art and Wisdom of Jewish Children.*
Philadelphia: Jewish Publication Society. 2000.

Humor, sincerity, and innocence set the tone of these remarks by children in response to questions about what it means to be Jewish, what is the most extraordinary miracle in Jewish history, what is the hardest part of being a *Bar/Bat Mitzvah*, what does Israel represent to you, and numerous others. The book is nicely designed, as well, with glossy paper, color illustrations by children, and varied type sizes.

Hintz, Martin. *Israel, Revised Edition.*
New York: Children's Press. 2006.

An accurate and unbiased nonfiction introduction to Israel for elementary and middle school students, with the text enhanced by outstanding color photographs. Geography, history, natural resources, education, the economy, and political issues are some of the subjects included. The coverage and organization is excellent for report writing; there is also a "fast facts" section, plus a bibliography and an index.

Leder, Jane Mirsky. *A Russian Jewish Family.*
Minneapolis, MN: Lerner. 1996.

A photo essay describing a Russian-Jewish family's struggle first to get to America and then to succeed in America. The text is pedestrian. Readers will probably be most interested in Boris, the younger of the two boys in the family, because of his transition from a refugee to a regular American kid.

Leiman, Sondra. *The Atlas of Great Jewish Communities: A Voyage through History.*
New York: UAHC Press. 2002.

An informative book, similar to a textbook, that covers the Diaspora experience— from the fall of the Second Temple to modern day Israel. Entries are wide-ranging and clearly written. Lists of sources are valuable for further research. Students en-counter such important historical figures as King Herod, the Rambam (Maimonides), Dona Grazia Nasi, and Eliezer Ben Yehuda, as well as events that shaped Jewish communities throughout history. Both attractive and accessible.

Matas, Carol. *The War Within.*
New York: Simon and Schuster. 2001.

After General Ulysses Grant issues an order expelling all Jews from the territory under his control, teenaged Hannah Green, a southern belle in the making, begins to question many of the values she took for granted, including slavery. Set mainly in Mississippi, this is an authentic portrayal of Jewish life in the South during the period of the Civil War.

Morgan, Anna. *Daughters of the Ark.*
Toronto: Second Story Press. 2005.

Based on interviews with former Ethiopian refugees, this chronicles the history of the *Beta Israel*, Ethiopian Jews, in a story set in two different time periods. Through the experiences of two girls—one who lives in 939 BCE and the other who lives in the present—the historic connection of the *Beta Israel* to *Eretz Israel*, their travails in Ethiopia, and their journey to Israel are portrayed.

Olswanger, Anna. **Shlemiel Crooks.** Illus. by Paula Goodman Koz.
Montgomery, AL: Junebug/New South Books. 2005.

This offbeat and funny story, set in St. Louis in the early 1900s, is based on the life of the author's grandfather. It involves the attempted robbery of Reb Olschwanger's saloon by two *shlemiel* crooks who are instigated by the ghost of Pharaoh and foiled by a talking horse and a neighborhood *shtuss*. Flavored heavily with a Yiddish-inflected narration and illustrated with earthy, heavily outlined linocuts, the story requires considerable practice before reading aloud. It appeals to children with some knowledge of both Yiddish and Jewish history, as well as to adults.

Rivlin, Lilly. **Welcome to Israel.**
Springfield, NJ: Behrman House. 2000.

Similar to Burstein's *Our Land of Israel* in coverage but newer and superior graphically, this discusses the people of Israel, regions of the country, and political issues. It also includes some discussion questions and activities, but overall it looks less like a textbook than Burstein's book. Unfortunately, it has no index.

Roseman, Kenneth. **Jeremiah's Promise: An Adventure in Modern Israel.**
New York: UAHC Press. 2002.

In one of his Do-It-Yourself Jewish Adventure Series, Roseman again links history with imagination. Here a young survivor of the concentration camps confronts post-war anti-Semitism and comes to Palestine in 1945. He lives the prophet Jeremiah's promise that Jews "would always have a right of ownership to this sacred place." The author presents his protagonist with various choices and their consequences, connecting them to a broad sweep of Israeli experience in the pre-state and early statehood period.

Roseman, Kenneth. **Until the Messiah Comes.**
New York: UAHC Press. 1999.

The reader is asked to make choices similar to those confronting Jews living in Russia or neighboring areas in the years 1881–1918. An array of possibilities is presented by the author, who knows his Eastern European history well. Real people and fictional characters are intermingled.

Rosenberg, Pam. **Jewish Americans.**
Chanhassen, MN: Child's World. 2004.

An introductory work in the Our Cultural Heritage Series, this is simple but mostly accurate. There are four chapters: A Scattered People, Coming to America, Becoming American, and Famous Jewish Americans (with the actor Nathan Lane incorrectly identified as Jewish). The format and succinct style are inviting.

Roy, Jennifer Rozines. *Discovering Cultures: Israel.*
Tarrytown, NY: Marshall Cavendish. 2004.

Excellent photographs enhance a text that presents many aspects of Israeli life, including dress, food, school, and relations with Arabs. There are also a recipe for *felafel*, instructions for dancing the *hora*, and profiles of Golda Meir, Itzhak Perlman, and Colonel Elan Ramon.

Ruby, Lois. *Swindletop.*
Austin, TX: Eakin. 2001.

Texas history—specifically Jewish life in Galveston after the devastating hurricane of 1901—is presented through a plot that just doesn't stop! An immigrant family is the focal point, and through them Ruby develops themes of finding opportunities in a new land and of building a Jewish community. There are several subplots involving an oil boom, a clairvoyant African-American boy, a mystery and a false accusation, and the aspirations of an independent-minded girl. The real life characters of Rabbi Henry Cohen and his wife, Molly, make appearances. Authentic details add to the appeal.

Schrier, Jeffrey. *On the Wings of Eagles: An Ethiopian Boy's Story.*
Brookfield, CT: Millbrook Press. 1998.

Sophisticated mixed-media illustrations resonate with the culture of the *Beta Israel* and the emotions of an Ethiopian Jewish boy telling the story of his family's hazardous yet wondrous journey to Israel. The evocative writing is especially effective in showing the awe that Ethiopians Jews felt when the legends they had preserved for centuries came true.

Silverman, Maida. *Israel: The Founding of a Modern Nation.* Illus. by Susan Avishai.
New York: Dial. 1998.

A readable and lucid introduction to the history of the Jewish people leading up to the founding of the modern state. Beginning with God's promise to Abraham, each short chapter builds on the next to both document and justify the Zionist dream. Brief portraits of Zionists and proto-Zionists, including women, are one of the book's many strong points.

Sofer, Barbara. *Ilan Ramon: Israel's Space Hero.*
Minneapolis, MN: Kar-Ben/Lerner. 2004.

Organized chronologically in short chapters, Sofer's account paints a compelling picture of Ramon the boy and man, the pilot and military hero, the husband and father, and the astronaut. Reminiscences of his friends, family, and colleagues add immediacy, and his desire to represent the unity of the Jewish people aboard the space shuttle *Columbia* is poignantly described. A full picture of an Israeli hero emerges, augmented by black-and-white photographs.

Speregen, Devra Newberger. *Albert Einstein: The Jewish Man Behind the Theory.*
Philadelphia: Jewish Publication Society. 2006

Through this book, readers familiar with Einstein's scientific contributions will learn about his development as a Jew and a Zionist. It is written in clear and easy-to-understand language, tracing his life from childhood on and illuminating his commitment to the establishment of a Jewish state.

Speregen, Devra Newberger. *Yoni Netanyahu: Commando at Entebbe.*
Philadelphia: Jewish Publication Society. 1995.

Jonathan Netanyahu died young in the service of his country. Remembered as the hero of Entebbe—the daring Israeli military operation to rescue Jewish hostages being held in Uganda's Entebbe Airport (July 4, 1976)—Yoni's full, short life is chronicled here in one of the publisher's JPS Young Biography Series. The writing is enlivened by many quotes from people who knew and admired the young IDF soldier, as well as by his own writing. Israel has many heroes, and Yoni is a particularly poignant one to young people, as are the circumstances of his life and death.

Stoppleman, Monica. *Jewish.*
North Mankato, MN: Sea-to-Sea. 2005.

An illustrated introduction to Judaism, part of the Beliefs and Cultures Series. Coverage includes the origins of Judaism, the *Torah*, synagogues, holidays, rituals, and anti-Semitism. A few activities, such as making a Rosh Hashanah card, are also included. The color photographs and other illustrations are clear, and there is a short glossary and index. For anyone needing a basic overview of Judaism, this is acceptable.

Teece, Geoff. *Judaism.*
North Mankato, MN: Smart Apple Media. 2005.

Originally published in England in 2003, this is part of the Religions in Focus Series on world religions. It includes many aspects of Jewish history, culture, and religion, reviewing origins, beliefs, different Jewish affiliations, holidays, and family life. Although the treatment is positive, some of the illustrations are misleading. A Hebrew verse with God's name on it is printed on every page. A set of questions, a glossary, and an index are included.

Waldman, Neil. *Masada.*
New York: Morrow. 1998.

Waldman narrates the history of the fortress built by Herod that became the site of the Jewish rebels' last stand against Rome in 73 CE. His story concludes with the site's excavation under the sponsorship of the reborn Jewish state in the 1960s. Handsome illustrations by the author and a timeline are included.

Wallace, Holly. *This Is My Faith: Judaism.*
Hauppage, NY: Barron's. 2006

Eleven-year-old Yoni Marcus and his family are the focal point of this attractive photographic introduction to American Judaism. Yoni's succinct comments, plus brief explanatory captions of the numerous photographs, inform readers about some of the fundamental aspects of Judaism: Its symbols, practices, beliefs, holy days, and important rituals.

MIDDLE SCHOOL

Altman, Linda Jacobs. *The Creation of Israel.*
Farmington Hills, MI: Lucent. 1998.

Beginning in ancient times, this book chronicles the Jewish experience of exile and persecution in country after country for 2,000 years. In response to the terror inflicted upon them in the Diaspora, Jews turned to political Zionism as the solution. The majority of the book deals with the establishment of the modern Jewish state. Well-illustrated and suitable for student research.

Banks, Lynne Reid. *Moses in Egypt.*
London: Puffin. 1998.

Inspired primarily by the animated film, "The Prince of Egypt," and secondarily by the biblical book of Exodus, this reads like a fast-paced adventure story. Moses is a larger-than-life hero, and others characters are vividly portrayed. Heavily and colorfully illustrated, the format is especially appealing.

Claybourne, Anna. *Golda Meir.*
Portsmouth, NH: Heinemann Library. 2003.

Golda Meir is one of the fortunate few who lived to see her life's work realized. This readable biography, part of the Leading Lives Series, combines information about her life from birth to death with an account of the founding of modern Israel. The effects of her devotion to Zionism on her personal life are dealt with sympathetically. An attractive format adds to the book's value as an introduction to Mrs. Meir and modern Israeli history.

Corona, Laurel. *Israel.*
Farmington Hills, MI: Lucent. 2003.

Part of the Modern Nations of the World Series, this is a balanced overview of Israel—its history, daily life, political issues, arts and culture, etc. Reference aids are appended. The drab format is the main drawback.

Corona, Laurel. *The Jewish Americans.*
Farmington Hills, MI: Lucent. 2004.

Part of the Immigrants in America Series, this is a well-crafted and well-researched history of Jews in America. Both negative and positive issues that have shaped the Jewish community are covered, and respected scholars are cited. A discussion of contemporary divisions in American Judaism is especially well presented.

Du Bois, Jill, and Mair Rosh. *Israel, Second Edition.*
Tarrytown, NY: Benchmark. 2004.

An inviting format and upbeat text characterize this overview of the State of Israel. The tone is positive, avoiding discussion of the Israeli-Palestinian conflict and concentrating on descriptive information about many aspects of the country, including its religious and cultural diversity. Thirteen chapters are well illustrated with color photographs and informational sidebars, covering subjects such as history, geography, environment, lifestyle, religion, language, arts, and food. Maps, a timeline, a glossary, a list of books, videos, and Web sites, and an index are included.

Finkelstein, Norman H. *Forged in Freedom: Shaping the Jewish-American Experience.*
Philadelphia: Jewish Publication Society. 2002.

From adaptation to integration, this is a history of American Jews in the twentieth century. The organization is topical, and each major topic is treated chronologically. Many photographs, succinct and thorough in coverage, well researched and carefully documented. Exemplary nonfiction writing!

Finkelstein, Norman H. *Friends Indeed: The Special Relationship of Israel and the United States.*
Brookfield, CT: Milbrook Press. 1998.

An exploration of United States–Israel relations since the founding of Israel in 1948, highlighting particular events that helped shape it. Organized chronologically, Finkelstein's lucidly written book shows how the Arab-Israeli conflict, strategic interests, and shared democratic values all affected the relationship.

Fisher, Leonard Everett. *To Bigotry No Sanction: The Story of the Oldest Synagogue in America.*
New York: Holiday House. 1998.

Handsome black-and-white photographs of Rhode Island's Touro Synagogue and reproductions of historic portraits and documents accompany Fisher's text. He has written several capsule histories into this volume: The history of the first Jewish settlers—*Sephardim* who were heirs to the rich Iberian culture destroyed by the Inquisition; the history of Roger William's Rhode Island Colony that welcomed diverse religious groups; and the history of the development of religious freedom in North America, exemplified by George Washington's assurance to Touro congregants that the new society would give "to bigotry no sanction."

Greenfeld, Howard. *A Promise Fulfilled: Theodor Herzl, Chaim Weizmann, David Ben Gurion, and the Creation of the State of Israel.*
New York: HarperCollins/Greenwillow. 2005.

A concise history of modern Zionism is delivered through the biographies of three men who shared what seemed like an impossible dream. Spanning 90 years, it chronicles events, achievements, and setbacks that led to the founding of the State of Israel. The personality of each man is revealed, showing how their backgrounds, experiences, and personal traits influenced history.

Lester, Julius. *Pharaoh's Daughter.*
San Diego: Harcourt/Silver Whistle. 2000.

A dazzling portrait of ancient Egypt and a provocative story of religious and cultural identity are created in this free interpretation of the youth of Moses and his older sister. The latter character, named Almah, not Miriam, becomes a priestess of the Egyptian gods—a plot strand that deviates so markedly from the biblical account that not all readers will be satisfied with it. A more traditional novel on the same subject is Bernice Gormley's *Miriam.*

Levitin, Sonia. *The Return.*
New York: Fawcett Books. 1988.

When twelve-year-old Desta, an Ethiopian Jew, learns there are camps in the Sudan where transport to Israel is waiting, she sets out with her brother and younger sister on a journey to freedom. After her brother is killed, Desta must take the lead as they struggle to reach their destination. This dangerous exodus was made by thousands of Ethiopian Jews in 1984–1985 during the Israeli airlift called "Operation Moses."

Matas, Carol. *After the War.*
New York: Simon Pulse. 1997.

This story of a Holocaust survivor who makes her way to Palestine is told in a choppy first-person narrative. The plot is eventful and exciting: Ruth, the protagonist, guides readers through the pain of surviving, the danger of continuing anti-Semitism, the barriers to entering Israel and the joy of success—a dream come true. Sadness floods each new problem but hope follows despair and love follows hope, all vital ingredients in fiction for teens.

Matas, Carol. *The Garden.*
New York: Simon and Schuster. 1997.

Amidst an action-filled plot set in Israel on the eve of independence, this sequel to *After the War* deals with some of the themes implicit in the founding of the Jewish state, such as the aspirations of refugees to create a haven and the necessity to defend the country against Arab attacks. Peace and conflict, hope and fear are thrown into sharp relief.

Miklowitz, Gloria. *Masada.*
Grand Rapids, MI: Eerdmans. 1998.

Antagonists in the Roman siege of Masada—one a teenage zealot boy and the other the Roman general leading the attack—tell their stories as the conflict moves to its tragic conclusion. Through the eyes on the teenage son of Masada's leader, the human side of the siege is revealed, culminating with the decision of the Jewish zealots to commit suicide rather than surrender.

Oswald, Nancy. *Nothing Here But Stones.*
New York: Henry Holt. 2004.

Historical fiction about an agricultural colony of Jewish immigrants, struggling to eke out a living in Colorado in the late 1800s. Based on the Cotopaxi Jewish Colony that lasted only a few years, this portrays the hardships that the colonists faced while trying to maintain a Jewish way of life. It is narrated by a girl named Emma, whose love for a horse named Mazel gives her something to cherish when everything seems to go wrong. Not a cheerful story but it has the ring of authenticity, and readers will empathize with the characters.

Rubin, Susan Goldman. *L'Chaim! To Jewish Life in America.*
New York: Harry Abrams. 2004.

This chronicle of Jewish life from 1654 to the present is graced with lively writing and splendid illustrations. It provides for the lay reader—adults as well as children—an account of a rich and varied history, with each chapter dealing with a different topic: Jews in the American Revolution, the labor movement, Jewish cowboys, and Jewish contributions to American society, to name a few. The many illustrations are superbly reproduced; a glossary, endnotes, references, illustration credits, and an index are included. Published in association with the Jewish Museum.

Sandell, Lisa. *The Weight of the Sky.*
New York: Viking. 2006.

Narrating this novel in a free-verse form that reads like prose, 16-year-old Sarah tells the story of the summer she spends on an Israeli *kibbutz.* For an American girl from a small, mostly Christian town, it is a transformative experience. Along with the thrill of belonging as a Jew in a Jewish country, Sarah experiences her first taste of independence and her first romantic encounters with boys. Her experiences and feelings are conveyed realistically, including her shock when a friend is killed. Political issues take a back seat here to personal experience but that does not detract from the story's emotional authenticity.

Sherman, Josepha. *Your Travel Guide to Ancient Israel.*
Minneapolis, MN: Lerner. 2004.

Readers are taken on a trip back in time to experience life in ancient Israel at the time of King Solomon. Clothing, housing, food, local customs, transportation, a few notable personalities, and more are described. The differences between now and then are highlighted when readers are alerted to the fact that there are no video games, hair dryers, sunscreen, cell phones, or watches. Acceptable as an introduction to the era.

Slavicek, Louise Shipley. *Israel.*
New York: Chelsea House. 2003.

This is a welcome exception to the anti-Israel books usually published by Chelsea House. It gives an objective account of the birth and growth of modern Israel, from the Jewish people's bond with the land since biblical times up until the present. Important issues are discussed and analyzed, and the book is illustrated with documentary photographs. It includes a chronology, bibliography, Internet sources, and an index.

Talbert, Marc. *Star of Luis.*
New York: Clarion. 1999.

After his father goes off to fight in World War II, Luis's mother takes him from their home in Los Angeles to New Mexico, where her parents and other family members live. There, the teenager discovers that his maternal relatives are descended from Jewish victims of the Inquisition and that many of them still practice selected Jewish rites. Upon returned to Los Angeles, Luis tries to reconcile and understand both dimensions of his identity.

Webster, Matt. *Inside Israel's Mossad: The Institute for Intelligence and Special Tasks.*
New York: Rosen. 2003.

A brief but informative account of the *Mossad*, Israel's formidable foreign intelligence agency initiated by David Ben Gurion in 1951. The organization's structure and goals are described along with some of its successes and failures. Photographs, an index, bibliography, and glossary are included.

Zakon, Nachman. *The Jewish Experience: 2,000 Years: A Collection of Significant Events.*
New York: Shaar Press/Mesorah. 2002.

Written from an Orthodox point of view, this volume contains selectively chosen events from *Maccabean* times (165 BCE) to 1999 when Ehud Barak was elected Prime Minister of Israel. Each event is portrayed as a "time capsule," which consists of a brief summary and a discussion of the Jewish historical significance of the event. Information sidebars, illustrations, and graphics are used throughout the book and for each event; both its date on the Jewish calendar and the corresponding Common Era date are given. Includes a bibliography and index.

HIGH SCHOOL

Alex: Building a Life.
Jerusalem: Gefen. 1996.

Alex Singer was a young American who made *aliyah* to Israel and was killed in battle on his 25th birthday. His parents, through the Alex Singer Project, collected his letters, journal entries, and drawings to create this book as a tribute to a life well lived. It is a moving and evocative experience for American teenagers to read, a reminder of the truth of the words of Rabbi Abraham Joshua Heschel (quoted in the book): "Let [young people] remember that there is meaning beyond absurdity. Let them be sure that every deed counts, that every word has power... And, above all, let them remember to build a life as if it were a work of art."

Bard, Mitchell (Editor). *At Issue in History: The Founding of the State of Israel.*
Farmington Hills, MI: Greenhaven. 2003.

The publisher's Opposing Viewpoints Series attempts to provide balanced collections of pro and con viewpoints on many of the world's thorniest political issues. Of the 14 essays selected for inclusion, half support the Jewish position and half the Arab. Included are important documents pertaining to the founding of Israel. The editor is executive director of the American-Israeli Cooperative Enterprise and editor of the Jewish Virtual Library (www.jewishvirtuallibrary.org). Useful for debates with a good bibliography and index.

Elkeles, Simone. *How to Ruin a Summer Vacation.*
Woodbury, MN: Flux. 2006.

A teenager is dragged to Israel by a father from whom she is estranged to meet a family she didn't know existed and who didn't know she existed, either. Learning first that "*moshav*" doesn't mean " shopping mall," Amy is reluctantly drawn into a circle of teenagers that include a cousin whom she doesn't like. In fact, Amy doesn't like anything or anyone, except her new found grandmother. Over the course of the summer, all of that changes, and a teenage *kvetch* eventually becomes a *mensch*. The changes happen too quickly to be completely believable, but Amy's transformation from a self-centered and truculent girl into a loving and caring young woman are heartening. Life in modern Israel is presented positively, with the emphasis on love of country, responsibility, and Israeli determination.

Garfinkle, Adam. *Israel.*
Broomall, PA: Mason Crest. 2004.

Part of the Modern Middle East Nations and Their Strategic Place in the World Series, sponsored by the Foreign Policy Research Institute. It gives students an introduction to the land, people, and history of Israel. The writing is clear, succinct, and incisive in its analysis of Israel's politics and relations with its neighbors. The point of view is positive toward Israel, debunking some Arab propaganda while acknowledging legitimate Arab grievances. Includes maps, photographs, a bibliography, and an index. One of the best recent nonfiction books about Israel for teenagers.

Hitzeroth, Deborah. *The Importance of Golda Meir.*
Farmington Hills, MI: Lucent. 1998.

This detailed account of Golda Meir's life presents her as a human being instead of a legend. Fully half of the biography is about her formative years in Russia and the United States. Paralleling the narrative of political struggle is one of the personal toll that her activism had on Meir's life. Well illustrated and useful for reports.

CHAPTER 12

Perseverance

"Perseverance prevails even against Heaven."

Talmud

PRESCHOOL

Figley, Marty Rhodes. *Noah's Wife.* Illus. by Anita Riggio.
Grand Rapids, MI: Eerdmans. 1998.

The exasperated but devoted wife of Noah endures the jibes of her neighbors, the irritations of Noah's work, and the excessive demands of keeping the ark in order. The story emphasizes the practical aspects of preparing to ride out the Flood, and the illustrations show the humorous side of that grand endeavor.

Gilman, Phoebe. *Something from Nothing.*
New York, Scholastic. 1992.

A lovable story based on a Yiddish song, this book shows a little boy named Joseph growing older and his beloved blanket diminishing into successively smaller articles made by Grandpa as the fabric wears out. The remarkable illustrations tell several stories at once and show a mouse family living underneath the floor of Joseph's house recycling all the discarded fabric. One of several appealing versions of the story, this was the winner of a Sydney Taylor Book Award.

Howland, Naomi. *Matzah Man.*
New York: Clarion. 2002.

A Jewish version of the nursery tale, "The Gingerbread Man," that is set during Passover and involves a chase after a runaway *matzah* man who eludes a *bubbe*, a *yenta*, and a fox but still winds up in the soup. The lilting rhyme, repetitive refrains, superb illustrations, and fine book design combine to create an outstanding story.

Newman, Leslea. *Runaway Dreidel.* Illus. by Kyrsten Brooker.
New York: Henry Holt. 2002.

"Twas the first night of Chanukah and on the fifth floor, There was holiday hustling and bustling galore." If these opening lines have a familiar ring, Newman's clever story and Brooker's engaging illustrations are totally fresh. While everyone is busy with Hanukkah preparations, a little boy's shiny new *dreidel* runs away, leading the boy, his family, and neighbors on a chase through the city neighborhood where they live, through a forest, to the shores of an ocean, and up into the sky where the dreidel becomes a star. Written in rhyming couplets that sparkle with vivid images, the story is enhanced by outstanding illustrations.

Simpson, Lesley. *The Shabbat Box.* Illus. by Nicole in den Bosch.
Rockville, MD: Kar-Ben Copies. 2001.

When Ira loses his class's treasured *Shabbat* box, he solves the problem by making a new one, all by himself. This empowering story portrays a loving family, a multi-cultural preschool class, and a child with imagination and perseverance. Instructions for making a *Shabbat* box, containing candles, a *challah* cover, and a *kiddush* cup, are included.

Taback, Simms. *Joseph Had a Little Overcoat.*
New York: Viking. 1999.

This illustrated version of a Yiddish song won the Caldecott Award. It is a version of the Sydney Taylor Book Award winner entitled *Something from Nothing* by Phoebe Gilman. The clever artwork includes die-cut shapes and the theme suggests that an imaginative creation—a story—is more lasting, useful, and nourishing than something material.

Topek, Susan Remick. *A Costume for Noah.* Illus. by Sally Springer.
Rockville, MD: Kar-Ben Copies. 1995.

As the kids in his Jewish preschool class plan their costumes for the holiday of Purim, Noah is worried. He'd like to be someone different this year. The family's new baby arrives at just the right time and decides Noah's costume: He is a big brother for Purim. Preschoolers see themselves in Noah and his friends, with the illustrations adding to the appeal. Other books about Noah are *A Turn for Noah* and *A Taste for Noah*.

PRIMARY

Bierman, Carol, and Barbara Hehner. *Journey to Ellis Island: How My Father Came to America.* Illus. by Laurie McGaw.
New York: Hyperion. 1998

An effective combination of documentary photographs, postcards, and realistic sepia-tone illustrations highlight this engrossing true story, based on the experiences of the author's father, who had to prove he was healthy enough to enter the United

States at Ellis Island. The lively story presents a stirring look at the immigrant experience as lived by courageous, believable characters.

Glaser, Linda. *The Borrowed Hanukkah Latkes.* Illus. by Nancy Cote.
Morton Grove, IL: Albert Whitman. 1997.

When Rachel's Mama runs out of potatoes to make *latkes* for all the family's expected guests, Rachel borrows some from Mrs. Greenberg. As more ingredients run short, Rachel keeps borrowing from Mrs. Greenberg, eventually persuading the elderly widow to join the Hanukkah celebration. Nicely told and illustrated.

Hest, Amy. *When Jesse Came across the Sea.* Illus. by P. J. Lynch.
Cambridge, MA: Candlewick. 1997.

Richly colored illustrations enhance this story of a young girl who travels alone to New York at the turn of the twentieth century to build a new life. Jessie earns a living as a lacemaker—a skill learned from her grandmother—and after several years, she is able to pay her grandmother's passage to America. The panoramic pictures and heartfelt text combine to present a memorable look at the immigrant experience.

Icenoggle, Jodi. *'Til the Cows Come Home.* Illus. by Normand Chartier.
Honesdale, PA: Boyds Mills Press. 2004.

A version of the folktale about making something from nothing, this has no Jewish content but retains the story's theme. The setting is the American West, the main character who excels at "making something from nothing" is a cowboy, and the style is rich with Western colloquialisms. Chartier's large, vivid illustrations capture the movement and vigor of the story.

Kimmel, Eric A. *A Cloak for the Moon.* Illus. by Katya Krenina.
New York: Holiday House. 2001.

In this elaboration of a tale by the *Hasidic* storyteller, Rabbi Nachman of Bratslav, Haskel, a tailor with mystical leanings, travels to exotic places in search of the secret of weaving the moon a garment for all seasons. The elegant illustrations in jewel-like tones reflect the lucidity and polish of the narrative.

Lasky, Kathryn. *Marven of the Great North Woods.* Illus. by Kevin Hawkes.
San Diego: Harcourt Brace. 1997.

Large color illustrations are a stunning backdrop to this appealing story of a small Jewish boy and a huge French-Canadian lumberjack who become friends in a logging camp in the great North Woods. Little Marven—a character based on the author's father—is sent to the camp to avoid the influenza epidemic raging in the city. His intrepid trip to the camp—alone on a train and then on skis across a snow covered wilderness—will amaze today's children.

Levine, Arthur. *All the Lights in the Night.* Illus. by James Ransome.
New York: Tambourine Books. 1991.

To escape persecution by soldiers of the Czar, two young brothers are sent away by their family. Traveling on their own, they make their way to Palestine. During the hazardous journey, a small, dented brass lamp that their mother has given them upholds their courage and their spirits. Dark, dramatic illustrations add to a moving story.

Prose, Francine. *The Demon's Mistake: A Story from Chelm.* Illus. by Mark Podwal.
New York: HarperCollins/Greenwillow. 2000.

Informed by a tongue-in-cheek urban sensibility, this story begins in *Chelm*, where demons delight in ruining the plans and parties of those easy marks, the *Chelmniks*. When the demons emigrate to the New World and finally descend upon the Big Apple, they discover to their chagrin that blasé New Yorkers aren't fazed by their mischief. That is, until a street smart demon tells them about traffic signals and computers. . . . Throughout this witty story, told in a folkloric style, Podwal's smudgy pictures charm and entertain. The demons are funny-scary, and the city scenes are a delight.

Rael, Elsa Okon. *Rivka's First Thanksgiving.* Illus. by Marryann Kovalski.
New York: Simon and Schuster. 2001.

The author of *What Zeesie Saw on Delancey Street* and *When Zayde Danced on Eldridge Street* again draws on childhood memories to create a story about Jewish immigrants living on New York's Lower East Side. Rivka's efforts to convince her family and their rabbi that Thanksgiving is indeed a holiday that Jews should celebrate are related with warmth, respect, and an understanding of the relevance of this American holiday to Jewish tradition and history. The softly colored illustrations reflect the ambience of the story, imbuing it with atmosphere and portraying its characters with affection and humor. Winner of a Sydney Taylor Book Award.

Sanfield, Steve. *Bit by Bit.* Illus. by Susan Gaber.
New York: Penguin Putnam. 1995.

In this version of a well-known Jewish tale, Zundel the tailor's coat gets smaller as his family gets bigger. The illustrations are delightful, and the theme of making the most of what you have is conveyed with conviction. Other versions of this beloved story are *Joseph Had a Little Overcoat* by Taback, *Something from Nothing* by Gilman, and *'Til the Cows Come Home* by Icenoggle. Because each one treats the essential story in a slightly different way, and with excellent illustrations, they will all be enjoyed by young children.

Schanzer, Rosalind. *Escaping to America: A True Story.*
New York: HarperCollins. 2000.

In the early twentieth century, a family of Polish Jews, headed by a determined father, risk their lives to escape the Old Country, surviving *pogroms*, Cossacks, and war before joyfully settling in to their new life. This boldly illustrated story, with a dynamic and generous layout, expresses their courage and their pride in becoming Americans.

Stuchner, Joan Betty. *The Kugel Valley Klezmer Band.* Illus. by Richard Row.
New York: Crocodile. 2001.

"Practise, practise, practise" is the advice given to young Shira, when she reveals her dream of someday playing fiddle in the Canadian village's *klezmer* band. Set around the turn of the twentieth century and illustrated with robust, richly colored realistic pictures, this book shows a girl persevering to realize her dreams.

Ungar, Richard. *Rachel Captures the Moon.*
Toronto: Tundra. 2001.

The foolish folk of *Chelm*, not content to wait for the moon to rise each evening, try to capture its luminescence permanently. When neither a ladder, a net, nor fragrant soup can lure the moon down to earth, a little girl captures its reflection in a barrel of water. A vividly illustrated version of a well-known Chelm tale.

Waxman, Sydell. *My Mannequins.* Illus. by Patty Gallinger.
Toronto: Napoleon Publishing. 2000.

A little girl named Dora helps out at her father's tailor shop after school. Frustrated by its rigid rules, Dora imagines designing flamboyant clothes for the mannequins. When some of her mannequins appear in the store windows wearing Dora's designs and customers are impressed, her aspirations to be a designer are affirmed. Set in the early 1900s in a Canadian garment district populated mainly by Jewish immigrants, the story has no overt Jewish content and no real climax.

Wieder, Joy Nelkin. *The Secret Tunnel.*
New York: Hachai. 2004.

This easy-to-read chapter book is part of Hachai's Fun-to-Read Series, which features brave children acting courageously to exemplify fundamental Jewish values. It is set in Jerusalem in the time of King Hezekiah, at a time when the Assyrian army, having already conquered Israel, was marching on Judea and preparing to lay siege to Jerusalem. The main character is an eleven-year-old boy who labors to save the city by helping dig the tunnel that will keep it supplied with fresh water. The historical setting, mildly exciting plot, and characterization are woven into a readable story that will interest newly independent readers.

Winter, Jonah. *Once Upon a Time in Chicago: The Story of Benny Goodman.*
Illus. by Jeanette Winter.
New York: Hyperion. 2000.

A short, easy-to-read, and vividly illustrated biography of Benny Goodman. It tells of his childhood, his large, poor family, his shyness, his discovery of the clarinet, and of his rise to fame as the "King of Swing." The illustrations have a jazzy look, and the book design is attractive. Jewish content is secondary to music, but this is still a charming introduction to a great Jewish American musician.

ELEMENTARY

Bial, Raymond. *Tenement: Immigrant Life on the Lower East Side.*
Boston: Houghton Mifflin. 2002.

Through striking photographs and clear writing, readers gain an understanding of how people lived and worked in tenements and how these dwellings helped shape the acculturation process. Although Bial is positive about the courage and perseverance of immigrants, his book makes the hardships they endured in tenements very clear.

Bunin, Sherry. *Dear Great American Writers School.*
Boston: Houghton Mifflin. 1995.

A wry look at life in a small southern town during World War II is conveyed through the letters of a girl who aspires to be a writer. Lured by the come-on tactics of a shady correspondence school, Bobby Lee Pomeroy records her impressions of several of the town's characters, including a quiet Jewish girl whose father is a storekeeper. Although the Jewish content is minimal, Bobby Lee's sincerity, juxtaposed with the Great American Writers School's demands for payment, make for a humorous story.

Celenza, Anna Harwell. *Gershwin's "Rhapsody in Blue."* Illus. by JoAnn Kitchel.
Watertown, MA: Charlesbridge. 2006.

The origins of an American musical masterpiece are explored in this delightfully written and illustrated book about the challenge that faced George Gershwin when he discovered that a jazz concert work he had promised to conductor Paul Whiteman was due in five weeks. An audio CD of "Rhapsody in Blue" is included and it is invaluable in helping children experience the New York sounds that inspired Gershwin and which he incorporated into the music.

Cooper, Ilene. *The Dead Sea Scrolls.* Illus. by John Thompson.
New York: Morrow. 1997.

Written with as much suspense as a mystery, this is a true account of the discovery of the Dead Sea Scrolls, the efforts to translate them, the battle over their possession, and their meaning to Jews and Christians. It is an intriguing accompaniment to the more fictionalized *Mystery of the Dead Sea Scrolls* by Hagit Allon and Lena Zehavi.

Dublin, Anne. *Bobbie Rosenfeld: The Olympian Who Could Do Everything.*
Toronto: Second Story Press. 2004.

An outstanding biography of the Canadian athlete, Fanny "Bobbie" Rosenfeld, who starred in the 1928 Olympics in Amsterdam, Holland. Besides being an engrossing account of this remarkable woman's life, the writing places Rosenfeld's achievements in the context of both social history and the politics of being a woman athlete at a time when resistance to women in sports was strong. The clarity of the writing is matched by an excellent format, with photographs, text boxes that add information and context to the main text, and helpful appended material. Without fictionalizing, Anne Dublin tells an engaging and exciting real-life story.

Fleischman, Sid. *Escape! The Story of the Great Houdini.*
New York: HarperCollins. 2006.

The author, a former magician, brings an admirable combination of skills and life experience to the writing of this biography about Harry Houdini, born Ehrich Weiss, the poor rabbi's son who grew up to become a world-famous magician and escape artist. A lively style and numerous photographs make the book appealing.

Freedman, Zelda. *Rosie's Dream Cape.* Illus. by Silvana Bevilacqua.
Vancouver: Ronsdale Press. 2005

Based on the experiences of the author's mother, this is set in Toronto in 1921. Rosie is an eleven-year-old immigrant child who works in a sweatshop. Her attempts to make herself a cloak from discarded fabric scraps reveal the hardships of such a life, as well as some of the rewards of perseverance.

Goldman, David J. *Jewish Sports Stars: Athletic Heroes Past and Present.*
Minneapolis, MN: Kar-Ben/Lerner. 2004.

Short biographies of Jewish athletes and sports figures, past and present. The writing is brisk, with facts and gossip interspersed. Sports enthusiasts who love statistics will find them here, along with a chronology of important medals, records and career highlights, a short bibliography, and an index. A revised edition was published in 2006.

Granfield, Linda. *97 Orchard Street, New York: Stories of Immigrant Life.*
  Photographs by Arlene Alda.
Toronto: Tundra Books. 2001.

This photo essay highlights several immigrant families of different ethnic backgrouds who lived at 97 Orchard Street, now the home of New York's Lower East Side Tenement Museum. Excellent photographs and a clear text illuminate the way tenement dwellers lived, worked, socialized, and acculturated. Because there is no table of contents or index, and the organization of the material is not strictly chronological, this is a supplementary work.

Hesse, Karen. *Letters from Rivka.*
New York: Puffin Books. 1993.

A perennially popular novel written in the form of letters from a 12-year-old girl who flees with her family from Russia and finds the path to freedom filled with obstacles. Prevented from boarding the ship to America with the rest of her family because of a disease, Rivka manages on her own with the help of Jewish aid societies, spends some tense days at Ellis Island, and is finally reunited with her family.

Hopkinson, Deborah. *Shutting Out the Sky: Life in the Tenements of New York, 1880–1924.*
New York: Orchard/Scholastic. 2003.

A well-written account of tenement life on New York's Lower East Side. Primarily told in the voices of five young immigrants, this chronicles the hardships they faced and the dreams they strived to fulfill. Documentary photographs add to an attractive and readable format, with useful appendices and impeccable documentation.

Kale, Shelly. *A Suitcase of Dreams: Immigration Stories from the Skirball Cultural Center.*
Los Angeles: Skirball Cultural Center. 2001.

Paintings, family photographs, and objects found in the collection of the Skirball Cultural Center are used to tell the story of Jewish immigration from Eastern Europe. Sharp reproductions of each item—painting or photo—and a wide, paperback format both suggest and show the reasons for leaving one's homeland, what was taken and what was left behind, and what the journeys were like. The succinct text asks readers questions that involve them in the immigration process and help create meaning.

Matas, Carol. *Rosie in Chicago—Play Ball!*
New York: Aladdin Paperbacks. 2003.

Rosie's family has moved to Chicago and she has problems making friends. Everything changes when she disguises herself as a boy and fills in for an injured player on her brother's baseball team. She becomes a star in disguise because girls aren't allowed to play baseball. The stricture against Jewish girls who desire a life outside the home and an education is a major theme of this book, a slower-moving sequel to *Rosie in New York—Gotcha!*

O'Connell, Rebecca. *Penina Levine Is a Hard-boiled Egg.* Illus. by Majella Lue Sue.
New Milford, CT: Roaring Brook Press. 2007

Eleven-year-old Penina sticks to her guns, refusing to complete a school assignment because she feels that it violates her Jewish faith. Parents, an annoying little sister, a bossy best friend, a supportive grandmother, and a religiously clueless teacher are all part of the mix in this funny story.

Shulevitz, Uri. *The Travels of Benjamin of Tudela through Three Continents in the Twelfth Century.*
New York: Farrar, Straus and Giroux. 2005.

Benjamin of Tudela, known only from the book he wrote about his travels, left his home in Spain in 1159 and spent 14 years traveling dangerous roads, seas, and deserts to reach

(Cont'd.)

> **The Travels of Benjamin of Tudela through Three Continents in the Twelfth Century.**
> *(Continued)*
>
> Genoa, Rome, Constantinople, Cairo, Baghdad, Jerusalem, and China. In this slightly fictionalized account, Benjamin relates what he saw and learned, telling stories of the Arch of Titus, the Assassins, the Crusaders, a false messiah, Jerusalem, and more. Each episode occupies a large, double-page spread, with stunning illustrations predominating.

Tal, Eve. *Double Crossing.*
El Paso, TX: Cinco Puntos Press. 2005.

Themes of hardship, adaptation, and courage are common to immigration stories, but this one has the added feature of a plot that involves being rejected at Ellis Island, being sent back to Europe, and having to make the second attempt at entry more successful. Smoothly written with an appealing, almost-12-year-old protagonist, it is by turns thoughtful and adventurous.

Watts, Irene. *Remember Me: A Search for Refuge in Wartime Britain.*
Toronto: Tundra Books. 2000.

Twelve-year-old Marianne, who was introduced in *Goodbye, Marianne*, is sent on the *Kindertransport* to England. Missing her parents and yearning for the familiarity of Jewish family life, she struggles in a series of foster homes. A fascinating picture of wartime England—of courage and narrow social attitudes—is painted. The sequel—and final book in the trilogy—is *Finding Sophie*.

MIDDLE SCHOOL

Greenfeld, Howard. *After the Holocaust.*
New York: HarperCollins/Greenwillow. 2001.

Focusing on eight Holocaust survivors now living in the United States, this powerful work of non-fiction shows the hardships faced by young survivors, many of whom were without homes, families, identities, or hope. It is organized into sections called "Liberation," "After the Liberation," and "The DP Camps," and includes first-person testimonies and many excellent photographs.

Hirschfelder, Arlene B. *Photo Odyssey: Solomon Carvalho's Remarkable Western Adventure, 1853–54.*
New York: Clarion. 2000.

Carvalho, a Baltimore Jew of *Sephardic* ancestry, was a tenderfoot when he joined an expedition led by the explorer, John Charles Fremont, in 1853–1854 as its painter/photographer. An account of the hazardous journey is accompanied with documentary photographs from the period, although none that Carvalho himself took. Well researched and documented, this biography recounts a stirring adventure.

Hotchkiss, Ron. *The Matchless Six: The Story of Canada's First Women's Olympic Team.*
Toronto: Tundra Books. 2006.

A dry, highly detailed account of the Canadian women's track-and-field team that starred in the 1928 Olympics. Readers have been introduced to their exploits in Anne Dublin's *Bobbie Rosenfeld: The Olympian Who Could Do Everything*. Here, Bobbie gets equal billing with Jane Bell, Myrtle Cook, Ethel Smith, Ethel Catherwood, and Jean Thompson. Each of these women was a star in one or more track-and-field events, setting records and winning medals. Their individual stories of motivation, training, determination, disappointment, and success are set within the larger struggle of women to be accepted in sports.

Johnson, Sheila Golburgh. *After I Said No.*
Santa Barbara, CA: Fithian Press. 2000.

A strong teenage character is at the center of this historical novel. After Pearl is sent to America by her family, she refuses the man chosen for her to marry and must support herself by working in the garment industry. The story portrays Pearl's struggle for independence, set against a background of sweatshop labor and union organizing among immigrant women.

Levine, Anna. *Running on Eggs.*
Chicago: Front Street/Cricket Books. 1999.

There are no villains, only misunderstandings, in this story of a tentative friendship between an Israeli girl and an Arab girl who are teammates on their school track team. Although the Arab-Israeli conflict is the central issue, it is viewed through a personal, rather than political, lens and integrated into many other aspects of contemporary Israeli life.

Levitin, Sonia. *Journey to America.* Illus. by Charles Robinson.
New York: Atheneum. 1993.

The first in a historical fiction trilogy about the Platt family who flee Germany to make a new life in America. In 1938, with conditions for German Jews worsening, Mr. Platt leaves for America in the middle of the night. The plan is for Mrs. Platt and the three girls to move to Switzerland, under the pretext of going on a vacation, where they will live until Mr. Platt has amassed enough money to send for them. Their train travel to Switzerland is harrowing enough, but once there, their money all but runs out, and they have to endure living conditions that none of them ever imagined before being able to endure, before they can join Mr. Platt in New York. Told by Lisa, the middle Platt sister, the story is suspenseful and believable. Family relationships are well portrayed, and each of the characters is a distinct individual. Today's readers will empathize with the family's plight and develop respect for the courage required of Jews uprooted by World War II. The other books in the trilogy are *Silver Days* and *Annie's Promise*.

Levitin, Sonia. *Silver Days.*
New York: Atheneum. 1989.

Adjustment to America for the middle-class Platt family is not easy. As refugees, the three sisters' parents have an especially difficult time earning a living. Mrs. Platt, who had a maid in Germany, becomes one in the U. S. in order to make ends meet. The three girls adjust better than their parents, doing well in school, working to help out, and making new friends. When Mr. Platt—an optimistic, ebullient character—decides he can do better in California, the Platts move to Los Angeles, where life does improve somewhat. Although word of her mother's death at Auschwitz causes Mrs. Platt to have a breakdown, the family supports one another and eventually has some reason to be optimistic about the future. Told by Lisa, the middle sister, the story reveals some of the adjustments to America that non-English speaking immigrants must make.

Orlev, Uri. *Run, Boy, Run.*
Boston: Houghton Mifflin. 2003.

Separated from his mother in the Warsaw Ghetto when he is only eight, a boy endures the Holocaust through a combination of luck, courage, the kindness of strangers, and a fierce instinct for survival that enables him to overcome even the loss of an arm in a farming accident. Assuming the identity of a Polish Catholic, Srulik/Jurek is known as "the blond, one-armed Jewish boy" among the villages and woods where he lurks. Self-protection has caused him to forget his past and his Jewish identity, and for a while after the war he resists the efforts of Jewish refugee groups to help him. An understated, almost reportorial style, keeps the story—based on a real person—from being unbearably painful.

Ruby, Lois. *Shanghai Shadows.*
New York: Holiday House. 2006.

A fast-paced and suspenseful piece of historical fiction, this is set in Shanghai during World War II. Its main characters are an Austrian-Jewish family who have fled the Nazis and become "stateless refuges" in a city occupied by Japan. Besides a stirring plot, this has fully developed characters—both major and minor—and a well-established sense of place. The protagonist, Ilse Shpann, grows in maturity throughout her family's increasingly difficult sojourn; she and her older brother work for a resistance group and even manage to have some fun during a very harrowing time. Written with a sure grasp of a complex plot and with a sure sense of teenage emotions.

Sandler, Martin W. *Island of Hope: The Story of Ellis Island and the Journey to America.*
New York: Scholastic. 2004.

Instead of focusing on the difficulty of leaving Europe and the tribulations encountered on the ocean voyage to America, this book examines the legal, physical, medical, and emotional experiences of immigrants once they arrived on Ellis Island. Well documented, with archival photos, excerpts from diaries and journals, and comments from Ellis Island employees, inspectors, and medical staff. Brief stories of well-known immigrants are included but there is no special emphasis on Jewish immigrants, some of whom are identified as Polish or Russian rather than Jewish. The illustrations and design of the book augment an engrossing narrative, providing both intimacy and immediacy.

Saturen, Myra. *Julietta.*
Unionville, NY: Royal Fireworks Press. 2003.

A historical novel set in Troyes, France in 1283. Julietta wants to be a doctor, but the eminent doctor she lives with doesn't want girls in his laboratory. Through perseverance and her own talents in healing people, she overcomes his opposition. Lore about medical practice of the period and herbal remedies is combined with a portrayal of aspects of medieval anti-Semitism and, in particular, how it affected Jewish doctors.

Stanley, Jerry. *Frontier Merchants: Lionel and Barron Jacobs and the Jewish Pioneers Who Settled the West.*
New York: Random House. 1998.

Sons of a Polish merchant who settled in California, Lionel and Barron Jacobs were in their twenties when they set off for the Arizona Territory in 1867 to start a new business venture. Their adventures and accomplishments are interspersed with information about Jews in America, nineteenth-century business development, and larger historical events.

Yavin, T. S. *All Star Season.*
Minneapolis, MN: Kar-Ben/Lerner. 2007

Baseball fans will enjoy this story for its attention to baseball skill development, as practiced by two teenage brothers who are both excellent and passionately dedicated players. Told mainly from the point of view of Reuven, the older and more intensely competitive of the two boys, the story also explores sibling relationships, school friendships, and what it's like to be part of a team.

CHAPTER 13

Recognizing and Resisting Evil

"These are the things that you are to do: Speak the truth to one another, render true and perfect justice in your gates. And do not contrive evil against one another, and do not love perjury, because all those are things that I hate—declares the Lord."

Tanakh

PRIMARY

Bunting, Eve. ***Terrible Things.*** Illus. by Stephen Gammell. Philadelphia: Jewish Publication Society. 1989.

In an allegory about perpetrators, victims, and bystanders, the animals of the forest are carried away, one kind after another, by the Terrible Things. The others do nothing, not realizing that they might be next or that they might have had the power to stop the Terrible Things. Originally published by Harper and Row in 1980.

Burg, Ann E. ***Rebekkah's Journey: A World War II Refugee Story.***
   Illus. by Joel Iskowitz.
Chelsea, MI: Sleeping Bear Press, 2006.

This picture book introduces children to the story of the 982 World War II refugees who were interned at a vacant army base in Oswego, New York in 1944–1945. A child and her mother are the main characters, and it is through their experiences that readers learn something about the Oswego camp and the plight of all refugees. Part of the Tales of Young Americans Series. Other stories for older children with the same setting are *Two Suns in the Sky* by Miriam Bat-Ami and *Good Night, Maman* by Norma Fox Mazer.

Gelman, Rita Golden. ***Queen Esther Saves Her People.*** Illus. by Frane Lessac.
New York: Scholastic. 1998.

A hint of danger, a dash of humor, and a touch of class characterize both the writing and the artwork in this delightful retelling of the Purim story. A striking page layout showcases the Persian-inspired illustrations, which match the story in detail and wry wit.

Gerstein, Mordicai. *Queen Esther, the Morning Star.*
New York: Simon and Schuster. 1999.
A faithful retelling of the story of Queen Esther is decorated with glowing pictures and a humorous attitude toward the two villains, Ahasuerus and Haman. Character traits are captured by the illustrations.

Hirsh, Marilyn. *The Rabbi and the Twenty Nine Witches.*
New York: Holiday House. 1976.

In this Talmudic legend, witches dance and witches melt when a rabbi uses his wits and courage to drive them out of town. Smoky blue, grey, and black illustrations add to the air of magic. Excellent for telling or reading aloud.

Kimmel, Eric A. *Hershel and the Hanukkah Goblins.* Illus. by Trina Schart Hyman.
New York: Holiday House. 1989.

Hershel of Ostropol, one of the central characters in Eastern European Jewish folklore, is the hero of this suspenseful tale. Vowing to help some villagers whose synagogue is haunted and whose Hanukkah celebrations are ruined by goblins, he stations himself in the spooky synagogue and, night after night, outwits an evermore ferocious goblin, including their king on the eighth night. The illustrations and text are in perfect harmony, making this one of children's most beloved Hanukkah stories.

Klein, Gerda Weissmann. *Promise of a New Spring: The Holocaust and Renewal.*
Illus. by Vincent Tartaro.
Houston: Rossel Books. 1981.

Comparing the Nazi destruction of the Jews during the Holocaust with a forest fire that devastates the animals and other wildlife in its path, this story for younger children is an effective introduction to the Holocaust. The illustrations, in two-tone and full color, extend the book's message.

Rouss, Sylvia. *Tali's Jerusalem Scrapbook.* Illus. by Nancy Oppenheimer.
New York: Pitspopany. 2003.

The feelings of an Israeli girl about the Israeli-Palestinian conflict are explored in this short illustrated book. Tali, her family, and her friends all express their fears, their sorrows, and their hope for a peaceful future. The illustrations are expressive and realistic, although not always in sync with the text. A constructive and very useful book to present the Israeli point of view.

Singer, Isaac Bashevis. *The Wicked City.* Illus. by Leonard Everett Fisher.
New York: Farrar, Straus and Giroux. 1972.

A classic tale of good and evil, expanded from the biblical account of the destruction of Sodom and Gomorrah. Fisher's strong scratch board illustrations leave no doubt as to who is wicked and who is good—the faces reveal all. Lot and his family are the human counterparts to a city known for its cruelty. Abraham is a less compelling figure but that is because the focus of the story—both the narrative and pictures—is on wickedness and its punishment. There is a depiction of God on the first page, which will make the book inappropriate for many Jewish libraries and families.

ELEMENTARY

Altman, Linda Jacobs. *Crimes and Criminals of the Holocaust.*
Berkeley Heights, NJ: Enslow. 2004.

After summarizing World War II and the Holocaust, the book briefly discusses the end of the war, liberation of the concentration camps, displaced person camps, and England's blockade of ports to prevent survivors from reaching Palestine. It then gives an account of the trials of 24 Nazi leaders in Nuremberg, Germany, presenting the prosecution's accusations, the witnesses' testimony, and the war criminals' defense. Reference aids are included. Part of The Holocaust in History Series.

Altman, Linda Jacobs. *Forgotten Victims of the Holocaust.*
Berkeley Heights: NJ: Enslow. 2003.

Part of a series called "The Holocaust in History" that incorporates information published in other books by Enslow and adds new information, geared to younger readers. The content includes information on Germany's relationship with the Soviet Union during World War II, Christian victims of the Nazis, and the treatment of Romany people, the disabled, political opponents of Hitler, homosexuals, and others considered to be defilers of racial purity.

Altman, Linda Jacobs. *Hitler's Rise to Power and the Holocaust.*
Berkeley Heights, NJ: Enslow. 2003.

Part of the "Holocaust In History" Series, this shows how Hitler's duplicity, ruthlessness, and obsession with racial purity, as well as his megalomania, led to both his success and then his failure.

Altman, Linda Jacobs. *The Jewish Victims of the Holocaust.*
Berkeley Heights, NJ: Enslow. 2003.

The information here includes a brief history of the Holocaust and anti-Semitism, the ghettos of Eastern Europe, the organization of genocide, concentration camps, and why the Germans persisted in their slaughter of Jews up until the very end of the war in Europe. Many survivors are quoted and attention is paid to the dilemma of those in the *Judenrat*, the Jewish council in the ghettos, and the Jewish police force. Part of The Holocaust in History Series.

Boyne, John. *The Boy in the Striped Pajamas.*
New York: David Fickling/Random House. 2006.

The horror dawns slowly. Bruno is a lively nine-year-old German boy through whose innocent and limited understanding the story unfolds. He leaves his beautiful home in Berlin when "the Fury" appoints his father to a very important job in a place that Bruno thinks is called "Out With." Written for readers who know something about the Holocaust and who will experience the shock of recognition when they realize the evil that pervades Bruno's world. Very discussable.

Cormier, Robert. *Tunes for Bears to Dance To.*
New York: Delacorte 1992.

A short, disturbing novel that explores—but does not explain—the nature of evil. The setting is somewhere outside of Boston, a depressed urban environment that reflects the almost-ruined lives of several of its characters. A boy named Henry, whose older, beloved brother has been killed, falls into the clutches of a man who exploits Henry and his parents' vulnerability and seeks to destroy Henry's innocence by bribing him to commit a senselessly cruel crime against a Holocaust survivor. The style is terse, almost cryptic, and it will leave readers with many questions.

Crowley, Bridget. *Feast of Fools.*
New York: Margaret K. McElderry/Simon and Schuster. 2003.

Set in a cathedral town during the Middle Ages, this mystery involves corrupt priests, deadly sins, and murder. The medieval setting is very well realized and an essential background to the characterization and plot. Two Christian boys are the main characters, and a subplot involves the Jews of the town, whose treatment epitomizes the anti-Semitism of the age.

Gellman, Marc. *And God Cried, Too.* Illus. by Harry Bliss.
New York: HarperCollins. 2002.

Similar to several other books by Rabbi Gellman but specifically situated in the events of September 11, 2001, this is a wholesome book of consolation and advice for younger children, their teachers, rabbis, and parents. Each chapter is based on a theological subject—evil, justice, anger at God, for example—and presented as a fictional vignette. Most of the values expressed are thoroughly Jewish, but the book is addressed to readers of all creeds, including those who do not believe in God at all.

Gellman, Marc, and Thomas Hartman. *Lost and Found.* Illus. by Debbie Tilley.
New York: Morrow. 1999.

The authors—a rabbi and a priest—discuss losses that children may face, from losing a toy, to loss of confidence and faith, to severe losses like the death of a family member or a pet. The tone is chatty and the approach is practical rather than religious, emphasizing the importance of moving forward while retaining fond memories.

Gerstein, Mordicai. *The Old Country.*
New Milford, CT: Roaring Brook Press. 2005.

The award-winning illustrator has created an allegory about war and prejudice without illustrations but with imaginative images and rhythmic language. It centers on a girl who becomes a fox, and is filled with talking animals and insects, form-changing sprites, idiotic royalty, and a great deal of humor. Although not overtly Jewish, it resonates with Jewish historical experience.

Glatshteyn, Yankev. *Emil and Karl.*
New Milford, CT: Roaring Brook Press. 2006.

Originally written in Yiddish in 1940 and now translated by Jeffrey Shandler, the story of Emil and Karl is set in Vienna on the brink of World War II. Since the Nazi takeover of Austria, ordinary citizens are encouraged to prey upon their Jewish neighbors, humiliating and torturing them. Emil and Karl, friends and about nine years old each, have both lost their parents in the political upheaval and are trying to survive on their own. Through their frightening experiences, readers are taken on a journey into the maelstrom that was to become the Holocaust.

Holm, Anne. *I Am David.*
San Diego: Harcourt Brace. 2004.

Originally published in 1965 under the title *North to Freedom*, this story of a child's escape from a German concentration camp has been criticized by some for making the rigors of escape appear too easy. There is a movie based on the book, also called *I Am David.* Translated from the Danish by L. W. Kingsland.

Ish-Kishor, Sulamith. *A Boy of Old Prague.*
New York: Pantheon. 1963.

A Christian peasant boy is punished by his cruel and all-powerful lord by being sent to the Prague Ghetto to be a servant in the household of a Jew. Tomas is bright but his mind has been filled from birth with anti-Semitic superstitions and hatred. How his thinking changes as he lives with a Jewish family and experiences life in the Ghetto is at the heart of this beautifully written and illustrated story, one of the best novels ever to be written for children about anti-Semitism.

Kacer, Kathy. *Clara's War.*
Toronto: Second Story Press. 2001.

Thirteen-year-old Clara and her family are deported from Prague to the concentration camp of Terezin. Through their experiences, the grimness and terror of the camp are shown in contrast to its rich cultural life. Friedl Dicker-Brandeis, the subject of a non-fiction book called *Fireflies in the Dark* by Susan Goldman Rubin and the opera, Brundibar, whose plot is retold in a book of the same title by Tony Kushner and Maurice Sendak, are part of *Clara's War*.

Kacer, Kathy. *The Night Spies.*
Toronto: Second Story Press. 2003.

In another of Kacer's novels set during the Holocaust, she returns to Gabi, the character based on her own mother whom she introduced in her first book, *The Secret of Gabi's Dresser*. Gabi—now 13—and her mother have been joined by Max, an 11-year-old cousin who, alone of his family, has escaped a Nazi roundup. Gabi's courageous mother arranges for them to go into hiding with a Christian farm family she and her late husband know. Driven to rashness by boredom, Gabi and Max sneak out of the confined space in the barn where they hide. They prowl around the nearby forest, making friends with a group of partisans, and spying on the Nazis for the partisans. The suspense of the plot is combined with a thoughtful exploration of what it was like to be hated and hunted and with the portrayal of several heroic non-Jews, based on real people.

Kacer, Kathy. *The Underground Reporters.*
Toronto: Second Story Press. 2004.

Turning her attention once again to the Holocaust, Kathy Kacer has taken a minor event and written an entire book about it. For children avid to read more and more about the Holocaust, this is about a group of young Jews in a Czechoslovakian town, who published a newspaper under the very eyes of the Nazis. The newspaper, entitled *Klepy*, or "gossip" in Czech, increased in length and content through its 22 issues; it ceased publication when most of the Jews of the town were deported to Terezin, where only two of the children mentioned in the book survived. Kacer based her book on events related to her by a survivor. Illustrated with photographs and maps, this is a minor, although absorbing, addition to Holocaust literature.

Mazer, Norma Fox. *Good Night, Maman.*
San Diego: Harcourt Brace. 1999.

In the first part of this Holocaust story, two French-Jewish children and their mother hide and run from the Nazis. Maman insists that Marc and Karin leave her behind in order to board a ship that is taking refugees to the United States. The second part of the story is set in Oswego, New York, where refugees were interned. Although, once there, life gets better for the two children, they yearn for their mother to join them. Ruth Gruber, who persuaded the U.S. government to bring refugees to this country, is one of the characters.

Melnikoff, Pamela. *Prisoner in Time: A Child of the Holocaust.*
Philadelphia: Jewish Publication Society. 2001.

When the Nazis begin to deport Jews from Prague, 12-year-old Jan Weiss is hidden by Gentile friends. His carelessness results in the arrest of his benefactors. Desperate, he is drawn to the grave of Rabbi Judah Loewe, known as the Maharal, one of the most famous sites in Old Prague. At the grave, he finds an amulet that allows him to time travel back to the time of Rabbi Loewe. Jan helps the rabbi make the *Golem*, which saves the Jewish community from its enemies. When he returns to the present, he is sent to Terezin and reunited with his dying mother. His promise to her leads him to search for a present-day *Golem*.

Moscowitz, Moshe. **The Queen of Persia.** Illus. by David Sokoloff.
Chicago: Shazak Productions. 2004.

Drawing heavily from the *Midrash* on *Megillat* Esther, this is a comic book presentation of the story of Purim. It follows the Megillah chapter by chapter, and each chapter concludes with a short multiple choice quiz. The illustrations are cartoon style, with sound effects sometimes incorporated into them. Most of the action is explained through dialogue, with occasional explanatory passages at the top or bottom of the frame. An enjoyable introduction to the Purim story.

Rappaport, Doreen. **The Secret Seder.** Illus. by Emily McCully.
New York: Hyperion. 2005.

In this somberly illustrated Holocaust story, a boy and his father, hiding from the Nazis in occupied France, climb to the top of mountain to share a Passover *Seder* with other Jewish men in the same circumstances. With very little food and in fear for their very lives, their somber observance is a testament to courage and faith. Poignantly written and very well illustrated, the story confronts the tragedy of the Holocaust while offering hope that the human spirit will prevail. For readers with some knowledge of the Holocaust.

Roy, Jennifer Rozines. **Yellow Star.**
Tarrytown, NY: Marshall Cavendish. 2006.

A story written in free verse about the author's aunt, who was one of only 12 children to survive the Lodz Ghetto. It recaps the subject's memory from the time she was about five, in 1939, until the ghetto was liberated in 1945. The quiet heroism of her family and friends throughout their daily struggle to remain alive imbues the narrative with hope.

Rubin, Susan Goldman. **Fireflies in the Dark: The Story of Friedl Dicker-Brandeis and the Children of Terezin.**
New York: Holiday House. 2000.

A Bauhaus-trained Jewish artist from Prague is imprisoned in Terezin. There she teaches traumatized children to express themselves and their fears through art. An inspiring biography with memorable illustrations by Dicker-Brandeis and her students. Paired with the poems and drawings in *I Never Saw Another Butterfly* by Volavkova, it presents one of the most moving explorations of the Holocaust.

Steele, D. Kelley. **Would You Salute? One Child's Story of the Holocaust.**
Illus. by Becky Hyatt Rickenbaker.
Statesville, NC: Hidden Path Publication. 2006.

This illustrated biographical story of a girl named Margot growing up in Germany during Hitler's rise to power challenges readers to think about what they would have done in a similar situation. Would you salute Hitler in school along with all of the other children and teachers? Would you feel proud wearing the uniform of the Hitler Youth? Would you watch as soldiers terrorized an elderly Jewish man on the street? Designed to create empathy in today's readers, it tackles many difficult subjects, including Margot's father's suicide.

Suhl, Yuri. *Uncle Misha's Partisans.*
New York: Four Winds Press. 1973.

The exciting story of Motele, a Jewish orphan who joins a band of resistance fighters. Using his talent as a violinist, Motele is able to deliver a devastating blow against the Nazis. Winner of a Sydney Taylor Book Award. Other books about Jewish resistance during the Holocaust include *Escaping into the Night* by D. Dina Friedman, *Greater Than Angels* by Carol Matas, and *To Live and Fight Another Day* by Bracha Weisbarth.

Vos, Ida. 1995. *Dancing on the Bridge at Avignon.*
Boston: Houghton Mifflin.

Set in Holland in 1942, this sad story reveals the terror that Nazi restrictions on normal life aroused in Jews. A 10-year-old girl emotionally recounts daily routines under siege and her family's reactions to threat and danger. Translated from the Dutch and winner of a Sydney Taylor Book Award.

MIDDLE SCHOOL

Adlington, L. J. *The Diary of Pelly D.*
New York: HarperCollins. 2005.

This science-fiction dystopia uses the device of a war diary to recast the Holocaust as a futuristic event. By replacing real ethnic groups with fictional ones, the outrageous nature of prejudice is cast into sharp relief. It will appeal to readers who enjoy thought-provoking science fiction like Sonia Levitin's *The Cure* and Lois Lowry's *The Giver*.

Altman, Linda Jacobs. *Adolf Hitler: Evil Mastermind of the Holocaust.*
Berkeley Heights, NJ: Enslow. 2005.

One of several books in the "Holocaust Heroes and Nazi Criminals" Series, this is a succinct and well-written biography of the uneducated Austrian ex-corporal who captured the hearts and minds of the German people. A concise overview of Hitler's life is given, from his humble beginnings to his macabre suicide in a Berlin bunker in 1945. Includes chapter notes, a bibliography, timeline, glossary, Internet addresses, and index.

Attema, Martha. *When the War Is Over.*
Custer, WA: Orca. 2003.

Sixteen-year-old Janke Visser risks her life working with the Dutch underground during the Nazi occupation of Holland, yet she also has a secret romantic relationship with a young, "good" German whose uncle is a vicious Nazi. Girls especially will be interested in this story of a daring heroine. The many Jewish characters in the novel all appear briefly.

Axelrod, Toby. *Hans and Sophie Scholl.*
New York: Rosen. 2001.

A biography of two of the founders of the White Rose, a courageous organization of German students and academics who resisted Hitler. Includes photographs, documents, a glossary, bibliography, and index.

Baer, Edith. *Walk the Dark Streets.*
New York: Farrar, Straus and Giroux. 1998.

In this powerful and absorbing sequel to Baer's 1980 novel, *A Frost in the Night*, Eva Bentheim has become a teenager trying to develop and assert her sense of self in the nightmare of Nazi Germany. Understated and at times almost documentary in style, it chills the heart with its artfully arranged accumulation of details showing the deterioration of life for German Jews.

Bartoletti, Susan. *Hitler Youth: Growing Up in Hitler's Shadow.*
New York: Scholastic. 2005.

An excellent nonfiction account of Hitler Youth, founded in 1926 as a Nazi organization dedicated to turning German teenagers into ardent followers of the Fuhrer. The lives of 12 young Germans are described; all are connected to Hitler Youth, either as eager members or staunch resisters. Profusely illustrated with many authentic photographs; includes a timeline, notes, bibliography, and index.

Burstein, Shmuel. *The War Against God and His People: A Guide to the Holocaust for Young People.*
Southfield, MI: Targum/Feldheim. 2000.

This is an introduction to the Holocaust for Orthodox students in middle school and high school. An extensive part of the book is devoted to an examination of why the Jewish people were singled out for destruction and to the question, "Where was God?" Both are discussed from a traditional point of view. Many black-and-white illustrations fill the book, but the format leaves much to be desired in its lack of reference aids. The absence of an index makes it extremely difficult to use except for browsing.

Callahan, Kerry P. *Mordechai Anielewicz: Hero of the Warsaw Ghetto Uprising.*
New York: Rosen. 2001.

Part of the publisher's Holocaust Biographies Series, this gives background information on Polish anti-Semitism between the two world wars, details of the Nazi's program of genocide, and an account of the uprising. Although not much is known about Anielewicz, who died young, he emerges as a hero. The style is straightforward and the information accurate. The format is not particularly attractive, but the book has the reference aids and illustrations necessary for student research.

Cheng, Andrea. *Marika.*
Ashville, NC: Front Street Books. 2002.

A Holocaust novel about an unhappy family of assimilated, self-hating Hungarian Jews. Spanning about 10 years in Marika's life, it chronicles the decline of her family's fortunes during World War II in Hungary. Despite having converted to Christianity, the family is still persecuted. The personal affairs of Marika's family occupy center stage here, in a departure from the historical focus of most novels taking place during the Holocaust.

Chotjewitz, David. *Daniel, Half Human, and the Good Nazi.*
New York: Simon and Schuster/Atheneum. 2004.

A powerful novel told through flashbacks from 1945 to the 1930s in Hamburg, Germany. Daniel and his best friend, Armin, are schoolboys who admire the Nazis until Daniel finds out, to his horror, that he is what the Nazis call a *mischling*, or "mongrel," because his mother was born a Jew. As life for Jews deteriorates, so does life as Daniel has known it. His feelings, his school experiences, his family's anguish, and his friend Armin's divided loyalties are all skillfully developed in a thought-provoking story that begs for discussion. Translated from the German by Doris Orgel.

Friedman, D. Dina. *Escaping into the Night.*
New York: Simon and Schuster. 2006.

This Holocaust novel is based on factual accounts of encampments that saved Jews. Hidden deep in the forests of Eastern Europe, the camps provided refuge to women, children, and sick people, as well as to men who fought as partisans against the Germans. Halina, the main character, is a 13-year-old girl whose mother has been killed. She and her two good friends, Reuven and Batya, have many hair-raising and at times bloodcurdling adventures. Halina's memories of her mother, her love of music, and her questioning mind help sustain her, as does perseverance and courage.

Giblin, James Cross. *The Life and Death of Adolf Hitler.*
New York: Clarion. 2002.

Oriented to readers in eighth grade and up, this is an account of the twentieth century's greatest monster, from his birth in 1889 to his death in 1945. The material on Hitler's early life and his rise to power is especially strong. His role in directing the Third Reich's destiny in World War II is amply documented, as is his hatred of Jews. The biography ends with a section discussing Hitler's legacy: Modern neo-Nazi and skinhead movements. Excellent photographs, a glossary, bibliography, and index enhance the value of yet another outstanding biography from Clarion.

Gottfried, Ted. *Deniers of the Holocaust.* Illus. by Stephen Alcorn.
Brookfield, CT: Twentieth Century Books/Millbrook. 2001.

The Holocaust is treated as a modern chapter in the long history of anti-Semitism in this comprehensive work for middle school students. Prominent denial leaders and organizations are profiled, and the author explains their core beliefs and tactics. He also explores the conflict between free speech rights and the need to restrain deniers. An excellent format enhances the book, which is one of several in a series about the Holocaust by this publisher.

Hautzig, Esther. *The Endless Steppe.*
New York: Crowell. 1968.

When the author was 11 years old during World War II, she and her family were arrested by the Soviets as political enemies and exiled to Siberia. Her unforgettable story is about their five years as prisoners trying to survive under the most dire of circumstances. Winner of the first Sydney Taylor Book Award.

Isaacs, Ann. *Torn Thread.*
New York: Scholastic. 2000.

Based on the experiences of a Holocaust survivor, this is the story of two teenaged sisters who survive a Nazi slave labor camp where they were imprisoned for several years. Through a large cast of characters, the author touches on some central Holocaust issues.

Katz, Samuel M. *Global Counterstrike: International Counterterrorism.*
Minneapolis, MN: Lerner. 2005.

Part of a series called Terrorist Dossiers, this contains information not easily found elsewhere. It is divided into chapters on Europe, the Middle East, and on international forces in places like Canada, Poland, and South Korea. Within each chapter there are lists called "Who's Who and What's What," and sections that discuss terrorist activities in various countries and the steps those countries have taken to combat terrorism. The writing style is clear and easy to follow; the format is drab. Appended material includes several reliable Web sites, a timeline dating from 1921 to 2004, a bibliography, suggestions for further reading and viewing, and a detailed index.

Katz, Samuel M. *Jerusalem or Death: Palestinian Terrorism.*
Minneapolis, MN: Lerner. 2003.

Part of the Terrorist Dossiers Series, this chronicles Palestinian terrorism, including the multiple PFLP jetliner hijackings of 1968–1970 and the massacre of Israeli schoolchildren at Maalot. Readers will also learn how old is the terrorist tactic of using shocking and spectacular deeds to grab world attention.

Kubert, Joe. ***Yossel April 19,1943: A Story of the Warsaw Ghetto Uprising.***
New York: ibooksgraphic novels/Simon and Schuster. 2003.

A talented graphic artist, Kubert writes a fictional account of a boy involved in the Warsaw Ghetto uprising. The boy is based on Kubert himself and his family, who escaped from Europe in time to avoid the fate of many of their relatives. Using the medium of the graphic novel, where drama, fear, tedium, danger, torture, heightened reality, and a host of other feelings can be communicated visually, Kubert portrays the suffering of the Holocaust.

Lawton, Clive. ***Auschwitz: The Story of a Nazi Death Camp.***
Cambridge, MA: Candlewick. 2002.

A graphically striking account of the Nazi death camp, from its origins as the Polish town of Oswiecim to the present. The text is concise and easy to follow, and the illustrations—mainly photographs and documents—are clear and explanatory. In relatively few pages, readers are given what Francine Prose called a "guided tour of Hell." Includes a glossary, timeline, and index.

Lawton, Clive. ***The Story of the Holocaust.***
New York: Franklin Watts. 2000.

Lawton, a British Holocaust educator, asks how the Holocaust could happen in a civilized society in the modern era. He discusses the historical roots of anti-Semitism and contemporary factors that increased the appeal of Nazism to Germans. There is a detailed presentation of measures that led to the Final Solution. The book is copiously illustrated with photographs and maps. Its information is divided into 20 different topics, each no more than two pages long. A list of important dates, a glossary, and an index are included. The photos and text often are quite gruesome.

Levitin, Sonia. ***The Cure.***
San Diego: Harcourt Brace. 1999.

Fusing science fiction with historical fiction, this somber story moves in time from a sterile future civilization to the rich but troubled world of medieval European Jewry, and then back again. The hero, a "misfit" who loves music and yearns for human intimacy, is "cured" by living the life of a young Jewish man who meets a tragic end, along with all of his fellow Jews, during the Black Death epidemic in Strasbourg, France.

McNeese, Tim. ***Masada: Sieges That Changed the World.***
New York: Chelsea House. 2003.

Written much like a brief textbook, this gives a dispassionate account of the mass suicide at Masada and includes information about Yigael Yadin's excavations at the site. Well organized and clearly written, there are illustrations and maps to inform the reader and heighten the book's eye appeal.

Matas, Carol. *In My Enemy's House.*
New York: Simon and Schuster. 1999.

Fifteen-year-old Marissa, who has lost most of her family, hides from the Nazis by posing as a Polish Catholic worker in Germany. She is assigned to help the family of a Nazi official to which she becomes deeply attached. Later, in the last days of the war, she is transferred to a Berlin factory where she barely survives Allied bombing attacks. Isolated, Marissa struggles to maintain her identity. This is a skillful portrait of a heroine making her way in a world of random cruelty and awful choices.

Miklowitz, Gloria. *The Enemy Has a Face.*
Grand Rapids, MI: Eerdmans. 2003.

Aspects of the Israeli-Palestinian conflict are skillfully explored in this novel about the disappearance of an Israeli teen living in Los Angeles. By giving the suspenseful story an American setting and centering most of the action on teenage students, Miklowitz succeeds in creating both a readable mystery and a balanced portrayal of Israeli and Palestinian points of view. Add to this the important role that the Internet plays in the story, and you have an outstanding blend of issues and action. Following a recent trend in novels for this age group, the ending is unhappy. Excellent for class discussion and book groups.

Miklowitz, Gloria. *Secrets in the House of Delgado.*
Grand Rapids, MI: Eerdmans. 2001.

In a gripping story about "New Christians" and the Spanish Inquisition, the author captures the terror of the times and the varying degrees of Jewish loyalty among members of one family. The narrator is a Christian servant girl who is bullied by a priest to spy on the family for whom she works.

Pressler, Mirjam. *Malka.*
New York: Philomel. 2003.

As a mother and her two daughters flee from the Nazis, the younger child becomes sick and unable to travel. The mother, a doctor, leaves her in the care of a family who later abandons her during a Nazi raid. Malka, at age seven, is on her own. The story alternates between chapters written from the point of view of Malka and that of her mother. A searing portrayal of a mother-daughter relationship under the most difficult of circumstances.

Rabinovici, Schoschana. *Thanks to My Mother.*
New York: Dial. 1998.

From the Vilna ghetto to the camps and a death march, young Susie's survival depended on her indomitable mother. This Holocaust memoir portrays the extremes of human endurance and includes Germans who behaved decently and Jews who did not.

Radin, Ruth. *Escape to the Forest: Based on a True Story of the Holocaust.*
   Illus. by Janet Hamlin.
New York: HarperCollins. 2000.

Despite harassments and random killings, young teen Sarah and her family manage to stay together in their German-occupied Polish town. Their "luck" runs out when the ghetto is liquidated. At the urging of her parents, Sarah evades deportation and makes her way into the forest where she joins a group of Jewish partisans. Based on real-life experiences, this book celebrates the exploits of Tuvia Bielski and his brothers, who not only attacked the Nazis, but sheltered numerous Jews in their stronghold. This is a well-written account of Jews who fought back.

Richter, Hans. *Friedrich.*
New York: Holt, Rinehart and Winston. 1970.

A chilling novel set during the Holocaust, this is the story of two German friends—one Jewish and one Christian—and the impact of Nazism on their lives. Several teaching guides are available for a story that is frequently taught.

Rogasky, Barbara. *Smoke and Ashes, Revised and Expanded.*
New York: Holiday House. 2002.

The first edition of this unflinching look at the Holocaust was written in 1988 and represented a significant contribution to books about the Holocaust for young people. Here, much new information has been added: The role of "ordinary" Germans in the Final Solution, the Germans' attempts to hide their crimes, the Allies' decision not to bomb the rail lines to Auschwitz, and more. A chapter called "The Uniqueness of the Holocaust" lists recent atrocities and hate crimes, such as the murder of a gay man, Matthew Shepard, and of a black man, James Byrd Jr. The Holocaust denial trial, in which David Irving sued Deborah Lipstadt and lost, is also mentioned. One of the very best treatments of the Holocaust for young people.

Rogow, Sally M. *Faces of Courage: Young Heroes of World War II.*
Vancouver: Granville Island. 2003.

Inspiring stories about 12 European teenagers (Danish, French, Jewish, German, Polish, and Romany) who resisted the Nazis. All are based on factual materials and drawn from documented sources. Contains a map of Europe during WWII, a foreword, introduction, references, and a glossary.

Roleff, Tamara L. *The Holocaust: Death Camps.*
Farmington Hills, MI: Greenhaven. 2002.

The History Firsthand series explores historical events through eyewitness accounts culled from other published sources. In this volume, excerpts describe every aspect of the death camps from the train ride to Auschwitz through liberation and beyond.

A detailed introduction and chapter prefaces provide context for the quotations, and there is a brief biography of each eyewitness. The first-person perspective is an effective way to present this material but also makes it more disturbing. For teens who have some basic understanding of the Holocaust. A table of contents, timeline, bibliography and index are included.

Rubin, Susan Goldman. *The Flag with Fifty-six Stars: A Gift from the Survivors of Mauthausen.* Illus. by Bill Farnsworth.
New York: Holiday House. 2005.

A stunningly illustrated account of a flag made secretly by prisoners at Mauthausen concentration camp to welcome their American liberators. Mistakenly, an extra row of stars was added, thus the 'fifty-six.' Based on interviews with survivors and liberating soldiers, this story of courage and resistance is inspiring.

Schmidt, Gary. *Mara's Stories: Glimmers in the Dark.*
New York: Henry Holt. 2001.

In the night and fog of a concentration camp, women and children gather at night to listen to stories told by a prisoner named Mara, the daughter of a rabbi. The stories are adapted from Jewish lore and modern Jewish literature. Sources and notes are included. Outstanding!

Smith, Frank Dabba. *Elsie's War: A Story of Courage in Nazi Germany.*
London: Frances Lincoln. 2003.

This photo-essay is similar in format to Smith's *My Secret Camera*, about life in the Lodz ghetto. The subject here is Elsie Leitz, a young German woman whose wealthy family manufactured cameras. Elsie and her father protected Jews, helped them escape, and eased their lives when they could. Because of this, Elsie was arrested and imprisoned, although later released when a friend bribed the SS. The black-and-white photographs are large, clear, and dramatic; the text is brief. A good high-interest, low-vocabulary choice for teens.

Sonneborn, Liz. *Murder at the 1972 Olympics in Munich.*
New York: Rosen. 2003.

A readable and informative account of the murder of 11 Israeli athletes at the 1972 Olympic Games in Munich by Palestinian terrorists. Many photographs, a glossary, a pathfinder to more information, a bibliography and suggested reading list, and an index are included and make the book suitable for reports.

Taylor, Peter Lane, and Christos Nicola. *The Secret of Priest's Grotto.*
Minneapolis, MN: Kar-Ben/Lerner. 2007.

A remarkable nonfiction Holocaust survival story is combined with accounts of cave exploring in this engrossing book. It tells the true story of a group of 32 Ukrainian

Jews who hid from the Nazis in a cave and managed to survive against incredible odds for almost one year. Stunning color photographs are spread throughout the book, which is written on a fairly adult level in the style of a *National Geographic* article. A note states that an article about Priest's Grotto appeared in *National Geographic Adventure* in 2004, and that the story is now being developed into a movie and TV documentary.

Tunnell, Michael O. *Brothers in Valor: A Story of Resistance.*
New York: Holiday House. 2001.

A historical novel recounting the activities of the Hubener Group, a small band of German teenagers who printed and distributed anti-Nazi literature during World War II. The story, told in the voice of one of the teenagers, is a remarkable one; it includes their Mormon background, their arrest, torture, and trial.

Uschan, Michael V. *The Holocaust.*
Farmington Hills, MI: Lucent. 2005.

Books in the World History Series attempt to present a broad, balanced, and penetrating view of the march of history. *The Holocaust* is succinct but thorough, with quotes from survivors, photographs, and a timeline. The coverage includes the roots of the Holocaust, how Jews were stripped of their rights, ghettoes, the Final Solution, life and death in the camps, resistance, liberation, the trials of Nazi war criminals, and the founding of Israel. Appended material includes notes, a reading list, bibliography, and an index.

Volavkova, Hana, Editor. *I Never Saw Another Butterfly.*
New York: Schocken. 1993.

Originally published in 1954, this collection of art and poetry created by children imprisoned in the Terezin concentration camp is one of the most moving records of the Holocaust. There are several other books for children about Terezin, and an excellent companion to this one is *Fireflies in the Dark: The Story of Friedl Dicker-Brandeis and the Children of Terezin* by Susan Goldman Rubin.

Warren, Andrea. *Surviving Hitler: A Boy in the Nazi Death Camps.*
New York: HarperCollins. 2001.

An inspiring account of the Holocaust experiences of Jack Mandelbaum, who survived three years as a teen in several camps. His zest for life and ability to form friendships helped him begin a new life in the United States.

Weisbarth, Bracha. **To Live and Fight Another Day: The Story of a
Jewish Partisan Boy.**
Jerusalem: Mazo. 2004.

An exciting novel based on the experiences of the author's family during the Holocaust. The main character is her brother, Benny, who led the family out of the ghetto before a Nazi "Final Solution" and then into the forests, where they eventually joined partisans fighting the Nazis. Pathos, ingenuity, adventure, tragedy, tenderness, and a hero with whom readers will identify are all part of this fine story. Other stories about Jewish partisans are *The Night Spies* by Kathy Kacer, *Escape to the Forest* by Ruth Radin and *Uncle Misha's Partisans* by Yuri Suhl.

Winter, Kathryn. *Katarina.*
New York: Farrar, Straus and Giroux. 1998.

Outcast and struggling, virtually alone, to survive in Slovakia during the Holocaust, a Jewish child is sustained by a combination of imagination, hope, and faith in the Catholic saints. A remarkable—at times—nightmarish, story about identity and difference.

Wiseman, Eva. *My Canary Yellow Star.*
Toronto: Tundra Books. 2001.

The grim fate of the Jews of Budapest during World War II is chronicled in this well-written novel. The suffering of teenage Marta and her family worsens as the Nazis, along with the Hungarian fascists who eagerly abetted them, implement their extermination program late in the war. Raoul Wallenberg is a character in the novel, portrayed convincingly as the hero that he was. Marta's friendship with a Christian boy adds a touch of romance to the story, but over it, too, hangs menace and the threat of death. Eva Wiseman is the author of *A Place Not Home*, and her writing here is even more polished, more absorbing.

Yolen, Jane. *The Devil's Arithmetic.*
New York: Viking Kestrel. 1988.

Sixteen-year-old Hanna is an American teen who is uninterested in her Jewish heritage. Through a time travel fantasy, she is transported to Poland during the Holocaust and into a journey of life, death, and survival. Winner of a Sydney Taylor Book Award.

HIGH SCHOOL

Barth-Grozinger, Inge. *Something Remains.*
New York: Hyperion. 2006.

This somber novel is based on research that a German high school English teacher and her students conducted. It chronicles the effects of Nazism on a Jewish family in a small town that had previously accepted them as full and equal citizens and good neighbors. As the doctrine of National Socialism perverts the educational and social systems, the Levi family suffers both emotional and material persecution. Erich, the teenage son, is the protagonist, and through his experiences—portrayed in great detail—a personal and civic tragedy is revealed.

Crew, David F. *Hitler and the Nazis, a History in Documents.*
New York: Oxford University Press. 2005.

The author uses documentary material—usually German in origin—to give the reader a succinct history of Germany, from the Weimar Republic after World War I, through the rise of Hitler and Nazism, the German racist state, Hitler's wars, the Holocaust, and its aftermath. Useful bibliographies, Web sites, and an index are included.

Greif, Jean-Jacques. *The Fighter.*
New York: Bloomsbury. 2006.

From the time he was a child in Warsaw, Moshe was a fighter. As he matures, moves to Paris, marries, and embraces a life relatively free of fear and anti-Semitism, Moshe continues his hobby as an amateur boxer. His fighting spirit is tested to the limit when the Nazis invade France and deport him to Auschwitz, where the camp guards force him to fight dying prisoners for their entertainment. This hard-hitting story, based on the experiences of a real person who survived the camps, shocks and horrifies.

Hoffman, Alice. *Incantation.*
New York: Little Brown. 2006

Set in Spain during the time of the Inquisition, this is the story of Estrella/Esther, a girl whose family are Conversos—Jews who outwardly embrace Catholicism but who secretly cling to their Jewish faith. As the noose of the Inquisition tightens around her family and neighbors, she flees Spain, realizing, in a sobering message to teenage readers, that "A Jew can never be attached to a place . . . We cannot have roots in the earth of any country, only in the garden that we carry inside us."

Kass, Pnina Moed. *Real Time.*
New York: Clarion. 2004.

A minute-by-minute account in real time of a terrorist bombing in Jerusalem, told from many different perspectives and in varying narrative styles. The plot is suspenseful, involving teenagers whose need to discover their pasts has taken them to Israel, and the denouement is chilling. In addition to its outstanding literary qualities, this is a very rare objective look at modern Israel, Palestinians, and terrorism. Teachers searching for thought-provoking and unbiased fiction about the current Israeli-Palestinian conflict could not do better than to assign this book. Winner of a Sydney Taylor Book Award.

Senesh, Hannah. *Hannah Senesh: Her Life and Diary: The First Complete Edition.*
Woodstock, VT: Jewish Lights. 2004.

This edition reprints most of the material first published in 1972 by Schocken. It contains Hannah Senesh's diaries from ages 13 to 22, along with a selection of her letters and poems. There are two essays about her childhood and about her final days in prison by her mother, and essays by two of Hannah's fellow soldiers. New to this edition is a foreword by Marge Piercy and a preface by Hannah's nephew, Eitan Senesh.

McKain, Mark. *Anti-Semitism.*
Farmington Hills, MI: Gale/Greenhaven. 2005.

This volume in the At Issue Series discusses the many aspects of anti-Semitism and their impact on today's world. Using material culled from magazines, speeches, essays, and newspapers, it treats many controversial topics, including Moslem anti-Semitism. Included are a bibliography, index, and list of contact agencies.

Peet, Mal. *Tamar.*
Cambridge, MA: Candlewick Press. 2007.

Filled with suspense from beginning to end, this dark novel for older teens and adults combines two stories. One is set in wartime Holland and involves espionage, resistance, and a passionate love affair. The modern-day story is about a teenage English girl who has been named Tamar after the heroic Tamar of the resistance. There are many characters in the novel, all so well drawn that they can never be confused with one another except when such is the author's intention. The plot and setting are perfectly realized and the style is clipped, as befits a novel so full of suspense, danger, and secrets. The Jewish content is very slight, almost nil, but the place and action are of Jewish interest. Winner of England's Carnegie Award.

Zusak, Marcus. *The Book Thief.*
New York: Random House. 2006.

Death is the omnipresent commentator in this compelling novel set in Germany during World War II. Genial as he muses on human existence, Death is sometimes frightened at the extent of human cruelty. Germany under Hitler was the epicenter of cruelty, as shown through several years in the life of a German child, the "book thief," her foster family, friends, and the town near Munich where she lives. The style is cryptic and allusive, studded with lists, single, standalone sentences, and several illustrated stories written within the story. The "good German" characters, reminiscent of those in Ursula Hegi's *Stones from the River*, are earthy, flawed, and unforgettable. And while Death (always) has the final word, it is to say "I am haunted by humans." For high school and up and not to be missed!

CHAPTER 14

Remembrance

"The memory of the righteous shall be for a blessing."

Tanakh

PRESCHOOL

Harnick, Sheldon. ***Sunrise, Sunset.*** Illus. by Ian Schoenherr.
New York: HarperCollins. 2005.

This charmingly illustrated story version of the song by Sheldon Harnick and Jerry Bock, written for the musical *Fiddler on the Roof* is perfect for storytelling and a subtle, non-didactic way to introduce young children to the concept of the Jewish lifecycle. Full-page pictures of *shtetl* life and *shtetl* dwellers predominate, with a few lines of the song on each double-page spread. The tone is wistful and life-affirming, as parents watch their children grow up, marry, and have children of their own. Words and music of the song are printed on the last two pages.

Zalben, Jane Breskin. ***Pearl's Marigolds for Grandpa.***
New York: Simon and Schuster. 1997.

The pain of loss and the solace of memory are expressed in this warm story about the death of Pearl's grandpa. Small, delicate illustrations of animals and floral motifs are appealing. Included is information about the funeral customs of various religions.

PRIMARY

Baker, Sharon Reiss. ***A Nickel, a Trolley, a Treasure House.*** Illus. by Beth Peck.
New York: Viking. 2007

In a time gone by, a Jewish boy who loves to draw is taken by his teacher on the trolley to a treasure house—the Metropolitan Museum of Art. The illustrations are muted paintings that softly mimic impressionism. The art and the story gently capture place and time of 100 years ago: City streets, transportation, furnishings at home and school, clothing, and games.

Blumenthal, Deborah. *Aunt Claire's Yellow Beehive Hair.* Illus. by Mary GrandPre. New York: Dial. 2001.

A very handsomely illustrated story about the collecting of family memories. With the help of some older relatives, a little girl assembles memorabilia and reconstructs some of her family's past. There is no Jewish content except for an adult's remark that the album they assemble is like *Kaddish*, a way of remembering the dead.

Borden, Louise. *The Journey That Saved Curious George: The True Wartime Escape of Margaret and H. A. Rey.* Boston: Houghton Mifflin. 2005.

An illustrated nonfiction book that is a triple biography of *Curious George* and his two creators. It echoes the spirit of the Curious George books, with short, pithy sentences and loose, amusing illustrations that include watercolor drawings, maps, diary pages, and photographs. The story documents the lives of H. A. and Margaret Rey, who fled the Nazis from Paris on bicycles with the manuscript of *Curious George* (then called *Fifi*) in their backpacks. The playful style brings life-affirming values to a grim time in history. Except for the fact that the Reys were Jewish, there is no Jewish content.

Cohen, Miriam. *Mimmy and Sophie.* Illus. by Thomas F. Yezerski. New York: Farrar, Straus and Giroux. 1999.

Four mini-stories highlight the relationship between two young sisters growing up in Depression-era Brooklyn. The plots evoke nostalgic images of the past, and the illustrations in comic book format are designed to conjure memories of a world gone by.

Edwards, Michelle. *Papa's Latkes.* Illus. by Stacey Schuett. Cambridge, MA:: Candlewick. 2004.

A sad, sweet and unsentimental story that takes place at Hanukkah, the first a father and his two daughters have observed since Mama died. The theme of the book is "choose life" and this is what the family does, as they remember Mama and bravely celebrate the holiday. Strong illustrations express actions and emotions.

Hoeslandt, Jo. *Star of Fear, Star of Hope.* Illus. by Johanna Kang. New York: Walker. 1996.

A strikingly illustrated story set in France during the Holocaust. A nine-year-old girl fears for the safety of a Jewish friend, who has suddenly disappeared. Her fear is compounded by guilt, because the girls have had an argument. With no comfortable answers to the child's questions, this portrays both personal loss and a communal tragedy involving perpetrators and bystanders. Winner of a Sydney Taylor Book Award.

Hyde, Heidi Smith. *Mendel's Accordion.* Illus. by Johanna Van Der Sterre. Minneapolis, MN: Kar-Ben/Lerner. 2007.

A wistful story about a *klezmer* band. After traveling throughout Eastern Europe playing at weddings and other events, the band members immigrate to the United States to escape persecution and hard times. They all find decent jobs, marry and raise families, and continue playing until their music no longer interests the younger generation. Then, Mendel's great-grandson finds Mendel's old accordion, has it fixed, and starts his own *klezmer* band, playing sad music that made people cry and happy music that made people laugh—just like before. The stylized illustrations are bold and expressive.

Morris, Ann. ***Grandma Esther Remembers: A Jewish-American Family Story.***
   Photographs by Peter Linenthal.
Brookfield, CT: Millbrook Press. 2002.

In this photo essay about a Jewish woman who lives in Brooklyn, Grandma Esther recalls her past, retrieved in part by old family photographs, and is shown volunteering at YIVO (*Yidisher visnshaftlekher institut*, or Institute for Jewish Research) and socializing with her two granddaughters. The photographs that comprise the heart of the book are mostly in color, clear, and well defined. A balanced look at Grandma Esther's past and present life is achieved.

Nivola, Claire. ***Elisabeth.***
New York: Farrar, Straus and Giroux. 1997.

Years after fleeing from the Nazis, a young woman—now living in the United States with a daughter of her own—is reunited with the beloved doll she left behind in Germany. The writing style and illustrations are elegant, restrained, and moving.

Oberman, Sheldon. ***The Always Prayer Shawl.*** Illus. by Ted Lewin.
Honesdale, PA: Boyds Mills Press. 1995.

Expressively illustrated, this moving story shows how Jewish tradition is handed on from one generation to another. From life is Tsarist Russia to present-day America, continuity, pride and devotion to tradition are exemplified by a grandfather, grandson, and a cherished *tallit*. Winner of a Sydney Taylor Book Award.

Oberman, Sheldon. ***By the Hanukkah Light.*** Illus. by Neil Waldman.
Honesdale, PA: Boyds Mills Press. 1997.

Parallels between ancient and modern Jewish history are shown in a story celebrating religious freedom through the symbol of a family's Hanukkah menorah that survived the Holocaust. A warm tone suffuses hope into chilling history.

Pastor, Melanie Joy. ***Wishes for One More Day.*** Illus. by Jacqui Grantford.
New York: Flashlight Press. 2006.

When Anna and Joey's grandfather dies, they assuage their grief by making a list of all of the things they would do with Poppy if they had had just one more day. Jewish mourning customs are briefly shown, and the story empowers children dealing with the death of a loved one.

Poole, Josephine. *Anne Frank.* Illus. by Angela Barrett.
New York: Alfred A. Knopf. 2005.

Most illustrated books with Holocaust settings are for older children, but this one serves as both an introduction to Anne Frank and to the cataclysmic times in which she lived. The experiences of the Frank family are placed in historical context, from their move to Holland, their exclusion from normal life, their hiding in the secret annex, their betrayal, and the death of all of the family but Otto Frank, whose survival resulted in Anne's diary becoming known to the world. Barrett's elegant illustrations are an essential part of the story that is told because they place the Franks and their confined existence within expressively rendered scenes of both historic and domestic significance. An endnote describes the publication of the diary and gives a detailed chronology.

Regelson, Abraham. *The Dolls' Journey to Eretz Israel.*
Miami, FL: Biblio Books International. 2005.

Abraham Regelson emigrated to Israel with his family in 1933. His daughter had to leave her beloved dolls behind and they were later sent to her by a friend. Regelson wrote this story for his daughter, publishing it first in serial form in the Friday children's supplement to the Hebrew newspaper, *Davar*. It was well-received and was published in book form, going through several editions and becoming beloved by a generation of Israeli children. It has now been re-published in Hebrew and English, with a translation by Sharona Regelson Tel-Oren and with its verses translated by Naomi Regelson Bar-Natan. The story is a fanciful one, written in a quaint style that at times resembles biblical prose. The pen-and-ink illustrations are from earlier editions. Of historical significance, the story will still have appeal to little girls.

Ross, Lillian Hammer. *Bubbe Leah and Her Paper Children.* Illus. by Mary Morgan.
Philadelphia: Jewish Publication Society. 1985.

A little girl named Chava wonders who these paper children are that her aunt, *Bubbe* Leah, talks about so wistfully. What she learns mixes the sadness of separation from family and friends with hope for a better future in America. The softly colored, pretty illustrations make the *shtetl* setting rather idyllic looking.

Rothenberg, Joan. *Matzah Ball Soup.*
New York: Hyperion. 1999.

When Rosie helps her grandmother make *matzah* balls for the family *Seder*, she wonders why they make so many. Grandma explains to her the family tradition of having four in each bowl. Rosie is shown how traditions are made and why they are worth preserving. Good for reading aloud.

Rouss, Sylvia. *Reach for the Stars: A Little Torah's Journey.* Illus. by Rosalie Ofer.
New York: Pitspopany. 2004.

Joachim Joseph, nicknamed Yoya, gave the "little *Torah*" to Israeli astronaut, Ilan

Ramon, to take with him on the ill-fated space shuttle *Columbia*. It was given to Joseph in Bergen-Belsen by Rabbi Simon Dasberg, who had smuggled it into the camp and used it to tutor Joseph for his *Bar Mitzvah*. This juxtaposition of events, lives, and deaths is the scaffolding upon which the story rests. It is poignantly written, telling of incredible courage with simplicity and conviction. Children reading the story will be moved but not shattered by the loss, because the narrative focuses on positive human ideals rather than tragedy. An excellent format, with large color illustrations, reinforces this positive focus.

Russo, Marisabina. *Always Remember Me.*
New York: Simon and Schuster/Atheneum. 2005.

The author-illustrator tells the story of her own family history, focusing on the four strong Jewish women (her grandmother, mother, and two aunts) who most influenced her life. It is told by a grandmother to a little girl about her first life, before she came to America, and is a story of love, courage, and tragedy, as the four women are caught up in the Holocaust, suffering but surviving. Each character is carefully individualized, with illustrations made to look like real-life photographs and documents. The story is reassuring and non-threatening, making it appropriate for somewhat younger children than is usual for Holocaust stories.

Sasso, Sandy Eisenberg. *Abuelita's Secret Matzahs.* Illus. by Diana Bryer.
Cincinnati, OH: Emmis Books. 2005.

Jacobo notices that his grandmother, or *abuelita*, celebrates Easter a little differently from everyone else: She doesn't serve ham and makes tortillas without yeast. When he asks her why, she answers, "It is the way of our family." After Jacobo meets a Jewish child, visits with him, and attends his family's *Seder*, he sees more similarities between Jewish customs and those practiced by *abuelita*. When he presses her for an answer, she reveals the family's long kept secret: Their ancestors were Spanish Jews who converted but continued to pass some Jewish practices down through the generations. When Jacobo asks her what he is, Christian or Jewish, she tells him that he will have to decide that for himself as he grows older. The illustrations are excellent, in a folk art style that extends the Southwestern setting and adds some emotional depth.

Schnur, Steven. *The Tie Man's Miracle.* Illus. by Stephen T. Johnson.
New York: Morrow. 1995.

Told by a little boy, this is the sad yet hopeful story of an elderly man who sells ties and no longer celebrates Hanukkah, because his own family has all perished in the Holocaust. Urged by the child's family to join them in lighting the eighth light, he reveals his sadness but tells them another story that, when it appears to come true later that evening, gives them hope. Large color illustrations are excellent in presenting realistic details and, in particular, the characters' emotions and individual faces.

Sim, Dorrith. *In My Pocket.* Illus. by Gerald Fitzgerald.
San Diego: Harcourt Brace. 1997.

On a July morning in 1939, a young Jewish child sails from Holland to the safety of a new life in Scotland. A simply told, strikingly illustrated story of the *Kinder-transport*—a rescue operation initiated by British Jews for Jewish children in Nazi-occupied countries, following the *Kristallnacht* on November 9, 1938.

Sofer, Barbara. *Shalom, Haver: Goodbye, Friend.*
Rockville, MD: Kar-Ben Copies. 1996.

The assassination of Israeli Prime Minister Yitzhak Rabin inspired this moving photo-essay about his life and death. It is written in Hebrew and English and emphasizes his human qualities, using family reminiscences and photographs. Winner of a Sydney Taylor Book Award.

Tarbescu, Edith. *Annushka's Voyage.* Illus. by Lydia Dabcovich.
New York: Clarion. 1998.

A simply told and charmingly illustrated story about two sisters who leave their native village and grandparents to be reunited with their widowed father in New York City. They endure the confusion and difficulties of the voyage yet savor each new experience. For these heroines, past and future are linked by a pair of ancestral candlesticks that they take with them as they make the transition from one way of life to another.

Watts, Irene. *A Telling Time.* Illus. by Kathryn E. Shoemaker.
Vancouver: Tradewind Books. 2004.

An illustrated version of the Purim tale, set within two framing stories. In the slightest of them, a present-day grandmother tells her granddaughter about an incident that happened during her last Purim in Vienna. The story then moves back in time to Nazi-occupied Vienna, where a group of children listens to their rabbi tell them the story of Queen Esther. Nazis come to arrest him, but after he sees the children to the street, he vanishes. The grandmother—one of the children who was with the rabbi—ascribes this to a miracle, thus ending the Holocaust strand of the story with hope. The illustrations are an important part of the story, especially in establishing mood and setting. This novel way of remembering two epochal Jewish narratives is very effective.

Woodruff, Elvira. *The Memory Coat.* Illus. by Michael Dooling.
New York: Scholastic. 1999.

How clever, imaginative Rachel saves her cousin Grisha from being turned back at Ellis Island is fluently told and artfully illustrated in this story of emigration from Tsarist Russia. The historical notes at the back of the book document the inspiration for, and accuracy of, the story.

ELEMENTARY

Ashby, Ruth. *Anne Frank: Young Diarist.*
New York: Simon and Schuster. 2005.

Part of the Childhood of World Figures Series, this book for children too young to read the actual diary closely resembles the format of the paperback edition of the diary. The narrative includes many conversational quotes and Anne's reflections from the diary.

Ben-Zvi, Hava. *Eva's Journey: A Young Girl's True Story.*
Lincoln, NE: iUniverse. 2004.

A survivor's memoir, this is set in Poland and Israel, moving chronologically through the Nazi terror and on to Communist domination. The spare, first-person narrative speaks to readers, connecting history with hope. Naive pen-and-ink drawings, maps, and family photographs add interest.

Brown, Jonatha A., and Elizabeth Hudson-Goff. *Anne Frank.*
    Illus. by Guus Floor, D. McHargue, and Jonathan Timmons
Milwaukee, WI: World Almanac Library. 2006.

The well-known story of Anne Frank is given a new twist as a graphic novel in this addition to the World Almanac Library's Graphic Biographies Series. The Frank family's life before the war, in hiding, and their final fate are depicted in large, realistic, brightly-colored panels. The format may appeal to younger children, but some grim pictures of women and children huddled inside the gas chambers of Birkenau make it more appropriate for children ages 10–12 and not for the 4–8 age range that the publisher recommends.

Dublin, Anne. *Written on the Wind.* Illus. by Avril Woodend.
Vancouver: Hodgepog Books. 2001.

A historical novel set in Toronto in 1954 at the time of a disastrous hurricane. Readers get a "keyhole" glimpse into the life of a Jewish immigrant family from the perspective of eight- or nine-year-old Sara who, with her brother, is rapidly learning how to be a Canadian while her parents seem to retain their old world ways. Sara's friendship with a neighborhood storekeeper and some sessions with a Ouija board precipitate the story's conflict and suspense. The story ends with the aftermath of the hurricane, which changed Toronto forever. Songs, jump rope rhymes, and commercial brand names are sprinkled through the narrative, adding authenticity to an appealing story.

Ferber, Brenda A. *Julia's Kitchen.*
New York: Farrar, Straus and Giroux. 2006.

A moving story about death, grief, and acceptance. Eleven-year-old Cara's mother and younger sister have just died in a house fire when the story opens; how Cara and her father deal with the aftermath is the central part of the plot. Written in a sincere style, with believable, empathetic characters and an upbeat tone despite the sadness of the plot, *Julia's Kitchen* reveals the centrality of Judaism to the character's lives. Winner of a Sydney Taylor Book Award.

Finkelstein, Norman H. *The Other 1492: Jewish Settlement in the New World.*
New York: Scribner's. 1989.

A well-written account of Jewish life in Spain, the expulsion, flight, and eventually freedom. Succinct sketches of outstanding Jews of the period are included, along with a bibliography and index. A good introduction for teaching children about 350 years of Jewish life in America, celebrated in 2004.

Finkelstein, Norman H. *Remember Not to Forget: A Memory of the Holocaust.*
    Illus. by Lars Hokanson and Lois Hokanson.
Philadelphia: Jewish Publication Society, 2004.

A straightforward presentation of anti-Semitism, the Holocaust, and its aftermath, illustrated with stark black-and-white pictures. Finkelstein is a consummate writer of non-fiction for children, and while this book is much simpler than most of his others, it is clear, direct, and powerful. Intended as an introduction to the subject for children in grades 3 through 5, this edition of the book—originally published in 1985—is a paperback reissue.

Friedman, D. Dina. *Playing Dad's Song.*
New York: Farrar, Straus and Giroux. 2006.

Gus mourns for his father who has been killed in the attack on the World Trade Centers. He's an insecure, lonely boy who spends a lot of his free time with a blanket over his head, remembering Dad and wishing he would come back. Several events mark a turning point for Gus. Through music lessons, a school assignment on the composer and violinist Nicolo Paganini, and his sister's encouragement to try out for a part in the school play, Gus's confidence begins to build and he finds he can honor his father's memory best when engaged with the world. The author develops Gus's character with disarming honesty, melding it with an absorbing plot and a theme that exalts the healing powers of creativity and imagination. The slight Jewish content is an integral part of the story, and sensitive readers will cheer for Gus's quiet achievements.

Goldman, Alex J. *I Am a Holocaust Torah: The Story of the Saving of 1,564 Torahs.*
Jerusalem: Gefen. 2000.

The subject of this story is the confiscation and/or destruction of Jewish religious objects during the Holocaust. The author tells how many *Torah* scrolls, which the Nazis stored in Prague, were rehabilitated and distributed to synagogues around the world as memorials to the Holocaust. The focus is on a 300-year-old *Torah* from Kosava Hors, a Czech village. Although told with reverence and filled with information about how *Torahs* are written and cared for, a story featuring a talking *Torah* to which human characteristics are ascribed reads rather awkwardly.

Hautzig, Esther. *A Picture of Grandmother.* Illus. by Beth Peck.
New York: Farrar, Straus and Giroux, 2002.

Set in Vilna, Lithuania, in 1939, this is the story of Sara's discovery that her grandmother is really her step-grandmother. As the story unfolds with a hint of mystery and a trace of family conflict, the reader gets a glimpse into the life of a cultivated Jewish family on the brink of unthinkable disaster. The events to come are not part of the story, which looks back fondly at a once-loved place and at family memories. The soft black-and-white sketches have the quality of old photographs. A quiet gem of a story, based on the author's childhood.

Hermann, Spring. *Anne Frank: Hope in the Shadow of the Holocaust.*
Berkeley Heights, NJ: Enslow. 2005.

The author includes salient facts of Holocaust history, interweaving them with excerpts from the diary, a map, photographs, anecdotes, and personal characteristics gleaned from every book written about Anne Frank and interviews from oral sources, including many remarks by Anne's close friends, neighbors, teachers, and Miep Gies. In addition to a timeline, there are chapter notes (in which all sources used are noted by chapter), a glossary, further reading, Internet addresses, and an index. Part of the Holocaust Heroes and Nazi Criminals Series.

Hesse, Karen. *The Stone Lamp.* Illus. by Brian Pinkney.
New York: Hyperion. 2003.

Eight powerful poems in free verse, arranged chronologically and told in the voices of Jewish children who lived during periods of crisis in Jewish history. Each poem is matched by a succinct statement about the historical event and dramatic illustrations. The massacre of the Jews of York, the burning of Jewish books in Paris, the Inquisition, the Holocaust, and the assassination of Yitzhak Rabin are among the subjects of the poems, which the author says she chose because they show that the light of the Jewish people may flicker but never goes out.

Kacer, Kathy. *The Secret of Gabi's Dresser.*
Toronto: Second Story Press. 1999.

The narrator tells her American grandchildren of a happy childhood in rural Slovakia and a near-miraculous escape from Nazi occupiers. Based on the experiences of the author's grandmother, the story is presented as historical fiction.

Kramer, Ann. *Anne Frank: The Young Writer Who Told the World Her Story.*
Washington, DC: National Geographic. 2007

An appealing format, with many photographs, maps, and quotes, will draw intermediate level readers to this brief biography of Anne Frank. It traces her life from birth to death, adding information about the Holocaust and about the young writer's lasting legacy.

Krinitz, Esther Nisenthal, and Bernice Steinhardt. *Memories of Survival.*
New York: Hyperion. 2005.

Esther Krinitz survived the Holocaust and lived to raise a family in the United States. Years after the war, she shared her memories with her children by sewing embroidered fabric collages depicting scenes from her early life. Her daughter, Bernice Steinhardt, has taken some of these amazing embroideries, added to the comments written by her mother, and created a book that is outstanding in its immediacy and beauty.

Lasky, Kathryn. *Dreams in the Golden Country: The Diary of Zipporah Feldman,*
   a Jewish Immigrant Girl.
New York: Scholastic. 1998.

Zippy emigrates from Russia to the United States in the early 1900s. Her diary tells readers about many aspects of the immigrant experience. Its tone is of hope and optimism as her dreams come true. Part of a popular series, written by a notable author.

Lee, Carol Ann. *Anne Frank's Story: Her Life Retold for Children.*
Mahwah, NJ: Troll Communications. 2002.

In a chatty and readable style, the author traces Anne Frank's life from a comfortable and happy childhood in Germany and the Netherlands, through almost two years in hiding, to a horrendous death in Bergen-Belsen just two weeks before the camp was liberated. The diary is the centerpiece of the narrative, but some lesser known facts emerge, and Anne's lively, sometimes abrasive, personality is captured. Especially for readers who are not yet ready to read the diary.

Lee, Carol Ann, and Jacqueline Van Maarsen. *A Friend Called Anne.*
New York: Viking. 2005.

A heartfelt memoir that explores the friendship between Anne Frank and Jacqueline Van Maarsen, told in Jacqueline's voice. The two girls attended school together in Amsterdam, and the story recalls many of the adventures that they had. Only after the war did Jacqueline learn what had happened to Anne, her mother, and sister. She herself survived because her mother convinced the Gestapo that they were Catholic. Accompanied by black-and-white photographs, a timeline, and a recommended book list.

Lehman-Wilzig, Tami. *Keeping the Promise: A Torah's Journey.*
   Illus. by Craig Orback.
Minneapolis, MN: Kar-Ben/Lerner. 2004.

A fictionalized and illustrated account of the little *Torah* that was taken aboard the space shuttle *Columbia* by Israeli astronaut, Ilan Ramon. The focus is on Rabbi

Jacob Dasberg of the Netherlands, who secretly took the little *Torah* with him when he was deported by the Nazis to Bergen-Belsen. Rabbi Dasberg used the *Torah* to tutor a boy in his barracks for his *Bar Mitzvah*, afterwards giving the *Torah* to the boy. That boy escaped and later, in Israel, gave the *Torah* to Ramon to take into space, telling its story to the world.

Levine, Karen. *Hana's Suitcase.*
Toronto: Second Story Press. 2002.

This true story unites decency across time, space, and nationality to honor the memory of a child who died in the Holocaust. Hana Brady perished at Auschwitz, but a suitcase with her name on it became the centerpiece of a small Holocaust museum in Japan. Motivated by the questions of children who visited the museum, the museum's director searched until she found not only some of Hana Brady's artwork but also her brother, George, who had survived and lived in Canada. This is based on a Canadian Broadcasting Company's radio program produced by the author and is published in the United States by Albert Whitman Company (2003). Winner of a Sydney Taylor Book Award.

Levine, Karen, and Emil Sher. *Hana's Suitcase on Stage.*
Toronto: Second Story Press. 2007.

Emil Sher has written a stage adaptation of Levine's Sydney Taylor Award-winning true story, *Hana's Suitcase*. Able to be performed with a minimum amount of staging, lighting and props, this nine-character play can be used for teaching about the Holocaust or performed on Yom Ha Shoah in remembrance of the Holocaust, extending the message of tolerance to all classroom students who read or perform it.

Littlesugar, Amy. *Willy and Max: A Holocaust Story.* Illus. by William Low.
New York: Philomel. 2006.

When Willy was a boy in Antwerp, he became friends with a Jewish boy named Max, whose father purchased a painting of "The Lady" from Willy's father's antique shop. Lushly colored, soft-edged illustrations and a gentle text evoke a world of childhood camaraderie clouded by war and the Nazi invasion of Belgium. Before Max and his father flee Antwerp, they bring the painting to Willy's father, asking that he hide it for them. That is not to be: The painting is stolen by a German. At this point, the story fast-forwards to the present, when Will—now an old man living in America—is called by a museum curator who has traced the painting to him. Will sees that it is turned over to Max's family, in memory of his friendship with Max. As well as being a very moving story, Willy and Max also deals with a subject—stolen art—that has not appeared in Judaic children's literature previously. It is highly recommended and accessible to children as young as third grade.

McDonough, Yona A. *The Doll with the Yellow Star.*
Illus. by Kimberly Bulcken Root.
New York: Henry Holt. 2003.

Claudine is an eight-year-old French Jewish child with a loving family, a charming home, and a new doll, whom she names Violette and who appears to be the same age as Claudine. When the Nazis occupy France, countless hardships and dangers beset the Jews, and Claudine especially hates having to wear a yellow star. In fact, she gives Violette the option of not wearing one. When Claudine is evacuated to the United States, she loses her doll and remains in despair for both the doll and her parents. Her father does return and, in a surprise ending, so does Violette, inspiring Claudine to find a new way to be closer to the memory of her mother. An emotionally authentic story with illustrations by the illustrator of the Sydney Taylor Award winner, *The Peddler's Gift.*

Millman, Isaac. *Hidden Child.*
New York: Farrar, Straus and Giroux. 2005.

Vivid memories of his boyhood as a hidden child during the Holocaust in France permeate Millman's moving account. It is told in short chapters or episodes, illustrated copiously with his illustrations that sketch—in color—scenes, people and experiences from his life during the span of the narrative. Exceptional for the immediacy and ease of the writing and the engrossing nature of the art.

Moss, Marissa. *Hannah's Journal.*
San Diego: Harcourt/Silver Whistle. 2000.

The exciting story of Hannah's voyage from Russia to America is told through her journal entries. The format, with lined pages, hand lettering, and Hannah's drawings and comments in the margins, is especially appealing.

Nerlove, Miriam. *Flowers on the Wall.*
New York: Simon and Schuster. 1996.

An illustrated story about the life of a Polish Jewish family under the Nazis. First, there is no money and very little food. Then come roundups of Jews. The family paints flowers on the wall to keep up their spirits but they, too, are taken—to Treblinka, "gone forever." Although this looks like a picture book, it is an emotionally engaging, very sad introduction to Holocaust study and more appropriate for elementary grade children.

Oirich, Alan, and Ron Randall. *Jewish Hero Corps #1.*
New York: Judaica Press. 2003.

The superheroes in this new comic book series include *Menorah* Man, *Dreidel* Maidel, and *Minyan* Man. Their superpowers are used to fight the evil Fobots, who seek to destroy Jewish memories. This initial issue shows how the superheroes acquired their powers. Readers learn about Judaism and Jewish symbols as they follow the adventure. Teacher's guide is available at www@jewishsuperhero.com.

Pushker, Gloria Teles. *Toby Belfer Visits Ellis Island.* Illus. by Judith Hierstein. Gretna, LA: Pelican. 2003.

Toby's Gram tells her the story of Gram's mother, Raezel, who came to America from Poland with her parents and six siblings. Reasons why Jews emigrated, their experiences aboard ship and at Ellis Island, and their subsequent absorption into American life are all touched upon, making this a pleasant introduction to immigration for primary age children. The illustrations are, as usual for the Toby Belfer stories, stylish and engaging.

Ringel, Robert, and Susan S. Ringel. *Inside the Rain Barrel.* Cleveland, OH: Susan S. Ringel. 2005.

Subtitled "A grandfather tells his granddaughter the true story of how a Jewish prayer book—and a young man—survived the Holocaust," this is based on the authors' family history. Illustrated with color photographs, it chronicles the events that led to an old family prayer book, dated at around 1890, being found after World War II by an ancestor of its original owner. Suggestions for researching one's own family history are included.

Rocklin, Joanne. *Strudel Stories.*
New York: Delacorte Press. 1999.

Several generations of a Jewish family are brought to life in this charming collection of linked stories. Strudel and stories are the connecting threads of a tradition that begins in Russia, is brought to America, and changed but continued through the process of acculturation. Short chapters offer vignettes of family members at different stages of their lives and, in some of the settings, that typify Eastern European Jewish immigration.

Rubin, Susan Goldman, and Ela Weissberger. *The Cat with the Yellow Star: Coming of Age in Terezin.*
New York: Holiday House. 2006.

Impeccably documented and abundantly illustrated with photographs and reproductions of artwork by the children of Terezin concentration camp, this is a memoir of a child who survived. Written with clarity and an emphasis on hope rather than cruelty, it shows how important strong human bonds, dedicated teachers, and art were to sustaining hope. Ela was chosen to play the part of the cat in the children's opera, *Brundibar*, which was performed many times in Terezin by prisoners, including adult musicians who had performed the opera before the Nazi takeover of Czechoslovakia. Ela and many of her girlfriends reunited after the war, and the final part of the book is one of triumph, not tragedy.

Senker, Cath. *Anne Frank—Voice of Hope.*
Austin, TX: Raintree Steck-Vaughn. 2001.

If another simplified biography of Anne Frank is needed, this photographic essay is more than acceptable. It is a succinct and respectful treatment of Anne's life, set in its historical context. The numerous photographs—mostly black-and-white—are clearly captioned and convey to readers in grades 3–5 the human tragedy of the Holocaust.

Toll, Nelly. *Behind the Secret Window: A Memoir of a Hidden Childhood During World War Two.*
New York: Puffin. 2003.

Originally published by Dial in 1993, this outstanding memoir of the Holocaust is now available in paperback, with the illustrations of the original here in black and white. As a testament to the redemptive power of the imagination, it is akin to *The Key is Lost* by Ida Vos, *Samir and Yonatan* by Gabrielle Carmi, *Katerina* by Kathryn Winter, and *Fireflies in the Dark* by Susan Goldman Rubin.

Waldman, Neil. *Say-Hey and the Babe: Two Mostly True Baseball Stories.*
New York: Holiday House. 2006.

Lore and legend, fact and fiction are blended into an absorbing exploration of baseball and its Depression variant, stickball, in one of Waldman's most readable books. An excellent format, with short, dated chapters, supports an interesting plot and captivating information. Even those who are not sports fans will be drawn into the story, which is enhanced by very fine illustrations.

Whiteman, Dorit Bader. *Lonek's Journey: The True Story of a Boy's Escape to Freedom.*
Long Island City, NY: Star Bright Books. 2005.

Based on an adult book by the author, this tells the story of the escape of thousands of Polish Jews from the Nazis through the experiences of one boy. After fleeing with his family from Poland to Siberia, he is separated from his mother and finds himself to be one of the more than 900 Jewish children known as the "Teheran children." This version covers Lonek's two year journey over thousands of miles by land and sea to find freedom in Palestine. There are maps and photographs throughout.

Woronoff, Kristen. *Anne Frank: Voice of Hope.*
Farmington Hills, MI: Blackbirch Press. 2002.

This entry in the publisher's Famous Women Series is more photo illustration than text. What text there is presents an adequate outline of Anne's life and death. Its brevity and accessibility will make this a useful work. Suggested for readers in grades 3–5, it also will attract older readers who want a thin book about a serious subject.

MIDDLE SCHOOL

Anne Frank in The World.
New York: Alfred A. Knopf. 2001.

Compiled by the Anne Frank House, this slim volume contains more than 225 black-and-white photographs. They reveal the Frank family, the Nazi era, and modern neo-Nazis. The text and photographs are good background material for the study of World War II and the Holocaust but, alas, there is no index.

Bayer, Linda. *Elie Wiesel: Spokesman for Remembrance.*
New York: Rosen. 2000.

A clear portrait of Elie Wiesel emerges in this well-organized biography that treats both its subject in particular and Holocaust survivors in general perceptively. Excerpts from Wiesel's writing are given along with many black-and-white photographs.

Berenbaum, Michael. *A Promise to Remember: The Holocaust in the Words and Voices of Its Survivors.*
New York: Bulfinch Press. 2003.

An oversize book that is part text, part illustration, part audio, and part interactive. An audio CD presents survivors' testimonies. The text is organized into 15 short chapters on such subjects as the assault against the Jews, the Warsaw Ghetto uprising, and liberation. It is illustrated with documentary photographs. Inserted in many of the pages are replicas of documents, which can be pulled out and handled independently of the book. They are its most powerful feature and include false identity papers, a color photo of a burning synagogue, two recipes written by women prisoners in Terezin, a copy of a Nazi "resettlement" order, an invitation to the Wansee Conference, etc. Excellent as an introduction to the Holocaust for middle school students and for families to read together.

Beyer, Mark. *Emmanuel Ringelblum: Historian of the Warsaw Ghetto.*
New York: Rosen. 2001.

Through the archival work of social historian Ringelblum and the secret group he led, primary source documents of the Nazis' extermination of Jews, particularly in the Warsaw Ghetto, were assembled and have survived. This factual biography imparts information about Ringelblum and his family, about the historical times in which he worked, and about his professional dedication to preserving a record of what he rightly inferred would be an epochal period in human history.

Bovson, Mara, and Allan Zullo. *Survivors: True Stories of Children of the Holocaust.*
New York: Scholastic. 2005.

Nine innocent children tell of the horror that entered their lives with the Holocaust. How did they survive? What depths of belief in self, in the ultimate defeat of evil and the return to normalcy, help them survive? What did luck have to do with it? Their stories are moving, captivating, and inspiring.

Denenberg, Barry. *Shadow Life: A Portrait of Anne Frank and Her Family.*
New York: Scholastic. 2005.

This work of "faction" is derived from all of the known information about the life of Anne Frank and her family, with the addition of a fictional diary written by Anne's older sister, Margot. A chronology; a bibliographic essay explaining the sources used, including books, videos, and films; a bibliography; and an index are included. Although the book gives Margot Frank a role she did not actually have, a valid picture of these disastrous times for Jews is painted.

Faigen, Anne G. *New World Waiting.*
Pittsburgh, PA: The History Company. 2006.

Set in Pittsburgh in 1906, this novel depicts Willa Cather as a high school teacher who sets high standards for her students and helps Molly, a 15-year-old Jewish immigrant from Poland, adjust to life in America. Under the author's skillful writing, the characters of Molly, her family and her friends—Victor (Vittorio), who is Italian, and Cleo, who is African-American—come alive. Faigen shows how Willa Cather based her ideas for short stories on her Pittsburgh experiences and the lives of people like Molly, Cleo, and Vittorio.

Frank, Anne. *The Diary of a Young Girl: The Definitive Edition,*
edited by Otto H. Frank and Mirjam Pressler.
New York: Doubleday. 1995.

This edition contains material, much of it having to do with Anne's emerging physical and emotional maturity, that was not included in the first edition of the *Diary*. There are many books about Anne Frank, but this is essential reading.

Giddens, Sandra. *Escape: Teens Who Escaped the Holocaust to Freedom.*
New York: Rosen. 1999.

Four accounts of teens who escaped extermination are given, mostly by the survivors themselves. Although they lost most of their families, they went on to build new lives. The author provides historical background and sketches of important Holocaust-era figures. Illustrated with photographs and maps giving escape routes.

Goldberg, Neal, and Miriam Liebermann. *Saying Goodbye: A Handbook for Teens Dealing with Loss and Mourning.*
Southfield, MI: Targum/Feldheim. 2004.

This informative handbook confronts death from a Jewish perspective, based on Jewish law and custom. The authors are a therapist and a social worker. The first section of the book discusses death through real-life stories, citing Jewish legal sources and customs when appropriate. Each chapter in this section ends with recommended reading from the second section of the book. This section is a collection of writings by lay people and professionals. There is no bibliography or index. A constructive and helpful book, written from an Orthodox perspective.

Hillman, Laura. *I Will Plant You a Lilac Tree: A Memoir of a Schindler's List Survivor.*
New York: Simon and Schuster/Atheneum. 2005.

In this autobiography of Hannelore Wolff, who was born in 1924 in Germany, she recalls in simple, direct, and unassuming language what happened to her and her family from 1940 to 1945. Through Polish ghettoes and eight concentration camps, her nightmare journey is made bearable by fellow Jews who helped each other endure the mental and physical torture of the Nazis. The last miracle to save Hannelore was becoming part of the group of Jews whom Oskar Schindler kept from death.

Lasky, Kathryn. *Blood Secret.*
New York: HarperCollins. 2004.

Mute since she was five, when her hippie mother abandoned her, Jerry has been sent by Catholic Charities to live with her elderly great-great-aunt in rural New Mexico. When she discovers a trunk in the basement filled with very old family relics, Jerry is able to travel back in time to fourteenth-century Spain, where the blood secret that her family has kept for over 600 years began. Through her experiences in the past at various times in the tragic saga of Spanish Jewry, Jerry begins to understand why her aunt—a practicing Catholic—lights candles on Friday nights, doesn't mix milk with meat, and throws pieces of dough into the oven before she bakes bread. Her new awareness of her Jewish heritage and the understanding that grows between teenage Jerry and 90-year-old Aunt Costanza give her the courage to speak and to engage with life once again. Lasky's grasp of this complicated material is deft. Each of the many characters speaks in a distinctive voice that helps establish both the setting and personality. The plot is complex and suspenseful, with the past and present woven together flawlessly. Some gruesome scenes of burnings are juxtaposed with lyrical descriptions of the New Mexican countryside. All in all, this is one of an accomplished writer's most accomplished novels.

Lee, Carol. *Anne Frank and the Children of the Holocaust.*
New York: Penguin. 2006.

For young people to comprehend that one million Jewish children died in the Holocaust and that thousands of others survived only by hiding, it is helpful for them to learn about the individual lives of individual children. Most of this book concerns Anne Frank's life before and during the Holocaust, but on a much more comprehensive level than that found in her famous diary. Anne's story is interspersed with accounts written by other young people, as well as reminiscences of surviving family and friends, who were eyewitnesses to Hitler's growing influence and the effect of anti-Jewish laws on Anne and other Jewish children as they lost their childhood to arrest, imprisonment, hiding, concentration camps, illness, and death. This factual account is a worthwhile companion to fictional versions such as *Walk the Dark Streets* by Edith Baer and *Something Remains* by Inge Barth-Grozinger.

Lobel, Anita. *No Pretty Pictures: A Child of War.*
New York: HarperCollins/Greenwillow. 1998.

Anita Lobel is a well-known illustrator of children's books. This memoir of her childhood during the Holocaust is frank and unsentimental, showing the horrors of concentration camp imprisonment and the contradictions of refugee life.

Matas, Carol. *Turned Away: The World War II Diary of Devorah Bernstein: Winnipeg, Manitoba, 1941.*
Markham, ON: Scholastic Canada. 2005.

Part of the Dear Canada Series, this is written in a diary format, combining chatty observations with deep ponderings, including thoughts about relatives stranded in Europe and brothers fighting on the European and Pacific fronts. Canadian and world history, including news headlines, are woven smoothly into Devorah's journal. Devorah is a likable character, and readers will learn something about the World War II period as they enjoy a readable story.

Meltzer, Milton. *Remember the Days.* Illus. by Harvey Dinnerstein.
New York: Zenith. 1974.

This sober chronicle of Jewish life in America emphasizes anti-Semitism and the losses that Jews faced as they became Americanized. It traces migration to America from 1654 to what was the present when the book was published and Jewish–African American relations were taking a downturn. The focus is almost entirely on *Ashkenazic* Jews. The format is also somewhat grim: Close set type and dark, charcoal drawings.

Moore, Lisa. *Elie Wiesel: Surviving the Holocaust, Speaking Out Against Genocide.*
Berkeley Heights, NJ: Enslow. 2005.

This fully documented biography, part of the Holocaust Heroes and Nazi Criminals Series, depicts the life of the great humanitarian, writer, and Nobel Peace Laureate (1986), who survived the horrors of Auschwitz to become the world's foremost champion for human rights, anti-racism, and anti-genocide. Includes chapter notes, a bibliography, glossary, timeline, Internet addresses, and an index.

Nir, Yehuda. *The Lost Childhood: A World War II Memoir.*
New York: Scholastic. 2002.

The author's Polish-Jewish family led a comfortable life until the Nazi occupation. After his father was arrested, Nir—then 11 years old—his mother and sister began a four-year odyssey of false identity. Because they had the good fortune to look Polish and were lucky enough to know a skilled forger, they lived, worked, and socialized with Nazis and anti-Semitic Poles. Today, Nir is a psychiatrist who speaks regularly to groups about his lost childhood.

Ollendorff, Valli. *Fate Did Not Let Me Go: A Mother's Farewell Letter.*
Gretna, LA: Pelican. 2003.

A letter written by a woman to her middle son, who had escaped to America, just before she was deported by the Nazis to Terezin. The small format book features the letter in English and the original German, plus family portraits and photographs. It has been made into a film documentary.

Patz, Nancy. *Who Was the Woman Who Wore the Hat?*
New York: Dutton. 2003.

Inspired by the author-illustrator's reaction to a woman's hat she saw in a glass case in Amsterdam's Jewish Historical Museum, this is a prose poem meditating on the identity of the woman and on her probable fate during the Holocaust. The fate of other Dutch Jews and, indeed, of every human being is implicated in the text and in the striking illustrations, which consist of somber-toned watercolors, pencil drawings, and old photographs. The overall effect is deeply moving and accessible to a wide range of readers. Winner of a Sydney Taylor Book Award.

Reiss, Johanna. *The Upstairs Room.*
New York: Crowell. 1992

For two years during the German occupation of Holland, Annie and her younger sister were hidden in a cramped room in a Dutch farmhouse. This fictionalized account of their experiences are continued in a sequel called *The Journey Back.*

Rubin, Susan Goldman. *Searching for Anne Frank: Letters from Amsterdam to Iowa.*
New York: Harry A. Abrams/Simon Wiesenthal Center. 2003.

Based on the author's research at the Wiesenthal Center's archives, this is an account of a very brief correspondence between Anne and Margot Frank and Juanita and Betty Wagner from Iowa. Despite this slim connection, the author instills a sense of personal involvement between the two families and provides an interesting contrast between life in America during World War II and in Nazi-occupied Holland. Extensively illustrated with photographs and maps.

Schroeder, Peter W., and Dagmar Schroeder-Hildebrand. *Six Million Paper Clips: The Making of a Children's Holocaust Memorial.*
Minneapolis, MN: Kar-Ben/Lerner. 2004.

Color photographs expand on the written account of a Holocaust memorial project in a town with no minorities. Whitwell, Tennessee is the setting; a school principal decided that diversity should be part of the curriculum, and the Holocaust was chosen as a unit of study. As the students became more involved with the subject, they began to collect paper clips to represent the number of Jews killed in the Holocaust. Coincidences mounted, and a German connection was found. The story of how they were able to create an actual museum makes for fascinating and inspiring reading. There is also a documentary film on the same subject.

Smith, Frank Dabba, and Mendel Grossman. *My Secret Camera: Life in the Lodz Ghetto.*
San Diego: Harcourt/Gulliver Books. 2000.

Mendel Grossman, who was imprisoned in the Lodz Ghetto for several years, secretly took pictures of the horrors unfolding around him. Grossman did not survive the Holocaust but his remarkable photographs did. They are heartbreaking reminders of everyday life in a community marked for destruction.

Speregen, Devra Newberger. *Ilan Ramon: Jewish Star.*
Philadelphia: Jewish Publication Society. 2004.

After a few chapters that introduce the reader to Ilan Ramon's boyhood and his service in the Israeli Air Force, the rest of this biography concentrates on his career as an astronaut. The author skillfully balances personal details, such as how the crew of the *Columbia* space shuttle bonded and became "like family," with technical information about training, how a space shuttle works, preparations for living in space, and life in orbit. The writing is cogent and lively, but the format is rather drab. Appended material includes a glossary and an index.

Stern, Ellen. *Elie Wiesel: A Voice for Humanity.*
Philadelphia: Jewish Publication Society. 1996.

A detail-rich biography that captures Wiesel's past and present life and the individuals who figured prominently in both. It traces the impact that his experiences had on making him the world's most prominent Holocaust spokesman. Clearly written with an accessible format.

Watts, Irene, and Lillian Boraks-Nemetz. *Tapestry of Hope: Holocaust Writing for Young People.*
Toronto: Tundra. 2003.

An anthology of writing about the Holocaust, this contains both previously published works and new first-person accounts, many of them by Canadian writers. Fiction, personal narratives, biographical sketches, and poetry are included. A powerful collection.

Woog, Adam. *Anne Frank.*
Farmington Hills, MI: Lucent. 2005.

Anne Frank's life is presented within the context of the larger historical events that surrounded it. Her story is systematically unfolded, using vignettes from the diary. Of special interest are the details describing the diary's publishing history and its evolution from a little-known family remembrance to a contemporary literary icon. Supplemented by the inclusion of clear and useful historical maps and charts. Especially helpful to young readers are individual drawings of the Frank family's accommodations and a cross-section view of the building and the annex in which they hid. Useful for both Jewish and non-Jewish readers. Part of the Heroes and Villains series.

Wukovits, John F. *The Importance of Anne Frank.*
Farmington Hills, MI: Lucent. 1999.

An exploration of the Frank family's life in Germany, their ancestral home, and in Amsterdam where they hoped to escape Nazism. The author summarizes life in the Secret Annex as recorded by Anne in her diary against the background of total war and implementation of the Final Solution. This title is intended as a conscious rebuttal of Holocaust denial and covers a lot of material well.

HIGH SCHOOL

Bauer, Yehuda. *A History of the Holocaust, Revised Edition.*
    Illus. by Leah Malka Diskind.
New York: Franklin Watts. 2001.

A noted Holocaust scholar has revised his 1982 work, adding much new material and correcting errors. The main thrust of the new edition is to provide an objective, factual account of what actually happened during the Holocaust. Well-researched, the narrative presents a brief overview of pre-Holocaust Jewish history and then goes on to cover all major aspects of the Final Solution, including German anti-Semitic policy, the formation of the ghettoes, the concentration and death camps, the resistance, the effects on Eastern and Western European Jewry, and the aftermath. Extensive notes, an excellent bibliography, and an index are included.

Bitton-Jackson, Livia. *I Have Lived a Thousand Years: Growing Up in the Holocaust.*
New York: Simon and Schuster. 1997.

Moving, powerful, and beautifully written, this is the memoir of a 13-year-old girl and her mother who survived the horrors of Auschwitz in the final year of World War II. The sequels are *My Bridges of Hope* and *Hello, America*.

Pressler, Miryam. *Anne Frank: A Hidden Life.*
New York: Puffin. 2001.

Pressler is an expert on the life of Anne Frank and the editor of the definitive edition of the diary. This book, originally published in Germany and translated into English by Anthea Bell, is a remarkable piece of biographical and historical reconstruction. Written in a conversational style, with the author's personal and sometimes passionate impressions recorded, it describes the Frank family's life before they went into hiding, gives short but precise portraits of the eight people who lived in the Secret Annex, speculates about their relationships using evidence from the various editions of the diary, and fills in many of the details that surrounded the development of Anne as a young woman and a writer. The final chapter—an account of Anne and Margot's final few months—is harrowing.

Waldman, Neil. *Out of the Shadows: An Artist's Journey.*
Honesdale, PA: Boyds Mills Press. 2006.

Waldman—a painter and book illustrator—has written an absorbing autobiography in which he explores the dark places of his childhood and the way in which art became a refuge. Many of Waldman's paintings appear in the book, along with those by his relatives.

CHAPTER 15

Repairing the World

"Rabbi Tarfon taught: It is not up to you to complete the work (of perfecting the world), but neither are you free to refrain from doing it."

Talmud

PRESCHOOL

Abraham, Michelle Shapiro. *Good Night, Lilah Tov.* Illus. by Selina Alko. New York: UAHC Press. 2001.

A companion to *Good Morning, Boker Tov*, this slight story shows parents tucking a little boy into bed and asking him what he did that day to make the world a better place. The examples of what he might have done are all *mitzvot* that preschoolers could perform, like greeting a friend, *tikun olam*, or giving *tzedakah*. An audio CD is available.

Watson, Sally. *The Butterfly Seeds.* New York: Tambourine Books. 1995.

A beautifully illustrated picture book that universalizes the immigrant experience by centering the story on a little boy who comes to New York's Lower East Side with a package of seeds given him by his grandfather, who has stayed behind. Grandpa has told Jake to plant the seeds in his new garden and "like magic, you'll have hundreds of butterflies." With no gardens to be found among the tenements where he lives, Jake gets the help of neighbors of various ethnic groups who live in his diverse community. He fears that the magic Grandpa has told him about won't work in America, but after a hard rain—and to the neighbors' delight—butterflies do emerge from the window box that Jake has lovingly cared for.

PRIMARY

Biers-Ariel, Matt. *Solomon and the Trees.* Illus. by Esti Kiss-Silverberg. New York: UAHC Press. 2001.

Drawing on legends about King Solomon and Jewish teachings about humankind's responsibility to care for nature, this serious, dramatically illustrated story stresses personal responsibility. In it, the mighty king revisits the forest that inspired him as a youth and realizes that, in harvesting its timber to build the Temple, he has all but destroyed it.

Cone, Molly. *Listen to the Trees.*
New York: UAHC Press. 1995.

A diverse collection of quotations expressing Judaism's concern for the environment, a few photographs, stories, comics, cartoon, blessings, and a glossary. Like *Solomon and the Trees*, it is a good choice for reading on Earth Day and on the Jewish holiday of *Tu B'Shevat*.

Davis, Aubrey. *Bagels from Benny*. Illus. by Dusan Petricic.
Toronto: Kids Can Press. 2003.

Based on a Jewish folktale, this is a whimsical yet serious story of a little boy's attempts to connect with God. To thank God for His gift of the wheat that makes his Grandpa's delicious bagels, Benny takes bagels to the synagogue and hides them in the *Holy Ark*. When the bagels disappear, week after week, Benny is delighted that his gift has been accepted. Then he is disappointed to learn that the bagels have been eaten all along by a hungry, tattered man. Grandpa explains that by feeding a hungry person, Benny has shown his thanks to God by helping make the world a better place. Petricic's illustrations are slightly surreal and colored mainly in shades of bagel brown. They extend the story by showing characters' emotions and personalities. Winner of a Sydney Taylor Book Award.

Fenton, Anne Lobock. *Tikun Olam: Fixing the World.*
Brookline, MA: Brookline Books. 1997.

A story about two good men, Mr. Mitzvah Fixit and Dr. Mender, who exemplify the importance of doing *mitzvot*, especially those of *tikun olam*, visiting the sick, and taking care of one's health. The sadness of Dr. Mender's death is mitigated by the holiness that *mitzvot* bring into the world.

Gershator, Phillis. *Honi's Circle of Trees.* Illus. by Mim Green.
Philadelphia: Jewish Publication Society. 1995.

Honi is a character from the *Talmud*, known for his magical circle-making powers and his love of trees. In this version, Honi plants carob trees, falls asleep, and wakes many years later to find that, although all of the people he knew are long gone, he is privileged to see his trees bear fruit. Soft, expressive black-and-white illustrations enhance this classic story.

Kushner, Lawrence, and Gary Schmidt. *In God's Hands.*
Woodstock, VT: Jewish Lights. 2005.

Illustrated handsomely with vivid, slightly stylized artwork, this is a picture book version of the Jewish folktale known as "Challahs in the Ark." A rich man and a poor man are opposites in their needs and motivations—one bakes bread and places it in the *Holy Ark* while the other takes the bread to feed his family—but they become united in the realization that God works miracles through human hands. *Bagels from Benny* by Aubrey Davis is a more childlike, more lilting version of the story.

Levine, Arthur. *Pearl Moskowitz's Last Stand.* Illus. by Robert Roth.
New York: Tambourine Books. 1993.

A wonderful story, with equally wonderful illustrations, about an elderly woman who decides she will save the last tree on her street from being cut down. She and a group of ethnically diverse friends use their wiles as *bubbes* to divert an earnest young bureaucrat from his efforts at urban renewal. He is no match for them, and the tree survives. Written in tongue-in-cheek style, this is a delightful look at not-so-passive resistance on behalf of the environment.

Michelson, Richard. *Across the Alley.* Illlus. by R. B. Lewis.
New York: G. P. Putnam's Sons. 2006.

Set in an urban neighborhood where blacks and whites don't mix, it is the story of a friendship between a white boy and a black boy who live across the alley from one another. From the nearness of their bedrooms, Abe teaches Willy how to play the violin and Willy teaches Abe how to pitch. Although these skills are contrary to the wishes of their parents, both boys succeed, bringing the adults along with them in sharing their pride. If readers don't find the premise absurd—that it is possible to learn to play the violin and to pitch "across the alley," secretly, and at night—then they may feel good about the interracial harmony that results. The illustrations are excellent.

Sasso, Sandy Eisenberg. *A Prayer for the Earth.* Illus. by Bethanne Anderson.
Woodstock, VT: Jewish Lights. 1996.

Noah's wife comes into her own in this didactic story. He saves the fauna, she saves the flora, gathering and sowing seeds and replenishing the land after the flood. Like many of Sasso's books, this is wordy and written from an adult perspective, intended to deliver an unmistakable message to children. The illustrations surpass the writing. A shorter board book version is called *Na'amah, Noah's Wife*.

ELEMENTARY

Bankston, John. *Jonas Salk and the Polio Vaccine.*
Hockessin, DE: Mitchell Lane. 2003.

Part of a series called Unlocking the Secrets of Science, this book presents scientific and biographical information in a somewhat chatty style. Documentation is lacking but the facts are accurate. After a chapter giving historical background on polio, short chapters describe Salk's work. Of slight Jewish content, this includes a chronology of the disease, a glossary, a list of books and Web sites, and an index.

Biers-Ariel, Matt. *The Seven Species: Stories and Recipes Inspired by the Foods of the Bible.* Illus. by Tama Goodman.
New York: UAHC Press. 2003.

Attractively designed and illustrated but mediocre in text, the main justification for this book is that it is useful for the holiday of *Tu Bi'Shevat* and for an insight into biblical ecology. For each fruit or grain, there is some background information, a story, and a few recipes. Most of the stories are familiar ones, based on traditional lore. The recipes include no safety precautions in recognition of the fact that children may be using them.

Burstein, Chaya. *The Kids' Catalog of Animals and the Earth.*
Philadelphia: Jewish Publication Society. 2006.

Like the other *Kids' Catalogs*, this is a useful and fact-filled compendium, written in Burstein's sprightly style and illustrated, in part, with her appealing cartoons. The content is comprehensive, including factual information, history, lore, legend, short stories, experiments, crafts and activities, a mini-encyclopedia, and an index. The focus is on Israel and Judaism, and the broad sweep includes ecology, zoology, and non-Jewish eco-heroes like Jane Goodall. Fine for *Tu Bi'Shevat* and any time of year.

Codell, Esme Raji. *Hanukkah, Shmanukkah!* Illus. by LeUyen Pham.
New York: Hyperion. 2005.

Three rabbis from Hanukkah past, present, and future haunt old man Scroogemacher's dreams in this parody of Dickens's *A Christmas Carol*. Packed into the story are capsule summaries of the immigration experience, Jewish American labor history, and a vision of an ideal, multicultural world where children learn in peace and harmony and women become rabbis. The narrative style is heavy in Yiddishisms, and the illustrations are bold. An author's note, an illustrator's note, a glossary, and a list of books for further reading complete an instructive message, told with verve.

Codell, Esme Raji. *Vive la Paris.*
New York: Hyperion. 2006

Paris is a black fifth-grader whose inner thoughts about family and friendships, plus her growing knowledge about the world, are revealed in a combination of lyrical prose and the natural language of children. As she learns about the Holocaust and man's inhumanity to man, she struggles with that burden and comes into her own as a *mensch* helping heal the world.

Cohn, Janice. *The Christmas Menorahs: How a Town Fought Hate.*
Illus. by Bill Farnsworth.
Mortons Grove, IL: Albert Whitman. 1995.

A story based on a well-publicized hate crime in Billings, Montana, showing how people of all faiths rose up to fight bigotry. The handsome illustrations make the book accessible to younger children, while the story itself is often studied by middle school students and included in curricula on tolerance.

The Eleventh Commandment: Wisdom from Our Children.
Woodstock, VT: Jewish Lights. 1996.

A charming and ecumenical collection written and illustrated by children in response to the question, "If there were an eleventh commandment, what would it be?" Divided into five sections: Living with Other People, Living with the Earth, Living with Family, Living with Ourselves, Living with God.

Gaines, Ann, and Jim Whiting. *Robert A. Weinberg and the Search for the Cause of Cancer.*
Hockessin, DE: Mitchell Lane. 2003.

Part of a series called Unlocking the Secrets of Science, this presents scientific and biographical information in a somewhat chatty style. Documentation is lacking but the facts are accurate. After a chapter giving the historical background on cancer, short chapters describe Weinberg's cancer research. Of slight Jewish content, this includes a chronology of the disease, a glossary, a list of books and Web sites, and an index.

Gellman, Marc, and Thomas Hartman. *Bad Stuff in the News: A Guide to Handling the Headlines.*
New York: SeaStar/North-South Books. 2002.

Written in response to the terrorist attacks of September 11, 2001, this imparts wholesome advice about many of the issues that frighten children: Violence, natural disasters, catastrophic accidents, abuse, hatred, pollution, addiction, sickness, dying, and generational conflict. Written by a rabbi and a priest, each chapter gives some examples of "bad stuff," discusses its sources and motivation, and then provides readers with suggestions for positive actions they can take to allay their fears and repair the world.

Gordon, Karen. *Selman Waksman and the Discovery of Streptomycin.*
Hockessin, DE: Mitchell Lane. 2003.

Part of a series called Unlocking the Secrets of Science, this presents scientific and biographical information in a somewhat chatty style. Documentation is lacking but the facts are accurate. After a chapter giving historical background on tuberculosis, short chapters describe Waksman's work. Of slight Jewish content, this includes a chronology of the disease, a glossary, a list of books and Web sites, and an index.

Kornblatt, Mark. *Understanding Buddy.*
New York: Margaret K. McElderry/Simon and Schuster. 2001.

A fifth-grader discovers that the sad, silent new boy in class is grieving over the sudden death of his mother. Rebuffed by Buddy when he tries to be friendly, Sam searches for answers—including Jewish answers—to the disturbing questions that arise as he tries to understand Buddy. A soccer subplot and realistic characterizations of contemporary children and a Jewish-American family add interest.

Littlefield, Holly. *Fire at the Triangle Factory.* Illus. by Mary O. Young. Minneapolis, MN: Carolrhoda/Lerner. 1996.

This fictionalized account of the Triangle Shirtwaist Factory fire is told in an easy-reader format, with limited text and illustrations on every page. It focuses on two 14-year-old girls, one Jewish and one Italian, who are typical of the sweatshop labor of the period. Factual material and fictional elements are blended into a rather bland plot.

McPherson, Stephanie. *Jonas Salk: Conquering Polio.* Minneapolis, MN: Lerner. 2002.

This work, part of the Lerner Biography Series, offers a chronological presentation of Salk's life and career. Although the text wanders, teenagers curious about the mechanics and poliltics of scientific research should be interested. Salk was a Jew but the book has no Jewish content.

Parks, Peggy J. *Jonas Salk: Polio Vaccine Pioneer.* Farmington Hills, MI: Blackbirch Press. 2004.

A well-documented biography of Jonas Salk, giving information about his early life, education, and achievements. Many archival photographs plus an index, timeline, and glossary. Short on Jewish content; useful for students doing reports. Part of the publisher's Giants of Science Series.

Rappaport, Doreen. *In the Promised Land: Lives of Jewish Americans.*
    Illus. by Ying-Hwa Hu and Cornelius Van Wright.
New York: HarperCollins. 2005.

Short, readable biographies of 13 Jewish Americans are enhanced by outstanding color illustrations. The subjects are diverse, and the focus is on life-defining moments. Included are Ernestine Rose, Pauline Newman, Ruth Bader Ginsburg, Jacob Davis, Jonas Salk, and Steven Spielberg.

Rosen, Sybil. *Speed of Light.*
New York: Simon and Schuster/Atheneum. 1999.

In a small Southern town during the 1950s, Audrey Ina's father puts his family's livelihood and safety at risk by championing the cause of a man who wants to become the town's first black policeman. The author captures the ambivalent situation of Southern Jews during the Civil Rights era and writes with an insight of a young person's awakening to the existence of evil in her world. A rich and meaningful work, which won a Sydney Taylor Book Award.

Zalben, Jane Breskin. *Let There Be Light: Poems and Prayers for Repairing the World.*
New York: Dutton. 2002.

A lyrical collection of prayers and poems from Buddhism, Christianity, Hinduism, Judaism, Native cultures, and Islam. Zalben illustrates each one with striking art that varies from her usual style and reflects the text beautifully. An ecumenical collection based on a central Jewish concept.

MIDDLE SCHOOL

Bohannon, Lisa Frederiksen. *Women's Work: The Story of Betty Friedan.*
Greensboro, NC: Morgan Reynolds. 2004.

In this dense biography of Betty Friedan, the author includes details about her family history and how her Jewish identity affected her life growing up in Peoria, Illinois. Extensive coverage of Friedan's role in founding the National Organization for Women and her numerous contributions to the Women's Movement are provided. Poorly reproduced black-and-white photographs are sparsely sprinkled throughout the text.

Cytron, Barry, and Phyllis Cytron. *Miriam Mendilow, Mother of Jerusalem.*
Minneapolis, MN: Lerner. 1991.

A biography of Myriam Mendilow, founder of Israel's Lifeline for the Old and other services for the elderly. Illustrated with many black-and-white photographs, it chronicles Myriam's life and does a good job of capturing the facets of her personality that made all of her efforts—often against formidable odds—successful.

Dash, Joan. *We Shall Not Be Moved: The Women's Factory Strike of 1909.*
New York: Scholastic. 1996.

A well-written account of the lives of young working women in 1909. Individuals who were involved in the burgeoning labor movement—of which the garment workers' strike was a seminal event—are brought to life, and the story of their struggles is tense and exciting. An interesting and rare perspective on class issues is given, as Dash shows how working-class strikers—mostly Jewish and Italian girls—were aided by upper-class women who were able to bring national attention to the plight of workers.

Finkelstein, Norman H. *Heeding the Call: Jewish Voices in America's Civil Rights Struggle.*
Philadelphia: Jewish Publication Society. 1997.

An even-handed and accurate account of the conflicts and commonalities between American Jews and African Americans as they have been played out in the arena of civil rights. Includes reference aids.

Rose, Or N. *Abraham Joshua Heschel: Man of Spirit, Man of Action.*
Philadelphia: Jewish Publication Society. 2003.

An overview of the life of one of the most influential Jewish thinkers of modern times, this brief biography covers Rabbi Heschel from birth to death, 1907–1972. His impassioned activism on behalf of civil rights and his involvement with Vatican II concerning Jewish issues also are explored.

Sachs, Marilyn. *Call Me Ruth.*
New York: Beechtree/Morrow. 1982.

A mother and daughter's different responses to their new life in America is the central part of the plot of this fine historical novel. The labor movement within the women's garment industry is an important part of the setting and plot. Winner of a Sydney Taylor Book Award.

HIGH SCHOOL

Bitton-Jackson, Livia. *My Bridges of Hope: Searching for Life and Love after Auschwitz.*
New York: Alfred A. Knopf. 1999.

A companion volume to *I Have Lived a Thousand Years* and *Hello America*, this is a concrete and suspenseful account of the main character's teenage years, once it is possible to rebuild a life shattered by the Holocaust and always shadowed by it. Comfortable American teens, perhaps searching for meaning, will find this revelatory.

Houston, Julian. *New Boy.*
Boston: Houghton Mifflin. 2005.

Based on the author's own experiences, this is the story of an African-American boy who becomes the first student of color at an exclusive private school in the 1950s. Incidents of prejudice against Italians and Jews open his eyes to discrimination and lead him to become involved in the struggle for civil rights. Of minimal Jewish content, this well-written novel would make a good tie-in with studies of prejudice and civil rights.

Levitan, David. *Wide Awake.*
New York: Alfred A. Knopf. 2006.

The theme of this thought-provoking political novel is that teens can change the world for the better if they set aside their differences and adopt a sense of community. It is set in the near future and involves the challenged election of the country's first gay, Jewish president. Many of the main characters are gay, making this the first book of Jewish content for teens to deal frankly with gay relationships. The Jewish content is slight because some of the teachings attributed to Jesus are the characters' moral inspiration. Levitan writes with flair, and *Wide Awake* has the potential to jolt teen readers wide awake.

CHAPTER 16

Repentance and Forgiveness

"Return to me . . . and I will return to you."

Tanakh

PRESCHOOL

Anderson, Joel. ***Jonah's Trash, God's Treasure.*** Illus. by Abe Goolsby.
Nashville, TN: Thomas Nelson. 1998.

The biblical story of Jonah is told in simple rhyming couplets and illustrated with clever, innovative artwork fashioned from throwaway items. Not only is this a well-designed and written picture book, but it also has the potential to inspire creative art projects.

Feinberg, Miriam. ***A Yom Kippur Think.*** Illus. by Karen Ostrove.
New York: United Synagoue of Conservative Judaism. 1994.

Simple language and engaging pictures convey the meaning of Yom Kippur as a day of reflection and soul searching. A little girl who is restless in services is helped by her father to find meaning in the day.

Jules, Jacqueline. ***The Hardest Word: A Yom Kippur Story.***
    Illus. by Katherine Janus Kahn.
Minneapolis, MN: Kar-Ben/Lerner. 2001.

The Ziz, a giant bird from Jewish legend, is a softy at heart. He confesses to accidentally doing wrong, and God assigns him a penance—to find the hardest word. The subtitle is misleading because the story does not depict any other aspect of Yom Kippur besides the concept of forgiveness. The illustrations are confusing: Some depict a modern setting, others a medieval.

Marzollo, Jean. ***Jonah and the Whale (and the Worm).***
New York: Little Brown. 2004.

The biblical story of Jonah is told and illustrated in Marzollo's casual, child-friendly style, with a running commentary by octopi at the bottom of each page.

Nondenominational, true to the Bible, and fun for young children. The fourth of Marzollo's Bible stories, all following the same format.

Zucker, Jonny. **Apples and Honey: A Rosh Hashanah Story.**
   Illus. by Jan Barger Cohen.
Hauppauge, NY: Barron's. 2002.

Double-spread illustrations of a family observing Rosh Hashanah will engage the attention of preschoolers. Each action is described by a few simple sentences. The ritual of *tashlikh* is explained as saying goodbye to the "sad things of last year by throwing crumbs into the river." A pleasant introduction, part of the Festival Time series.

PRIMARY

Blitz, Shmuel. **The Artscroll Children's Book of Yonah.** Illus. by Tovah Katz.
New York: Mesorah. 2006.

Augmented by questions and comments and read from right to left, this brightly illustrated book contains the text of the *Book of Jonah* in Hebrew and in English. The *Book of Jonah*, with its themes of transgression and repentance, is traditionally read in synagogues on Yom Kippur, the Day of Atonement.

Brodsky, Beverly. **Jonah.**
New York: Lippincott. 1977.

Brodsky's loose, deeply colored illustrations are in vivid contrast to the stark white pages of the book. Both animals and humans are rendered to resemble ancient Near Eastern art. They dramatically portray the biblical story of Jonah, which Brodsky tells seriously and with dignity.

Geller, Beverly Mach. **The Mystery of the Missing Pitome.** Illus. by Lisa Perel.
Jerusalem: Gefen. 2000.

A Sukkot story that explains the requirements for the pitom that makes the *etrog* kosher. Its main character is a curious little boy named Yosef who takes a peek at the *etrog* his father has carefully chosen and then mistakenly believes he has been the cause of its missing *pitom*. Gently acknowledging Yosef's mistake and his subsequent attempts to make amends, *Abba* explains the *Halakhic* requirements for the pitom. Marred by weak binding and mediocre illustrations.

Gerstein, Mordicai. **The Legend of Jonah and the Two Great Fish.**
New York: Simon and Schuster. 1997.

Strands of legend embellish a fancifully illustrated version of the Bible story. The novelty of two fish and the decidedly different contents of their interiors captivate children. The biblical story of Jonah is well known to children, and Gerstein's slyly offbeat version is a treat.

Hoffman, Amalia. *Purim Goodies.*
Jerusalem: Gefen. 2007.

When two servant girls, Groyseh Adella and Kleineh Adella, eat all of the Purim treats that they are sent to deliver, they cause a rift between the two families they work for. When the rabbi reminds them that there are people in their town with nothing to eat, they repent, bake a whole new batch of *hamentaschen*, and share them with everyone. Based on a story by Sholom Aleichem, the story has appeal that extends beyond the holiday of Purim.

Jaffe, Nina. *The Way Meat Loves Salt.* Illus. by Louise August.
New York: Henry Holt. 1998.

A Jewish version of the *Cinderella* story with a touch of *King Lear*, this relates the initially sad but ultimately happy tale of a young woman named Mireleh. The fairy godmother is transformed into Elijah, and the setting is Eastern Europe. August's illustrations are superb, and Jaffe's source notes are, as usual, impeccable.

Kassirer, Sue. *Joseph and His Coat of Many Colors.*
    Illus. by Danuta Jarecka.
New York: Simon and Schuster. 1997.

Colorful illustrations decorate this easy-to-read Bible story about Joseph and his brothers. Kassirer's simplified version of a story about excess pride, sibling rivalry, and forgiveness retains the core of its meaning while avoiding its darker themes. Youngsters will enjoy reading it on their own.

Kimmel, Eric A. *Gershon's Monster: A Story for the Jewish New Year.*
    Illus. by Jon J Muth.
New York: Scholastic. 2000.

The teachings of the *Baal Shem Tov* are woven into this satisfying folktale about *tashlikh* and *teshuvah*. Not until his precious children are threatened by a fearsome sea monster composed of all the sins he has carelessly tossed away does Gershon truly repent. The moody watercolors are the perfect companions to a story that personifies abstract concepts in a way that makes them meaningful to primary grade children. Winner of a Sydney Taylor Book Award.

Koralek, Jenny. *The Coat of Many Colors.* Illus. by Pauline Baynes.
Grand Rapids, MI: Eerdmans. 2004.

An economical retelling of the biblical story of Joseph, in which details about the dreams are condensed, the storyline is simplified, and the episode involving Potiphar's wife is omitted. The essence and truth of the story are maintained, however, by graceful writing and outstanding illustrations.

MacGill-Callahan, Sheila. *When Solomon Was King.* Illus. by Stephen T. Johnson. New York: Penguin Putnam. 1995.

A formally narrated and illustrated story that offers an explanation of why Jews don't hunt for sport. The style is dignified, the vocabulary is rich, the illustrations are handsome, and the story is engrossing. Of the many stories about King Solomon written for children, this is one of the best and a good example of the power of language to stimulate imagination.

Manushkin, Fran. *Sophie and the Shofar: A New Year's Story.* Illus. by Rosalind Charney Kaye.
New York: UAHC Press. 2001.

The meaning of repentance—of being sorry—is conveyed to readers through the story of a little girl who wrongly accuses her Russian cousin of stealing the family *shofar*. The story is warm and wholesome, but Kaye's illustrations are less effective, especially in depicting the characters, whose faces are hard to distinguish one from another.

Michelson, Richard. *Grandpa's Gamble.* Illus. by Barry Moser.
Tarrytown, NY: Marshall Cavendish. 1999.

Sepia-tone illustrations capture the introspective mood of this story about *teshuvah*. Knowing that his grandchildren think he is boring because he is always praying, an old man tells them of how he learned to cheat and gamble when he was newly arrived in the United States. When his daughter—the children's mother—got sick, he made his last gamble by betting on God to cure her. The children now see him in a new light. The picture book format is inappropriate to the complexities of this story, and the ending is contrived.

Schur, Maxine Rose. *The Peddler's Gift.* Illus. by Kimberly Bulcken Root.
New York: Dial. 1999.

Superb watercolor and pencil illustrations enhance a story about a simple peddler who is the butt of jokes among the boys in the *shtetl*. After a boy named Leibush steals a *dreidel* from Shnook the peddler, he is overcome with guilt and returns the *dreidel*, discovering as he does so that Shnook is much more than he seems. Set during Hanukkah, the theme of this Sydney Taylor Book Award-winning story is the contrast between external appearance and moral stature. Shnook is a version of the wise fool of legend.

Siegel, Bruce. *The Magic of Kol Nidre.* Illus. by Shelly O. Haas.
Minneapolis, MN: Kar-Ben/Lerner. 1998.

A gentle story, warmly illustrated, about the meaning of the *Kol Nidre* prayer to three generations of a family and to Jews everywhere. A grandfather, a father, and a little boy each exemplify some of the magic of the beloved prayer, which opens the evening Yom Kippur service. Realistic watercolor illustrations reflect the text.

Silverman, Erica. *When the Chickens Went on Strike: A Rosh Hashanah Tale.*
Illus. by Matthew Trueman.
New York: Dutton. 2003.

Sholom Aleichem wrote a story called *Kapores*, which Silverman, the author of *Raisel's Riddle* and *Sholom's Treasure*, has adapted. It is told by a boy whose father sends him out of the *shul* for misbehaving on Rosh Hashanah. He sees a strange sight: A "parade of poultry" marching out of the village and assembling in a field to demand freedom from *kapores*. When services end, he tells the villagers what has happened and, out of deep concern for their cherished custom, they attack the chickens, who counterattack. Torn between custom and change, the boy sides with the chickens and helps them escape, observing that "customs come and customs go . . . all things change with time." Without preaching about the merits of either ritual or inner intent, the story and the illustrations make a strong point about repentance and its meaning.

Tarbescu, Edith. *The Boy Who Stuck Out His Tongue.* Illus. by Judith Christine Mills.
Cambridge, MA: Barefoot Books. 2000.

Sassy, disobedient Hershel learns a much-needed lesson in this story, written in a folkloric style. Sly humor runs through it, and the moral is gently revealed. The illustrations and format are striking, all in an ethnic mode evocative of the Hungarian setting.

Tregobov, Rhea. *The Big Storm.* Illus. by Maryann Kovalski.
Toronto: Kids Can Press. 1992.

When Jeanette forgets her cat, who is waiting for her in a snowstorm, she is stricken with guilt. Finding the cat, named Kitty Doyle, and making sure she is not sick, is the essence of this story. It is set in a Jewish milieu in Canada and has a pleasant, old-fashioned feel to it.

Tregobov, Rhea. *What-If Sara.* Illus. by Leanne Franson.
Toronto: Second Story Press. 1999.

Sara's daydreaming often interferes with her hardworking Jewish family's tasks. She redeems herself when she writes a letter on behalf of her father to an irate customer. This very slight story is set in a Jewish neighborhood in Toronto. The illustrations are its high point.

Weilerstein, Sadie Rose. *K'tonton's Yom Kippur Kitten.* Illus. by Joe Boddy.
Philadelphia: Jewish Publication Society. 1995.

After blaming a stray kitten for spilling the milk, K'tonton is stricken with guilt at Yom Kippur services. The Jewish Tom Thumb demonstrates the meaning of repentance in this delightful edition of a story first published in Weilerstein's *The Adventures of K'tonton*. K'tonton is one of the most appealing of modern Jewish characters, and every Jewish child deserves to make his acquaintance.

ELEMENTARY

Morris, Gerald. *The Princess, the Crone, and the Dung Cart Knight.*
Boston: Houghton Mifflin. 2004.

An adventure-fantasy based on Arthurian legends and set in the England of Camelot. The heroine is an orphan named Sarah whose mother and Jewish guardian have been burned at the stake. She vows vengeance and becomes involved with several of Camelot's most famous knights and sorceresses, plus two girls of her own age. After many adventures and quests, Sarah overcomes her thirst for vengeance and opts for mercy, but not until a lot of blood has flowed. Fast-paced, engaging, and often quite humorous, this is part of a series.

Waldron, Kathleen Cook. *Joseph, Master of Dreams.*
Quebec: Roussan/Beloved Books. 2001.

A fresh retelling of the familiar story from *Genesis*, with well-drawn characters and some details added by the author. Joseph is appealing: Self-centered and vain but also strong in values and leadership. True to the original, the author sees God's hand in the unfolding events. The publisher's imprint, Beloved Books, seeks to offer "stories of faith" from an ecumenical perspective, and this story succeeds without preaching.

MIDDLE SCHOOL

Cohen, Barbara. *King of the Seventh Grade.*
New York: Lothrop, Lee and Shephard. 1982.

As his *Bar Mitzvah* approaches, Vic does everything he can to get out of it. As the coolest of seventh-graders, he has a sense of invulnerability that is shattered when he discovers that he isn't really Jewish, because his mother never converted. Shaken by this discovery and by the fact that he actually cares, Vic's arrogance is further eroded when he is arrested for shoplifting with some friends. Issues like divorce, peer relationships, and Jewish practice are part of a flawless plot peopled by convincing characters and delivered with suspense and a positive Jewish message.

Williams, Laura E. *The Spider's Web.*
Minneapolis, MN: Milkweed Editions. 1999.

A fast-paced and engrossing novel about teenage neo-Nazis, this story juxtaposes the experiences and emotions of a 13-year-old skinhead with those of an old woman who was once an ardent supporter of Hitler. There are only two minor Jewish characters in the book, but it makes a strong statement against racist extremism.

CHAPTER 17

Saving Life

"Saving a single life is a mitzvah equal to saving the entire world."

Talmud

PRIMARY

Altman, Linda Jacobs. ***The Legend of Freedom Hill.***
Illus. by Cornelius Van Wright and Ying-Hwa Hu.
New York: Lee and Low. 2000.

California during the Gold Rush is the setting for this story of an interracial friendship. Two little girls, one Jewish and the other African-American, find enough gold to ransom the runaways that the slave catcher has in his clutches. An engaging story is enhanced by excellent illustrations.

Bishop, Claire Huchet. ***Twenty and Ten.*** Illus. by William Pene Du Bois.
New York: Viking. 1952.

In an early story about Holocaust rescuers, 20 French schoolchildren are watched over by their teacher, Sister Gabriel. When they agree to hide 10 Jewish children whose parents have been taken by the Nazis, bonds of friendship form and hold strong when German soldiers come to the school looking for Jews. Told by one of the children, the story is filled with bravery and suspense. It is often used as classroom reading and as one of the first books that children read about the Holocaust.

Blatt, Evelyn Mizrahi. ***More Precious than Gold.*** Illus. by Eli Toron.
New York: Hachai. 2002.

Torah and *mitzvot* are more precious than gold, which is the theme of this historical novel. Set in Spain in 1492, the plot involves a Spanish-Jewish family's flight to Turkey following the Edict of Expulsion. Ten-year-old Sarah smuggles a Jewish orphan aboard the ship taking them to Turkey, thus saving her life. Large print and short chapters are appropriate for the intended readership.

Gerstein, Mordicai. *The White Ram.*
New York: Holiday House. 2006.

According to the *midrash*, a white ram was created by God on the sixth day for the sole purpose of saving the future Abraham from sacrificing his son, Isaac. Residing in the Garden of Eden, the white ram leaves it and travels to the mountain where he will serve as the scapegoat and be sacrificed in Isaac's place. On his way, he is repeatedly tempted to turn aside from his task but he perseveres, fulfills God's will, and saves Isaac. The illustrations that accompany the story are as fanciful and evocative as any that Gerstein has created.

Kushner, Tony. *Brundibar.* Illus. by Maurice Sendak.
New York: Hyperion. 2003.

Brundibar is a fairy tale opera for children, composed by Hans Krasa—who died at Auschwitz—and performed many times by the doomed children imprisoned in the Terezin concentration camp. On one level, it is a typical fairy tale, with magic animals, a creepy villain, determined little children, and an ending in which good triumphs. Kushner's sassy text captures this flavor. On another level, *Brundibar* is full of menace, with yellow stars on many of the characters and a villain who resembles Hitler. The illustrations in particular portray the opera's tragic provenance. They are among Sendak's finest achievements and must be seen and studied to be appreciated. This remarkable book will be enjoyed and appreciated by all ages, for different reasons.

Oppenheim, Shulamith. *The Lily Cupboard.* Illus. by Ronald Himler.
New York: HarperCollins. 1992.

A deeply moving, sensitively illustrated story about a little Dutch Jewish girl whose parents hide her from the Nazis with a Christian farm family. The trauma of being separated from her parents is mitigated by the kindness of the family and by a pet rabbit that they give her, which Miriam names after her father. Danger lurks in this story, and readers do not find out if Miriam and her parents are ever reunited.

Singer, Isaac Bashevis. *The Golem.* Illus. by Uri Shulevitz.
New York: Farrar, Straus and Giroux. 1982.

In one of several outstanding illustrated versions of the *Golem* legend, the saintly *Maharal*, Rabbi Loew, creates a giant of clay. The *Golem* saves the life of a Jew falsely accused of a crime. Set in medieval Prague during the reign of Emperor Rudolf II.

Wieder, Joy Nelkin. *The Great Potato Plan.*
New York: Hachai. 1999.

The outbreak of World War I strands a Jewish family in Warsaw. With Papa already in the United States, Simcha, the oldest son, must help his mother in the struggle against starvation and marauding Cossacks. Fraught with danger and suspense, the story also embodies sound Jewish values.

Wisniewski, David. *Golem.*
New York: Clarion. 1996.

A superbly illustrated and powerfully told version of the classic *Golem* tale, emphasizing his role in protecting the Jews of Prague. The violence in the story alarms some adults, who do not find it appropriate for primary grade children. Although it is a picture book, Wisniewski's version of the story appeals to a wide age range. Winner of a Caldecott Award.

ELEMENTARY

Altman, Linda Jacobs. *Resisters and Rescuers: Standing Up Against the Holocaust.*
Berkeley Heights, NJ: Enslow. 2003.

A lucid account of rescue and resistance during the Holocaust, beginning with German resistance to Hitler. Heroes of various resistance movements are discussed, along with the different forms resistance took. Part of the Holocaust in History Series, with notes, a glossary, Web sites, and an index.

Attema, Martha. *Daughter of Light.*
Custer, WA: Orca. 2001.

During the harsh winter of 1944 in Holland, when food is scarce and electricity has been turned off, a nine-year-old girl confronts the town's Nazi-collaborationist mayor to get electricity and heat for her pregnant mother.

Attema, Martha. *Hero.*
Custer, WA: Orca. 2004.

A gently written story set during the Holocaust about a hidden child and his love for the stallion, Hero. Themes of bravery, looking past appearances, and consideration for others are woven into the story. Izaak, the main character, grows from being a self-absorbed child to a selfless young man.

Forest, Jim. *Silent as a Stone: Mother Maria of Paris and the Trash Can Rescue.*
   Illus. by Dasha Pancheshnaya.
Crestwood, NY: St. Vladimir's Seminary Press. 2007.

A well-illustrated, fictionalized biography of an Orthodox Christian nun who rescued Jewish children from a Nazi roundup in Paris during World War II. The emphasis is on Mother Maria's saintliness, and she was indeed made a saint by her church. This little-known episode in the annals of Holocaust rescue and resistance deserves to be better known.

Hesse, Karen. *The Cats in Krasinski Square.* Illus. by Wendy Watson.
New York: Scholastic. 2004.

A little Jewish girl who lives with her older sister under false identities outside of the Warsaw Ghetto tells this spare, memorable story. Having befriended the many stray cats who come through the cracks in the ghetto wall, she uses them to foil a Gestapo raid on some underground workers who are smuggling food into the ghetto. Told in the present tense, the narrative's tone draws readers into a setting whose surface normality is belied by the presence of soldiers and war-damaged buildings. Watson's illustrations evoke both the mood and the setting to perfection. Not a picture book for younger readers but rather an illustrated Holocaust story, this will require some setting of historical context for the elementary age children who read it.

Kacer, Kathy. *Saving Edith.*
Toronto: Second Story Press. 2006

A true story about a Jewish family's flight from the Nazis through Europe during the Holocaust and of the brave people who hid and protected them. Told from the point of view of a girl of seven when the story begins, it is a touching tale.

Kaplan, William, and Shelley Tanaka. *One More Border.* Illus. by Stephen Taylor.
Toronto: Groundwood/Douglas and McIntyre. 1998.

Fans of fiction and non-fiction alike will enjoy this suspenseful memoir of a family's escape from war-ravaged Europe during World War II. The Japanese diplomat and Righteous Gentile, Chiune Sugihara, issues them exit visas, allowing them to continue on their dangerous journey eastward across Asia and the Pacific until they reach safety in Canada. The format blends documentary photographs, maps, and illustrations.

Lasky, Kathryn. *The Night Journey.*
New York: Viking. 2005.

An introduction by the author has been added to this new edition. Its release coincides with the publication of *Broken Song*, also by Kathryn Lasky. A few of the characters and one pivotal incident overlap: Reuven of *Broken Song* helps Sashie and her family of *The Night Journey* escape from Russia, and later the two are reunited and married. Winner of a Sydney Taylor Book Award.

Lowry, Lois. *Number the Stars.*
Boston: Houghton Mifflin. 1973.

A highly praised story about a friendship between a Jewish girl and a Christian girl, set in German-occupied Denmark. With disarming simplicity, Lowry portrays a brave Danish family, the dangers involved in smuggling Jews to neutral Sweden, and the true meaning of both courage and friendship. One of the most widely read of Holocaust stories, this is the winner of a Sydney Taylor Book Award.

McCann, Michelle R., and Luba Tryszynska-Frederick. *Luba: The Angel of Bergen-Belsen.* Illus. by Carol Marshall.
Berkeley, CA: Tricycle Press. 2003.

Another illustrated story about the Holocaust, this book tells of a woman prisoner who rescued and hid 54 abandoned children in her barracks in the concentration camp of Bergen-Belsen. A prologue and endnotes supply background material and introduce readers to the real Luba, who participated in the writing of the book. A more gentle story than most set during the Holocaust, this is graced with stunning full-page illustrations.

Maguire, Gregory. *The Good Liar.*
New York: Clarion. 1999.

Probing moral ambiguities, this novel set during the Holocaust in rural France lends itself to class discussion. It is told by an old man about himself and his brothers when they were mischievous boys who became good liars to evade their strict, pious mother's restrictions on their fun. When their area is occupied by Nazis, they learn the difference between lies and the truth, sport and life. And they see their mother's courage and integrity in a new light.

Mochizuki, Ken. *Passage to Freedom: The Sugihara Story.* Illus. by Dom Lee.
New York: Lee and Low. 1997.

Strong, sepia-tone illustrations enhance this moving brief biography of the Japanese diplomat who saved thousands of Jews by issuing exit visas to them during the Holo-caust. For younger readers than Gold's biography of Sugihara entitled *A Special Fate*, it is told by Sugihara's young son. This child's-eye perspective brings to light family rela-tionships, the desperate situation of Lithuanian Jews, the circumstances under which Sugihara disobeyed his government's orders, and the importance of his courageous act.

Perrin, Randy. *Time Like a River.*
Muskegon, MI: RDR Books. 1998.

In this time-travel fantasy, a 13-year-old girl living in California's Bay Area travels back 100 years to find the key to her mother's undiagnosed illness from a Chinese man. The Jewish content is slight, but the story—a collaboration between the author and his two daughters—is engrossing.

Polacco, Patricia. *The Butterfly.*
New York: Philomel. 2000.

During the Nazi occupation of France, a child discovers that her mother is hiding Jews. The "little ghost" who appears in her bedroom at night is one of them. Monique and Sevrine become friends, sharing hope for a brighter future symbolized by a butterfly. A poignant story whose illustrations express its moods.

Rogasky, Barbara. *The Golem.* Illus. by Trina Schart Hyman.
New York: Holiday House. 1996.

Told in 12 chapters, Rogasky's tales of the *Golem* emphasize the recurrent threat of anti-Semitism, linking the *Blood Libel* that endangered the Jews of sixteenth-century Prague with the Holocaust. From his creation to his death, the *Golem* is a compelling figure, but the hero of the stories is Rabbi Loew, the *Maharal*, who created and destroyed him. The outstanding illustrations, several per chapter, capture both the outward and inward qualities of the characters and the distinctive look of Prague.

Schwartz, Ellen. *Jesse's Star.*
Custer, WA: Orca. 2000.

A time-travel fantasy that takes a modern Canadian boy back to the *shtetl* where his ancestors lived. Jesse becomes his great-great-grandfather, Yossi, who outwits a garrison of Russian soldiers despite his clumsiness. The historical setting is well realized, and the characterization is believable. Readers enjoy an appealing central figure as they absorb daily Jewish life in a by-gone era.

Steiner, Connie Colker. *Shoes for Amelie.* Illus. by Denis Rodier.
Montreal: Lobster Press. 2001.

The heroism of the people of the town of le Chambon-Sur-Lignon in Vichy-controlled France during World War II is portrayed through a story of one courageous and "ordinary" family who hid a Jewish child from the Germans.

Toksvig, Sandi. *Hitler's Canary.*
New Milford, CT: Roaring Brook Press. 2007.

Sparkling writing and memorable characters are the outstanding characteristics of this story set during the German occupation of Denmark. Eleven-year-old Bamse is the narrator and through him we meet his theatrical family, all of whom become involved in the rescue of Danish Jews.

Vander Zee, Ruth. *Erika's Story.* Illus. by Roberto Innocenti.
Mankata, MN: Creative Editions. 2003.

The story told by Erika is so shocking that few readers will be able to even contemplate it happening to them. Taken as an infant aboard a cattle car with her parents, she was thrown from the train—a tiny bundle swaddled in pink—and rescued. As the adult Erika tells this story, she wonders: "How many hours did my parents stand crushed together?...I wonder where [my mother] stood. Was my father next to her?...Did they talk about what to do?...When did they make their decision?" Innocenti's illustrations match the narrative in drama: They are almost all in somber shades of grey, except for the pink bundle and two non-Holocaust scenes. The gentle style of writing contrasts with the incredible events recounted, adding to the story's impact. Only the cover illustration—of a historically inaccurate five pointed yellow star—hits a false note.

Vos, Ida. **The Key Is Lost.**
New York: Morrow/HarperCollins. 2000.

Separated from their parents, in hiding from the Nazis, and always in the gravest danger, two Dutch-Jewish sisters become finely attuned to the skills of survival. Showing how the girls are affected, how they adapt, and how they protect themselves psychologically from constant threat, the story is enlivened by a spirit of hope and even humor. This Sydney Taylor Book Award winner is based on the author's personal experiences. Translated from Dutch.

Watts, Irene. **Good-Bye, Marianne: A Story of Growing Up in Nazi Germany.**
Toronto: Tundra Books. 1999.

A story based on the author's childhood in Nazi Germany. As life grows more terrifying for Jews, 11-year-old Marianne is emotionally battered. When space opens on the first *Kindertransport* in December 1938, Marianne's mother insists that she leave. The sequels are *Remember Me* and *Finding Sophie.*

Wolkstein, Diane. **Esther's Story.** Illus. by Juan Wijngaard.
New York: Morrow. 1996.

A sophisticated and elegant rendering of the Purim story, told at the start by the young Hadassah and then in her later role as a rather bewildered Queen Esther. The *Megillat* Esther is combined with *midrash* and original fictional elements to create a story of a reluctant heroine. Luscious illustrations accompany the narrative: A framed, full-page painting done in deep, dark tones is matched with each page of text.

MIDDLE SCHOOL

DeSaix, Deborah Durland, and Karen Gray Ruelle. **Hidden on the Mountain: Stories of Children Sheltered from the Nazis in Le Chambon.**
New York: Holiday House. 2007.

The village of Le Chambon in France is famous for sheltering Jews during the Holocaust under the leadership of Pastor Andre Trocme. Many of the people who, as children, were hidden there were interviewed by the authors of this engrossing nonfiction account. After some historical background—including the history of "La Montagne Protestante," or "Protestant Mountain"—the balance of the book is about the hidden children, the Resistance, the pastors and their families, and Christians who lived in the village. Excellent photographs, a glossary, pronunciation guide, recommended reading, bibliography, source notes and index round out this handsome addition to Holocaust literature for young people.

Draper, Allison Stark. *Pastor Andre Trocme: Spiritual Leader of the French Village Le Chambon.*
New York: Rosen. 2001.

Le Chambon-Sur-Lignon is a village in southeastern France that saved about 5,000 Jews during the Holocaust. Its residents were Protestants, with a history of religious persecution and Huguenot resistance in Catholic France. It is partly for that reason that Pastor Trocme was able to inspire them to the nonviolent resistance that he espoused. Neither the villagers' motivation nor Trocme's is adequately explained in this biography, another in Rosen's acceptable but not outstanding Holocaust Biography Series.

Glick, Susan. *Heroes of the Holocaust.*
Farmington Hills, MI: Lucent. 2003.

After an introductory chapter giving a history of the Holocaust, the author discusses the personality, motivation, and conditions that prompted Oskar Schindler, Raoul Wallenberg, Vladka Meed, Andre Trocme, Hannah Senesh, and Jan Karski to aid and rescue Jews. An economically and gracefully written work, this is part of Lucent's History Makers Series.

Gold, Alison Leslie. *A Special Fate: Chiune Sugihara, Hero of the Holocaust.*
New York: Scholastic. 2000.

The biography of a Japanese diplomat and Righteous Gentile, Chiune Sugihara, is interwoven with the stories of two Holocaust survivors whose lives he touched. A personal portrait of Sugihara is drawn, showing him as a man of integrity, compassion, and deep family loyalties. His wife, Yukiko, emerges as an equally strong person whose support for her husband's decision to issue thousands of exit visas to desperate Jews was crucial. Some black-and-white photographs round out a well-researched and readable biography.

Harrison, Barbara. *Theo.*
New York: Clarion. 1999.

A story set in Greece during World War II. Orphaned Theo and his older brother flee to a mountain village where the village priest and his wife are setting up an escape network for Jews. Greek heroism is celebrated, and the plot involves puppets, Greek legends, and the circumstances that led to the Greek Civil War. The Jewish content is slight.

Lasky, Kathryn. *Broken Song.*
New York: Viking. 2005.

After his parents are killed in a *pogrom* and he becomes responsible for his baby sister, a budding young musician flees the *shtetl* and finds refuge in Vilna. There, Reuven becomes a member of the Bund and an underground fighter trying to overthrow the Czar. A companion to Lasky's earlier book, *The Night Journey*, this involves some of the same characters and events. It is an excellent evocation of the historical period and of a young man's struggle to fulfill his aspirations and his duties.

Leapman, Michael. *Witnesses to War.*
New York: Viking. 1998.

Accounts of eight children who suffered under Nazism. Included are Anne Frank and several other Jewish children, Roman Catholics, and Romany. Written clearly and illustrated with maps and photographs, the perspective is universalistic rather than specifically Jewish.

Levine, Ellen. *Darkness over Denmark: The Danish Resistance and the Rescue of the Jews.*
New York: Holiday House. 2000.

Interviews with individuals involved in the Danish resistance, documentary photographs, and a lucid text combine to tell an inspiring true story. Along with several well-written novels about the same period, it shows readers how the lives of Danish Jews were saved because ordinary Danish citizens refused to remain mere bystanders.

Levitin, Sonia. *Room in the Heart.*
New York: Dutton. 2003.

A powerful and accomplished historical novel set in Denmark during the Nazi occupation. It begins in April 1940, when the Germans invaded under the ruse of protecting the Danes, and ends in 1943, when the valiant secret evacuation of Danish Jews to Sweden began. A Danish Jewish teenage girl and a Danish Gentile teenage boy are the main characters; all of the numerous characters are masterfully portrayed, functioning within a fully-realized plot and setting. Among Levitin's finest achievements, it is a testament to individual courage during a dark and dangerous time.

Matas, Carol. *Greater Than Angels.*
New York: Simon and Schuster. 1998.

A courageous teenage heroine joins the Righteous Gentiles of Le Chambon-Sur-Lignon, France in resisting the Nazis and smuggling her fellow Jews over the border to Switzerland. A notable feature of the story is the portrayal of different responses to the existential questions raised by the Holocaust.

McArthur, Debra. *Raoul Wallenberg: Rescuing Thousands from the Nazis' Grasp.*
Berkeley Heights, NJ: Enslow. 2005.

An account of Wallenberg's rescue of 100,000 Hungarian Jews and his eventual disappearance when the war had ended. The bravery of his deeds and the variety of means that he used to save people is an engrossing story, here part of the publisher's Holocaust Heroes and Nazi Criminals Series.

Rabb, M. C. *Missing Persons: The Rose Queen.*
New York: Penguin Putnam. 2004.

This is the first book in a mystery series about two Jewish sisters who change their identities after their father's death to evade a mercenary stepmother. Taking to the road, they settle in a small Indiana town and try very hard to mask their New York accents and big-city outlook. The town's people are welcoming, except for a high school classmate of the youngest sister. When that girl—the not-yet annointed Rose Queen of Venice, Indiana—disappears, the sisters become sleuths, solving the case with clever detective work. Although it is established clearly that the sisters are Jewish, that doesn't make much of a difference to the story. The writing is fresh and fun and the characters lively, so this is a welcome addition to that small collection of lighthearted reading for teens. Equally as readable are *The Chocolate Lover*, *The Unsuspecting Gourmet*, and *The Venetian Policeman*.

Roberts, Jeremy. *Oskar Schindler: Righteous Gentile.*
New York: Rosen. 2000.

A celebrated figure in the aftermath of Keneally's novel and Spielberg's film, Schindler was not an admirable man in many ways. He was an alcoholic, an adulterer, a Nazi Party member and a war profiteer employing slave labor. Yet, he took enormous risks to save Jews and is credited with saving over 1,000 lives. The author records Schindler's deeds while describing the events of World War II and the progress of the Final Solution. Roberts probes the conflicting instincts within Schindler's psyche and his possible motivations. Photographs and reference aids are included. Part of Rosen's Holocaust Biography Series.

Streissguth, Thomas. *Raoul Wallenberg: Swedish Diplomat and Humanitarian.*
New York: Rosen. 2001.

This account introduces a flesh-and-blood Wallenberg to readers. It sets the scene for Wallenberg's mission, with a background on Jewish life in World War II Hungary, Hungary's role as a German ally, and the machinations of various Hungarian political and military leaders, which affected the Jewish population. The daring manner in which Wallenberg operated is described, illustrated with photographs and one of the passes he handed out to Hungarian Jews. The last chapter speculates on Wallenberg's fate. A timeline, glossary, and other reference aids are included. Eva Wiseman's *My Canary Yellow Star* could be read as a fictional companion to this book.

Taylor, Marilyn. *Faraway Home.*
Dublin: O'Brien Press. 1999.

An Austrian brother and sister are sent on the *Kindertransport* to Northern Ireland, where a farm for Jewish refugees from Hitler was established near Belfast. Actual events are integrated with sympathetic characters, believable relationships, well-paced action, and a portrayal of lives forever changed by war.

Vogiel, Eva. *Facing the Music.*
New York: Judaica Press. 2002.

This is the third of Vogiel's novels set in an Orthodox girls' school in England shortly after World War II. Like the others, its characters include teachers and students and its plot is intricate and rather suspenseful. In this book, identical twin girls who were separated during the Holocaust are finally reunited. The role of music in both of their lives is a factor in the conclusion. The characters are not particularly well developed, but girls who enjoy school stories and especially those who have read the first two books will enjoy this one.

Wukovits, John F. *Oskar Schindler.*
Farmington Hills, MI: Lucent. 2002.

A chronicle of Schindler's life, especially his wartime activities, including his evolution from profiteer to rescuer and his post-war struggles with normalcy. While his motivations are pondered, his actions are recorded so that readers can decide for themselves why Schindler did what he did. The clearly written text is broken up by photographs and sidebars on almost every page. The sidebars are relevant and provide extra context without breaking up the flow of the main text. The photographs are pertinent. Footnotes, bibliography, notes of works consulted, and an index are included. Part of the Heroes and Villains Series.

Wulf, Linda Press. *The Night of the Burning.*
New York: Farrar, Straus and Giroux. 2006.

War, revolution, influenza, and *pogroms* all conspired to create tens of thousands of homeless refugee children during and after World War I. This moving historical novel is based on the lives of two Jewish sisters who were rescued—along with several hundred others like them—by a Jewish philanthropist named Isaac Ochberg and taken in by South Africa's Jewish community. The personal struggle of the older sister to overcome the trauma of losing her parents and home, to revere her memories of them, and yet to forge a new, happy life for herself is as compelling as any historical drama.

HIGH SCHOOL

Opdyke, Irene Gut. *In My Hands: Memoirs of a Holocaust Rescuer.*
New York: Alfred A. Knopf. 1999.

The author grew up in an independent Poland, with solid ethical and moral values imparted by caring parents. Forced to work for the Germans during World War II, she used her relatively advantageous position to help Jews who were used as slave laborers in the hotel laundry she supervised. Later, she emigrated to the United States.

Sokolow, Reha. *Defying the Tide: An Account of Authentic Compassion During the Holocaust.*
New York: Devora. 2003.

A Holocaust memoir written by a survivor's daughter in her mother's voice. The author's family survived by hiding and passing as Gentiles in Germany during World War II. They were greatly assisted by a friend, a non-Jewish woman. The stories of both women are told in the first person, and the experiences described are graphic but not harrowing. The shift in the point of view from one woman to the other is somewhat confusing.

Spinelli, Jerry. *Milkweed.*
New York: Alfred A. Knopf. 2003.

A searing portrayal of life in the Warsaw Ghetto. The main character is a homeless orphan who lives by his wits and initially finds the Nazi occupation of Warsaw exciting. When he attaches himself to a Jewish family who is forced into the Ghetto, he has his first experiences of being part of a family and acting to help others. Because the child's frame of reference is so radically limited by the circumstances of his life, his point of view—and the author's—tends to perceive the destruction of the Jews as an existential absurdity, with no moral or historical resonance. This is not at all a Jewish view and it compromises the story's thematic thrust.

CHAPTER 18

Self-Worth

"If I am not for myself, who will be for me?
If I am not for others, what am I?
And if not now, when?"

Talmud

PRESCHOOL

Anderson, Joel. ***David and the Trash-Talkin' Giant.*** Illus. by Abe Goolsby.
Nashville, TN: Thomas Nelson. 1999.

The story of David and Goliath is retold in rhyme, with clever illustrations assembled from scrap and digitally photographed. Some pages challenge readers to discover hidden objects. The message: It's what's inside that counts!

Baer, Julie. ***I Only Like What I Like.***
Peoria, IL: Bollix Books. 2003.

Author-illustrator Julie Baer's full-page collages are the book's most prominent feature, creating impressionistic portraits of a little boy's willingness to change his mind. The text is brief and very childlike, told as a series of vignettes by the boy. The emotional and imaginative content of each vignette is imparted through illustrations resembling quilts, filled with vivid colors, lines, shapes, faces, and human and animal images. The effect is both personal and symbolic, drawing the reader into a young child's imaginative perceptions of his small world. The Jewish content is presented as a natural part of that world.

Hodes, Lauren. ***Too Big, Too Little . . . Just Right!***
New York: Judaica Press. 2002.

This is the story of a middle child who begins to doubt her place in the family after a little brother is born. She is always too big for some things and too little for others. Her loving grandmother finds her crying and comforts her by showing her that for some things, like a big hug, she's just right.

Rouss, Sylvia. *The Littlest Pair.* Illus. by Holly Hannon.
New York: Pitspopany. 2001.

Two termites that board Noah's ark are rejected by the other animals. When they make sawdust that creates traction on the slippery, wet decks, the other animals accept them. Noah sums it up: "So let's put an end to any more hurtful chatter. We're all God's creatures and to God we all matter." This cute but distorted version of the Noah story will make sense to young children once they know what termites are.

Rouss, Sylvia. *The Littlest Frog.* Illus. by Holly Hannon.
New York: Pitspopany. 2001.

A rhymed story about the smallest of the frogs that plague Pharaoh and the only one to actually frighten him. Part of the publisher's "Littlest" series, it is meant to enhance self-esteem among children who may also be the littlest.

Wing, Natasha. *Jalapeno Bagels.* Illus. by Robert Castillo.
New York: Simon and Schuster/Atheneum. 1996.

Pablo's mother is a Latina and his father is Jewish. Together, they own a bakery that his mother calls a panaderia. When Pablo has to bring some food from his culture to school, he ponders his choices from among the delicious treats his parents make and decides on jalapeno bagels, "Because they are a mixture of both of you. Just like me." A sweet story, cheerfully illustrated, this takes a very positive look at an inter-married family, omitting any discussion of religious differences or practices and emphasizing the positive nature of ethnic diversity.

PRIMARY

Hughes, Shirley. *The Lion and the Unicorn.*
New York: DK. 1999.

A picture story about a little boy named Lenny Levi, who is evacuated from London during the Blitz. Filled with authentic visual details that place the story, the narrative and superb illustrations allow the reader to see a cinematic unfolding of Lenny's experiences in the countryside.

Kimmel, Eric A. *Onions and Garlic.*
New York: Holiday House. 1996.

Based on a poem by Hayyim Nahman Bialik, this is a tale of the foolish son whose father despairs of him, whose brothers scoff at him, but who eventually makes good. The motif is a common one in folk literature, and there is nothing here but the characters' name to mark it as Jewish. Nevertheless, Kimmel's fluid, fast-paced style and vibrant, angular illustrations distinguish it. Arnold's art is all line and movement, with heavily outlined shapes enfolding the bold black type.

Naliboff, Jane. *The Only One Club.* Illus. by Jeff Hopkins.
New York: Flashlight Press. 2004.

A refreshing look at being different is depicted in this picture book about a girl who is the only Jewish child in her class. She forms "The Only One Club" for herself, but all of her classmates want to join because they are the "only one" of something, as well. Set during Hanukkah, this delivers a wholesome message about individual uniqueness and sameness.

Rosenfeld, Dina. *Yossi and Laibel on the Ball.* Illus. by Norman Nodel.
New York: Hachai. 1998.

A new boy moves into Yossi and Laibel's neighborhood, showing the brothers that, even though he uses a wheelchair, he's a great baseball pitcher. One of several books about Yossi and Laibel, this imparts a wholesome message in a child-centered manner. The rhyming narrative and realistic illustrations lend themselves to reading aloud.

Schotter, Roni. *Purim Play.* Illus. by Marilyn Hafner.
New York: Little Brown. 1997.

Set during a play rehearsal, the story of Purim is filtered through the personalities and perspectives of several children and their reaction to an elderly neighbor asked to play the part of Haman. Rollicking illustrations add to the fun of a picture book that probes the relations of children with the elderly.

Steinberg, Bracha. *Just Like. . . Me!* Illus. by Lisa Perel.
Nanuet, NY: Feldheim. 2001.

"Be yourself" is the lesson that is delivered in this short, easy-to-read, illustrated story. Brown-haired, freckle-faced, chubby Rivka isn't content to be herself. She tries to be like one friend after another—the prettiest one, the most athletic, the smartest, the nicest—but she can't be. When she tearfully confesses to her mother why she has been acting out of character, *Imma* shows her that she is important to God. The obvious moralizing is sweetened by the portrayal of a loving mother-daughter relationship.

ELEMENTARY

Bietz, Barbara. *Like a Maccabee.* Illus. by Anita White
St. Paul, MN: Yaldah. 2006.

Hanukkah and soccer are the twin subjects of this heartwarming novel that will especially appeal to boys. As Ben learns about the *Maccabees'* struggle against overwhelming odds from his grandfather, he develops the courage and self-confidence to overcome his own fears.

Blume, Judy. *Are You There, God? It's Me, Margaret.*
New York: Simon and Schuster. 1970.

A classic novel about growing up, fitting in, and identity. After moving from Manhattan to the suburbs, 11-year-old Margaret Simon needs advice about her changing body, friends, boys, and religion. She turns to God, asking questions that still resonate with adolescent readers. One of the main reasons for this book's enduring popularity is that Margaret speaks in the voice of Everygirl. She is direct, genuine, and not at all coy—a child becoming a teenager who expresses herself honestly, without the self-conscious cuteness of so many of the Margaret wannabes that this book inspired. The Jewish content—Margaret has a Christian mother and a Jewish father and is being raised with no religion—is integral to Margaret's questions about her identity.

Hurwitz, Johanna. *Faraway Summer.* Illus. by Mary Azarian.
New York: Morrow. 1998.

In 1910, orphaned 12-year-old "Dossi" (Hadassah) Rabinowitz is sent by the Fresh Air Fund for a vacation on a Vermont farm. During her two-week stay, her horizons widen, while her hosts—a Protestant family—make some discoveries, too. The story emphasizes the hopeful aspects of the immigrant experience and the commonalities among American groups. The sequel is entitled *Dear Emma*.

Kacer, Kathy. *A Bit of Love and a Bit of Luck: Margit: Book Two.*
New York: Penguin Putnam. 2005.

The second book about a Jewish refugee child and her family in the Our Canadian Girl series, this is set in 1946, when Margit's father joins them after being liberated from a concentration camp. The well-developed plot involves the difficulties that immigrants experienced in their efforts to make a new life and Margit's school experiences as a new girl.

Littman, Sarah Darer. *Confessions of a Closet Catholic.*
New York: Dutton. 2005.

Like Margaret in *Are You There, God? It's Me, Margaret*, she questions. Like Heather in *What Happened to Heather Hopkowitz?*, she searches for religious identity. Eleven-year-old Justine, a middle child, is upset with her socially insecure, twice-a-year Jewish family and is drawn to a friend's Catholicism. Her closet secrets are funny and also poignant, as is her search for a comfortable place within her family and meaning within Judaism. Many Jewish children will feel an affinity with this lovable character. Winner of a Sydney Taylor Book Award.

Matas, Carol. *Sparks Fly Upward.*
New York: Clarion. 2002.

A historical novel set in Winnipeg, Canada at the beginning of the twentieth century. A timid adolescent girl is sent to a foster home when her father cannot find work.

Her foster family is Ukrainian, and while some are kind, several of the men are anti-Semites. How she gains confidence and learns to make her own choices are the main themes.

Meiseles, Shayna. *The Bat Mitzvah Club: Debbie's Story.*
New York: Merkos. 2002.

Twelve-year-old Debbie faces her *Bat Mitzvah* with trepidation until her parents enroll her in a preparatory class called the Bat Mitzvah Club. The weekly club sessions, taught by a talented teacher, engage Debbie and other students and teach them to look forward to the responsibilities of an observant Jewish woman. Swimming competitions and a Holocaust mystery form part of the plot. Characterization is strong, especially of Debbie's family, who appear to have become recently observant. A firmly traditional view of the *Bat Mitzvah* is embedded in an earnest and absorbing narrative.

Peterseil, Tehila. *Unjust Cause.*
New York: Pitspopany. 1998.

Davy suffers from dysgraphia, a learning disability that makes it difficult for him to correctly write what he is thinking. His problem is undiagnosed and now in fifth grade, he is angry, frustrated, and desperate to please his demanding father. The story is set within an Orthodox community, and David eventually benefits from the special education program of the religious school system. As a literary work, the writing is mediocre but it makes a strong point about learning disabilities.

Rocklin, Joann. *The Very Best Hanukkah Gift.*
   Illus. by Catherine O'Neil.
New York: Delacorte. 1999.

Eight-year-old Daniel, a middle child, has a problem. He's afraid of dogs, and a neighbor with one has just moved in next door. The author probes the subjects of sibling birth order and children's fears with humor and sensitivity.

Wishinsky, Frieda. *Just Call Me Joe.*
Custer, WA: Orca. 2004.

An easy-to-read and engrossing chapter book about Jewish immigrants in New York at the turn of the twentieth century. Ten-year-old Joseph and his 17-year-old sister Anna are sent by their parents to New York, where they live with their poor but kindly widowed aunt. Joe's experiences in school and on the New York streets, plus Anna's experiences working in a sweatshop, demonstrate some of the hardships that immigrants had to overcome. The Jewish values they learned in *cheder* and from their parents enable both young people to make the right decisions and choices.

MIDDLE SCHOOL

Adelman, Penina V. *The JGirls' Guide: The Young Jewish Women's Handbook for Coming of Age.*
Woodstock, VT: Jewish Lights. 2005.

A potpourri of information that covers many aspects of Jewish life for preteen and teenage girls who ask, "Where do I fit in?" The 10 chapters include such topics as friendship, parents, eating, body image, sexuality, *tikun olam*, and Jewish identity. Each chapter follows a given format that begins with a *mitzvah* statement from the Jewish text. There are suggestions for discussion, activities, historical information, things to think about, a glossary, a bibliography, and blank note pages in the back called "My Thoughts."

Almagor, Gila. *Under the Domim Tree.*
New York: Simon and Schuster. 1995.

Teenagers living in an Israeli youth village after the Holocaust search for lost parents and try to deal with survivor guilt. Based on the author's experiences, this is an absorbing look at Israel in the early days of statehood and at young Holocaust refugees dealing with issues of identity, community, and sorrow.

French, Jackie. *Hitler's Daughter.*
New York: HarperCollins. 2003.

Despite an off-putting title, this is a fascinating "what if?" story. Set in Australia, it involves a group of schoolmates who make up stories while they wait for the bus. One of their stories takes them into the privileged world of a disabled girl whose father is Adolf Hitler. Motivated by the story, one of the boys in the group begins to think about its implication: About good and evil, about prejudice, social responsibility, and about how they enter into his own life. There are no Jewish characters in the story but the issues raised are of interest to Jewish readers.

Cohen, Deborah Bodin. *Lilith's Ark: Teenage Tales of Biblical Women.*
Philadelphia: Jewish Publication Society. 2006.

Episodes from the teenage years of women in the *Book of Genesis* are found in this collection of modern *midrash* for girls. Eve, Sarah, Hagar, Rebecca, Rachel, Leah, Dinah, Tamar, and Asenath are included, each the subject of a story that deals primarily with their "first loves, blossoming spirituality, and developing bodies and identities." The author has provided a detailed discussion guide and that will help fulfill the book's pedagogical purpose in a mother-daughter book club, or as part of the curriculum of a pre- or post-*Bat Mitzvah* class.

Greene, Bette. *The Summer of My German Soldier.*
New York: Dial. 1973.

A powerful novel about a dysfunctional Jewish family, told by 12-year-old Patty Bergen. Patty's narration captures the atmosphere of a small Southern town during World War II—mainly its hyper-patriotism and small-mindedness. Even more unforgettable is the author's portrayal of a child's desperate search for love and acceptance in the face of an uncaring mother and an abusive father. Two things sustain Patty: The family's maid, Ruth, and a friendship she forms with an escaped German soldier. Judaism in this family takes the form of customs but not belief or the practice of Jewish values. There are very few books that give so unflinching a portrait of parental cruelty and its impact on a child.

Jung, Reinhardt. *Dreaming in Black and White.*
New York: Phyllis Fogelman. 2003.

A disabled German boy ponders his place in his family and the world by imagining himself into the Nazi era, when his status as an undesirable would have doomed him. A somber story, there are frequent shifts between the past and the present. This serves as the key to the story, as readers are led to examine their own prejudices against imperfection. The narrator thinks: "Back then I would have been killed. These days I ought not to exist at all, because of genetic testing." The Jewish content is minimal, but the book would be excellent for discussions about prejudice, including anti-Semitism. Translated from the German by Anthea Bell.

Kamen, Gloria. *Hidden Music: The Life of Fanny Mendelssohn.*
New York: Simon and Schuster/Atheneum. 1996.

Sister of the more famous Felix, Fanny Mendelssohn was a dutiful daughter, an adoring sister, and a talented musician in her own right. This well-crafted biography of a woman who lived in an era when most respectable women did not have careers has a subtle but strong feminist thrust.

Soumerai, Eve Nussbaum, and Carol D. Schulz. *A Voice from the Holocaust.*
Westport, CT. Greenwood Press. 2003.

The memoir of a *Kindertransport* child who was separated from her loving family and taken in by an English family who were emotionally frozen and probably mentally disturbed. At 15, she was sent to work at a home for children and began to recover from her traumatic experiences. Meant to be used in schools, there is a foreword to the teacher, an introduction, and a timeline. Good for discussion. Part of the Voices of Twentieth Century Conflict Series.

Vogiel, Eva. *Invisible Chains.*
New York: Judaica Press. 2000.

An Orthodox boarding school in England is the setting for this story of two sisters, one of whom is paralyzed. A wise headmistress and a concerned young teacher intervene to solve the girls' potentially destructive relationship. Traditional Judaism guides and supports them.

Weiss, Arnine Cumsky. **Becoming a Bat Mitzvah: A Treasury of Stories.**
Scranton, PA: University of Scranton Press. 2005.

Anecdotal in tone, the stories in this compilation span the decades and are the personal reflections of remarkable people of all ages who have interesting tales to tell. Many feature people with special needs, abilities, or interests.

Wiseman, Eva. *No One Must Know.*
Toronto: Tundra Books. 2004.

Thirteen-year-old Alexandra is pretty, popular in school and in her Catholic youth group, and not especially concerned that her immigrant parents won't talk about their lives before they came to Canada. It takes a set of coincidences to bring matters to a crisis: Alex's first boyfriend is Jewish, she finds some old pictures hidden in her mother's dresser, and a friend from her parents' past comes to visit. When Alex is finally told that she and her family are Jewish, that they conceal this to protect her from anti-Semitism, and that her parents are Holocaust survivors, she chooses honesty and compels her anxious parents to do likewise. Alex is a believable heroine, and her parents' dilemma is portrayed sympathetically.

HIGH SCHOOL

Bitton-Jackson, Livia. *Hello, America.*
New York: Simon and Schuster. 2005.

The third book in a trilogy that also includes *I Have Lived a Thousand Years* and *My Bridges of Hope*. Bitton-Jackson continues the saga of teenage Elli and her mother, who emigrate as refugees to New York following World War II. Warmly welcomed by family and friends, mother and daughter cope with the strangeness of a new country and gradually adapt. Elli becomes a teacher and is able to get the education she was deprived of in Europe. Much of the story is told through the lens of Elli's romantic life: Several men fall in love with her. A formal, somewhat self-conscious style underscores Elli's sense of distance from a country that seems much less respectful of tradition and much more liberal in its social customs than what she has known before coming to the United States.

Ehrenhaft, Daniel. *Tell It to Naomi.*
New York: Delacorte Press. 2004.

When Dave Rosen falls in love with a fellow student, he has to figure out a way to capture her attention and esteem. He assumes the guise of "Naomi" and writes an advice column for the school newspaper, which becomes wildly popular but soon careens out of control. By the end, Dave solves some but not all of his problems and gains some self-knowledge and self-confidence. Dave is Jewish, but this is an incidental part of the novel.

Garfinkle, D. L. *Storky: How I Lost My Nickname and Won the Girl.*
New York: G. P. Putnam's Sons. 2005.

Besides being laugh-out-loud funny, *Storky* is a perceptive portrayal of male adolescence. With a wonderfully drawn main character, it deals with issues of self-worth, friendship, sexuality, divorce, and even, very slightly, homosexuality in the characters of an aunt and her partner. Michael Pomerantz, a.k.a. Storky, tells the story and as it progresses, teenage readers will come to empathize with this lovable teen.

Kositsky, Lynne. *The Thought of High Windows.*
Toronto: Kids Can Press. 2004.

A Holocaust novel for mature teens, this convincingly blends teenage angst with the terrors of war. It is about a group of Jewish refugee children on a perilous and—for some—fatal journey across Europe. The main character is a homely girl who is derided by the other girls for being fat, ugly, and "Old Jewish." As their situation grows more perilous, Esther takes on false identities to evade the Nazis and to work with the French resistance. She grows in courage and self-esteem, gaining the strength to go on when her beloved friend, Walter, is captured and sent to Auschwitz. A "good German" makes a somewhat contrived appearance at a critical moment but aside from that, the novel rings true.

McKay, Sharon E. *Esther.*
Toronto: Penguin Canada. 2004.

Like her namesake, Esther, a French Jew, survived by hiding her real identity. This fast-paced historical novel is based on the life of Esther Brandeau, the first Jew to set foot in New France. Fleshing out the few facts known about Esther, including her frequent disguises as a boy, the author spins a rousing, romantic yarn that breathes life into French society of the 1700s. The characterization is especially strong.

Newman, Leslea. *Jailbait.*
New York: Delacorte. 2005.

A cautionary tale for teens about an overweight and unpopular girl who becomes trapped in a damaging sexual relationship with an older man. Told as a first-person confessional, it combines an absorbing plot and characters with a socially important theme.

Stein, Tammar. *Light Years.*
New York: Alfred A. Knopf. 2005.

An accomplished first novel about an Israeli girl who seeks both emotional and physical distance from Israel, where her boyfriend was killed in a suicide bombing. It is told in chapters that alternate between Charlottesville, Virginia, where she is attending college, and Israel. Maya's family and social life are revealed, along with interesting glimpses into the experiences of young Israeli soldiers. The characterization is quite strong: Maya is sympathetic and believable, as are the people she encounters in America and those she recalls in Israel. A much more polished book than Zenatti's *When I Was a Soldier*, this book gives an insight into the lives of many Israeli young people who are of the age for army service.

Woodson, Jacqueline. *If You Come Softly.*
New York: G. P. Putnam's Sons. 1998.

An accomplished young adult novel about a Romeo-Juliet relationship between an African-American boy and a white, Jewish girl. Racism is prevalent throughout the story, leading to a shocking conclusion. The girl's family is not religious and committed to secular, liberal ideals, which they don't always practice.

Zenatti, Valerie. *When I Was a Soldier.*
New York: Bloomsbury. 2005.

Zenatti's memoir, originally written in French, reveals what it is like to be an Israeli teenager and soldier. She writes about her home in Beersheva, school, friends, pop stars, romances, first sex, getting plastered—all with the same flippant, somewhat cynical tone used to describe her army experiences. Despite the subject, which should be interesting for its insider look at modern Israel and (some) modern Israeli teens, Zenatti's account is bogged down by too much self-absorption and not enough self-knowledge.

CHAPTER **19**

Many Stories, Many Values

"Turn it and turn it again for everything is in it."

Talmud

PRESCHOOL

Blitz, Shmuel. *Bedtime Stories of Jewish Values.* Illus. by Liat Binyamini Ariel.
New York: Mesorah. 1998.
Intended to teach children virtuous behavior through stories, this collection of short stories—part of a series by an Orthodox publisher—exemplifies values such as honesty, loyalty, piety, etc. Brightly illustrated and didactically written.

Blitz, Shmuel. *Bedtime Stories to Make You Smile.* Illus. by Tova Katz.
New York: Mesorah. 2003.
This collection of 21 humorous stories culled from the *Talmud*, Jewish folklore, contemporary Jewish life, and history is designed to instruct as well as to entertain. It is part of a series of bedtime story books by Shmuel Blitz and, like all of them, it is heavy on the preaching. Each story is accompanied by a large, color illustration and is two pages long.

Raanan, Ahuva, and Chaim Walder. *Stories Straight from Avi's Heart.*
    Illus. by Tirtsa Pelleg.
Nanuet, NY: Feldheim. 2004.

Avi's face, shown in large, full-page illustrations, reflects each of the emotions that the authors address in this book aimed at helping parents and their young children understand such feelings as anger, fear, shyness, worry, jealousy, happiness, etc. For each emotion, there is a common-sense discussion of it for adults plus a short, illustrated story that shows how Avi encounters and, with his parents' help, deals with the emotion. The plots are grounded in everyday life, the emotions are common ones, the perspective is Orthodox, and the purpose is bibliotherapeutic.

PRIMARY

Geras, Adele. *My Grandmother's Stories: A Collection of Jewish Folktales,*
Revised Edition. Illus. by Anita Lobel.
New York: Alfred A. Knopf. 2003.

A new edition of the 1990 Sydney Taylor Book Award winner (illusrated by Jael
Jordan) with fresh, colorful illustrations. Excellent for reading aloud, these traditional
Jewish tales are framed by a narrative involving a little girl and her grandmother in
Grandmother's apartment in Israel several decades ago.

Goldin, Barbara Diamond. *Journeys with Elijah: Eight Tales of the Prophets.*
Illus. by Jerry Pinkney.
San Diego: Harcourt/Gulliver. 1999.

Stunning color illustrations decorate these traditional stories that are set in different
parts of the world where Jews have lived, including China, Argentina, and Persia. The
focus is on Elijah's message of kindness and compassion, and the sometimes offbeat settings, rendered beautifully by the illustrations, add interest.

Krohn, Genendel. *Miracle at Sea and Other Stories: Timeless Tales from the*
Lives of Our Sages. Illus. by Tirtsa Pelleg.
Nanuet, NY: Feldheim. 2006

A collection of 16 stories taken from the *Talmud*, each telling of a Talmudic personality who exhibits positive character traits, including the performance of *mitzvot*.
Each story is only one or two pages long and accompanied by a full-page color
illustration and a summary of the lesson it teaches. It is targeted to Orthodox
Jewish readers.

Krohn, Genendel. *The Miracle of the Rock: Timeless Tales from the Lives of Our*
Sages. Illus. by Tirtsa Pelleg.
Nanuet, NY: Feldheim. 2003.

An excellent collection of short stories about rabbis and sages, intended to exemplify *mitzvot* and inspire children. Rabbi Chanina ben Dosa, Rabbi Akiva, Rabbi
Hillel, and Yehudah HaNasi are some of the notables who appear in these stories,
illustrated realistically, in color. A short note indicating what each story teaches is
included along with a glossary. The large format, with an illustration accompanying
each story, is inviting.

Lehman-Wilzig, Tami. *Tasty Bible Stories: A Menu of Tales and Matching Recipes.*
Illus. by Katherine Janus Kahn.
Minneapolis, MN: Kar-Ben/Lerner. 2003.

Fourteen well-known Bible stories are retold and matched with food relevant to the
story. Several recipes go with each story, and the many color illustrations—some full

page—are dynamic. Written in a breezy, colloquial style, this fun book includes a recipe index and a chart of metric conversions.

Maisel, Grace Ragues, and Samantha Schubert. *A Year of Jewish Stories: 52 Tales for Children and Their Families.* Illus. by Tammy L. Keiser.
New York: URJ Press. 2004.

A collection of 52 stories retold from Jewish tradition. The table of contents organizes them according to Jewish holidays, and there are indexes of both topics and virtues. Short enough to be read in one sitting, perhaps before bedtime, the stories suffer from being "updated," so that the timeless magic of folklore, which shows but does not tell readers its meaning, is replaced with truncated tales, told with far too many modern clichés. Mainly for parents or teachers in a hurry.

Prose, Francine. *The Angel's Mistake: Stories of Chelm.*
Illus. by Mark Podwal.
New York: Greenwillow. 1997.

In a charming marriage of words and pictures, this version of some of the *Chelm* stories—adapted successfully for a younger-than-usual audience—tells of how a botched mission by two angels created the legendary town of fools. A perfect introduction to Chelm for children too young to understand the irony of most other versions.

Schram, Peninnah. *Ten Classic Jewish Children's Stories.* Illus. by Jeffrey Allon.
New York: Pitspopany. 1998.

This collection of 10 highly abridged stories—each limited to two pages—seems intended more for educational purposes than literary enjoyment. Most of the stories are from *midrash*, including the ones about Honi the Circlemaker, Miriam, Jacob, and Rabbi Hillel. They will be welcomed by teachers with a few spare minutes to use constructively, and each is followed by a few study questions. The large, overly colored illustrations are banal, and the book design is pedestrian.

Schwartz, Howard, and Barbara Rush. *The Diamond Tree: Jewish Tales from Around the World.* Illus. by Uri Shulevitz.
New York: HarperCollins, 1991.

An outstanding collection of Jewish tales from Eastern Europe and the Middle East, told with folkloric clarity and charm. Readers will find stories from the *Talmud*, tales set in Chelm, and others about a foolish but lovable little boy named Chusham, a child no bigger than a walnut, and the giant Og, among others. Some of the motifs will be familiar: A bear who eats children; a witch who captures children; and a tiny person. They exemplify the values of the Jewish people and introduce children to some classic tales. The illustrations, the book design, and the authors' source notes are all excellent. Winner of a Sydney Taylor Book Award.

Spinner, Stephanie. *It's a Miracle! A Hanukkah Storybook.* Illus. by Jill McElmurry.
New York: Simon and Schuster/Atheneum. 2003.

On each night of Hanukkah, Grandma Karen tells Owen a bedtime story, all of which remind him of people in his family. As the stories are told, characters come alive, and strong Jewish values are expressed through a felicitous blend of dialogue and illustration. At dinner on the last night, all of the people in Grandma Karen's stories sit around the table, with pictures above their heads to remind Owen and readers of their individual stories. Charmingly written and illustrated, this is also an excellent example of the modern picture book, with every literary and artistic element plus size, format, and design contributing to an outstanding whole.

Taback, Simms. *Kibitzers and Fools: Tales My Zayda Told Me.*
New York: Viking. 2005.

Boundlessly exuberant, this collection of Yiddish stories, maxims, and jokes is illustrated in Taback's signature, award-winning style. Visual details abound, even to the endpapers and table of contents. In a short introduction, Taback introduces Yiddish and urges readers to have some *chutzpah* and try it. As in much Jewish lore from Eastern Europe, irony is the prevailing tone, so children need to have some sense of the disjunction between what is and what should be before they enjoy it. A gem!

ELEMENTARY

Geras, Adele. *The Kingfisher Treasury of Jewish Stories.* Illus. by Jane Cope.
Boston: Kingfisher. 2003.

The 15 stories in this book are a mixture of ones that are well known and others that are lesser known. The same can be said of the authors. The lesser-known stories are mainly by English authors, and readers learn nothing about them because there are no background notes or authors' biographies given. Folklore, historical fiction, and stories set in modern-day England, Israel, and South Africa are included. First published in 1996, this small paperback is the first American edition.

Gershator, Phillis. *Wise ... and Not So Wise: Ten Tales from the Rabbis.*
    Illus. by Alexa Ginsburg.
Philadelphia: Jewish Publication Society. 2004.

A delightful collection of stories adapted from the *Talmud* and *Midrash*. Each one is followed by the author's comments, giving sources, mentioning alternative versions, saying how she changed or embellished the tale, and asking questions that explore both the meaning of the story and how it reflects rabbinical thinking. Attractive illustrations in shades of black and gray are a pleasant addition to stories that beg to be read aloud or told.

Gold, Sharlya, and Mishael Maswari Caspi. *The Answered Prayer and Other Yemenite Folktales.* Illus. by Marjory Wunsch.
Philadelphia: Jewish Publication Society, 2004.

Twelve folktales, both sad and humorous, create an understanding of the lives of Yemenite Jews. The reader is struck by how often danger from their non-Jewish neighbors motivates these tales. Best for telling to children in third grade and up. This book is a paperback reissue of a collection first published in 1990.

Goldin, Barbara Diamond. *A Child's Book of Midrash: 52 Jewish Stories from the Sages.*
Northvale, NJ: Jason Aronson. 1993.

The retellings of these stories from the *Midrash* and the *Talmud* exemplify the rabbinic wisdom of the originals while adding plot elements that make them interesting to children. The author says she chose them for their ability to appeal to children while retaining their original values, messages, and meaning. Most of the 52 stories are quite short and can be easily woven into library programs. Bible heroes, rabbis, prophets, kings, talking animals, and ordinary folk are all found in this classic treasury.

Goldin, Barbara Diamond. *One Hundred and One Jewish Read Aloud Stories.*
New York: Black Dog and Levinthal, 2001.

A collection of short versions of stories from the Bible, *Talmud* and *Midrash*, folktales from various countries, and a section of holiday stories. Some non-fiction and poetry is included, as are stories by I. L. Peretz, I. B. Singer, Sadie Rose Weilerstein, Sydney Taylor, and other modern writers. It is acceptable as an introduction to some classic Jewish children's stories.

Goldin, Barbara Diamond. *While the Candles Burn: Eight Stories for Hanukkah.*
Illus. by Elaine Greenstein.
New York: Viking. 1996.

Faith, traditions, religious commitment, peace, honoring women, charity, and rededication are the themes of these stories. Most are folktales but one is set in modern Israel and another is about a Holocaust survivor.

Jaffe, Nina. *The Mysterious Visitor: Stories of the Prophet Elijah.*
Illus. by Elivia Savidier.
New York: Scholastic. 1997.

Spirited writing and sparkling illustrations portray Elijah in different guises, settings, and historical periods as he delivers his universal blessings of comfort and peace. This is the second collaboration between the author and illustrator to win a Sydney Taylor Book Award. The source notes are excellent.

Jaffe, Nina. *Tales for the Seventh Day.* Illus. by Kelly Stribling Sutherland.
New York: Scholastic. 2000.

Seven gracefully written tales follow an Introduction describing traditional observances that have maintained Jewish identity and continuity. The tales are adapted
from *Talmud*, folk literature, and Jewish legend.

Jaffe, Nina. *The Uninvited Guest and Other Jewish Holiday Tales.* Illus. by Elivia Savidier.
New York: Scholastic. 1993.

An outstanding collection of Jewish folktales for the holidays of Rosh Hashanah, Yom
Kippur, Sukkot, Hanukkah, Purim, Passover, and *Shabbat*. The Yom Kippur tale, "Miracles
on the Sea," is adapted from an I. L. Peretz story; sources for all the tales are given, and
Jaffe's retellings and Savadier's illustrations sparkle. The notes, as usual with books by
this author, are exemplary. Winner of a Sydney Taylor Book Award.

Kimmel, Eric A. *A Hanukkah Treasury.* Illus. by Emily Lisker.
New York: Henry Holt. 1998.

This compendium of stories, songs, poetry, recipes, legends, history, and tradition makes
for a wealth of information about Hanukkah. Included are a clear re-telling of the
Hanukkah story, selections from the First Book of Maccabees, the history of the *menorah*
and *hanukkiyah*, the origins of the *dreidel*, holiday foods from many communities, music,
poetry, and ritual. The bright acrylic paintings add style and energy.

Kimmel, Eric A. *The Jar of Fools: Eight Hanukkah Stories from Chelm.*
    Illus. by Mordicai Gerstein.
New York: Holiday House. 2000.

Too delicious to be enjoyed only at Hanukkah, these effervescent tales show how the
wisdom of fools might be the wisest kind of all. Not all of the stories are traditional
Chelm tales and not all of them follow the conventions of Chelm tales, which show
the absurdity of taking the truth too literally. Nevertheless, the intrinsic humanity of
the tales, the examples of making the best of things, are present in abundance, enhanced by outstanding illustrations that capture each story's spirit of silliness.

Oberman, Sheldon. *Solomon and the Ant and Other Jewish Folktales.*
    Introduction by Peninnah Schram.
Honesdale, PA: Boyds Mills Press. 2006.

An outstanding collection of 43 Jewish tales from the Bible, rabbinic sources, and all over
the world where Jews have lived. Peninnah Schram's introduction and commentary are
invaluable additions to the collection, which includes notes, sources and variants, and
motif numbers from the Israel Folk Archives (IFA) for each story. Not illustrated, it is an
excellent resource for teachers, librarians, and other storytellers.

Philip, Neil. *The Pirate Princess and Other Fairy Tales.* Illus. by Mark Weber.
New York: Arthur A. Levine/Scholastic. 2005.

Rabbi Nahman of Bratslav, one of the great Hasidic masters, told stories in Yiddish and Hebrew in the late eighteenth and early nineteenth centuries. His followers have preserved and interpreted them up to the present day. In this outstanding collection, seven of the more child-friendly stories are retold and illustrated. In an eloquent introduction, Philip presents the background on the tales and explains his own approach to changing them for a general readership.

Pollack, Gadi. *Once Upon a Tale: Twelve Illustrated Parables from the*
Dubno Maggid.
Nanuet, NY: Feldheim. 2004.

Rabbi Jacob Ben Wolf Kranz, better known as the Dubno Maggid for his storytelling abilities, was born in Vilna in 1741 and died in 1804. Twelve of his stories are offered in a graphic-novel format, each only two pages long followed by an explanation of their meaning, with references from the *Torah* and other writings. Primarily for observant readers.

Rossel, Seymour. *Sefer Ha-Aggadah: Volume One.* Illus. by Judy Dick.
New York: UAHC Press. 1996.

Based on *Sefer Ha-Aggadah*, the classic collection of *talmudic* legends and stories compiled by Hayim Nahman Bialik and Yehoshua Hana Ravnitzky, this book features stories about Adam and Eve, Noah, Abraham and Sarah, Joseph, Moses, and other biblical figures. The stories exemplify concepts such as obedience to God, keeping one's word, holiness, and honoring women. There is a second volume.

Schacht, Rebecca. *Lights along the Path: Jewish Folklore through the Grades*
for Children Ages Four to Twelve. Illus. by Jacqui Morgan.
Beverly Hills, CA: Chelsey Press. 1999.

A collection of folktales from sources in the *Talmud* and *Midrash*, each designated for an appropriate grade level and each credited to its source. The stories include animal fables, tales of magic and miracles, and retellings of the biblical narrative— all with a moral message. Intended to be used by teachers and other adults. The author is certified as a teacher in the Waldorf School movement.

Schwartz, Howard. T*he Day the Rabbi Disappeared: Jewish Holiday Tales of Magic.*
Illus. by Monique Passicot.
New York: Viking, 2000.

The magic in these tales—of dreams, heavenly journeys, and secret names—is used to protect and save the Jewish people. Several of the stories feature learned women and all 12 of them are associated with the major festivals, *Rosh Hodesh*, and the Sabbath.

Schwartz, Howard. *Invisible Kingdoms: Jewish Tales of Angels, Spirits, and Demons.* Illus. by Stephen Fieser.
New York: HarperCollins. 2002.

In this outstanding collection of folklore, angels serve as God's messengers, spirits of the dead haunt this world as ghosts, and evil forces known as demons try to lead humans astray. Stories are from a variety of places where Jews have lived. Source notes identify each tale. Schwartz's retellings preserve the fluid, concrete style of oral storytelling, and each story is fresh and engaging. They vary in length and will appeal to a wide age range, including adults.

Schwartz, Howard. *A Journey to Paradise and Other Jewish Tales.*
Illus. by Giora Carmi.
New York: Pitspopany. 2000.

These eight folktales from Eastern Europe, Tunisia, Yemen and Israel are filled with magic and adventure. Most are available in other versions, including some of Schwartz's other collections. Here, the large format and well-spaced print will invite independent reading. The illustrations are vividly colored, unsubtle, and awkwardly placed.

Schwartz, Howard, and Barbara Rush. *A Coat for the Moon and Other Jewish Tales.* Illus. by Michael Iofin.
Philadelphia: Jewish Publication Society. 1999.

A top-notch collection of folklore told by Jews in many geographical areas and historical periods. The values of charity, justice, loyalty, wisdom, cooperation, kindness, and love are illuminated in stories of demons, witches, giants, and other magical beings.

Serwer, Blanche Luria. *Let's Steal the Moon: Jewish Tales, Ancient and Recent.* Illus. by Trina Schart Hyman.
New York: Little Brown. 1970.

This engaging collection of 11 folktales from the Middle East and Eastern Europe contains stories about King Solomon, the *Golem*, the Fools of Chelm, and Rabbi Hillel, among others. Hyman's dark, dramatic illustrations portray characters, setting, and action as effectively as the text.

Sholom Aleichem. *A Treasury of Sholom Aleichem's Children's Stories.*
Selected and translated by Aliza Shevrin.
New York: Jason Aronson. 1996

Some of the great Yiddish writer's *Mayses far Yidishe Kinder* (Stories for Jewish Children), as well as those from his other works, are included in this anthology. They capture the experiences of children growing up in the *shtetls* of Eastern Europe while being sensitive to the universal experiences of childhood.

Simon, Solomon. *The Wise Men of Helm and Their Merry Tales.*
Springfield, NJ: Behrman House. 1961.

Originally published in 1942, *The Wise Men of Helm* was one of the first modern collections of Jewish folklore for children. The narration is deadpan and completely serious, as though nothing could be more sensible than Chelm logic. The life-affirming spirit of the *shtetl* is revealed in the stories, as well as a distinguishing human characteristic—the ability to laugh at ourselves. A classic, followed by *More Tales of the Wise Men of Helm*.

Singer, Isaac Bashevis. *Zlateh the Goat and Other Stories.* Illus. by Maurice Sendak.
New York: HarperCollins. 1994.

First published in 1976, this now classic collection of folktales translated from Yiddish is illustrated with some of Sendak's finest work. There are tales from Chelm and stories of the supernatural among the seven included. As Singer's first book for children, it also can be considered one of his finest and a landmark in Jewish children's literature. No Judaic library should be without it; all Jewish children should know these stories. Translated by the author and Elizabeth Shub, who translated most of Singer's books for children.

Wiesel, Elie. *King Solomon and His Magic Ring.* Illus. by Mark Podwal.
New York: HarperCollins. 1999.

Twenty wonder tales based on *Talmud* and *Midrash* are presented in a somewhat formal style. Demons, angels, flying carpets, and talking animals are featured, and the tales show Solomon's legacy to be a mixed one.

MIDDLE SCHOOL

Asher, Sandy. *With All My Heart, With All My Mind.*
New York: Simon and Schuster. 1999.

Eric A. Kimmel, Sonia Levitin, Johanna Hurwitz, and Gloria Miklowitz are some of the authors of these short stories about Jewish teens' search for independence, identity, and spiritual authenticity. Each story is accompanied by a short interview with the author and a biographical sketch.

Hautzig, Esther. *The Seven Good Years and Other Stories of I. L. Peretz.*
Philadelphia: Jewish Publication Society. 2004.

The stories of the Yiddish writer I. L. Peretz (1859–1915) are said to have captured the soul of the Eastern European Jewry. The award-winning author Esther Hautzig has translated and adapted 10 of these treasures for children. Each story is enhanced by Deborah Ray's smoky, evocative illustrations. Among them are Peretz's famous "Bontsche Zweig,"

(Continued)

> **The Seven Good Years and Other Stories of I. L. Peretz.** *(Continued)*
>
> "The Magician," "The Seven Good Years," and "If Not Still Higher." JPS has reissued these stories in a paperback edition. They were originally published in 1984. No Jewish child should miss them.

Krantz, Gershon. *Chanan and His Violin and Other Stories.*
New York: Merkos. 2000.

Sixteen stories and a play make up this collection. With settings that range from ancient to modern and plots often centered on a holiday, the pervasive theme is one of persecution. Although Jewish spiritual values prevail in the end, the point of view is somber, and the climax to some of the stories is violent. Written in the tradition of Yiddish storytelling, this is primarily for Orthodox readers.

Lazewnik, Libby. *The Burglar and Other Stories.*
Southfield, MI: Targum Press. n.d.

A collection of stories written for a primarily Orthodox audience about teens who learn important moral lessons. Useful for teaching character development.

Penn, Malka. *Ghosts and Golems: Haunting Tales of the Supernatural.*
  Illus. by Theodor Black.
Philadelphia: Jewish Publication Society. 2001.

The ghosts and *golems* in this collection of 10 original short stories are primarily devices used to propel plots and develop themes dealing with loss, conflict, change, and Jewish continuity. The writing is uneven in quality. A similar short story collection with a similar purpose and intended audience, *With All My Heart, With All My Mind* by Sandy Asher, is a better choice.

Weinfeld, Chaya Baila. *An Unexpected Detour and Other Stories.*
New York: Judaica Press. 2003.

A collection of historical short stories about the holidays, set mostly in Russia and Eastern Europe. The plots involve miracles and mysterious occurrences, and the settings range from antiquity to the present. An extensive glossary is included.

Yaffe, Rachel. *Lost and Found and Other Stories.* Illus. by Bryna Waldman.
New York: Merkos. 2002.

This is a collection of six short stories and a novella, written for adolescent girls from an Orthodox perspective. The settings are both contemporary and historical, and the focus is often on the courage of women. The overriding theme is God's love for the Jewish people.

APPENDIX A

Glossary

Definitions of words italicized in the text are found in this glossary.

Afikomen: A special piece of matzah that is hidden at the start of the Passover Seder and eaten at the end.

Akeda: Refers to the story of the binding of Isaac in *Genesis* 22:1–19.

Aliyah: One of the meanings of the term is immigration to Israel. Another refers to the honor given to those who are called to participate in the reading of the Torah in the synagogue. The literal meaning in Hebrew is "going up."

Ashkenazim (pl.): Jews tracing their origins to northwestern, central, and eastern Europe.

Aufruf: Yiddish for the calling up of a couple to the Torah on the Shabbat before their wedding.

Baal Shem Tov: Israel ben Eliezer (1698–1760), the founder of the religious movement of Hasidism.

Baal Teshuvah: A newly observant Jew. The literal meaning in Hebrew is "person who has repented or returned."

Bar Mitzvah: A ceremony marking the time when a boy of 13 becomes an adult in religious matters.

Baruch Hashem: Praise God.

Bat Mitzvah: A ceremony marking the time when a girl of 12 becomes an adult according to Jewish law.

Beta Israel: The name by which Ethiopian Jews refer to themselves. The literal meaning in Hebrew is "House of Israel."

BCE: Before the Common Era; alternative to BC.

Bikur holim: Visiting the sick.

Blood Libel: A false accusation that Jews used the blood of Christian children to make matzah for Passover.

Bris: see Brit milah.

Brit milah: A ceremony of circumcision performed on the eighth day of a Jewish boy's life. The literal meaning in Hebrew is "covenant of circumcision."

Brocha; brochot (pl.): Blessing.

Bubbe: Yiddish for grandma.

CE: Common Era, alternative to AD.

Caftan: A garment worn by some observant Jews, consisting of a long gown with sleeves reaching below the hands. It is generally fastened by a belt or sash.

Challah; challot (pl.): A loaf of yeast-leavened egg bread, usually braided, traditionally eaten on the Sabbath, holidays, and other ceremonial occasions.

Charoset: Mixture of nuts, fruit, wine, and other ingredients for the Passover ritual; represents the mortar used while Jews were slaves in Egypt.

Cheder: Jewish elementary school.

Chelm: Legendary town of fools.

Chelmnik: Resident of Chelm.

Chesed: Lovingkindness.

Chumash: Five Books of Moses.

Chuppah: A marriage canopy.

Chutzpah: Yiddish for insolence, nerve, audacity.

Days of Awe: The Ten Days of Repentance, beginning with Rosh Hashanah and ending with the holiday of Yom Kippur.

Dovid HaMelech: King David.

Dreidel: Yiddish for a four-sided, top-like toy with the Hebrew letters nun, gimel, hay, and shin on the sides. Used to play a traditional Hanukkah game.

Dybbuk: In Jewish legend, the restless soul of a deceased human being that enters the body of a living person and takes possession.

Elijah's Cup: A cup of wine customarily set apart in honor of the prophet Elijah at the Passover Seder.

Eretz Israel: The Land of Israel.

Etrog: Citron; one of the Four Species of plants used in the Sukkot ritual.

Felafel: Arabic for ground spiced chickpeas rolled into balls and fried.

Gelt: Yiddish for money.

Gematria: A system by which hidden truths and meanings are discovered within words. Each letter of an alphabet corresponds to a number.

Golem: In Jewish lore, an artificially created, man-like creature with supernatural strength.

Haggadah; Haggadot (pl.): The book read during the Passover Seder recounting the story of the Exodus.

Halakhah: Jewish law.

Hamentaschen: Yiddish for triangular fruit- or poppy seed-filled cookies traditionally served during Purim. The name comes from the hamentaschen's resemblance to the hat Haman wore.

Hanukkiyah; hanukkiyot (pl.): The nine-branched candelabrum lit during Hanukkah.

Haredi; haredim (pl.): A term for rigorously Orthodox Jews. The literal meaning in Hebrew is "fearful one(s)."

Hashavas aveidah: Returning lost things.

Hasidic/Hasidism: Pertaining to the Jewish religious movement called Hasidism (pious ones), founded by Israel ben Eliezer in Eastern Europe in the eighteenth century.

Havdalah: A ceremony marking the end of the Sabbath or another holy day.

Holy Ark: The cupboard or niche in the synagogue where the Torah Scrolls are kept.

Hora: An Israeli circle dance.

IDF: Israel Defense Forces.

Imma: Hebrew for mother.

Kabbalah: Mystical teachings that deal with concepts of creation and other spiritual matters.

Kaddish: Prayer for the dead chanted by the reader or mourners in public worship.

Kapores: Yiddish for the custom practiced just before the Day of Atonement for ridding oneself of sin. It involves swinging a live chicken above the head while reciting a prayer as a way to transfer the sins of a person to a chicken. It is no longer common practice. In Hebrew, the word is "kapporot," meaning "ridding of sin."

Kashrut: Dietary laws.

Ketubah: The wedding contract between a bride and groom.

Kibbutz: Israeli collective settlement.

Kiddush: A blessing recited over wine at the beginning of the Sabbath or holiday evening meal.

Kindertransport: German for the movement to evacuate children from Nazi Germany to Great Britain.

Kippah; kippot (pl.): Head covering, called a yarmulke in Yiddish.

Kol Nidre: A prayer recited on the eve of the Day of Atonement.

Kosher: See kashrut.

Kotel: The Western Wall in Jerusalem.

Kristallnacht: German for the state-organized pogrom against Jews that took place throughout Nazi Germany on November 9–10, 1938.

Kvetch: Yiddish for complainer.

Landsleit society: Yiddish for mutual aid society.

Lashon hara: Evil speech; gossip.

Latkes: Yiddish for potato pancakes.

Maccabees: A family of Jewish patriots of the second and first centuries BCE, active in the liberation of Judea from Greco-Syrian rule.

Maror: Bitter herbs; part of the Passover Seder.

Matzah: Unleavened bread used primarily at Passover.

Megillah: Scroll.

Melamud: Teacher.

Mensch: Yiddish for decent person.

Menorah: A candelabrum with seven branches. The Hanukkah menorah, or hanukkiyah, is a nine-branched candelabrum.

Mesirat nefesh: Self-sacrifice for the sake of a mitzvah.

Midrash; midrashim (pl.): A large collection of rabbinical writings that examine the Hebrew Bible in the light of oral tradition. The Midrashim are divided into two groups: Halakhah, which clarify legal issues; and Aggadah, nonlegal writings intended simply to enlighten.

Midrash Tanhuma: A section of the Midrash.

Minyan: The quorum required for public worship services.

Mitzvah; mitzvot (pl.): Commandment or good deed.

Modeh Ani: The prayer said upon waking, thanking God for returning our souls to us.

Moshav: An Israeli cooperative agricultural settlement.

Parashah: The weekly Torah reading, one of 54 parashiyyot into which the Torah is divided.

Pirke Avot: A work containing the moral and ethical teachings of about 60 Talmudic scholars; usually translated as "Ethics of the Fathers."

Pitom: A small growth at the tip of an etrog.

Pogrom: Russian for an organized, often officially encouraged massacre or persecution of a minority group, especially one conducted against Jews.

Rabbi Hillel: One of the greatest Jewish sages of the Second Temple period (ca. 70 BCE–10 CE).

Refuah shelaimah: A wish for a speedy recovery.

Rugelach: Yiddish for a type of pastry.

Schmaltz: Yiddish for rendered chicken fat.

Shabbat: The Sabbath.

Shabbos: Yiddish for Sabbath or Shabbat.

Seder: The home ceremony conducted as part of the Passover observance. In Israel, the Seder occurs on the first night of Passover. In the Diaspora, it is observed on the first two nights.

Seder Plate: A special plate containing symbolic foods used during the Passover Seder.

Sefer Torah: Torah scroll.

Sephardim (pl.): Jews who trace their ancestry to Spain, Portugal, and other countries around the Mediterranean. Distinguished from Ashkenazim, who originally came from Central and Eastern Europe.

Shamash: The extra, or ninth, light on the hanukkiyah, used as the "helper" to light all of the other candles.

Shehina: God's female presence.

Shema: The central prayer of Judaism, affirming the belief in the oneness of God.

Shema Yisrael: "Hear, O Israel, " the first two words of the Shema, the central prayer of Judaism.

Shlemiel: Yiddish for a dolt or fool.

Shmura Matzah: Passover Matzah made from grain that has been under special supervision from the time it was harvested to ensure that no fermentation has occurred.

Shtuss: Yiddish for commotion or nonsense.

Shofar: Ram's horn.

Shtetl: Yiddish for village where Jews lived in Eastern Europe.

Shul: Yiddish for synagogue.

Side locks (payes in Hebrew): Longer hair worn on each side of the face by some observant Jews.

Sofer: Scribe.

Sukkah: A temporary hut or booth with a roof of leafy boughs, straw, and so forth, built for the holiday of Sukkot.

Tallit (tallitot, pl.): A four-cornered shawl worn during prayers.

Talmud: The collection of rabbinical writing consisting of the Mishnah and Gemara, constituting the religious authority of Judaism.

Tam: Yiddish for flavor.

Tanakh: Torah, Prophets, and Writings; the Hebrew Scriptures.

Tashlikh: A ceremony performed on the first afternoon of the Jewish New Year, when crumbs are thrown into a body of water to represent the casting away of sins.

Teshuvah: Repentance.

Tikun olam: Repairing the world.

Torah: The Five Books of Moses/the entire corpus of Jewish law and teaching including the Tanakh, or Hebrew Scriptures, and the Talmud.

Tzedakah: Charity or righteousness.

Tzimmes: Yiddish for a traditional Jewish casserole made with fruit, meat, and vegetables. The word is also used to signify a fuss or outcry.

Wadi: In regions of the Middle East and North Africa, a stream bed or channel that only carries water during the rainy season.

Yenta: Yiddish for gossip or busybody.

Zayde/Zayda: Yiddish for grandpa.

Zayteem: Olives.

Zoftig: Yiddish for plump.

APPENDIX B

Jewish Holy Days and Festivals

Jewish holidays begin at sundown and last until approximately sundown of the next day. They are dated according to the Jewish calendar—an adjusted lunar calendar of 12 months—with the Sabbath celebrated every week and Rosh Hashanah beginning the new year. They are listed below in the order in which they occur during the Jewish year. For more information about Jewish holy days and festivals, consult a Jewish encyclopedia.

Shabbat: The Sabbath; the seventh day of the week; celebrated every week of the year.

Rosh Hodesh: Celebrates the new moon and the beginning of a new month.

Rosh Hashanah: New Year; the first and second days of Tishri (September/October).

Days of Awe: The 10 days of repentance between Rosh Hashanah and Yom Kippur.

Yom Kippur: Day of Atonement; a fast day observed at the end of the 10 days of repentance on the 10th of Tishri (September/October).

Sukkot: Festival of Tabernacles or Booths; observed from the 15th through the 22nd of Tishri (September/October).

Shemini Atzeret: Festival that concludes Sukkot.

Simhat Torah: Rejoicing in the Law; observed on the day after Shemini Atzeret.

Hanukkah: Festival commemorating the victory of the Maccabees, observed for eight days starting on 25th of Kislev (November/December).

Tu B'Shevat: The New Year for Trees; celebrated on the 15th of Shevat (January/February).

Purim: Celebrates the deliverance of Persian Jews from genocide; observed on the 14th of Adar (February/March). In leap years, an additional month is inserted after Adar, called Adar II. In leap years, Purim is observed during Adar II.

Passover: Commemorates the Exodus from Egypt; observed from the 15th through the 23rd of Nisan (March/April).

Yom ha Shoah: Holocaust Remembrance Day; occurs during the Jewish month of Nisan (March/April).

Yom ha Atzma'ut: Israel Independence Day, celebrating the founding of the State of Israel in 1948 on the 5th of Iyar (April/May).

Lag B'Omer: A holiday occurring in the period between Passover and Shavuot; observed on the 18th of Iyar (April/May).

Shavuot: Pentacost; observed on the 6th and 7th of Sivan (May/June).

Tisha B'Av: Fast day on the 9th of Av commemorating the destruction of the First Temple by the Babylonians in 586 BCE and the destruction of the Second Temple by the Romans in 70 CE (July/August).

Sydney Taylor
Book Awards

The Sydney Taylor Book Award was established by the Association of Jewish Libraries (AJL) in honor of the author of the classic All of a Kind Family stories to encourage the publication of outstanding books of Jewish content for children. The award, chosen by a committee of AJL members, is given to authors of the most distinguished contributions to Jewish children's literature published in the preceding year. The first award was given in 1968. In most years since then, two awards have been given, one to a book for younger readers and one to a book for older readers. In 2007, a third category—books for teens—was added. Honor books are also cited. In the list of winners below, the title of the winner for young readers is listed first. As with many longstanding awards, some of the older titles have limited appeal to today's readers, so not all of the winners are annotated in this guide. Those that are included are marked with an asterisk, and their location in the guide can be ascertained by using the author or title indexes. For more information on the Sydney Taylor Book Awards, see www.jewishlibraries.org

2007

*Krensky, Steven. *Hanukkah at Valley Forge.* Illus. by Greg Harlin. New York: Dutton, 2006.

*Ferber, Brenda. *Julia's Kitchen.* New York: Farrar, Straus and Giroux, 2006.

*Zusak, Markus. *The Book Thief.* New York: Alfred A. Knopf/Random House, 2006. (The first Association of Jewish Libraries Teen Book Award winner.)

2006

The year of the award was changed from the year in which the book was published to the year in which the award was given. Therefore, the next award after 2005 is 2007.

2005

*Silverman, Erica. *Sholom's Treasure: How Sholom Aleichem Became a Writer.* Illus. by Mordicai Gerstein. New York: Farrar, Straus, and Giroux, 2004.

*Littman, Sarah Darer. *Confessions of a Closet Catholic.* New York: Dutton, 2005.

2004

No award for Younger Readers given.

*Kass, Pnina Moed. *Real Time.* New York: Clarion, 2004.

2003

*Davis, Aubrey. *Bagels for Benny.* Illus. by Dusan Petricic. Toronto: Kids Can Press, 2003.

*Patz, Nancy. *Who Was the Woman Who Wore the Hat?* New York: Dutton, 2003.

2002

*Hershenhorn, Esther. *Chicken Soup by Heart.* Illus. by Rosanne Litzinger. New York: Simon and Schuster Books for Young Readers, 2002.

*Levine, Karen. *Hana's Suitcase: A True Story.* Toronto: Second Story Press, 2002 and Morton Grove, IL: Albert Whitman, 2003.

2001

*Rael, Elsa Okon. *Rivka's First Thanksgiving.* Illus. by Maryann Kovalski. New York: Simon and Schuster, 2001.

*Reef, Catherine. *Sigmund Freud: Pioneer of the Mind.* New York: Clarion, 2001.

2000

*Kimmel, Eric A. *Gershon's Monster.* Illus. by Jon J Muth. New York: Scholastic, 2000.

*Vos, Ida. *The Key Is Lost.* Trans. by Terese Edelstein. New York: Morrow/Harper-Collins, 2000.

1999

*Schur, Maxine Rose. *The Peddler's Gift.* Illus. by Kimberly Bulcken Root. New York: Dial, 1999.

*Rosen, Sybil. *Speed of Light.* New York: Atheneum, 1999.

1998

*Stillerman, Marci. *Nine Spoons.* Ilus. by Pesach Gerber. New York: Hachai, 1998.

*Napoli, Donna Jo. *Stones in Water.* New York: Dutton, 1997.

1997

*Rael, Elsa Okon. *When Zayde Danced on Eldridge Street.* Illus. by Marjorie Priceman. New York: Simon and Schuster, 1997.

*Jaffe, Nina. *The Mysterious Visitor: Stories of the Prophet Elijah.* Illus. by Elivia Savidier. New York: Scholastic, 1997.

1996

*Sofer, Barbara. *Shalom, Haver: Goodbye, Friend.* Rockville, MD: Kar-Ben Copies, 1996.

*Schur, Maxine Rose. *When I Left My Village.* Illus. by Brian Pinkney. New York: Dial, 1996.

1995

*Hoestlandt, Jo. S*tar of Fear, Star of Hope.* Illus. by Johanna Kang. Translated from French. New York: Walker, 1995.

*Vos, Ida. *Dancing on the Bridge of Avignon.* Translated from Dutch. Boston: Houghton Mifflin, 1995.

1994

*Oberman, Sheldon. *The Always Prayer Shawl.* Illus. by Ted Lewin. Honesdale, PA: Boyds Mills Press, 1994.

*Schnur, Steven. *The Shadow Children.* Illus. by Herbert Tauss. New York: Morrow, 1994.

1993

*Jaffe, Nina. *The Uninvited Guest.* Illus. by Elivia Savadier. New York: Scholastic, 1993.

*Matas, Carol. *Sworn Enemies.* New York: Bantam Doubleday Dell, 1993.

1992

*Gilman, Phoebe. *Something from Nothing.* Toronto: North Winds Press/Scholastic Canada, 1993.

*Hesse, Karen. *Letters from Rivka.* New York: Henry Holt, 1992.

1991

*Goldin, Barbara Diamond. *Cakes and Miracles: A Purim Tale.* Illus. by Erika Weihs. New York: Viking, 1991.

*Lanton, Sandy. *Daddy's Chair.* Illus. by Shelly O. Haas. Rockville, MD: Kar-Ben Copies, 1991.

*Schwartz, Howard, and Barbara Rush. *The Diamond Tree: Jewish Tales from Around the World.* Illus. by Uri Shulevitz. New York: HarperCollins, 1991.

1990

*Kimmel, Eric A. *The Chanukah Guest.* Illus. by Giora Carmi. New York: Holiday House, 1990

*Geras, Adele. *My Grandmother's Stories.* Illus. by Jael Jordan. New York: Alfred A. Knopf, 1990.

1989

*Blanc, Esther Silverstein. *Berchick.* Illus. by Tennessee Dixon. Volcano, CA: Volcano Press, 1989.

*Lowry, Lois. *Number the Stars.* Boston: Houghton Mifflin, 1989

1988

*Polacco, Patricia. *The Keeping Quilt.* New York: Simon and Schuster, 1988.

*Yolen, Jane. *The Devil's Arithmetic.* Viking Kestrel, 1988.

1987

Adler, David. *The Number on My Grandfather's Arm.* Illus. by Rose Eichenbaum. New York: UAHC Press, 1987.

*Levitin, Sonia. *The Return.* New York: Atheneum, 1987.

1986

*Hirsh, Marilyn. *Joseph Who Loved the Sabbath.* Illus. by Devis Grebu. New York: Viking Kestrel, 1986.

Pitt, Nancy. *Beyond the High White Wall.* New York: Charles Scribner's Sons, 1986.

1985

*Freedman, Florence B. *Brothers.* Illus. by Robert Andrew Parker. New York: Harper and Row, 1985.

Snyder, Carol. *Ike and Mama and the Seven Surprises.* New York: Lothrop, Lee, and Shepard, 1985.

1984

*Schwartz, Amy. *Mrs. Moskowitz and the Sabbath Candlesticks.* Philadelphia: Jewish Publication Society, 1984.

Orlev, Uri. *The Island on Bird Street.* Boston: Houghton Mifflin, 1984.

1983

Pomerantz, Barbara. *Bubbe, Me, and Memories.* Illus. by Leon Lurie. New York: UAHC Press, 1983.

Zar, Rose. *In the Mouth of the Wolf.* Philadelphia: Jewish Publication Society, 1983.

1982

*Heller, Linda. *The Castle on Hester Street.* Philadelphia: Jewish Publication Society, 1982.

*Sachs, Marilyn. *Call Me Ruth.* New York: Bantam Doubleday Dell, 1982.

1981

*Cohen, Barbara. *Yussel's Prayer.* Illus. by Michael Deraney. New York: Lothrop, Lee and Shepard, 1981.

*Lasky, Kathryn. *The Night Journey.* New York: Penguin USA, 1981.

1980

Fisher, Leonard Everett. *A Russian Farewell.* New York: Four Winds Press, 1980.

1979

Snyder, Carol. *Ike and Mama and the Block Wedding.* New York: Coward, McCann & Geoghegan, 1979.

1978

*Orgel, Doris. *The Devil in Vienna.* New York: Penguin USA, 1978.

1977

Heyman, Anita. *Exit from Home.* New York: Random House, 1977.

1976

*Meltzer, Milton. *Never to Forget.* New York: HarperCollins, 1976.

1975

Moskin, Marietta. *Waiting for Mama.* New York: Coward, McCann & Geoghegan, 1975.

1974

No award given.

1973

*Suhl, Yuri. *Uncle Misha's Partisans.* New York: Four Winds Press, 1973.

1972, 1971

No awards given.

1970

Lange, Suzanne. *The Year.* Ghent, NY: S. G. Phillips, 1970.

1969

Ish-Kishor, Sulamith. *Our Eddie.* New York: Pantheon, 1969.

1968

*Hautzig, Esther. The Endless Steppe. New York: HarperCollins, 1968.

Jewish Publishers

This list consists of Jewish publishers who, at the time of this writing, are publishing books for children and teens written in or translated into English. The author apologizes for any inadvertent omissions.

Alef Design
4423 Fruitland Avenue
Los Angeles, CA 90058
www.alefdesign.com

Behrman House
11 Edison Place
Springfield, NJ 07081
www.behrmanhouse.com

CCAR (Central Conference of American Rabbis)
355 Lexington Avenue
New York, NY, 10017
www.ccarnet.org

EKS
322 Castro Street
Oakland, CA 94607
www.ekspublishing.com

Feldheim Publishers
208 Airport Executive Park
Nanuet, N.Y. 10954
Feldheim Publishers Israel Office:
POB 46163, Jerusalem, 91431, Israel
www.feldheim.com

Gali Girls
48 Cranford Place
Teaneck, NJ 07666
www.galigirls.com

Gefen Books
600 Broadway
Lynbrook, NY 11563
Gefen Publishing Israel Office:
6 Hatzvi Street, Jerusalem, 94386 Israel
www.israelbooks.com

Hachai Publishing
527 Empire Boulevard
Brooklyn, NY 11225
www.hachai.com

Hamodia
Distributed by Feldheim

Jason Aronson (an imprint of Rowman and Littlefield Publishers, Inc.)
4501 Forbes Boulevard, Suite 200
Lanham, MD 20706
www.rowmanlittlefield.com

Jewish Lights Publishing
Sunset Farm Offices, Route 4,
P.O. Box 237
Woodstock, VT 05091
www.jewishlights.com

Jewish Publication Society
2100 Arch Street, 2nd Floor
Philadelphia, PA 19103
www.jewishpub.org

Jonathan David Publishers
68-22 Eliot Avenue
Middle Village, NY 11379
www.jdbooks.com

Judaica Press
123 Ditmas Avenue
Brooklyn, NY 11218
www.judaicapress.com

Kar-Ben Publishing/Lerner Publishing Group
1251 Washington Avenue N.
Minneapolis, MN 55401
www.karben.com

KTAV Publishing House
930 Newark Avenue, 4th Floor
Jersey City, NJ 07306
www.ktav.com

Mahrwood Press
31 Zevin Street, Suite 8
Jerusalem, 97450, Israel
www.Mahrwoodpress.com

Matzah Ball Books
13909 Old Harbor Lane, #304
Marina Del Rey, CA 90292
www.matzahballbooks.com

Merkos Publications/Kehot Publication Society
770 Eastern Parkway
Brooklyn, NY 11212
www.kehotonline.com

Mesorah Publications/Artscroll
4401 Second Avenue
Brooklyn, NY 11232
www.artscroll.com

Milk and Honey Press
700 N. Colorado Boulevard, Suite 180
Denver, CO 80206
www.milkandhoneypress.com

Nachshon Press
9175 Gross Point Road, Suite 186
Skokie, IL 60077·
www.nachshonpress.com

Pitspopany Press
40 East 78 Street, #16D
New York, NY 10021
www.pitspopany.com

Seraphic Press
1531 Cardiff Avenue
Los Angeles, CA 90035
www.seraphicpress.com

Shazak Productions
6415 N. Sacramento
Chicago, IL 60645
www.shazak.com

Targum Press
22700 W. Eleven Mile Road
Southfield, MI 48034
Targum Press Israel Office:
P.O. Box 43170
Jerusalem, Israel
www.targum.com

Torah Aura Productions
4423 Fruitland Avenue
Los Angeles, CA 90058
www.torahaura.com

URJ Press (Union of Reform Judaism)
633 Third Avenue
New York, NY 10017
www.urjbooksandmusic.com

United Synagogue of Conservative Judaism
The Rapaport House
155 Fifth Avenue
New York, NY 10010
www.uscj.org

Urim Publications
9 HaUman Street, 2nd Floor
P.O. Box 52287
Jerusalem, 91521, Israel
www.urimpublications.com

Yaldah Publishing
P.O. Box 18662
Saint Paul, MN 55118
www.yaldahpublishing.com

Author & Illustrator Index

A

Abraham, Michelle Shapiro, 11, 121, 195
Abrams, Judith Z., 60
Abulafia, Yossi, 57
Adelman, Nechama Dina, 11
Adelman, Penina V., 89, 226
Adelson, Leone, 75
Adler, David A., 70, 102, 252r
Adler, Tzivia, 12
Adlington, L.J., 160
Agranoff, Tracey, 102
Alcorn, Stephen, 163
Alcott, Louisa May, 3
Alda, Arlene, 147
Aleichem, Sholom, 205, 207, 238
Alexander, Sue, 123
Alko, Selina, 11, 12, 13, 195
Allen, Richard, 102
Allon, Hagit, 57, 146
Allon, Jeffrey, 68, 233
Almagor, Gila, 226
Altman, Linda Jacobs, 133, 209
Amler, Jane Frances, 52
Anderson, Bethanne, 197
Anderson, Joel, 203, 221
Andreasen, Dan, 60
Andriani, Renee, 80
Antin, Mary, 60
Apperley, Dawn, 87
Araten, Harry, 75
Aretha, David, 126
Argoff, Patti, 15, 39, 82, 84
Ariel, Liat Binyamini, 231
Aroner, Miriam, 65

Arrick, Fran, 3, 37
Ashby, Ruth, 179
Asher, Sandy, 239, 240
Attema, Martha, 160, 211
Auch, Mary Jane, 37
August, Louise, 49, 105, 205
Ausbinder, Odelia, 118
Avishai, Susan, 131
Avrech, Robert J., 72
Axelrod, Toby, 161
Azarian, Mary, 224

B

Backman, Aidel, 48
Baer, Edith, 161, 189
Baer, Julie, 12, 221
Baker, Sharon Reiss, 173
Banks, Lynne Reid, 133
Bankston, John, 60, 61, 197
Bard, Mitchell, 138
Barrett, Angela, 176
Barron, Rachel Stiffler, 61
Barth-Grozinger, Inge, 169, 189
Bartoletti, Susan, 161
Bastrya, Judy, 89
Bat-Ami, Miriam, 44, 153
Bauer, Yehuda, 193
Baum, Maxie, 75
Bayer, Linda, 187
Baynes, Pauline, 63, 205
Becker, Boruch, 87
Bell, Anthea, 227
Bell, William, 43
Ben-Zvi, Hava, 179

Ben-Zvi, Rebecca Tova, 102
Bender, Robert, 17
Benderly, Beryl Lieff, 126
Beneduce, Ann Keay, 51
Benenfeld, Rikki, 12, 75
Berenbaum, Michael, 187
Berger, Gilda, 102
Bernardin, James, 33
Bernstein, Robin, 27
Bevilacqua, Silvana, 52, 147
Beyer, Mark, 187
Bial, Raymond, 146
Bialik, Hayim Nahman, 222, 237
Bierman, Carol, 142
Biers-Ariel, Matt, 195, 198
Bietz, Barbara, 223
Billin-Frye, Paige, 82
Bishop, Claire Huchet, 209
Bittinger, Ned, 97
Bitton-Jackson, Livia, 193, 202, 228
Bjornson, Barb, 64
Black, Theodor, 240
Blanc, Esther Silverstein, 3, 65, 252
Blatt, Evelyn Mizrahi, 209
Blau, Fayge Devorah, 11
Bliss, Harry, 156
Blitz, Shmuel, 65, 204, 231
Bloom, Tzivia, 34
Blumberg, Marjie, 103
Blume, Judy, 224
Blumenthal, Deborah, 174
Blumenthal, Scott, 123
Boddy, Joe, 207
Bogot, Howard I., 12, 111
Bohannon, Lisa Frederiksen, 201
Bolam, Emily, 30
Boraas, Tracey, 126
Boraks-Nemetz, Lillian, 192
Borden, Louise, 174
Bosch, Nicole in den, 83, 142
Bovson, Mara, 187
Boyne, John, 156
Brandeis, Batsheva, 65
Bredeson, Carmen, 89
Brett, Jan, 63
Brichto, Mira, 12, 13
Brickman, Robin, 90

Brodman, Aliana, 27, 48
Brodsky, Beverly, 204
Broida, Marian, 126
Brooker, Kyrsten, 142
Brown, Don, 57
Brown, Jonatha A., 179
Broxon, Janet, 14
Bruna, Dick, 13
Bryer, Diana, 177
Bunin, Sherry, 146
Bunting, Eve, 153
Burg, Ann E., 153
Burstein, Chaya, 20, 65, 127, 130, 198
Burstein, Robin, 27
Burstein, Shmuel, 161

C

Callahan, Kerry P., 161
Capucilli, Alyssa Satin, 76
Carle, Eric, 112
Carlson, Lisa, 81
Carlstrom, Nancy White, 13
Carmi, Danielle, 5, 72, 186
Carmi, Gabrielle, 186
Carmi, Giora, 95, 121, 238, 251
Carnabuci, Anthony, 48
Carolan, Christine, 30
Carter, David, 76
Cartwright, Reg, 97
Caseley, Judith, 42
Caspi, Mishael Maswari, 235
Cassway, Esta, 20, 51
Castillo, Robert, 222
Catalanotto, Peter, 102
Cato, Vivian, 103
Celenza, Anna Harwell, 146
Chaikin, Miriam, 20, 21, 57
Chapman, Carol, 27
Chartier, Normand, 143
Cheng, Andrea, 162
Chotjewitz, David, 162
Chwast, Jacqueline, 97
Chwast, Seymour, 76, 92
Cisner, Naftali, 76
Claybourne, Anna, 133
Cleary, Brian P., 89

Clement, Gary, 66
Clements, Gary, 22
Codell, Esme Raji, 198
Cohen, Barbara, 3, 13, 33, 70, 226, 253
Cohen, Deborah Bodin, 13, 226
Cohen, Jacqueline M., 41, 114
Cohen, Jan Barger, 89, 204
Cohen, Miriam, 32, 174
Cohen, R.G., 77
Cohen, Santiago, 77
Cohen, Tod, 81
Cohn, Janice, 198
Cone, Molly, 90, 196
Connelly, Gwen, 68
Cooper, Alexandra, 77
Cooper, Ilene, 5, 57, 103, 114, 146
Cope, Jane, 234
Coplestone, Jim, 111
Coplestone, Lis, 111
Cormier, Robert, 3, 156
Corona, Laurel, 133
Correll, Cory, 79
Cote, Nancy, 92, 143
Cousins, Lucy, 47
Crew, David F., 170
Croll, Carolyn, 83
Crowley, Bridget, 156
Curtis, Sandra, 103
Cutchin, Marcia, 31
Cytron, Barry, 201
Cytron, Phyllis, 201
Czernecki, Stefan, 29

D

Dabcovich, Lydia, 178
Dacey, Bob, 97
Da Costa, Deborah, 5, 111, 112
Dahlberg, Maurine F., 43
Dash, Joan, 201
Davis, Aubrey, 1, 32, 196, 250
Deedy, Carmen Agra, 35
Delano, Marfe Ferguson, 58
Denenberg, Barry, 187
Deraney, Michael, 17, 253
DeSaix, Deborah Durland, 215
Desmoinaux, Christel, 84

Diamond, Donna, 107
Diaz, David, 72
Dick, Judy, 59, 237
Dickens, Charles, 198
Dion, L.N, 77
DiSalvo-Ryan, DyAnne, 40, 99
Diskind, Leah Malka, 193
Dixon, Tennessee, 65, 252
Dollinger, Renate, 90
Dolphin, Laurie, 5
Dooling, Michael, 178
Downey, Lynn, 13
Draper, Allison Stark, 216
Dublin, Anne, 146, 150, 179
Du Bois, William Pene, 209
DuBois, Jill, 134
Dubois, Liz Goulet, 113, 114
Ducharme, Dede Fox, 35
Duffy, Daniel Mark, 32

E

Eagle, Godeane, 65
Edelstein, Terese, 250
Edwards, Michelle, 27, 40, 174
Ehrenhaft, Daniel, 228
Eichenbaum, Rose, 252
Eisenberg, Ann, 39
Eisler, Colin, 17
Eitan, Ora, 64, 80
Elkeles, Simone, 5, 138
Emerman, Ellen, 77
Ephraim, Shelly Schonebaum, 88, 100, 112
Epstein, Sylvia, 90
Erlbach, Arlene, 90
Eshetie, Alemu, 124
Estes, Eleanor, 32
Evans, Clay Bonnyman, 17

F

Fagan, Cary, 28, 66, 114
Faigen, Anne G., 188
Farnsworth, Bill, 70, 167, 198
Feder, Harriet, 52
Feiler, Bruce, 23

Feinberg, Miriam, 203
Feinstein, Edward, 61
Fenton, Anne Lobock, 196
Ferber, Brenda, 179
Ferber, Brenda A., 179, 249
Fieser, Stephen, 238
Figley, Marty Rhodes, 141
Finkelstein, Norman H., 127, 134, 180, 201
Finkelstein, Ruth, 78
Finney, Kathryn Kunz, 16
Fisher, Adam, 103
Fisher, Leonard Everett, 4, 53, 134, 154, 253
Fishman, Cathy Goldman, 91
Fitzgerald, Gerald, 178
Flanagan, Alice, 91
Fleischman, Sid, 147
Floor, Guus, 179
Fontes, Justine, 123
Fontes, Ron, 123
Forest, Heather, 28, 31
Forest, Jim, 211
Fowles, Shelley, 28, 113
Frampton, David, 21
Frank, Anne, 5, 188
Frankl, Viktor, 62
Frankle, Pessie, 104
Franson, Leanne, 207
Frasconi, Anthony, 4, 50
Freedman, Florence, 66, 252
Freedman, Zelda, 147
French, Fiona, 17
French, Jackie, 226
Fridman, Sashi, 66, 78
Friedman, Aharon, 28
Friedman, D. Dina, 160, 162, 180
Friedman, Judith, 66, 101
Fuchs, Menucha, 25, 78

G

Gaber, Susan, 56, 144
Gadot, A.S., 63
Gaines, Ann, 199
Gallinger, Patty, 145
Gammell, Stephen, 153

Gamoran, Mamie, 3
Ganeri, Anita, 91
Ganz, Yaffa, 28, 104
Garfinkle, Adam, 139
Garfinkle, D.L., 229
Garrifson, Barbara, 115
Gaskins, Pearl, 23
Geller, Beverly Mach, 204
Gellman, Ellie, 66, 78
Gellman, Marc, 18, 156, 199
Gelman, Rita Golden, 153
Geras, Adele, 92, 232, 234, 252
Gerber, Pesach, 50, 69, 250
Gershator, Phillis, 196, 234
Gerstein, Mordicai, 56, 157, 236, 249
  Biblical stories by, 47, 66, 154, 204, 210
Getzel, 25
Gevry, Claudine, 77
Gibb, Sarah, 94
Giblin, James Cross, 162
Giddens, Sandra, 188
Gilbert, Yvonne, 21
Gilman, Phoebe, 92, 141, 142, 144, 251
Ginsburg, Alexa, 234
Glaser, Linda, 70, 92, 143
Glasthal, Jacqueline B., 35
Glatshteyn, Yankev, 157
Glazer, Devorah, 78
Glick, Susan, 216
Gold, Alison Leslie, 213, 216
Gold, Sharlya, 235
Gold-Vukson, Marji, 79
Goldberg, Malky, 39
Goldberg, Neal, 188
Goldin, Barbara Diamond, 78, 92, 112, 232, 235, 251
Goldman, Alex J., 180
Goldman, David J., 147
Goldstein, Margaret J., 128
Goodell, Jon, 49
Goodman, Tama, 198
Goolsby, Abe, 203, 221
Gorbaty, Norman, 12, 111
Gordon, Julie K., 21
Gordon, Karen, 199
Gordon-Lucas, Bonnie, 107
Gore, Leonid, 20, 123

Gormley, Beatrice, 58, 128, 135
Gottfried, Ted, 163
GrandPre, Mary, 174
Granfield, Linda, 147
Grantford, Jacqui, 175
Grebu, Devis, 94, 252
Green, Mim, 196
Greenberg, Kay, 79
Greene, Bette, 4, 227
Greene, Jacqueline Dembar, 128
Greene, Rhonda Gowler, 14
Greenfeld, Howard, 135, 149
Greengard, Alison, 18, 40, 49
Greenstein, Elaine, 84, 235
Greenstein, Susan, 28
Greif, Jean-Jacques, 170
Gresko, Marcia S., 123, 128
Griffis, Molly Levite, 42
Groat, Diane de, 104
Groner, Judyth, 14, 79, 121
Grossblatt, Ruby M., 79
Grossman, David, 42
Grossman, Laurie, 124
Grossman, Mendel, 192

H

Haas, Shelly O., 14, 19, 65, 122, 206, 251
Hafner, Marilyn, 86, 223
Hall, Melanie, 13, 69, 91
Halperin, Wendy Anderson, 19
Halpern, Joan, 70
Hamilton, Janet, 61
Hamlin, Janet, 166
Hanks-Henn, Judy, 65
Hannon, Holly, 85, 222
Harber, Frances, 66
Harlin, Greg, 96, 249
Harnick, Sheldon, 173
Harrison, Barbara, 216
Hartman, Thomas, 156, 199
Hass, Estie, 78
Hauser, Bill, 107
Hautzig, Esther, 5, 163, 181, 239, 253
Hawkes, Kevin, 143
Hayaski, Nancy, 113
Hegi, Ursula, 171

Hehner, Barbara, 142
Heiligman, Deborah, 93
Heller, David, 128
Heller, Linda, 252
Heller, Ruth, 40
Herman, Charlotte, 4, 93, 104
Herman, Debbie, 93
Hermann, Spring, 181
Hershenhorn, Esther, 67, 250
Hesse, Karen, 5, 147, 181, 212, 251
Hessel, Joui, 94
Hest, Amy, 40, 71, 94, 143
Heyman, Anita, 253
Hierstein, Judith, 185
Hildebrandt, Ziporah, 79
Hillman, Laura, 189
Himler, Ronald, 210
Himmelman, John, 81, 95
Hintz, Martin, 129
Hirschfelder, Arlene B., 149
Hirsh, Marilyn, 25, 94, 154, 252
Hitzeroth, Deborah, 139
Hodes, Lauren, 33, 221
Hodges, Margaret, 51
Hoestlandt, Jo, 174, 251
Hoffman, Alice, 170
Hoffman, Amalia, 205
Hoffman, Laurence A., 124
Hoffman, Mary, 18
Hogrogian, Nonny, 4
Hokanson, Lars, 180
Hokanson, Lois, 180
Holland, Cheri, 80
Holm, Anne, 157
Holtzman, Yehudit, 26
Holub, Joan, 80
Hopkins, Jeff, 223
Hopkinson, Deborah, 148
Horwitz, Brad, 21
Hotchkiss, Ron, 150
Houghton, Sarah, 115
Houston, Julian, 202
Howland, Naomi, 75, 94, 141
Hoyt-Goldsmith, Diane, 94
Hu, Ying-Hwa, 112, 209
Huck, Charlotte, 6
Hudson-Goff, Elizabeth, 179

Hughes, Shirley, 222
Hurwitz, Johanna, 115, 224, 239
Hyde, Heidi Smith, 174
Hyman, Trina Schart, 154, 214, 238

I

Icenoggle, Jodi, 143, 144
Innocenti, Roberto, 214
Iofin, Michael, 238
Isaacs, Ann, 163
Ish-Kishor, Sulamith, 3, 4, 157, 253
Iskowitz, Joel, 153
Ivanov, Anatoly, 49
Iwai, Melissa, 98

J

Jacobs, Laurie, 112
Jacobs, Michael, 89
Jaffe, Nina, 4, 29, 49, 51, 235, 236, 251
Janisch, Heinz, 49
Jarecka, Danuta, 205
Jarrett, Judy, 105
Jenkins, Debra Reid, 13
Johnson, Evelyne, 25
Johnson, Richard, 88
Johnson, Sheila Golburgh, 150
Johnson, Stephen T., 177, 206
Jones, Jan N., 90
Jones, Lara, 19
Jordan, Jael, 232, 252
Joselit, Jenna, 2, 10
Juhasz, George, 56
Jules, Jacqueline, 31, 47, 75, 80, 95, 203
Jung, Reinhardt, 227
Jungman, Ann, 113

K

Kacer, Kathy, 35, 157, 158, 169, 181, 212, 224
Kahn, Katherine Janus, 4–5, 31, 47, 86, 95, 122, 203, 232
Kale, Shelly, 148
Kamen, Gloria, 227
Kanefield, Teri, 37

Kanemoto, Dan, 82
Kang, Johanna, 174, 251
Kaplan, Kathy Walden, 71
Kaplan, William, 212
Karwoski, Gail Langer, 36
Kass, Pnina Moed, 5, 170, 250
Kassirer, Sue, 205
Katz, Avi, 104
Katz, Samuel M., 163
Katz, Tova, 65, 104, 204, 231
Kawasaki, Shauna Mooney, 27, 78, 88
Kaye, Rosalind Charney, 125, 206
Kehl, Drusilla, 67
Keiser, Tammy, 19, 233
Kelly, Sheila M., 22
Kendall, Jonathan P., 124
Kimmel, Eric A., 4, 33, 49, 55, 72–73, 75, 95, 108, 143, 154, 205, 222, 236, 239, 250, 251
Kimmelman, Leslie, 80, 81, 95
Kiss-Silverberg, Esti, 195
Kitchel, JoAnn, 87, 146
Klagsbrun, Francine, 2
Klein, Gerda Weissmann, 154
Klein-Higger, Joni, 81
Kline, Suzy, 95
Klineman, Harvey, 28, 33, 41
Kneen, Maggie, 84
Koelsch, Michael, 43
Koffsky, Anne D., 11, 93, 121
Kono, Erin Eitter, 86
Koons, Jon, 96
Koralek, Jenny, 63, 205
Kornblatt, Mark, 199
Koshkin, Alexander, 21
Kositsky, Lynne, 229
Kosofsky, Chaim, 67
Koss, Amy, 104, 116
Kovalski, Maryann, 144, 207, 250
Koz, Paula Goodman, 130
Kramer, Ann, 181
Krantz, Gershon, 240
Krantz, Jacob Ben Wolf (Rabbi), 237
Krantz, Sarah, 77, 78, 79
Krenina, Katya, 93, 143
Krensky, Stephen, 96, 249
Krinitz, Esther Nisenthal, 182

Kripke, Dorothy K., 96
Krohn, Genendel, 14, 28, 232
Kropf, Latifa Berry, 81
Krulik, Nancy, 96
Kubert, Joe, 36, 164
Kurtz, Jane, 73
Kushner, Karen, 14
Kushner, Lawrence, 14, 196
Kushner, Tony, 157, 210
Kuskin, Karla, 48

L

LaFrance, Marie, 63
Lakin, Patricia, 55
Lamstein, Sarah Marwil, 96
Lamut, Sonja, 29
Lane, Nancy, 93
Lang, Cecily, 96
Lange, Suzanne, 253
Lanton, Sandy, 97, 251
Lasky, Kathryn, 3, 143, 182, 189, 212, 216, 253
Lattimore, Deborah Noure, 69
Lattridge, Celia Barker, 22
Lawton, Clive, 164
Lazewnik, Libby, 240
Leapman, Michael, 217
Leder, Jane Mirsky, 129
Lee, Carol Ann, 182, 189
Leff, Tova, 29, 77, 81, 85
Lehman-Wilzig, Tami, 104, 182, 232
Leiman, Sondra, 129
Lemelman, Martin, 40
Lenski, Lois, 48
Lessac, Frane, 153
Lester, Julius, 22, 128, 135
LeTord, Bijou, 15
Levin, C., 28
Levine, Abby, 82
Levine, Anna, 150
Levine, Arthur, 144, 197
Levine, Ellen, 217
Levine, Gail Carson, 37
Levine, Karen, 183, 250
Levinson, Robin K., 67
Levitan, David, 202

Levitas, Alexandra, 65
Levitin, Sonia, 3–5, 108, 115, 117, 135, 150, 151, 160, 164, 217, 239, 252
Levy, Sarah G., 82
Lewin, Ted, 175, 251
Lewis, Patrick, 97
Lewis, R.B., 197
Liddle, Elizabeth, 19
Lieberman, Channah, 82
Lieberman, Syd, 40
Liebermann, Miriam, 188
Lindbergh, Reese, 15
Linenthal, Peter, 175
Lisker, Emily, 22, 90, 236
Lissy, Jessica, 82
Lister, Claire, 83
Littlefield, Holly, 200
Littlesugar, Amy, 183
Littman, Sarah Darer, 4, 224, 250
Litzinger, Rosanne, 67, 99, 250
Livney, Varda, 83, 87
Lobel, Anita, 190, 232
Lobel, Arnold, 27
Lottridge, Celia Barker, 22
Low, William, 183
Lowenstein, Sallie, 117
Lowry, Lois, 1, 160, 212, 252
Lucas, Margeaux, 87
Ludwig, Warren, 111
Lurie, Leon, 252
Lyampe, Rina, 85
Lynch, P.J., 143

M

MacGill-Callahan, Sheila, 206
Mack, Tracy, 73
MacLeod, Elizabeth, 58
Maggid, Dubno, 237
Maguire, Gregory, 213
Mahr, Aryeh, 58
Maisel, Grace Ragues, 233
Majewski, Dawn, 14
Mann, Kenny, 52
Manushkin, Fran, 42, 83, 97, 125, 206
Marshall, Carol, 213
Marzollo, Jean, 67, 203

Matas, Carol, 36, 51, 129, 135, 148, 160, 165, 190, 217, 224, 251
Mayer, Marianna, 53
Mazer, Norma Fox, 153, 158
McArthur, Debra, 217
McCann, Michelle R., 213
McCaughrean, Geraldine, 38
McClintock, Barbara, 95
McCully, Emily, 159
McDonough, Yona A., 33, 39, 184
McElmurry, Jill, 234
McGovern, Ann, 26
McGraw, Laurie, 103, 142
McGrory, Anik, 112
McHargue, D., 179
McKain, Mark, 171
McKay, Sharon E., 229
McKie, Todd, 16
McNeese, Tim, 164
McPherson, Stephanie, 200
Meade, Holly, 15
Medoff, Francine, 83
Meiseles, Shayna, 225
Mekibel, Shoshana, 69
Melmed, Laura Kraus, 29
Melnikoff, Pamela, 158
Meltzer, Milton, 190, 253
Meret, Sasha, 23
Metzger, Lois, 117
Michelson, Richard, 55, 197, 206
Migdale, Lawrence, 94
Migron, Hagit, 90
Miklowitz, Gloria, 136, 165, 239
Milgram, Goldie, 105
Millman, Isaac, 184
Mills, Judith Christine, 207
Mitten, Christopher, 125
Mochizuki, Ken, 213
Moore, Lisa, 190
Morgan, Anna, 129
Morgan, Jacqui, 237
Morgan, Mary, 176
Morris, Ann, 5, 175
Morris, Gerald, 208
Morris, Jackie, 18
Morris, Neil, 53
Moscowitz, Moshe, 105, 159

Moser, Barry, 51, 206
Moskin, Marietta, 253
Moss, Marissa, 184
Moxley, Sheila, 92
Musleah, Rahel, 105
Muth, Jon J., 205, 250
Mykoff, M., 28

N

Nahman, Rabbi, 237
Naliboff, Jane, 223
Napoli, Donna Jo, 61, 73, 250
Nason, Ruth, 97, 98
Nathan, Cheryl, 121
Natti, Susannah, 102
Navarro, Larry, 43
Naylor, Phyllis, 117
Neil, Philip, 29
Nerlove, Miriam, 83, 184
Newbery, Linda, 117
Newman, Leslea, 81, 84, 142, 229
Nicola, Christos, 167
Nir, Yehuda, 190
Nislick, June Leavitt, 36
Nivola, Claire, 94, 175
Nodel, Norman, 223
Norton, Mary, 95
Nutkis, Phyllis, 15

O

O'Connell, Rebecca, 148
Oberman, Sheldon, 175, 236, 251
Oeltjenbruns, Joni, 79
Ofer, Rosalie, 176
Oirich, Alan, 184
Older, Elfin, 113
Olivas, Daniel A., 33
Ollendorff, Valli, 191
Olson, Julie, 77
Olswanger, Anna, 130
Opdyke, Irene Gut, 219
Oppenheim, Shulamith Levy, 56, 116, 210
Oppenheimer, Nancy, 154
Orback, Craig, 182
Orgel, Doris, 253

Orlev, Uri, 151, 252
Ostow, Micol, 118
Ostrove, Karen, 203
Oswald, Nancy, 136
Oxley, Jennifer, 82

P

Paley, Joan, 15
Paluch, Beily, 84
Pancheshnaya, Dasha, 211
Papp, Robert, 36
Parker, Robert Andrew, 66, 92, 252
Parks, Peggy J., 200
Pasachoff, Naomi, 38
Paschkis, Julie, 75
Passicot, Monique, 237
Pastor, Melanie Joy, 175
Patz, Nancy, 191, 250
Pearlman, Bobby, 84
Peck, Beth, 173, 181
Peet, Mal, 171
Pelleg, Tirtsa, 14, 28, 231, 232
Penn, Malka, 115, 240
Perel, Lisa, 204, 223
Peretz, I.L., 49, 92, 235, 236, 239
Perez, Ito Esther, 12
Perkal, Yocheved Leah, 104
Perrin, Randy, 213
Pertzig, F., 29
Peterseil, Tehila, 225
Petricic, Dusan, 32, 196, 250
Pham, LeUyen, 198
Philip, Neil, 237
Phillis, Rachael, 91
Pillo, Cary, 80
Pinkney, Brian, 107, 125, 181, 251
Pinkney, Jerry, 17, 49, 232
Pinsker, Marlee, 43
Pirotta, Saviour, 58
Pitt, Nancy, 252
Podwal, Mark, 22–23, 50, 54, 105, 113, 144, 233, 239
Polacco, Patricia, 5, 68, 98, 213, 252
Pollack, Gadi, 237
Pomerantz, Barbara, 252
Poole, Josephine, 176

Poppel, Hans, 27
Portnoy, Mindy Avra, 19, 122
Posner, Marcia, 5
Potok, Chaim, 62
Potter, Giselle, 56
Pressler, Mirjam, 165, 193
Priceman, Marjorie, 19, 98, 250
Propp, Vera, 115
Prose, Francine, 50, 113, 144, 233
Provost, Gary, 71
Pushker, Gloria Teles, 106, 185

R

Raanan, Ahuva, 231
Rabb, M.C., 218
Rabinovici, Schoschana, 165
Racklin-Siegel, Carol, 18, 40, 49
Radin, Ruth, 166, 169
Rael, Elsa Okon, 19, 98, 144, 250
Rahlens, Holly-Jane, 118
Randall, Ron, 184
Randall, Ronne, 84
Ransome, James, 144
Rao, Anthony, 25
Rappaport, Doreen, 159, 200
Rauchwerger, Diane, 85
Rauchwerger, Lisa, 106
Ravnitsky, Yehoshua Hana, 237
Ray, Deborah, 239
Redenbaugh, Vickie Jo, 97
Redsand, Anna, 62
Reef, Catherine, 62, 250
Reeves, Mary Bell, 53
Regelson, Abraham, 176
Reid, Barbara, 64
Reingold, Alan, 35
Reinhart, Matthew, 48
Reiss, Johanna, 5, 191
Remkiewicz, Frank, 95
Renberg, Dalia, 40
Revell, Cindy, 34
Rey, H.A., 174
Rey, Margaret, 174
Ricci, Regolo, 28
Rice, Earle, Jr., 53
Richter, Hans, 166

Rickenbaker, Becky Hyatt, 159
Rifai, Amal, 118
Riggio, Anita, 141
Ringel, Robert, 185
Ringel, Susan S., 185
Rinn, Miriam, 116
Rivers, Ruth, 99
Rivlin, Lilly, 130
Roberts, Jeremy, 218
Robinson, Jessie B., 82
Rocklin, Joanne, 185, 225
Rodier, Denis, 214
Rogasky, Barbara, 53, 166, 214
Rogow, Sally M., 166
Roleff, Tamara L., 166
Romanenko, Vitaly, 99, 102
Root, Kimberly Bulcken, 184, 206, 250
Roraback, Robin, 79
Rose, Or N., 202
Roseman, Kenneth, 130
Rosen, Michael, 5, 98, 99, 116
Rosen, Sybil, 200, 250
Rosenbaum, Andrea Warmflash, 64
Rosenberg, Pam, 130
Rosenfeld, Dina, 15, 26, 64, 81, 85, 122, 223
Rosenthal, Betsy R., 99
Rosh, Mair, 134
Rosinsky, Natalie M., 99
Rosner, Gillian, 59
Ross, Lillian Hammer, 43, 176
Rossel, Seymour, 59, 237
Rossoff, Donald, 19
Roth, Matthue, 109
Roth, Robert, 197
Roth, Ruchela, 86
Roth, Susan, 85
Rothenberg, Joan, 31, 34, 176
Rothenberg, Joani Keller, 114
Rotner, Shelley, 22
Rouss, Sylvia, 4, 31, 85, 86, 113, 114, 122, 154, 176, 222
Row, Richard, 145
Roy, Jennifer Rozines, 131, 159
Rubin, Susan Goldman, 136, 157, 159, 167, 168, 185, 186, 191
Ruby, Lois, 71, 131, 151
Ruelle, Karen Gray, 215

Rush, Barbara, 4, 106, 108, 233, 238, 251
Russo, Marisabina, 41, 177

S

Sachs, Marilyn, 44, 202, 253
Salkin, Jeffrey, 106
Samut, Sonja, 71
Sandell, Lisa, 5, 136
Sanders, Nancy I., 86
Sandler, Martin W., 151
Sandman, Rochel, 68
Sanfield, Steve, 144
Sasso, Sandy Eisenberg, 16, 114, 177, 197
Saturen, Myra, 152
Savadier, Elivia, 84, 103, 235, 236, 251
Schacht, Rebbeca, 237
Schachter, Esty, 38
Schanzer, Rosalind, 144
Schanzer, Roz, 39, 80
Schecter, Ellen, 106
Schiffman, Jessica, 67
Schindler, S.D., 96
Schmidt, Gary, 167, 196
Schnur, Steven, 177, 251
Schoenherr, Ian, 173
Schon, Ruchy, 86
Schories, Pat, 76
Schorr, Melissa, 38
Schotter, Roni, 56, 86, 223
Schram, Peninnah, 68, 233, 236
Schrier, Jeffrey, 131
Schroeder, Peter W., 191
Schroeder-Hildebrand, Dagmar, 191
Schubert, Samantha, 233
Schuett, Stacey, 174
Schuh, Mari C., 87
Schulman, Goldie, 99
Schultz, Carol D., 227
Schuman, Burt, 125
Schur, Maxine Rose, 68, 107, 125, 206, 250, 251
Schwabach, Karen, 74
Schwartz, Amy, 252
Schwartz, Betty, 87
Schwartz, Cherie Karo, 106
Schwartz, Ellen, 29, 52, 118, 214

Schwartz, Howard, 4, 16, 233, 237, 238, 251
Schwartz, Ora, 70
Schweiger-D'mil, Itzhak, 64
Seeger, Pete, 19
Segal, Eliezer Lorne, 107
Seidman, Lauren, 122
Sendak, Maurice, 4, 157, 210, 239
Senesh, Hannah, 170
Senker, Cath, 185
Serwer, Blanche Luria, 238
Seshan, Priya, 125
Seva, 66, 78
Severance, John B., 59, 62
Shalant, Phyllis, 37
Shapiro, Michelle, 69
Sher, Emil, 183
Sheri, Shira, 20
Sherman, Josepha, 136
Sheshan, Priya, 125
Shevrin, Aliza, 238
Shoemaker, Kathryn E., 178
Shollar, Leah, 41, 50, 69
Shub, Elizabeth, 239
Shulevitz, Uri, 42, 148, 210, 233, 251
Shulman, Lisa, 99
Siegel, Bruce, 206
Sievert, Terri, 100
Silverman, Erica, 56, 69, 207, 249
Silverman, Maida, 92, 131
Sim, Dorrith, 178
Simon, Solomon, 239
Simpson, Lesley, 142
Singer, Isaac Bashevis, 1, 4, 50, 59, 112, 154, 210, 235, 239
Slavicek, Louise, 137
Slonim, David, 29
Smith, Dian, 87
Smith, Frank Dabba, 167, 192
Snyder, Carol, 252, 253
Sobel, Ileene Smith, 23
Sofer, Barbara, 131, 178, 251
Sokoloff, David, 159
Sokolow, Reha, 220
Sollish, Ari, 87
Sonneborn, Liz, 167
Sorenson, Henri, 35

Souhami, Jessica, 26
Soumerai, Eva Nussbaum, 227
Spark, 103, 116
Sper, Emily, 100
Speregen, Devra Newberger, 132, 192
Spier, Peter, 50
Spinelli, Jerry, 220
Spinner, Stephanie, 234
Spirin, Gennady, 51
Springer, Sally, 79, 80, 142
Stampler, Ann Redisch, 41, 114
Stanley, Jerry, 152
Steele, D. Kelley, 159
Steig, William, 116
Stein, Tammar, 229
Steinberg, Bracha, 223
Steinberg, Judy, 107
Steiner, Connie Colker, 125, 214
Steinhardt, Bernice, 182
Stern, Ellen, 192
Stern, Joel, 107
Stillerman, Marci, 69, 250
Stockwell, Gail Provost, 71
Stone, Phoebe, 16
Stone, Tanya Lee, 59, 87
Stoppleman, Monica, 132
Streissguth, Thomas, 218
Stuchner, Joan Betty, 145
Sucher, Laura, 78
Sugarman, Brynn Olenberg, 69
Suhl, Yuri, 29, 160, 169, 253
Sutherland, Kelly Stribling, 236
Swarner, Kristina, 16
Swartz, Daniel J., 100
Swartz, Nancy Sohn, 69

T

Taback, Simms, 26, 142, 144, 234
Tabs, Barbara, 107
Tal, Eve, 70, 149
Talbert, Marc, 137
Tanaka, Shelley, 212
Tanner, Suzy Jane, 88
Tarbescu, Edith, 178, 207
Tartaro, Vincent, 154
Tauss, Herbert, 251

Taylor, Marilyn, 218
Taylor, Peter Lane, 167
Taylor, Stephen, 212
Taylor, Sydney, 3, 7, 72, 235
Teece, Geoff, 132
Teis, Kyra, 43
Tempel, Sylke, 118
Thisdale, Francois, 43
Thompson, John, 146
Tilley, Debbie, 156
Timmons, Jonathan, 179
Toksvig, Sandi, 214
Toll, Nelly, 186
Topek, Susan Remick, 88, 142
Toron, Eli, 209
Touson, Esther, 78
Tregobov, Rhea, 207
Trueman, Matthew, 207
Tryszynska-Frederick, Luba, 213
Tunis, John, 3
Tunnell, Michael O., 168

U

Udovic, David, 89
Uhlberg, Myron, 29
Ungar, Richard, 30, 56, 145
Uschan, Michael V., 168

V

Van der Sterre, Johanna, 174
Van Kampen, Vlasta, 26
Van Maarsen, Jacqueline, 182
Van Wright, Cornelius, 112, 209
Vander Zee, Ruth, 214
Victor-Elsby, Elizabeth, 88
Vogiel, Eva, 219, 227
Volavkova, Hana, 168
Vorst, Rochel Groner, 88
Vos, Ida, 160, 186, 215, 250, 251

W

Walder, Chaim, 231
Waldman, Bryna, 240
Waldman, Debby, 34

Waldman, Neil, 55, 64, 106, 126, 132, 175,
186, 194
Waldron, Kathleen Cook, 208
Wallace, Holly, 133
Ward, Catherine, 89
Ward, Elaine, 45
Warren, Andrea, 168
Wasserman, Mira, 30
Watson, Sally, 5, 195
Watson, Wendy, 212
Watts, Irene, 44, 149, 178, 192, 215
Waxman, Sydell, 145
Weber, Ilse, 72
Weber, Mark, 237
Webster, Matt, 137
Weider, Joy Nelkin, 96
Weihs, Erika, 251
Weil, Sylvie, 59
Weilerstein, Sadie Rose, 2–4, 101, 207,
235
Weinfeld, Chaya Baila, 240
Weisbarth, Bracha, 160, 168
Weiss, Arnine Cumsky, 228
Weissberger, Ela, 185
Weissenberg, Fran, 60, 185
Wells, Rosemary, 60
Welsh, T.K., 54
White, Anita, 223
Whiteman, Dorit Bader, 186
Whiting, Jim, 44, 199
Wickstrom, Thor, 66
Wieder, Joy Nelkin, 145, 210
Wiesel, Elie, 239
Wijngaard, Juan, 215
Wikler, Madeline, 79
Wilder, Laura Ingalls, 3
Wildsmith, Brian, 20, 42
Wilkowski, Susan, 101
Williams, Laura E., 208
Wilson, Anne, 16
Wilson, Janet, 35
Wing, Natasha, 222
Winn-Lederer, Ilene, 15, 64, 122
Winter, Jeanette, 145
Winter, Jonah, 145
Winter, Kathryn, 169, 186
Wiseman, Eva, 169, 218, 228

Wishinsky, Frieda, 225
Wisniewski, David, 211
Wolf, Elizabeth, 104
Wolff, Jason, 85
Wolfson, Ron, 124
Wolkstein, Diane, 215
Woodend, Avril, 179
Woodruff, Elvira, 178
Woodson, Jacqueline, 230
Woog, Adam, 192
Woronoff, Kristen, 186
Wukovits, John F., 193, 219
Wulf, Linda Press, 219
Wunsch, Marjory, 235

Y

Yaffe, Rachel, 240
Yalowitz, Paul, 81
Yavin, T.S., 152
Yezerski, Thomas F., 32, 174
Yolen, Jane, 43, 169, 252
Yorinks, Arthur, 116

Young, Cybele, 114
Young, Mary O., 91, 200

Z

Zakashanskyi-Sverev, Chana, 68
Zakon, Nachman, 137
Zalben, Jane Breskin, 101, 107, 116, 173, 201
Zar, Rose, 252
Zehavi, Lena, 57, 146
Zeitlin, Steve, 51
Zelcer, Draizy, 102
Zeldis, Malcah, 33, 39
Zemach, Kaethe, 26
Zemach, Margot, 27, 29, 59
Zenatti, Valerie, 230
Ziefert, Harriet, 16, 30
Zolkower, Edie Stoltz, 88
Zorn, Steve, 94
Zucker, Jonny, 89, 204
Zullo, Allan, 187
Zusak, Markus, 171, 249
Zwerger, Lisbeth, 49

Title Index

A

Aaron's Bar Mitzvah: Growing Up Jewish with Sarah Leah Jacobs, 113

Abraham Joshua Heschel: Man of Spirit, Man of Action, 202

Abuelita's Secret Matzahs, 177

Across the Alley, 197

Adara, 58

Adolf Hitler: Evil Mastermind of the Holocaust, 160

Adventures of Jeremy and Heddy Levi, The, 104

Adventures of K'tonton, The, 2, 101, 207

Adventures of Yaakov and Isaac, The, 36

After the Holocaust, 149

After I Said No, 150

After the War, 135

AJL Newsletter, 7

Albert Einstein, 58

Albert Einstein: Genius of the Twentieth Century, 55

Albert Einstein: The Jewish Man behind the Theory, 132

Albert Einstein: A Life of Genius, 58

Albert Einstein and the Theory of Relativity, 60

Albert Einstein: Visionary Scientist, 58, 62

Alex: Building a Life, 138

Alexandra's Scroll, 57

All American, 3

All-of-a-Kind Family, 3, 72

All-of-a-Kind Family Downtown, 72

All-of-a-Kind Family Uptown, 72

All the Lights in the Night, 144

All Star Season, 152

Always Prayer Shawl, 175

Always Remember Me, 177

Ancient Hebrews, The, 52

Ancient Israelites and Their Neighbors: An Activity Guide, 126

And God Cried, Too, 156

And Shira Imagined, 121

Angel Secrets, 20

Angel's Mistake, The: Stories of Chelm, 233

Angels Sweep the Desert Floor: Bible Legends About Moses in the Wilderness, 21

Animals and the Ark, The, 47

Animals of the Bible, The, 18

Anne Frank, 176, 179, 192

Anne Frank and the Children of the Holocaust, 189

Anne Frank: A Hidden Life, 193

Anne Frank: Hope in the Shadow of the Holocaust, 181

Anne Frank in the World, 186

Anne Frank—Voice of Hope, 185

Anne Frank: Voice of Hope, 186

Anne Frank: Young Diarist, 179

Anne Frank: The Young Writer Who Told the World Her Story, 181

Anne Frank's Story: Her Life Retold for Children, 182

Annie's Promise, 5, 115, 150

Annie's Shabbat, 96

Annushka's Voyage, 178

Answered Prayer and Other Yemenite Folktales, The, 235

Anti-Semitism, 171

Anya's Echoes, 38

Apples and Honey: A Rosh Hashanah Lift-the-Flap Book, 80

Apples and Honey: A Rosh Hashanah Story, 89, 204

Apples and Pomegranates: A Family Seder for Rosh Hashanah, 105

Are You There, God? It's Me, Margaret, 224

Ariel Sharon, 127

Ark, The, 47

Artscroll Children's Book of Ruth, The, 65

Artscroll Children's Book of Yonah, The, 204

Ashes of Roses, 37

At Issue in History: The Founding of the State of Israel, 138

Atlas of Great Jewish Communities: A Voyage Through History, 129

Aunt Claire's Yellow Beehive Hair, 174

Auschwitz: The Story of a Nazi Death Camp, 164

Avram's Gift, 103

B

Baby's Bris, 101

Bachelor and the Bean, The, 28

Bad Stuff in the News: A Guide to Handling the Headlines, 200

Bagels from Benny, 1, 196

Baker's Portrait, A, 40

Bat Mitzvah Club, The: Debbie's Story, 225

B'Chol L'Vavchah, With All Your Heart: A Weekly Prayer Book, 21

Be Not Far From Me: The Oldest Love Story: Legends From the Bible, 72

Beautiful World That God Made, The, 14

Because Nothing Looks Like God, 14

Becky and Benny Thank God, 12

Becoming a Bat Mitzvah: A Treasury of Stories, 228

Bedtime, 11

Bedtime Stories of Jewish Values, 231

Bedtime Stories to Make You Smile, 231

Before You Were Born, 16

Behind the Secret Window: A Memoir of a Hidden Childhood During World War Two, 186

Behold the Trees, 123

Beni's First Wedding, 101

Benjamin and the Word, 33

Berchick, 3, 65

Best of K'tonton, The, 2

Bible from Alef to Tav, The, 89

Bible Heroes I Can Be, 39

Big Like Me! A New Baby Story, 78

Big Quiet House, A, 28

Big Storm, The, 207

Bim and Bom, 100

Birdland, 73

Biscuit's Hanukkah, 76

Bit by Bit, 144

Bit of Love and a Bit of Luck, A: Margit, Book Two, 35, 224

Blessing of the Animals, The, 116

Blood Secret, 189

Blue's Clues Holiday, A, 82

Boat of Many Rooms, The, 97

Bobbie Rosenfeld: The Olympian Who Could Do Everything, 146, 150

Bone Button Borscht, 32

Book Thief, The, 171

Booklist, 6

Borrowed Hanukkah Latkes, The, 92, 143

Borrowers, The, 95

Box of Candles, A, 112

Boy of Old Prague, A, 3, 156

Boy in the Striped Pajamas, The, 156

Boy Who Loved Words, The, 56

Boy Who Stuck Out His Tongue, The, 207

Braid the Challah, 84

Bridge to America, 70

Broken Song, 212, 216

Brothers: A Hebrew Legend, 66

Brothers in Valor: A Story of Resistance, 168

Brothers' Promise, The, 66

Brundibar, 156, 185, 210

Bubbe Leah and Her Paper Children, 176

Burglar and Other Stories, The, 240

Butterfly, The, 213

Butterfly Seeds, The, 195

By the Hanukkah Light, 175

C

Cain and Abel: Finding the Fruits of Peace, 114

Caleb's Ride on Noah's Ark, 13

Call Me Ruth, 202

Carp in the Bathtub, The, 70

Cat with the Yellow Star, The, 185

Cats in Krasinski Square, The, 212

Celebrate Hanukkah with Light, Latkes, and Dreidels, 93

Celebrate Passover with Matzah, Maror, and Memories, 93

Celebrate! Stories of the Jewish Holidays, 102

Celebrating Hanukkah, 94

Celebrating Passover, 94

Chanan and His Violin and Other Stories, 240

Chanukah Blessing, The, 68

Chanukah Bugs: A Pop-Up Celebration, 76

Chanukah Guest, The, 4, 75, 95

Chanukah Lights Everywhere, 98

Chanukah on the Prairie, 125

Chernowitz, 3, 37

Chicken Man, 27

Chicken Soup by Heart, 67, 100

Children of Israel, 124

Children's Bible Stories from Genesis to Daniel, 21

Children's Literature in the Elementary School, 7th Edition, 6

Child's Book of Midrash, A: 52 Jewish Stories from the Sages, 235

Chocolate Chip Challah, 106

Chosen, The, 62

Christmas Carol, A, 198

Christmas Menorahs, The: How a Town Fought Hate, 198

Clap and Count: Action Rhymes for the Jewish Year, 80

Clara's War, 156

Cloak for the Moon, A, 143

Clouds of Glory, 21

Coat of Many Colors, The, 205

Coat for the Moon and Other Jewish Tales, A, 238

Colors of Israel, 124

Colors of My Jewish Year, The, 77

Come, Let Us Be Joyful: The Story of Hava Nagila, 125

Company's Coming: A Passover Lift-the-Flap Book, 80

Confessions of a Closet Catholic, 4, 224

Confused Hanukkah, A, 96

Costume for Noah, A, 142

Could Anything Be Worse?, 25

Count with Mendel, 76

Cow in the Kitchen, The, 25

Cow in the House, The, 30

Cow of No Color, The, 51

Creation of Israel, The, 133

Crimes and Criminals of the Holocaust, 155

Cure, The, 160, 164

Curious George, 174

D

D Is for Dreidel, 87

Dance, Sing, Remember, 80

Dancing on the Bridge at Avignon, 160

Daniel, Half Human, and the Good Nazi, 162

Darkness over Denmark: The Danish Resistance and the Rescue of the Jews, 217

Daughter of the Great Zandini, 114

Daughter of Light, 211

Daughter of Venice, 61

Daughters of the Ark, 129

Daughters of Eve: Strong Women of the Bible, 43

Daughters of Fire: Heroines of the Bible, 42

Dave at Night, 37

David and Max, 71

David and the Trash-Talkin' Giant, 221

David's Songs: His Psalms and Their Story, 17

Day of Delight: A Jewish Sabbath in Ethiopia, 107, 125

Day the Rabbi Disappeared, The: Jewish Holiday Tales of Magic, 237

Dead Sea Scrolls, The, 57, 146

Dear Emma, 115, 224

Dear Great American Writers School, 146

Death on Sacred Ground, 52

*Defying the Tide: An Account of Authentic
   Compassion during the Holocaust,* 220

Demons' Mistake, The, 144

Deniers of the Holocaust, 163

Devil's Arithmetic, The, 169

*Diamond Tree, The: Jewish Tales from
   Around the World,* 4, 233

Diary of Pelly D., The, 160

Diary of a Young Girl, The, 5

*Diary of a Young Girl: The Definitive
   ˙ Edition,* 5, 188

Dinosaur on Hanukkah, 85

Dinosaur on Passover, 85

Dinosaur on Shabbat, 85

Discovering Cultures: Israel, 131

Does God Have a Big Toe?, 18

Dog of Knots, 71

Doll with the Yellow Star, The, 184

Dolls' Journey to Eretz Israel, The, 176

Dovid the Little Shepherd, 64

Double Crossing, 149

Dreaming in Black and White, 227

Dreams Come True Club, The, 34

*Dreams in the Gold Country: The Diary of
   Zipporah Feldman, a Jewish Immigrant
   Girl,* 182

Duel, 42

Dybbuk, 113

Dybbuk: A Version, 53

Elie Wiesel: A Voice for Humanity, 192

Elijah the Slave, 50

Elisabeth, 175

Ella of All of a Kind Family, 72

*Elsie's War: A Story of Courage in Nazi
   Germany,* 167

*Emmanuel Ringelblum: Historian of the
   Warsaw Ghetto,* 187

Emil and Karl, 156

Emily Goldberg Learns to Salsa, 118

Endless Steppe, The, 5, 163

Enemy Has a Face, The, 165

Erika's Story, 214

*Escape to the Forest: Based on a True Story
   of the Holocaust,* 166, 169

Escape! The Story of the Great Houdini, 147

*Escape: Teens Who Escaped the Holocaust
   to Freedom,* 188

Escaping to America: A True Story, 144

Escaping Into the Night, 160, 162

Esther, 229

Esther's Story, 215

Eva's Journey: A Young Girls' True Story,
   179

Eve and Her Sisters, 39

Even Higher, 49

*Excellence in Jewish Children's Literature:
   A Guide for Book Selectors, Reviewers,
   and Award Judges,* 6

Exodus, 20

E

*Edward Teller and the Development of the
   Hydrogen Bomb,* 60

Eight Candles to Light: A Chanukah Story, 89

Eight Lights for Eight Nights, 93

Eight Nights of Chanukah, The, 84

Eight Wild Nights: A Family Hanukkah, 89

*Eleventh Commandment, The: Wisdom from
   Our Children,* 199

*Elie Wiesel: A Holocaust Survivor Cries Out
   for Peace,* 115

Elie Wiesel: Spokesman for Remembrance,
   187

*Elie Wiesel: Surviving the Holocaust,
   Speaking Out Against Genocide,* 190

F

*Faces of Courage: Young Heroes of World
   War II,* 166

Facing the Music, 219

Faige Finds a Way, 65

Family Haggadah, The, 106

Faraway Home, 218

Faraway Summer, 115, 224

*Fate Did Not Let Me Go: A Mother's
   Farewell Letter,* 191

Feast of Fools, 156

Feathers, 31

Festival of Freedom, 92

Fighter, The, 170

Finding Sophie, 44, 149, 215

Fire at the Triangle Factory, 200

Fireflies in the Dark: The Story of Friedl Dicker-Brandeis and the Children of Terezin, 156, 159, 168, 186

First Gift, The, 63

First He Made the Sun, 16

Five Alive! My Yom Tov Five Senses, 85

Five Books of Moses for Young People, The, 20

Fixer, The, 28

Flag With Fifty-six Stars: A Gift from the Survivors of Mauthausen, 167

Flowers on the Wall, 184

Flying Latke, The, 116

For Heaven's Sake, 16

For Kids— Putting God on Your Guest List, 106

Forged in Freedom: Shaping the Jewish-American Experience, 134

Forgotten Victims of the Holocaust, 155

Four Good Friends and a Boat, 78

Four Sides, Eight Nights: A New Spin on Hanukkah, 102

Four Special Questions: A Passover Story, 89

Friday Nights of Nana, The, 94

Friedrich, 166

Friend Called Anne, A, 182

Friends Indeed: The Special Relationship of Israel and the United States, 134

Frontier Merchants: Lionel and Barron Jacobs and the Jewish Pioneers Who Settled the West, 152

Frost in the Night, A, 161

G

Gabriel's Ark, 103

Garden, The, 135

Gavriel and the Golden Garden, 25

Genius: A Photobiography of Albert Einstein, 58

Gershon's Monster: A Story for the Jewish New Year, 4, 205

Gershwin's Rhapsody in Blue, 146

Get Ready for Shabbos with Mendel, 77

Get Well Soon, 85

Ghosts and Golems: Haunting Tales of the Supernatural, 240

Gift, The, 47

Gittel's Hands, 69

Giver, The, 160

Global Counterstrike: International Counterterrorism, 163

Glory, 13

Go-Between, The, 40

God Around Us, The: A Child's Garden of Prayer, 12

God Around Us, The, Vol. 2: The Valley of Blessings, 13

God's Garden: Children's Stories Grown from the Bible, 103

God's Mailbox, 18

Golda Meir, 133

Golem, 211

Golem, The, 210, 214

Good-Bye, Marianne, 44, 149, 215

Good Liar, The, 213

Good Morning, Boker Tov, 11, 195

Good Night, Lilah Tov, 195

Good Night, Maman, 153, 158

Goy Crazy, 38

Grandma Esther Remembers: A Jewish-American Family Story, 175

Grandpa Like Yours, A; A Grandma Like Yours, 64

Grandpa's Gamble, 206

Great Hanukkah Party, The, 88

Great Israel Scavenger Hunt, The, 123

Great Potato Plan, The, 65, 210

Greater Than Angels, 160, 217

Guests Deserve the Best, 78

H

Had Gadya: A Passover Song, 92

Hammerin' Hank: The Life of Hank Greenberg, 33

Hana's Suitcase, 183

Hana's Suitcase on Stage, 183

Hannah Senesh: Her Life and Diary: The First Complete Edition, 170

Hannah's Journal, 184

Hannah's Sabbath Dress, 64
Hans and Sophie Scholl, 161
Hanukkah, 91, 99
Hanukkah!, 86
*Hanukkah: A Counting Book in English,
     Hebrew, and Yiddish,* 100
Hanukkah Cat, Revised Edition, 65
*Hanukkah: Celebrating the Holiday of
     Lights,* 90
Hanukkah Family Treasury, The, 94
*Hanukkah Fun: Great Things to Make and
     Do,* 89
Hanukkah Ghosts, The, 115
Hanukkah: Jewish Festival of Lights, 100
Hanukkah Lights, 87
Hanukkah Mice, The, 84
Hanukkah, Oh Hanukkah, 85
Hanukkah, Shmanukkah!, 198
Hanukkah Treasury, A, 236
Hanukkah at Valley Forge, 96
Happy Birthday to Me!, 82
*Happy Birthday, World: A Rosh Hashanah
     Celebration,* 81
Happy Hanukkah, Biscuit!, 76
Hardest Word, The, 47, 203
*Haym Solomon: Patriot Banker of the
     American Revolution,* 52
Hebrew Kid and the Apache Maiden, The, 72
*Heeding the Call: Jewish Voices in America's
     Civil Rights Struggle,* 201
Hello, America, 193, 202, 228
Hero, 211
*Hero and the Holocaust, A: The Story of
     Janusz Korczak and His Children,* 70
Heroes of the Holocaust, 216
Hershel and the Hanukkah Goblins, 4, 49,
     154
Hidden Child, 184
*Hidden on the Mountain: Stories of Children
     Sheltered from the Nazis in Le
     Chambon,* 215
*Hidden Music: The Life of Fanny
     Mendelssohn,* 227
History of the Holocaust, A, Revised Edition,
     193
*Hitler and the Nazis, a History in
     Documents,* 170

*Hitler Youth: Growing Up in Hitler's
     Shadow,* 161
Hitler's Canary, 214
Hitler's Daughter, 226
Hitler's Rise to Power and the Holocaust,
     155
Holocaust, The, 168
Holocaust, The: Death Camps, 166
Home Free, Margit: Book One, 35
Honi's Circle of Trees, 196
Hooray for Hanukkah!, 83
Hooray! It's Passover!, 81
Horn for Louis, A, 33
Horrible Harry and the Holidaze, 95
How Does God Make Things Happen?, 15
How I Saved Hanukkah, 104
*How the Rosh Hashanah Challah Became
     Round,* 90
How to Ruin a Summer Vacation, 5, 118,
     138
How Yussel Caught the Gefilte Fish, 93
Hundred Dresses, The, 32

I

I Am David, 156
I Am a Holocaust Torah, 180
I Am a Torah, 84
*I Believe In . . . Christian, Jewish, and
     Muslim Young People Speak about
     Their Faith,* 23
I Go to the Doctor, 12, 75
I Go to School, 75
I Go Visiting, 76
I Have a Little Dreidel, 75
*I Have Lived a Thousand Years: Growing Up
     in the Holocaust,* 193, 202, 228
I Never Saw Another Butterfly, 159, 168
I Only Like What I Like, 221
*I Will Plant You a Lilac Tree: A Memoir of a
     Schindler's List Survivor,* 189
I Wish I Were King, 28
If You Come Softly, 230
Ilan Ramon, Israel's First Astronaut, 59
Ilan Ramon: Israel's Space Hero, 131
Ilan Ramon: Jewish Star, 192
Impact of the Holocaust, 52

Importance of Anne Frank, The, 193
Importance of Golda Meir, The, 139
Importance of Simon Wiesenthal, The, 51
In God's Hands, 196
In God's Name, 16
In My Enemy's House, 165
In My Hands: Memoirs of a Holocaust Rescuer, 219
In My Pocket, 178
In Our Image: God's First Creatures, 69
In the Beginning: Bereishit, 18
In the Days of Sand and Stars, 43
In the Month of Kislev, 49
In the Promised Land: Lives of Jewish Americans, 200
Incantation, 170
Inside Israel's Mossad: The Institute for Intelligence and Special Tasks, 137
Inside the Rain Barrel, 185
Invisible Chains, 227
Invisible Kingdoms: Jewish Tales of Angels, Spirits, and Demons, 238
Is It Shabbos Yet?, 77
Island of Hope: The Story of Ellis Island and the Journey to America, 151
Israel, 123, 125, 126, 128, 133, 137, 139
Israel: The Founding of a Modern Nation, 131
Israel in the News: Past, Present, and Future, 126
Israel in Pictures, Revised and Expanded, 128
Israel, Revised Edition, 129
Israel, Second Edition, 134
It Could Always Be Worse, 4, 27
It Couldn't Be Worse, 26
It's Challah Time!, 81
It's Hanukkah!, 77
It's Hanukkah Time!, 81
It's a Miracle! A Hanukkah Storybook, 234
It's Not Worth Making a Tzimmes Over!, 99
It's Party Time! A Purim Story, 89
It's Purim Time!, 81
It's Seder Time!, 81
It's Shofar Time!, 81
It's Sukkah Time!, 81
It's Tu B'Shevat, 88

J

Jailbait, 229
Jalapeno Bagels, 222
Jar of Fools, The: Eight Hanukkah Stories from Chelm, 236
Jason's Miracle, 126
Jeremiah's Promise: An Adventure in Modern Israel, 130
Jeremy's Dreidel, 66
Jerusalem or Death: Palestinian Terrorism, 163
Jerusalem Sky: Stars, Crosses, and Crescents, 22
Jesse's Star, 214
Jewish, 132
Jewish Americans, 130
Jewish Americans, The, 133
Jewish Book Annual, 1992–1993, 5
Jewish Book World, 7
Jewish Experience, The: 2,000 Years: A Collection of Significant Events, 137
Jewish Faith, The, 97
Jewish Festivals Throughout the Year, 91
Jewish Hero Corps #1, 184
Jewish Holiday Origami, 107
Jewish Holidays All Year Round: A Family Treasury, 103
Jewish Sports Stars: Athletic Heroes Past and Present, 147
Jewish Victims of the Holocaust, The, 155
Jewish Year, The: Celebrating the Holidays, 108
JGirls' Guide, The: The Young Jewish Woman's Handbook for Coming of Age, 226
Jonah, 204
Jonah and the Whale (and the Worm), 203
Jonah's Trash, God's Treasure, 203
Jonas Salk: Conquering Polio, 200
Jonas Salk and the Polio Vaccine, 197
Jonas Salk: Polio Vaccine Pioneer, 200
Jonathan and the Waves/Yonatan v'Hagalim, 20
Joseph, 42
Joseph Had a Little Overcoat, 142, 144
Joseph and His Coat of Many Colors, 205

Joseph, Master of Dreams, 208
Joseph Who Loved the Sabbath, 94
Josh and Alisha Celebrate Chanukah, 79
Journey to America, 5, 115, 150
Journey Back, The, 191
Journey to Ellis Island: How My Father
    Came to America, 142
Journey to Paradise and Other Jewish Tales,
    A, 238
Journey That Saved Curious George, The:
    The True Wartime Escape of Margaret
    and H. A. Rey, 174
Journeys with Elijah: Eight Tales of the
    Prophet, 50, 232
Judaism, 132
Julia's Kitchen, 179
Julietta, 152
Just Call Me Joe, 225
Just Enough and Not Too Much, 26
Just Like... Me!, 223
Just Right: The Story of a Jewish Home, 77
Juvenile Judaica, ix

K

Katarina, 169, 186
Keeping the Promise: A Torah's Journey, 182
Key Is Lost, The, 186, 215
Key under the Pillow, The, 41
Kibitzers and Fools: Tales My Zayda Told
    Me, 234
Kids' Cartoon Bible, The, 20
Kids' Catalog of Animals and the Earth, The,
    198
Kids' Catalog of Bible Treasures, The, 127
Kids' Catalog of Hanukkah, The, 102
Kids' Catalog of Israel, A, Revised Edition,
    127
Kids' Catalog of Passover, The: A Worldwide
    Celebration of Stories, Songs,
    Customs, Crafts, Food, and Fun, 106
Kids Love Jewish Holiday Crafts, 102
Kind Little Rivka, 64
King of Mulberry Street, The, 73
King of the Seventh Grade, 208
King Solomon and the Bee, 40
King Solomon and His Magic Ring, 239

Kingdom of Singing Birds, The, 65
Kingfisher Treasury of Jewish Stories, The,
    234
K'tonton's Yom Kippur Kitten, 207
Kugel Vally Klezmer Band, The, 145

L

Last Pair of Shoes, The, 66
Latkes, Latkes, Good to Eat, 94
L'Chaim! To Jewish Life in America, 136
Lech Lecha: The Journey of Abraham and
    Sarah, 18
Legend of Freedom Hill, The, 209
Legend of Jonah and the Two Great Fish,
    The, 204
Lemuel the Fool, 29
Let There Be Light: Poems and Prayers for
    Repairing the World, 201
Let's Go Shopping, 75
Let's Go to Shul, 12, 75
Let's Steal the Moon: Jewish Tales, Ancient
    and Recent, 238
Let's Talk About the Sabbath, 96
Let's Visit Israel, 121
Letters from Rivka, 147
Liberty on 23rd Street, 35
Life and Death of Adolf Hitler, The, 162
Life of Moses, The, 53
Life and Times of Moses, The, 44
Light Years, 229
Lights along the Path: Jewish Folklore
    through the Grades for Children Ages
    Four to Twelve, 237
Like a Maccabee, 223
Lilith's Ark: Teenage Tales of Biblical
    Women, 226
Lily Cupboard, The, 116, 210
Lion and the Unicorn, The, 222
Lise Meitner and the Atomic Age, 61
Lise Meitner, Discoverer of Nuclear Fission,
    61
Lise Meitner: Pioneer of Nuclear Fission, 61
Listen to the Trees, 196
Little Boy Named Avram, A, 15
Little Girl Named Miriam, A, 122
Little, Little House, The, 26

Little Women, 3
Littlest Frog, The, 222
Littlest Pair, The, 85, 222
Lonek's Journey: The True Story of a Boy's Escape to Freedom, 186
Long Johns for a Small Chicken, 65
Lost in America, 44
Lost Childhood, The: A World War II Memoir, 190
Lost and Found, 156, 240
Lost and Found and Other Stories
Lots of Latkes, 97
Love Me Later, 12
Love You, Soldier, 71
Luba: The Angel of Bergen-Belsen, 213

M

Maccabee Jamboree: A Hanukkah Countdown, 80
Magic of Kol Nidre, The, 206
Magic Menorah, The: A Modern Chanukah Tale, 107
Magician's Visit, The, 92
Make a Wish, Molly, 90
Make Your Own Bar/Bat Mitzvah: A Personal Approach to Creating a Meaningful Rite of Passage, 105
Malka, 165
Man's Search for Meaning, 62
Many Ways: How Families Practice Their Beliefs and Religions, 22
Mara's Stories: Glimmers in the Dark, 167
Marika, 162
Market Wedding, The, 28
Marven of the Great North Woods, 143
Masada, 132, 136
Masada: Sieges That Changed the World, 164
Matchless Six, The: The Story of Canada's First Women's Olympic Team, 150
Matzah Ball Boy, The, 99
Matzah Ball Soup, 176
Matzah Man, 75, 81, 141
Matzah Meals: A Passover Cookbook for Kids, 107
Matzah That Papa Brought Home, The, 97

Matzo Ball Moon, 84
Mayses far Yidishe Kinder (Stories for Jewish Children), 238
Memories of Survival, 182
Memory Coat, The, 178
Mendel Rosenbusch: Tales for Jewish Children, 72
Mendel's Accordian, 174
Menorah Story, The, 22
Messes of Dresses, 29
Milkweed, 220
Mimmy and Sophie, 32, 174
Mimmy and Sophie All Around the Town, 32
Miracle of Hanukkah, The, 76
Miracle Lights: The Chanukah Story!, 105
Miracle of the Rock, The: Timeless Tales from the Lives of Our Sages, 232
Miracle at Sea and Other Stories: Timeless Tales from the Lives of Our Sages, 232
Miriam, 128, 135
Miriam Mendilow, Mother of Jerusalem, 201
Miriam's Cup, 97
Miriam's Journey: Discovering a New World, 67
Missing Girls, 117
Missing Persons: The Chocolate Lover, 218
Missing Persons: The Rose Queen, 218
Missing Persons: The Unsuspecting Gourmet, 218
Missing Persons: The Venetian Policeman, 218
Mitten, The, 63
Moishe's Miracle, 29
Molly's Pilgrim, 3, 32, 33, 35, 90
Mommy Never Went to Hebrew School, 122
Money in the Honey, The, 47
Mordechai Anielewicz: Hero of the Warsaw Ghetto Uprising, 161
More All-of-a-Kind Family, 72
More Precious than Gold, 65, 209
More Tales of the Wise Men of Helm, 239
More than Matzah: A Passover Feast of Fun, Food, Facts, and Activities, 93
Moses, 51
Moses and the Angels, 23
Moses Basket, The, 63
Moses in Egypt, 133

Moses: The Long Road to Freedom, 51
Most Magnificent Mosque, The, 113
Mother Goose Rhymes for Jewish Children, 82
Mountain of Blintzes, A, 112
Mouse in the Matzah Factory, The, Revised Edition, 83
Moxie Kid, The, 71
Mr. Belinsky's Bagels, 29
Mr. and Mrs. Noah, 48
Mrs. Greenberg's Messy Hanukkah, 92
Mrs. Honig's Cakes, 104
Mrs. Katz and Tush, 68
Much, Much Better, 67
Murder at the 1972 Olympics in Munich, 167
My Baby Brother, What a Miracle!, 113
My Bridges of Hope, 193, 202, 228
My Canary Yellow Star, 169, 218
My Cousin Tamar Lives in Israel, 121
My First Hanukkah, 83
My First Jewish Holidays Library, 83
My First Passover, 83
My First Shabbat, 83
My Grandmother's Stories: A Collection of Jewish Folktales, Revised Edition, 232
My Guardian Angel, 59
My Mannequins, 145
My Name Is Rachamim, 124
My Secret Camera: Life in the Lodz Ghetto, 167, 192
My Two Grams, 113
My Very Own Haggadah, 79
Mysterious Visitor, The: Stories of the Prophet Elijah, 235
Mystery Bear, The: A Purim Story, 75
Mystery of the Dead Sea Scrolls, 57, 146
Mystery of the Missing Pitome, The, 204

N

Na'amah, Noah's Wife, 197
Naftali the Storyteller and His Horse, Sus, 59
Nazi War Criminals, 53
Neve Shalom, Wahat al Salaam: Oasis of Peace, 5
Never-Ending Greenness, The, 126

Never Mind the Goldbergs, 109
New Boy, 202
New Boy, The/Yeled Hadash, 70
New World Waiting, 188
Nickel, a Trolley, a Treasure House, A, 173
Niels Bohr: Physicist and Humanitarian, 38
Night of the Burning, The, 219
Night Journey, The, 212, 216
Night Lights: A Sukkot Story, 78
Night Spies, The, 158, 169
Nine Spoons: A Chanukah Story, 69
97 Orchard Street, New York: Stories of Immigrant Life, 147
No Matzah for Me!, 96
No One Must Know, 228
No Pretty Pictures: A Child of War, 190
No Rules for Michael, 31
Noah and the Great Flood, 47
Noah and the Ziz, 47
Noah's Ark, 16, 49, 50
Noah's Bed, 111
Noah's Trees, 15
Noah's Wife, 141
North to Freedom, 156
Not the End of the World, 38
Nothing Here But Stones, 136
Number the Stars, 1, 212
Numbers of My Jewish Year, The, 79

O

Odd Boy Out: Young Albert Einstein, 57
Old Country, The, 156
Old Noah's Elephants, 111
Old Testament Women, 45
On Eagles' Wings and Other Things, 125
On Morning Wings, 15
On Noah's Ark, 63
On Passover, 91
On Purim, 91
On Rosh Hashanah and Yom Kippur, 91
On Shabbat, 91
On Sukkot and Simhat Torah, 91
On the Wings of Eagles: An Ethiopian Boy's Story, 131
Once Upon a Shabbos, 75, 95

Once Upon a Tale: Twelve Illustrated Parables from the Dubno Maggid, 237
Once Upon a Time, 102
Once Upon a Time in Chicago, 145
One Foot Ashore, 128
One Hundred and One Jewish Read Aloud Stories, 235
One More Border, 212
One More River: A Noah's Ark Counting Song, 15
Onions and Garlic, 222
Only One Club, The, 223
Open Your Doors: Margit, Book Three, 35
Opposites of My Jewish Year, The, 77
Oskar Schindler, 219
Oskar Schindler: Righteous Gentile, 218
Other 1492, The: Jewish Settlement in the New World, 180
Our Eddie, 4
Our Eight Nights of Hanukkah, 99
Our Land of Israel, 127, 130
Out of Many Waters, 128
Out of the Shadows: An Artist's Journey, 194

P

P Is for Passover: A Holiday Alphabet Book, 87
Papa's Latkes, 174
Paradise, 17
Parashah Plays, 102
Passage to Freedom: The Sugihara Story, 213
Passover, 86, 87, 91
Passover!, 86
Passover around the World, 104
Passover Is Here!, 84
Passover Seder, The, 100
Passover Splendor: Cherished Objects for the Seder Table, 108
Passover Story, The, 91
Pastor Andre Trocme: Spiritual Leader of the French Village Le Chambon, 216
Paths to Peace: People Who Changed the World, 116
Pearl Moskowitz's Last Stand, 197
Pearl Plants a Tree, 101
Pearl's Eight Days of Chanukah, 101

Pearl's Marigolds for Grandpa, 173
Pearl's Passover, 101
Peddler's Gift, The, 184, 206
Penina Levine Is a Hard-boiled Egg, 148
Perfect Porridge, 68
Perfect Prayer, The, 19
Pharaoh's Daughter, 128
Photo Odyssey: Solomon Carvalho's Remarkable Western Adventure, 1853–54, 149
Pickpocket's Tale, A, 74
Picture of Grandmother, A, 181
Pip and the Edge of Heaven, 19
Pirate Princess and Other Fairy Tales, The, 29, 237
Place Not Home, A, 169
Place That I Love, The, 77
Play to the Angels, 43
Playing Dad's Song, 180
Pocket Full of Seeds, 44
Prayer for the Earth, A, 197
Praying to A. L., 42
Prince of Egypt, The, 43
Prince William, Maximilian Minsky, and Me, 118
Princess, the Crone, and the Dung Cart Knight, The, 208
Prisoner in Time: A Child of the Holocaust, 158
Promise Fulfilled, A: Theodor Herzl, Chaim Weizmann, David Ben Gurion, and the Creation of the State of Israel, 135
Promise of a New Spring: The Holocaust and Renewal, 154
Promise to Remember, A: The Holocaust in the Words and Voices of Its Survivors, 187
Promised Land, The, 60
Prophets for Young People, The, 51
Purim, 89
Purim Goodies, 205
Purim Play, 223

Q

Quake! Disaster in San Francisco, 1906, 36
Queen Esther, the Morning Star, 154

Queen Esther Saves Her People, 153
Queen of Persia, The, 159

R

Rabbi and the Twenty Nine Witches, The,
  154
Rabbi Who Flew, The, 90
Rachel Captures the Moon, 145
Rachel's Gift, 30
Rachel's Library, 56
Raisel's Riddle, 56
*Raoul Wallenberg: Rescuing Thousands from
  the Nazis' Grasp,* 217
*Raoul Wallenberg: Swedish Diplomat and
  Humanitarian,* 218
Reach for the Stars: A Little Torah's Journey,
  176
Real Time, 5, 170
Rebecca, 40
Rebecca's Journey Home, 69
Rebecca's Passover
*Rebekkah's Journey: A World War II Refugee
  Story,* 153
Remember the Days, 190
*Remember Me: A Search for Refuge in
  Wartime Britain,* 44, 215
*Remember Not to Forget: A Memory of the
  Holocaust,* 180
*Remembering the Prophets of Sacred
  Scripture,* 53
Rescuing Einstein's Compass, 56
*Resisters and Rescuers: Standing Up
  Against the Holocaust,* 211
Return, The, 135
Rivka's First Thanksgiving, 144
Rivka's Way, 37
*Robert A. Weinberg and the Search for the
  Cause of Cancer,* 199
Room in the Heart, 217
Rosie in Chicago: Play Ball!, 148
Rosie in Los Angeles: Action!, 36
Rosie in New York: Gotcha!, 51, 148
Rosie's Dream Cape, 147
Run, Boy, Run, 151
Runaway Dreidel, 81, 142
Runaway Latkes, The Running on Eggs, 150

Russian Jewish Family, A, 129
Ruth and Naomi, 67

S

Sack Full of Feathers, A, 34
Sam I Am, 5, 114
Samir and Yonatan, 5, 72
Sammy Spider's First Haggadah, 86
Sammy Spider's First Passover, 86
Sammy Spider's First Purim, 86
Sammy Spider's First Rosh Hashanah, 86
Sammy Spider's First Shabbat, 86
Sammy Spider's First Sukkot, 86
Sammy Spider's First Trip to Israel, 122
Sammy Spider's Israel Fun Book, 122
Saturday Secret, The, 116
Saving Edith, 212
*Say Hey and the Babe: Two Mostly True
  Baseball Stories,* 186
*Saying Goodbye: A Handbook for Teens
  Dealing with Loss and Mourning,* 188
School Library Journal, 6
*Searching for Anne Frank: Letters from
  Amsterdam to Iowa,* 191
Secret of Gabi's Dresser, The, 158, 181
Secret Grove, The, 5
Secret of the Mezuzah, The, 53
Secret of Priest's Grotto, The, 167
Secret Seder, The, 159
Secret Tunnel, The, 65, 145
Secret World of Kabbalah, The, 60
Secrets in the House of Delgado, 165
Sefer Ha-Aggadah: Volume One, 237
Sefer Ha-Aggadah: Volume Two, 59
Sefer Torah Parade, The, 12
*Selman Waksman and the Discovery of
  Streptomycin,* 199
*Seven Good Years and Other Stories of I. L.
  Peretz, The,* 239
Seven Species, The: Stories and Recipes, 198
Seventh Day, The, 13
Shabbat, 83
Shabbat Box, 142
Shabbat Shalom, 88
Shabbat Shalom!, 11
Shadow of a Flying Bird, The, 66

Shadow Life: A Portrait of Anne Frank and Her Family, 187

Shadow Play: A True Story of Tefillah, 50

Shalom, Haver: Goodbye, Friend, 178

Shalom, Salaam, Peace, 111

Shanghai Shadows, 151

Shapes of My Jewish Year, The, 77

Shlemazel and the Remarkable Spoon of Pohost, 41

Shlemiel Crooks, 130

Shmuel Ha Nagid: A Tale of the Golden Age, 58

Shoes for Amelie, 214

Sholom's Treasure, 56

Shutting Out the Sky: Life in the Tenements of New York, 1880–1924, 148

Sigmund Freud: Pioneer of the Mind, 62

Silent as a Stone: Mother Maria of Paris and the Trash Can Rescue, 211

Silver Days, 5, 115, 150, 151

Simon Boom Gives a Wedding, 29

Simon Says, 42

Sing Praise, 14

Singing Mountain, The, 4, 108, 117

Sisterland, 117

Six Million Paper Clips: The Making of a Children's Holocaust Memorial, 191

Smoke and Ashes, Revised and Expanded, 166

Snow in Jerusalem, 5, 112

Solomon and the Ant and Other Jewish Folktales, 236

Solomon and the Trees, 195, 236

Something for Nothing, 114

Something from Nothing. 92, 141, 142, 144

Something Remains, 169, 189

Sophie and the Shofar, 206

Sound the Shofar, 95

Sounds of My Jewish Year, The, 77

Sparks Fly Upward, 224

Special Fate, A: Chiune Sugihara, Hero of the Holocaust, 213, 216

Speed of Light, 200

Spider's Web, The, 208

Spin the Dreidel, 77

Star of Fear, Star of Hope, 174

Star of Luis, 137

Starlight and Candles, 97

Stealing Home, 118

Stolen Words, 116

Stone Lamp, The: Eight Stories of Hannukah Through History, 5, 181

Stonecutter Who Wanted to Be Rich, The, 25

Stones from the River, 171

Stones in Water, 73

Stories from Adam and Eve to Ezekiel, 22

Stories Straight from Avi's Heart, 231

Storky: How I Lost My Nickname and Won the Girl, 229

Story of the Holocaust, The, 164

Story of Mimmy and Simmy, The, 28

Story of Ruth, The, 68

Story of Shabbat, The, 90

Storyteller's Beads, The, 73

Strange Relations, 4, 108

Streets Are Paved With Gold, The, 60

Streets of Gold, 60

Strudel Stories, 185

Such a Noise!, 27

Suitcase of Dreams: Immigration Stories from the Skirball Cultural Center, 148

Sukkah That I Built, The, 88

Summer of My German Soldier, The, 4, 227

Sunrise, Sunset, 173

Surviving Hitler: A Boy in the Nazi Death Camps, 168

Survivors: True Stories of Children of the Holocaust, 187

Sweet New Year, A: A Taste of the Jewish Holidays, 105

Swindletop, 131

T

Tale of Mishka the Kvetch, The, 27

Tales for the Seventh Day, 236

Tali's Jerusalem Scrapbook, 154

Tamar, 171

Tamar's Sukkah, 78

Tapestry of Hope: Holocaust Writing for Young People, 192

Taste for Noah, A, 142

Tasty Bible Stories: A Menu of Tales and Matching Recipes, 232

Tell It to Naomi, 228

Telling Time, A, 178

*Ten Classic Jewish Children's Stories,*233

Ten Commandments for Jewish Children, The, 83

Ten Good Rules, 88

Ten Old Men and a Mouse, 66

Ten Tzedaka Pennies, 81

Tenement: Immigrant Life on the Lower East Side, 146

Terrible, Terrible, 27

Terrible Things, 153

Thank You, God! A Child's Book of Prayer, 14

Thanks to My Mother, 165

Theo, 216

Thirty-One Cakes: A Hashavas Aveidah Story, 33

This Is the Dreidel, 82

This Is the Earth That God Made, 13

This Is the Matzah, 82

This Is My Faith: Judaism, 133

This Is Our Seder, 79

Thought of High Windows, The, 229

Thread of Kindness: A Tzedaka Story, 69

Ticket to Israel, A, 123

Tie Man's Miracle, The, 177

Tikkun Olam: Fixing the World, 196

Tikva Means Hope, 98

'Til the Cows Come Home, 143, 144

Time Like a River, 213

To Bigotry No Sanction, 134

To Build a Land, 5

To Live and Fight Another Day, 160, 168

Toby Belfer Never Had a Christmas Tree, 106

Toby Belfer Visits Ellis Island, 185

Too Big, Too Little . . . Just Right!, 221

Too Many Cooks: A Passover Parable, 88

Too Much of a Good Thing, 30

Too Much Noise, 26

Too Young for Yiddish, 55

Torah and Judaism, The, 103

Torn Thread, 163

Touch of Passover, A, 87

Touch of the High Holidays, A: A Touch and Feel Book, 78

Tough Questions Jews Ask: A Young Adult's Guide to Building a Jewish Life, 61

Tower of Babel, The: Migdal Bavel, 18

Travels of Benjamin of Tudela, The: Through Three Continents in the Twelfth Century, 148

Treasure in the Tiny Blue Tin, The, 35

Treasury of Sholom Aleichem's Children's Stories, A, 238

Trees of the Dancing Goat, The, 68

Tunes for Bears to Dance To, 3, 156

Tuning Up: A Visit with Eric Kimmel, 55

Turn for Noah, A, 142

Turn, Turn, Turn, 19

Turned Away: The World War II Diary of Devorah Bernstein: Winnipeg, Manitoba, 1941, 190

Twenty and Ten, 209

Two Brothers, The: A Legend of Jerusalem, 64, 66

Two By Two, 64, 75

Two Suns in the Sky, 44, 153

U

Un Toque De Pasaj, 87

Uncle Eli's Special-for-Kids, Most Fun Ever, Under-the-Table Passover Haggadah, 107

Uncle Misha's Partisans, 169

Under the Domim Tree, 226

Underground Reporters, The, 158

Understanding Buddy, 199

Unexpected Detour and Other Stories, An, 240

Uninvited Guest and Other Jewish Holiday Tales, The, 4, 29, 236

Unjust Cause, 225

Unresolved, The, 54

Until the Messiah Comes, 130

Upstairs Room, The, 5, 191

V

Very Best Hanukkah Gift, The, 225

Very Best Place for a Penny, The, 81

Viktor Frankl: A Life Worth Living, 62

Visit to Oma, A, 41

Visiting a Synagogue, 98

Viva la Paris!, 198
Voice from the Holocaust, A, 227

W

Waiting for Eugene, 117
Walk the Dark Streets, 161, 189
Walker's Crossing, 117
Walking the Bible, 23
War Against God and His People, The: Guide to the Holocaust for Young People, 161
War Within, The, 129
Way Meat Loves Salt, The, 205
Way Too Much Challah Dough, 99
We Gave the World Moses and Bagels: Art and Wisdom of Jewish Children, 128
We Just Want to Live Here: A Palestinian Teenager, an Israeli Teenager—an Unlikely Friendship, 118
We Shall Not Be Moved: The Women's Factory Strike of 1909, 201
Weight of the Sky, The, 5, 136
Welcome to Israel, 130
What Do I Say?, 39
What Does God Look Like?, 15
What Happened to Heather Hopkowitz?, 4, 104, 224
What I Like about Passover, 83
What If Sara, 207
What Makes Me a Jew?, 122
What You Will See Inside a Synagogue, 124
What Zeesie Saw on Delancey Street, 19, 98, 144
When the Beginning Began, 22
When the Chickens Went On Strike, 207
When I Fell Into My Kiddush Cup, 78
When I Left My Village, 107, 125
When I Was a Soldier, 230
When Jesse Came Across the Sea, 143
When Mindy Stole Hanukkah, 95
When Pirates Came to Brooklyn, 37
When the Soldiers Were Gone, 115
When Solomon Was King, 206
When the War Is Over, 160
When Will the Fighting Stop?, 5
When the World Was Quiet, 15

When Zayde Danced on Eldridge Street, 19, 144
Where Do People Go When They Die?, 19
Where Is God?, 15
Where the Wild Things Are, 4
Where's My Dreidel?, 87
While the Candles Burn: Eight Stories for Hanukkah, 235
White Ram, The, 210
Who Am I?, 86
Who Is the Builder?, 14
Who Knows Ten? Children's Tales of the Ten Commandments, Revised Edition, 90
Who Was the Woman Who Wore the Hat?, 191
Who's That Sleeping on My Sofabed?, 79
Why the Moon Only Glows, 26
Why Noah Chose the Dove, 1, 112
Why on This Night? A Passover Haggadah for Family Celebration, 105
Wicked City, The, 154
Wide Awake, 202
Willy and Max: A Holocaust Story, 183
Winter Witch, The, 17
Wise Men of Helm and Their Merry Tales, The, 239
Wise . . . and Not So Wise: Ten Tales from the Rabbis, 234
Wise Shoemaker of Studena, The, 40
Wishes for One More Day, 175
With All My Heart, With All My Mind, 239, 240
Witnesses to War, 217
Women's Work: The Story of Betty Friedan, 201
Wonders of America, The: Reinventing Jewish Culture, 10
Wonders and Miracles: A Passover Companion, 4, 108
Would You Salute? One Child's Story of the Holocaust, 159
Written on the Wind, 179

Y

Year of Jewish Stories, A: 52 Tales for Children and Their Families, 233

Yellow Star, 159
Yellow Star, The: The Legend of King Christian of Denmark, 35
Yettele's Feathers, 31, 34
Yom Kippur Think, A, 203
Yoni Netanyahu: Commando at Entebbe, 132
Yossel April 19, 1943: *A Story of the Warsaw Ghetto Uprising,* 164
Yossi and Laibel On the Ball, 223
Yossi's Goal, 52
You Never Know: A Legend of the Lamed Vavniks, 50

Your Travel Guide to Ancient Israel, 136
Yussel's Prayer, 17

Z

Zack, 43
Zayde Was a Cowboy, 36
Zigazak! A Magical Hanukkah Night, 49
Ziz and the Hanukkah Miracle, The, 31
Zlateh the Goat and Other Stories, 4, 239

Subject Index

A

Abel (Biblical), 114
Abraham, 14, 18, 210
abusive fathers, 4
adoption, 69
Afikomen, 241
African-Americans, 3, 22, 37, 68, 202
  entertainers, 33
  interracial relationships with, 197, 209, 230
  novels of mixed ancestry, 43, 118
  shared prejudice with Jews, 115, 201
age-appropriate books, 8
AJL. *See* Association of Jewish Libraries
Akeda, 21, 241
Alef Design (publisher), 255
Aleichem, Sholom, 56
Alex Singer Project, 138
Aliyah, 138, 241
All of a Kind Family stories, 249
Alzheimer's disease, 117
American Revolution, 52, 96, 136
American-Israeli Cooperative Enterprise, 138
American-Israeli relations, 134
angels, 16, 47, 113
  as helpers, 20–21, 23
  in folktales, 233, 238, 239
Anielewicz, Mordechai, 161–162
Ansky, S. Y., 113
anti-Semitism, 3
  as theme in novels, 54, 130, 157, 227, 228
  aspects of, 171
  in America, 190
  in medieval times, 152, 156
  in nonfiction, 125, 132, 155, 163, 164, 180
  in Poland, 161

Arab-Jewish relations, 5, 154
  in novels, 71, 72, 112, 135, 150, 165
  nonfiction examinations of, 118, 126
Armstrong, Louis, 33
Ashkenazim, 8, 241
Association for Library Service to Children
    (ALSC), 299
Association of Jewish Libraries (AJL), 6
  Newsletter, 7, 299
  School, Synagogue and Centers Division,
    299
  Sydney Taylor Book Awards and, 249
astronauts, 59, 131, 177, 182–183, 192
Aufruf, 101, 241
Auschwitz (concentration camp), 72, 183,
    190, 202, 210
  in novels, 151, 170, 229
  memoirs about, 193
  nonfiction accounts of, 164, 166

B

Baal Shem Tov, 50, 205, 241
Baal Teshuvah, 117, 241
Bar Mitzvah, 72, 129, 177, 183, 226, 241
  in novels, 103, 113, 208
  preparation for, 61, 105, 106
Barak, Ehud, 137
Baruch Hashem, 241
baseball, 116
  biographies of players, 33
  history of, 186
  in novels, 40, 119, 148, 223
  skill development in, 152
Bat Mitzvah, 103, 118, 129, 225, 226, 241
  in novels, 118, 225

preparation for, 61, 105, 106
stories for, 228
BCE (Before Common Era), 241
bedtime rituals, 11–12, 195
bees, 40
Behrman House (publisher), 255
Bell, Jane, 150
Benjamin of Tudela, 148–149
Bergen-Belsen (concentration camp), 177,
182, 183, 213
Beta Israel, 124, 129–130, 131, 241
Bikur holim, 85, 241
birthdays, 81, 82, 90, 138
Black Death, 164
blindness, 66, 73. *See also* disabilities
blood libel, 214, 241
Bohr, Niels, 38
Book Thief, The (Zusak), 249
Booklist, 6
Borrowers, The (Norton), 95
Brady, Hana, 183
Braille, 66. *See also* blindness
bris, 101, 241
Brit milah, 101, 242
brochot, 82, 242
Brooklyn Dodgers, 119
Bubbe, 242. *See also* grandmothers
Byrd, James Jr., 166

C

caftan, 242
Cain (Biblical), 114
Caldecott Awards, 4, 50, 142, 211
Camelot, 208
Canadian Broadcasting Company, 183
cancer research, 199
Carnegie Awards, 171
Case-Western Reserve University, 299
Carvalho, Solomon, 149
Cather, Willa, 188
Catherwood, Ethel, 150
Catholic Charities, 189
caves, 167–168
CCAR (Central Conference of American
Rabbis), 255
CE (Common Era), 242

challah bread, 84, 90, 142, 242
baking of, 77, 197
humorous stories about, 99
recipes for, 81, 106
Chambon-sur-Lignon, le (French village),
214–217
Chanukah. *See* Hanukkah
charity
by children, 48, 68, 81
Charles W. Follett Award, 3
charoset, 88, 91, 242
cheder, 56, 59, 225, 242
Chelm, 29, 112, 233, 238, 242
"logic" of, 239
as location in stories, 57, 59, 114, 144, 145
in holiday tales, 96, 112, 236
Chelmnik, 242
chesed, 67, 68, 242
Christian X (King of Denmark), 35
Christmas, 17, 68, 106, 126, 198
family tensions during, 114
Chumash, 18, 242
chuppa, 242
chutzpah, 242
Civil War (American), 129
Civil War (Greek), 216
collection development guidelines, 9–10
comic books, 36, 184
Comprehensive Children's Literature
Database, 7
concentration camps. *See* individual camp
names
Cook, Myrtle, 150
Cossacks, 70, 144, 211
Cotopaxi Jewish Colony, 136
counting books, 15, 79, 80, 81, 100
cowboys, 36, 143
creation stories, 13–17, 21–22
Cullen, Countee, 38
Curious George (Rey), 174

D

Dasberg, Jacob (Rabbi), 183
dating
interfaith dating, 38
interracial dating, 117

David (King of Israel), 48, 67, 121, 242
  psalms of, 17
Davis, Jacob, 200
Days of Awe, 242, 247
Dead Sea Scrolls, 57, 146
demons, 29, 144, 238, 239
Diaspora, 53, 59, 129, 133, 245
Dicker-Brandeis, Friedl, 159
disabilities, 103, 225, 227. *See also* blindness
doctors, 12, 152, 165
Dovid HaMelech, 242. *See also* David (King of Israel)
dreidels, 79, 93, 206, 242
  alphabet books with, 87
  Braille lettering on, 66
  directions on making, 89, 100
  directions on using, 75, 77
  Dreidel Maidel (superhero), 184
  history and customs of, 102, 236
  in holiday stories, 81, 99, 106, 142
  in pop-up books, 76
  letter identification on, 82
dybbuk, 53, 67, 113, 242
dysgraphia, 225

E

earthquakes, 36
Easter, 177
Ecclesiastes, 19
Edict of Expulsion (Spanish decree), 209
Einstein, Albert, 55–58, 60–62, 116, 132
EKS (publishers), 255
Eldridge Street Synagogue, 19
Elijah (prophet), 232, 235
  as slave, 50
  in folktales, 1, 69, 92, 205
  in Hanukkah stories, 68
Elijah's cup, 30, 79, 242
Ellis Island
  as location in novels, 147, 178, 185
  fictional rejections at, 149
  nonfiction accounts of, 142–143, 151–152
Eretz Israel, 242
etrog, 204, 242
Eve (Biblical), 43

biographical sketches of, 39
Exodus, Book of, 20, 51, 81, 91, 96, 133

F

fabric collages, 182
factories, 201
  in fiction, 37, 51–52, 83, 115, 165, 200
Fanny Goldstein Merit Award, 299
felafel, 242
Feldheim Publishers, 255
Festivals, 247–248. *See also* individual festival names
Frank, Anne, 116, 176, 217
  biographies for middle school and above, 189, 192–193
  biographies for young readers, 176, 179, 181–182, 185
  diary as literary milestone, 5
  Diary of a Young Girl, 188
  historical fiction about, 187
  legacy of, 193
  photo illustrations of, 186
Frankl, Viktor, 62
Fremont, John Charles, 149
Freud, Sigmund, 62
Friedan, Betty, 201
funerals, 118, 173

G

Gali Girls (publishers), 255
Garden of Eden, 17, 23, 210
Gefen Books (publishers), 255
gelt (money), 48, 76, 85, 87, 242
gematria (numerology), 60, 242
General Slocum (steamship), 54
Genesis, 21, 22, 26, 40, 208, 226
genies, 56
Gershwin, George, 146
ghosts, 54, 67, 115, 130, 238, 240
giants, 221
Ginsburg, Ruth Bader, 200
goblins, 4, 49, 154
Gold Rush, 209
golem, 214, 238, 240
  as saviors of Jewish communities, 158–159

definition of, 242
stories for young children, 210, 211, 238
Gomorrah, 154
Goodall, Jane, 198
Goodman, Benny, 145
gossip, 34
grandfathers, 119, 130, 173, 206, 252
  as teachers, 19, 55, 185, 223
  death of, 16, 175
  separation from, 71, 195
grandmothers, 55, 138, 148, 221, 252
  as keepers of tradition, 176
  as storytellers, 73, 232, 234
  as teachers, 16, 92, 94, 143
  death of, 118
  Holocaust experiences of, 69, 117, 178, 181
  in blended families, 113, 177
  romantic lives of, 112
grandparents, 26, 80, 94
  as protectors, 111
  celebration of, 64
  in blended families, 122
  separation from, 178
Grant, Ulysses S., 129
Great Mosque, 113
Greenberg, Hank, 33
grief, 188
Gurion, David Ben, 135, 137

H

Ha Nagid, Shmuel (Rabbi), 58
Hachai Publishing, 255
Haggadot, 79, 242
Halakhah, 243
Hamentaschen, 243
Hamodia (publishers), 255
Hanukkah, 29, 31, 83–86, 174, 225, 247
  activity books, 89, 93
  alphabet books, 87
  appreciation for, 97, 104, 126, 223
  bedtime stories during, 234
  charity during, 48, 68
  compendiums for, 102, 235, 236
  counting books for, 80, 100
  customs of, 82, 88, 90–91
  dreidel stories for, 66, 75, 77, 82, 87, 142

ghost stories, 115, 154, 198
history of, 57, 94, 100, 105
increased emphasis on, 2
interfaith themes and, 17, 95–96, 99, 106, 114, 198
menorahs and, 22, 69, 107, 175
picture books for, 49, 65, 79, 81, 98, 142
poetry collections for, 5
pop-up books for, 76
songs for, 75
stories of family tensions during, 114, 116
stories of kindness at, 92, 143, 177
Hanukkah at Valley Forge (Krensky), 249
Hanukkiyah, 22, 31, 76–77, 83, 85, 236, 243
haredi, 124, 243
Harlem Renaissance, 37
Hashavas aveidah, 33, 243
Hasidism, 8, 243
hate crimes, 198
Havdalah, 243
heaven, 16, 17, 19, 21, 49
Hebrew Scriptures, 1
Herod (King of Judea), 79, 129, 132
Herschel, Abraham Joshua, 202
Herzl, Theodor, 135
Heschel, Abraham Joshua, 138
Hitler Youth, 161
Hitler, Adolf, 168, 170, 171, 210
  biographies of, 155, 160, 162
  in novels, 208, 214, 218, 226
  influence on Nazi Germany, 159, 189
  resistance to, 161, 211
holidays. *See* individual holiday names
Holocaust, 185, 212, 229
  aftermath of, 52, 115–116, 149, 170
  anthologies, 192
  biographies of survivors, 51, 115, 184, 187–188
  children's experiences during, 151, 156, 174, 181, 187–190, 217
  denials of, 163, 166
  guides to, 155, 161, 164, 166–168, 180, 187
  heroes of, 70, 209, 211, 215–219
  history of, 181, 193
  illustrated stories about, 213, 214
  in Jewish consciousness, 5

memoirs, 165, 177, 182, 186, 227
memoirs by rescuers, 219, 220
memorials, 180, 183, 191–192
moral dilemmas in, 159
nonfiction accounts for elementary
  grades, 155, 176
novels for high school, 44
novels for middle school, 38
resistance to, 158–160, 162
stories for young children, 35, 53, 71,
  114, 154, 175
survival stories during, 167, 169
survivor adjustments to new life, 44, 117,
  126, 135, 149, 202, 226
world impact of, 52
Holocaust Remembrance Day, 52
Holy Ark, 243
holy days, 247–248. *See also* individual holy
  days
homosexuality, 117, 229
hora, 243
hospitals, 72, 85
Houdini, Harry, 147
Hubener Group, 168
Hughes, Langston, 38
hunting, 206
hurricanes, 179
hydrogen bomb, 60–61

I

IDF. *See* Israel Defense Forces
illustrated books
  selection criteria for, 9
Imma, 243
influenza, 143
Inquisition, 134, 137, 165, 170, 181
intermarriage, 4–5, 112, 114, 222
Irving, David, 166
Isaac Siegel Memorial Award, 3
Israel, 15, 82, 198, 232, 235
  early statehood of, 179, 226
  emigration from, 229
  gift of Torah to, 15
  God's love for, 73
  history of, 53, 123–124, 126–130, 133–139
  immigration to, 70, 107, 176

Jewish-Arab relations in, 5, 71, 72, 118,
  154, 165
jingles about, 82
kibbutz in, 27, 121, 122, 124,
modern life in, 131, 150, 163, 170
picture books of, 70, 121–123
stories of ancient times, 41, 57, 58
travel guides to, 121–122, 125
Israel Defense Forces (IDF), 243
Israeli-American relations, 134

J

Jacobs, Barron, 152
Jacobs, Lionel, 152
Jason Aronson (publisher), 255
jazz, 73
Jewish Book Council, 3, 5, 7
Jewish Book Month, 5
Jewish Book World (serial), 7
Jewish children's literature
  collection development guidelines for, 9–10
  history of, 1–3
  promotion of, 5–6
  standards for, 1, 6–9
Jewish Historical Museum, 191
Jewish identity, 12
Jewish Lights Publishing, 255
Jewish National Fund, 123
Jewish Publication Society, 2, 255
Jewish Valuesfinder, the (Web site), 7
Jewish Virtual Library, 138
Jewish-Arab relations, 5, 154
  in novels, 71, 72, 112, 135, 150, 165
  nonfiction examinations of, 118, 126
Jonah (Biblical), 18–19, 145, 203–204
Jonathon David Publishers, 256
Joseph (Biblical), 205
Judah the Prince (Rabbi), 30
Judaica Press, 256
Julia's Kitchen (Ferber), 249

K

K'tonton (folktale character), 2, 101, 207
Kabbalah, 60, 243
Kaddish, 174, 243

kapores, 207, 243
Kar-Ben Publishing/Lerner Publishing
    Group, 256
Karski, Jan, 216
kashrut (dietary laws), 104, 243
ketubah, 101, 243
kibbutz, 27, 121, 122, 124, 136, 243
Kiddush, 243
Kiddush cups, 78, 142
Kimmel, Eric A., 55
Kindertransport, 243
    in biographies, 215, 227
    in historical fiction, 44, 149, 178, 218
kippot, 11, 36, 243
Kol Nidre, 206, 243
Korczak, Janusz, 70
kosher, 76, 106, 204, 243
Kotel, 243
Krantz, Jacob Ben Wolf (Rabbi), 237
Krasa, Hans, 210
Kristallnacht, 178, 243
KTAV Publishing House, 256
kvetch, 243

L

Lag B'Omer, 248
landsleit society, 244
Lansky, Aaron, 55
lashon hara, 244
latkes, 49, 77, 87, 244
    humorous stories about, 81
    in folktales, 29
    in Hanukkah stories, 49, 92–97, 99, 106,
        143, 174
    recipes for, 75
Lester, Julius, 128
Lifeline for the Old (service), 201
Lincoln, Abraham, 42
Lipstadt, Deborah, 166
Lodz Ghetto, 159, 167, 192
logging camps, 143
logotherapy, 62
Lower East Side (New York City), 54, 98
    immigrant experience in, 3, 52, 144, 195
    life and culture of, 72, 98, 115
    tenements in, 146–148

M

Maccabees, 65, 80, 91, 94, 105, 126, 236
    definition of, 244
    victory over Greco-Syrian army, 93, 95,
        96, 126, 223
Maggid, Dubno, 237
magicians, 92, 114–115, 147, 240
Mahrwood Press, 256
Maimonides, 129
Mandelbaum, Jack, 168
Manhattan Project, 38
maror, 79, 87, 93, 244
Masada (fortress), 122, 132, 136, 164
matzah, 244
Matzah Ball Books, 256
Mauthausen (concentration camp), 167
Meed, Vladka, 216
megillah, 65, 159, 215, 244
Meir, Golda, 131, 133, 139
Meitner, Lisa, 61
melamud, 244
Mendelssohn, Fanny, 227
Mendilow, Myriam, 201
menorahs, 55, 69, 107, 175, 198, 244
    as source of light, 17
    as superhero, 184
    history of, 22, 236
    in preschool books, 77, 82, 87
mensch, 244
mental illness, 117
Merkos Publications/Kehot Publication
    Society, 256
mesirat nefesh, 69, 244
Mesorah Publications/Artscroll, 256
Metropolitan Museum of Art, 173
Mezquita, La, 113
Midrash Tanhuma, 244
midrashim, 244
Milk and Honey Press, 256
Minneapolis Jewish Day School, 21
minyan, 21, 184, 244
Mitzvot, 75–109, 195–196, 209, 232, 244
Modeh Ani (prayer), 244
Moses, 20, 23, 63
    death of, 66
    historical treatments of, 44, 51

pictorial accounts of, 53
Ten Commandments and, 83–84
moshav, 138, 244
Mother Goose, 82
mourning, 188
Mt. Ararat, 23
Mt. Sinai, 23
multicultural library collections, 10

N

Nachshon Press, 256
Nasi, Dona Grazia, 129
National Jewish Book Awards, 4
National Organization for Women, 201
National Yiddish Book Center, 55
Native Americans, 52
Nazis, 38, 62, 164, 183, 189, 191
  abductions by, 73
  as fugitives, 51
  escapes from, 167, 168, 178, 181, 186, 217
  in France, 84, 174, 184, 213, 215, 217
  in novels, 43, 73, 151, 157–163, 165, 229
  in stories for young children, 126, 154,
      179, 209–213, 215
  Jewish socialization with, 190
  neo-Nazis, 53, 187, 208
  post-war trials of, 52, 155, 168
  resistance to, 166, 169
Nazism, 166, 170, 186, 193, 217
  in novels, 35, 227
  in post-war Germany, 52
Netanyahu, Yoni, 132
New Jewish Values Finder, 1, 299
New York Yankees, 119
Newbery-Caldecott Committee, 299
Newman, Pauline, 200
9/11, 156, 180, 199
Noah's Ark stories
  counting books, 15
  for elementary grades, 21
  for high school students, 38
  for preschoolers, 13, 15–16, 18, 47–48,
      64, 111–112, 142, 222
  for primary grades, 49–50, 97
  modern interpretations of, 38
  Noah's wife as central character, 141, 197

novels about, 38
religious emphasis in, 237
secular version of, 63
Nobel Prize for Literature, 4
noise, 26, 30
Norton, Mary, 95
nuclear fission, 61
nuclear power, 38
nuns, 209, 211
nursing homes, 42

O

oceans, 20
Ochberg, Isaac, 219
Old Bailey (London prison), 74
Old Testament. *See* Hebrew Scriptures
Olympic Games, 146, 150, 167
origami, 107

P

paintings, 45, 183
Parashah, 102, 103, 244
Passover, 79, 90, 247
  activity books for, 79, 93, 101, 105, 106
  alphabet books, 87
  anthologies for, 108
  books for preschoolers, 86–87, 100, 141
  cookbooks for, 107
  customs, 104
  history of, 97
  in fantasy adventures, 78
  in folktales, 30, 236
  in novels, 96, 159
  in picture books, 51, 80–84
  introductory books to, 91, 94–95
  songs for, 92
Perlman, Itzhak, 131
physics, 38, 60, 62
pickpockets, 74
picture books
  selection criteria for, 9
pioneers, 3, 152
Pirke Avot, 244
Piscopia, Elena, 61
pitom, 156, 204, 244

Pitspopany Press, 256
plays, 183
pogroms, 144, 216, 219, 243, 244
polio, 197, 200
Priest's Grotto, 167–168
Purim (festival), 56, 75, 142, 205, 223, 247
    folktales for, 236
    introduction to, 85, 89
    kiddush for, 78
    Queen Esther and, 153, 159, 178, 215

Q

Queen of Sheba, 40

R

Rabbi Hillel, 244
Rabin, Yitzhak, 178, 181
Ramon, Ilan, 59, 131, 177, 182–183, 192
refuah shelaimah, 39, 244
refugee camps
    American, 36, 44, 158
    Sudanese, 73
refugees, 35, 124, 190, 219, 229
    in America, 128, 129, 151, 153, 158,
        228
    in Canada, 224
    in Ireland, 218
    in Israel, 125, 126, 135, 226
regelach, 244
Revolutionary War. *See* American
    Revolution
Rey, H.A., 174
Rey, Margaret, 174
riddles, 40, 56, 127, 207
Ringelblum, Emmanuel, 187
Robinson, Jackie, 119
Rose, Ernestine, 200
Rosenfeld, Bobbie, 146, 150
Rosh Hashanah, 80, 89, 90, 207, 247
    activities for, 132
    folktales for, 236
    guides for, 105
    history and customs of, 91
    in novels, 103
    preschool introductions to, 81, 85, 204

Rosh Hodesh, 237, 247
Rudolf II (Holy Roman Emperor), 210
Ruth, Book of, 65, 68

S

saints, 169, 211
Salk, Jonas, 197, 200
Sammy Spider (literary character), 5
Satan, 21
scavenger hunts, 123
Schindler, Oskar, 189, 216, 218, 219
schmaltz, 244
School Library Journal, 6
sea monsters, 205
seder plate, 80, 245
seder, 245. *See also* Passover
Sefer Torah, 12, 245
Seneca Reservation (New York), 52
Senesh, Hannah, 170–171, 216
Sephardim, 245
September 11, 2001, 156, 180, 199
Seraphic Press, 256
Shabbat (Sabbath), 91, 142, 245, 247
    folktales for, 236
    in novels, 104
    in picture books, 93, 99
    in preschool literature, 11, 78, 83, 88
    preparations for, 81, 94, 96
    significance of, 83, 90, 97
Shabbos, 75, 77, 95, 245
shamash, 76, 245
Sharon, Ariel, 127
Shavuot (holy day), 15, 85, 112, 248
Shazak Productions, 256
Shehina, 21, 245
Shema (prayer), 19, 39, 78, 245
Shema Yisrael, 245
Shemini Atzeret (festival), 247
Shepard, Matthew, 166
shlemiel, 245
Shmura Matzah, 245
shofar, 18, 79, 95, 103, 123, 206, 245
Sholom's Treasure (Silverman), 56
Shrine of the Book (Israel Museum), 57
shtetl, 245
shtuss, 245

shul, 245
side locks, 245
Simhat Torah (holy day), 12, 19, 84, 85, 91, 247
Singer, Alex, 138
Six Day War, 36
Skirball Cultural Center, 148
slavery, 42, 50, 68, 128, 218
Smith, Ethel, 150
soccer, 118, 200, 223
Sodom, 154
sofer, 103, 245
Solomon (King of Israel), 137, 206, 239
  in folktales, 236, 238
  legends of, 64, 195
  preschool books about, 40
Solomon, Haym, 52
space shuttle, 59, 131, 177, 182, 192
Spielberg, Steven, 200
Steinhardt, Bernice, 182
storms, 111
story poems, 5
streptomycin, 199
Sugihara, Chiune, 212, 213, 216
sukkah, 78, 88, 98, 245
Sukkot (festival), 32, 78, 88, 98, 204, 247
Sydney Taylor Book Awards, 3–6, 67, 141, 169, 180
  as models of best American Jewish children's literature, 10
  committee for, 299
  for acculturation stories, 144
  for Biblical story adaptations, 235
  for biographies, 62
  for books examining Jewish-Arab relations, 5, 170
  for books on faith, 19, 224
  for civil rights stories, 200
  for folktales, 196, 205, 232–233, 236
  for Hanukkah stories, 69, 206
  for historical fiction, 56, 65, 73, 96
  for Holocaust themes, 160, 174, 191, 215
  for immigration stories, 125
  for nonfiction, 163, 175, 178, 183
  for refugee stories, 36, 107, 125, 202, 212
  for Yom Kippur stories, 17
  list of winners 1968–2007, 249–253

on Jewish Valuesfinder Web site, 7
Sydney Taylor Manuscript Awards
  for elementary grade books, 36
  for historical fiction, 36, 60
  for middle school books, 73
synagogues, 10, 19, 32, 66, 95, 96, 196
  burning of, 187
  guides to, 98, 124
  haunted, 154
  Kabbalah traditions in, 60
  origins of, 132
  readings in, 204
  services in, 97
  Torahs in, 12, 180
  Touro Synagogue, 134

T

tallitot, 245
Talmud, 52, 122, 245
  characters in, 196
  legends from, 154
  story adaptations of, 41, 50, 231–237, 239
tam, 245
Tanakh, 20, 73, 245
Targum Press, 256
tashlikh, 89, 204, 205, 245
"Teheran children," 186
Teller, Edward, 60
Ten Commandments, 83–84, 88
Ten Plagues, 18–19
tenements, 51, 146–148, 195
Terezin (concentration camp), 157–159, 168, 185, 187, 191, 210
terrorism, 156, 163, 167, 170, 229
teshuvah, 117, 205, 206, 246
Thanksgiving, 32, 144, 250
Thompson, Jean, 150
tikun olam, 195, 196, 226, 246
time travel, 158, 214
Tisha B'Av (holy day), 248
Torah, 246
  importance in Jewish children's literature, 12
  in preschool literature, 12, 15
  values of, 8
Torah Aura Productions (publisher), 256

Tower of Babel, 18
Treblinka (concentration camp), 184
Triangle Shirtwaist Factory, 37, 115, 200.
  See also factories
Trocme, Andre (Pastor), 215, 216
Tu B'Shevat (festival), 247
tzedakah, 33, 81, 98, 195, 246. *See also*
  charity
as holiday custom, 82
as way of reaching heaven, 49
at Sabbath, 11, 77
community projects, 105
tzimmes, 99, 246

U

United Nations, 52
United Synagogue of Conservative Judaism,
  256
Urim Publications, 257
URJ (Union of Reform Judaism) Press, 256

V

Valley Forge, 96
Van Maarsen, Jacqueline, 182
Vatican II, 202

W

wadi, 71, 246
Waksman, Selman, 199
Wallenberg, Raoul, 216–218
Wansee Conference, 187
Warsaw Ghetto, 151, 187, 212, 220
Warsaw Ghetto Uprising, 36, 161, 164, 187
Weimar Republic, 170
Weinberg, Robert A., 199
Weisenthal Center, 191
Weiss, Ehrich (Harry Houdini), 147
Weizmann, Chaim, 135
White Rose (Nazi resistance group), 161
white supremacists, 117
Whiteman, Paul, 146
Wiesel, Elie, 115, 116, 187, 190, 192, 239
Wiesenthal, Simon, 51, 53
witches, 154, 238

Wolff, Hannelore, 189
Women's League of Conservative Judaism, 2
World Trade Center (New York City), 180.
  See also 9/11
World War I, 2, 3, 170, 210, 219
World War II. *See also* Holocaust, 5, 227, 228
effect on Jewish literature, 3
heroes of, 166, 168, 211, 214
memoirs of, 190, 193, 212, 219, 220
nonfiction accounts for elementary
  grades, 155
nonfiction accounts for high school, 170
nonfiction accounts for middle school,
  162, 186, 191, 218
novels for elementary grades, 42, 71, 146,
  157, 185
novels for high school, 171
novels for middle school, 44, 73, 117,
  137, 150–151, 169, 216
occupation of Denmark, 35
pre-war Jewish literature, 2
refugee stories, 153
writing process, 55

Y

Yadin, Yigael, 164
Yaldah Publishing, 257
Yehuda, Eliezer Ben, 129
yenta, 99, 141, 246
Yom ha Atzma'ut (festival), 248
Yom ha Shoah, 183, 247
Yom Hashoah, 52
Yom Kippur, 95, 203, 207, 247
folktales for, 236
introduction to, 85, 203
picture books about, 207
prayers for, 17, 206
Yom Kippur War, 71

Z

Zayda, 234, 246
zayteem, 123, 246
Zionism, 125–126, 131, 133, 135
Ziz (mythical bird), 31, 47, 203
zoftig, 246

About the Author

Linda R. Silver is a specialist in Jewish children's literature, the creator and editor of an online guide called "The Jewish Valuesfinder" (www.ajljewishvalues.org), co-editor of book reviews for children and teens for the quarterly *Newsletter of the Association of Jewish Libraries* (AJL), author of several publications and many articles and book reviews, a frequent speaker at conferences, and a teacher at workshops. She has a degree in library science from Case-Western Reserve University and worked in public, school, synagogue, and special libraries before retiring in 2006. As a public librarian, she served on the Board of Directors of the ALA's Association for Library Service to Children (ALSC) and as a member of the Newbery-Caldecott Committee, as well as on many other ALSC committees. As a Judaic librarian, she has been active in the AJL, serving in numerous capacities including chair of the Sydney Taylor Book Award Committee, president of AJL's School, Synagogue and Centers Division, and president of AJL's Greater Cleveland Chapter. In 2004, Linda received the AJL's Fanny Goldstein Merit Award in recognition of her contributions to the Association and to the profession of Judaic librarianship.